Readings in Wes

Vere dignum

University of Chicago Readings in Western Civilization

John W. Boyer and Julius Kirshner, General Editors

1. **The Greek Polis**
   Edited by Arthur W. H. Adkins and Peter White
2. **Rome: Late Republic and Principate**
   Edited by Walter Emil Kaegi, Jr., and Peter White
3. **The Church in the Roman Empire**
   Edited by Karl F. Morrison
4. **Medieval Europe**
   Edited by Julius Kirshner and Karl F. Morrison
5. **The Renaissance**
   Edited by Eric Cochrane and Julius Kirshner
6. **Early Modern Europe: Crisis of Authority**
   Edited by Eric Cochrane, Charles M. Gray, and Mark A. Kishlansky
7. **The Old Régime and the French Revolution**
   Edited by Keith Michael Baker
8. **Nineteenth-Century Europe: Liberalism and Its Critics**
   Edited by Jan Goldstein and John W. Boyer
9. **Twentieth-Century Europe**
   Edited by John W. Boyer and Jan Goldstein

University of Chicago
Readings in Western Civilization
John Boyer and Julius Kirshner, General Editors

2
Rome:
Late Republic and Principate

Edited by Walter Emil Kaegi, Jr., and Peter White

The University of Chicago Press
Chicago and London

Eric Cochrane, 1928–1985

ἀθάνατος μνήμη
Immortal memory

The University of Chicago Press, Chicago 60637
The University of Chicago Press, Ltd., London

Printed in the United States of America
07 06 05 04 03 02 01 00 99 98 5 6 7 8 9

Library of Congress Cataloging-in-Publication Data
Main entry under title:

University of Chicago readings in Western civilization.

Includes bibliographies and indexes.
Contents: — v. 2. Rome / edited by Walter Emil Kaegi, Jr. and Peter White— —v. 4, Medieval Europe / edited by Julius Kirshner and Karl F. Morrison.
1. Civilization, Occidental—History—Sources. 2. Europe—Civilization—Sources. I. Boyer, John W. II. Kirshner, Julius. III. Readings in western civilization.
CB245.U64 1986 909′.09821 85-16328
ISBN 0-226-06934-6 (v. 1)
ISBN 0-226-06935-4 (pbk.: v. 1)
ISBN 0-226-06936-2 (v. 2)
ISBN 0-226-06937-0 (pbk.: v. 2)

∞ The paper used in this publication meets the minimum requirements of the American National Standard for Information Sciences—Permanence of Paper for Printed Library Materials, ANSI Z39.48-1992.

Contents

Series Editors' Foreword

This series is the result of almost four decades of teaching the History of Western Civilization course at the College of the University of Chicago. The course was founded in its present form in the late 1940s by a group of young historians at Chicago, including William H. McNeill, Christian Mackauer, and Sylvia Thrupp, and has been sustained during the past twenty-five years by the distinguished teaching of Eric Cochrane, Hanna H. Gray, Charles M. Gray, and Karl J. Weintraub. In the beginning it served as a counterpoint to the antihistorical and positivistic thrust of the general education curriculum in the social sciences in the Hutchins College. Western Civilization has since been incorporated as a year-long course into different parts of the College program, from the first to the last year. It now forms part of the general intercivilizational requirement for sophomores and juniors. It is still taught, as it has been almost constantly since its inception, in discussion groups ranging from twenty to thirty students.

Although both the readings and the instructors of the course have changed over the years, its purpose has remained the same. It seeks not to provide students with morsels of Western culture, nor to nourish their moral and aesthetic sensitivities, and much less to attract recruits for the history profession. Its purpose instead is to raise a whole set of complex conceptual questions regarding the nature of time and change and the intended and unintended consequences of human action and consciousness. Students in this course learn to analyze past events and ideas by rigorously examining a variety of texts. This is in contrast to parallel courses in the social sciences, which teach students to deploy synchronic and quantitative techniques in analyzing society, usually without reference to historical context or process.

Ours is a history course that aims not at imparting relevant facts or exotic ideas but at providing students with the critical tools by which to analyze texts produced in the distant or near past. It also serves a related purpose: to familiarize students with major epochs of that Western historical tradition to which most of them, albeit at times unknowingly, are heirs. The major curricular vehicle of the course is the *Readings in Western Civilization*, a nine-volume series of primary sources in translation, beginning with Periclean Athens and concluding with Europe in the twentieth century. The series is not meant to be a comprehensive survey of Western history. Rather, in each volume, we provide a large number of documents on specific themes in the belief that depth, not breadth, is the surest antidote to superficiality. The very extensiveness of the documentation in each volume allows for a variety of approaches to the same theme. At the same time the concentrated focus of individual volumes makes it possible for them to serve as source readings in more advanced and specialized courses.

Many people contributed to the publication of these volumes. The enthusiastic collaboration and labors of the members of the Western Civilization staff made it possible for these *Readings* to be published. We thank Barbara Boyer for providing superb editorial direction to the project and Mary Van Steenbergh for her dedication in creating beautifully text-edited manuscripts. Steven Wheatley's advice in procuring funding for this project was invaluable. Members of the University of Chicago Press have given their unstinting support and guidance. We also appreciate the confidence and support accorded by Donald N. Levine, the Dean of the College at the University of Chicago. Above all, we are deeply grateful for the extraordinary dedication, energy, and erudition which our late colleague and former chairperson of the course, Eric Cochrane, contributed to the *Readings in Western Civilization*.

We are grateful to the National Endowment for the Humanities for providing generous funding for the preparation and publication of the volumes.

John W. Boyer and Julius Kirshner

General Introduction

The dimensions of Roman history are vast with respect to both time and space. Archaeological investigation reveals that the earliest habitation at Rome long preceded the traditional date of her foundation in 753 B.C. Historians disagree concerning the appropriate date for the end of the Roman Empire, with dates varying from as early as A.D. 180 and as late, for Edward Gibbon, as 1453. The principal divisions of Roman history are usually considered to be those of the Republic, traditionally dated between 509 and 27 B.C.; the Empire or Principate, beginning in 27 B.C.; and the Later Roman Empire, beginning as early as A.D. 150 or 180 or as late as 395, although a third-century date, whether or not 284, the beginning of the important reign of Diocletian, seems most reasonable. Historians also disagree about the date for the end of the Later Roman Empire in western Europe, which they date from as early as A.D. 395 to as late as 750 or 800, although the traditional date is 476, and the fifth century was, in any event, a watershed for the empire's political, intellectual, and military history. Roman history naturally focuses on the city of Rome and the adjacent countryside in central Italy, but the borders of the empire eventually stretched from the Euphrates River in the east to the Atlantic Ocean in the west, and from the First Cataract of the Nile River in the south to Scotland in the north.

Because of the large amount and scope of available material, the editors of this volume were forced to be selective. The earliest document, written by Cato the Censor, or Cato the Elder, dates from the first half of the second century B.C., and the latest one, the *Institutes* of Justinian I, from the sixth century A.D. These documents, which have been selected for their relevance to the broader history of Western civilization, concentrate on the western European provinces even though the empire also included substantial areas and populations in North Africa and western Asia.

The investigation and interpretation of Roman history has changed substantially since the Renaissance. In the nineteenth century, B. G. Niebuhr began the critical evaluation of literary histories, while the most famous historian of Rome, Theodor Mommsen, emphasized political history, especially the study of Roman constitutional and institutional problems.

Twentieth-century historians turned to social and economic history. Matthias Gelzer pioneered the study of familial ties, which he considered a prerequisite to any understanding of the politics of republican Rome. Even more influential was Michael Rostovtzeff, the most important investigator of Roman social and economic history. By asking new questions and by making extensive use of nonliterary sources, especially archaeological findings, inscriptions, coins, and papyruses, he transformed the study of Roman history, even though succeeding generations of Roman historians—especially Ronald Syme, Anton von Premerstein, Ernest Badian, Pierre Grenade, and Erich Gruen—returned to political questions, particularly those concerning the transformation from the Republic to the Principate. Moses Finley, Richard Saller, and many other historians reopened the investigation of economic topics, raising new questions and offering new analyses. Since the 1960s, some of the greatest contributions to Roman history have come from the discovery of new nonliterary sources—especially valuable for the understanding of social and economic conditions—but no new synthesis has emerged. Archaeology, epigraphy (the study of inscriptions), and papyrology continue to furnish the greatest amount of new evidence for the study of Roman history.

Many historians, especially in the past half-century, have investigated the Later Roman Empire. In particular, the work of A. H. M. Jones, P. Brown, Alan and Averil Cameron, Arnaldo Momigliano, Ramsay MacMullen, and many art historians, most notably Richard Delbrueck, has achieved a new appreciation of Late Roman values, endurance, and culture. There has been a decisive trend in recent research to analyze and appreciate Late Roman values and esthetics and culture in their own right, and not to attempt to evaluate them by the standard of classical values of the first century B.C. or A.D. The transformation of classical values into the different spiritual values of the late classical period has been one of the most intensively investigated subjects of recent decades.

Historians have often endeavored to find some single cause for the end of the Roman Empire, yet most of their "causes"—ranging from lead poisoning to slavery to climatic change—have failed to explain why it was possible for the empire, with a new capital at Constantinople, to retain its control over much of the eastern provinces for many more centuries. Semantic problems (i.e., what is being explained, the end of an empire, a civilization, a people?) have also complicated the investigations. Although many modern historians have questioned the validity of the word "fall" in discussions of the end of the Roman Empire, as early as the fifth century the philosopher Damascius reported the use of that word to describe the contemporary condition of Rome. The voluminous writings by historians have not resulted in any consensus on the definition or solution of the controversy. The problem or fact of the Roman Empire's endurance for a relatively long time has often been ignored in scholarly debates about the reasons for its decline.

Scholars have learned much in recent years concerning the empire's diverse subject peoples and their cultures, which were influenced, but not necessarily overwhelmed, by elite Greco-Roman civilization. The assimilation and adaptation of classical civilization by these peoples has received intensive study. Modern methodologies from the social sciences have provided insights into the society and cultures of many subject peoples who left no written records. One people—the Greeks—did leave major written records, and among the most significant trends in recent scholarship (since the 1960s) has been the new attention given to these writings, especially in the important publications of G. W. Bowersock, C. P. Jones, and Fergus Millar.

Many of the older historical questions remain unanswered. Thus the nature and causes of Roman imperialism, passionately debated early in this century by Tenney Frank and his contemporaries, have recently been reappraised by R. M. Errington and W. V. Harris and still remain controversial. To apply techniques of quantitative measurement, such as statistical and computer analyses, future Roman historians will need to master the rapidly increasing archaeological evidence, which sometimes provides very specific information about such diverse topics as chronology, family life, technology, diet, and trade.

The problem of technology in the Roman world, including the issue of the influence of slavery on the Romans' readiness to adapt new technological innovations, has received new scrutiny. Yet a rereading of the literary sources as well as comparison with new archaeological evidence does not indicate absolute technological stagnation, especially in harnessing energy. The subject deserves and will receive more research. Municipal decline, especially the deterioration of municipal public life, is another discernible process that is being investigated, and about which archaeology should eventually offer much more information.

For an empire of Rome's size, it would be incorrect to assume the universality of every development or trend. Some provinces and municipalities flourished, for many different reasons, while others stagnated or even declined. The reader should not assume that the readings accurately represent real conditions at every point in the Roman Empire at any given moment. "Eternal Rome" is a cliché, yet Roman institutions, society, thought, and economy did change, however slowly, during the course of centuries—and much could and did change in any given century.

Other unsolved problems of Roman history include the elite's failure to reproduce itself, the nature and intentions of Augustus Caesar, the ways in which Rome evolved from a city-state into an empire, and Roman methods of transportation and uses of mechanics. The readings include a number of discussions, from different periods of Roman history, on the problem of governmental corruption, a topic on which there is surprisingly little scholarly consensus.

Centuries of writings on Roman history have not exhausted the subject. The field is changing, and our understanding of its fundamental lines is likely to alter considerably. Many opportunities for research await the scholars who have the necessary training and tools.

The editors of this volume have divided the source readings into five clusters, each concerning a major aspect of Roman civilization. As with other volumes in this series, only primary sources have been included, as substantial blocks rather than as excerpted paragraphs whenever possible. Many of the readings shed light on multiple dimensions of Roman society.

The first topic, entitled "Political Ideas and Practices, from Republic to Principate," includes contemporary descriptions—by both rulers and subjects—of Roman political institutions and principles, as well as the idealizations of Polybius and Pliny the Younger. These readings indicate some gaps between ideals and realities, but do provide insight into political Rome, fundamental to any understanding of Roman history.

The second cluster of texts, "Rome and Its Subjects," concerns Roman political and fiscal policies in the provinces and in the municipalities. Municipal life outside Rome remained vigorous for centuries. Aelius Aristides' speech *To Rome* provides one provincial perspective on the benefits of Roman rule for the empire's non-Latin-speaking subjects and additional testimony on the vitality of municipal life in the provinces.

"Legal Foundations of Roman Society: The Status of Persons under the Law" is the third topic. Justinian's *Institutes* include discussions of civil and natural law, the differences between freedom and slavery, and the status of minors, men, and women. They also provide an introduction to Roman legal reasoning and methods of developing law. Roman law was one of Rome's most important contributions to Western civilization, a rare intellectual dimension in which Roman thought decisively triumphed over Greek. This selection introduces the reader to both some basic aspects of mature Roman law and some essential social concepts and categories.

Readings on Roman law lead into the fourth topic, "Preoccupations of

Public and Private Life," which includes readings on a number of fundamental subjects: devotion to agriculture; attitudes toward slaves and free labor by tenant farmers who enjoyed free but dependent status; accumulation and expenditure of wealth; private versus public concerns; the idealized position of noble women; concern about rebellion of slaves; and personal and public prayer (although the editors had difficulty finding texts that accurately described principal features of Roman religion under either the Republic or the Empire). The Christianization of the empire is the subject of the succeeding volume in this series; therefore, sources on this very important transformation and its consequences for Rome are not included herein, except for some significant remarks by Pliny and Trajan. The selection from Quintilian focuses on the elementary education that he thought should precede the rhetorical training of influential Romans and is particularly revealing of Roman values in education and culture. Although these readings discuss details of daily life and personal concerns, they also offer more general insights into Roman social and economic life, diet, and technology.

The fifth topic, "Problems of the Later Roman Empire," includes readings on institutional, economic, and technological problems of organization and survival. The readings in the last grouping are largely limited to secular subjects, both governmental and private. Important omissions include readings on the final stages of non-Christian thought, including the last pagan apologetics, and on relations with barbarians other than the Huns. Diocletian's *Price Edict* is a document from the early years of the Later Roman Empire (according to many scholars' periodization); it describes the crisis of the empire and the interrelationship between economic and military problems and also provides clues about daily life as well as the relative prestige of differing occupations. Selections from the *Theodosian Code* serve as a document on law in the Later Roman Empire, particularly concerning the conflicting interests of wealthy landowners, dependent farmers (*coloni*), and the government, which urgently needed reliable sources of tax revenues. *On Military Matters* is a rare analysis of the internal causes of the empire's crisis in the late fourth century, with emphasis on technological, fiscal, and military responses. The selection from Priscus introduces the challenge of the barbarians and the readiness of some Romans to prefer barbarian rule to that of Rome. It also reviews some criticisms of the gap between Roman political ideals and realities in the final decades of Roman government in western and central Europe.

The readings may appear to overrepresent the Roman elite, but it was the elite who left most of the written records. This may be regrettable but it is a fact, and readers should approach the sources with an appropriate critical caution. It is likewise very difficult to find appropriate works written by Roman women. One of Rome's most important and distinctive institutions, her army, also receives relatively little attention.

The emphasis of the volume is on Roman civilization, not Latin literature, of which there are ample studies. Roman philosophy and other important aspects of Roman intellectual life may best be studied by consulting separately published lengthy works by Cicero and Seneca the Younger. Descriptions of public spectacles, including gladiatorial combat and the circus, have been omitted. Roman art and architecture are important, but those wishing to study them as well can more fruitfully choose their own slides of such sites as Pompeii, Herculaneum, Ostia, the Pont du Gard, Vaison-la-Romaine, Jerash, Caesarea, Timgad, Ephesus, and Palmyra, or of objects from the Roman collections of great museums, such as the Metropolitan Museum of Art, the British Museum, the Louvre, and the museums of Rome, Naples, and Cologne. Art objects and architecture are revealing not only of Roman aesthetics and values, but also of daily living conditions, housing, dress, hydraulics, tools, food, jewelry, health, trade and manufactures, metallurgy, and diverse specific topics such as the nature of storehouses and granaries.

Note

Two editorial points deserve mention. The internal numbering of documents follows that of the editors of the original texts. Second, most footnotes from previously published translations have been deleted. A few footnotes have been added by the editors of this volume.

Select Bibliography

Supplementary Texts

A useful supplement to this volume would be *Roman Civilization: Sourcebook*, edited by Naphtali Lewis and Meyer Reinhold, which contains sources organized by topic, including many inscriptions and papyruses, and is divided into one volume on the Republic and one on the Principate (New York: Columbia University Press, 1955; reprint, New York: Harper Row, Harper Torchbooks, 1966). Alternative or additional source readings include inexpensive editions of Cicero's *De Re Publica* (On the commonwealth) (Library of Liberal Arts, 1929), and *Offices and Selection of Letters* (Everyman, 1953), which includes the valuable "Laelius, On Friendship," and "Cato, On Old Age" (readings from Cicero provide important texts concerning Roman philosophical and humanistic values); Plutarch's *Lives*, under the title *Fall of the Roman Republic* (Penguin Books, 1974); Livy's *The Early History of Rome* (Penguin Books, 1960); and texts of Tacitus, for example, *Annals of Imperial Rome* (Penguin Books, 1956), and *Complete Works* (Modern Library, 1964).

Suggestions for Further Reading

Classics

Bury, John B. *History of the Later Roman Empire: From the Death of Theodosius to the Death of Justinian*. 2d ed. New York: Macmillan, 1923. Reprint. New York: Dover, 1957.

Cary, Max, and H. Scullard. *A History of Rome*. 3d ed. New York: St. Martin's, 1976.

Gelzer, Matthias. *The Roman Nobility*. Oxford: Blackwell, 1975.

Gibbon, Edward. *History of the Decline and Fall of the Roman Empire*. Edited by John B. Bury. London: Methuen, 1909, and other editions.

Hammond, Mason. *The Antonine Monarchy*. Rome: American Academy in Rome, 1959.

Mommsen, Theodor. *History of Rome*. 2d ed. Translated by W. P. Dickson. New York: Scribner's, 1895.

Rostovtzeff, Michael. *The Social and Economic History of the Roman Empire*. Oxford: Oxford University Press, 1957.

Syme, Ronald. *The Roman Revolution*. Oxford: Oxford University Press, 1939.

Taylor, Lily Ross. *Party Politics in the Age of Caesar*. Berkeley and Los Angeles: University of California Press, 1962.

Recent Scholarship

Badian, Ernst. *Roman Imperialism in the Late Republic*. 2d ed. Ithaca, N.Y.: Cornell University Press, 1969.

———. *Studies in Greek and Roman History*. Oxford: Blackwell, 1964.

Bowersock, G. W. *Augustus and the Greek World*. Oxford: Oxford University Press, 1965. Reprint. Westport, Conn.: Greenwood, 1982.

Brown, Peter. *The World of Late Antiquity*. London: Thames & Hudson, 1971.

Brunt, Peter A. *Social Conflicts in the Roman Republic*. London: Chatto and Windus, 1971; New York: Norton, 1974.

Crook, John Anthony. *Law and Life of Rome*. Ithaca, N.Y.: Cornell University Press, 1967.

Errington, R. M. *Dawn of Empire: Rome's Rise to World Power*. Ithaca, N.Y.: Cornell University Press, 1972.

Finley, M. I. *The Ancient Economy*. Berkeley and Los Angeles: University of California Press, 1973.

Garnsey, Peter, and Richard P. Saller *The Roman Empire:* Economy, Society, and Culture. Berkeley: The University of California Press, 1987.

Gruen, Erich. *The Last Generation of the Roman Republic*. Cambridge: Harvard University Press, 1974.

Harris, W. V. *War and Imperialism in Republican Rome*. Oxford: Oxford University Press, 1979.

Jones, A. H. M. *The Later Roman Empire*. Oxford: Blackwell, 1964. Reprint. Norman, Okla.: University of Oklahoma Press, 1968.

Jones, C. P. *Plutarch and Rome*. Oxford: Oxford University Press, 1971.

Kaegi, Walter Emil, Jr. *Byzantium and the Decline of Rome*. Princeton, N.J.: Princeton University Press, 1968.

MacMullen, Ramsay. *Paganism in the Roman Empire*. New Haven, Conn.: Yale University Press, 1981.

———. *Roman Government's Response to Crisis*. New Haven, Conn.: Yale University Press, 1976.

Millar, Fergus. *The Emperor in the Roman World*. Ithaca, N.Y.: Cornell University Press, 1977.

Petit, Paul. *Pax Romana*. Berkeley: University of California Press, 1976.

Saller, Richard P., and Peter Garnsey. *The Early Principate*. Greece and Rome Monographs. Oxford: Oxford University Press, 1982.

Sherwin-White, A. N. *The Roman Citizenship*. 2d ed. Oxford: Oxford University Press, 1980.

1 Political Ideas and Practices, from Republic to Principate

1. Polybius, *History* (Selections)

The most distinguished Greek historian who described and interpreted the Roman Republic was Polybius of Megalopolis (in Arcadia), who lived from about 200 B.C. to sometime after 118 B.C. The son of the Achaean statesman and landowner Lycortas, his political career included service as an envoy to Egypt in 180 B.C. and then as a cavalry commander of the Achaean Confederation. The Romans deported him to Rome without trial, together with a thousand other Achaeans, after Rome's victory over the Achaeans at the battle of Pydna in 168 B.C. There he was befriended by the eminent Roman statesman Scipio Aemilianus and became a member of his intellectual circle. Polybius may have accompanied Scipio to Spain in 151 B.C.; in any case, he witnessed Scipio's destruction of Carthage in 146 B.C. He helped to organize government in Greece after his return.

Polybius was a prolific author, but all of his works are lost except for sections of his forty books of histories, published in about 150 B.C., of which the first five survive in their entirety and the rest only in fragments. He intended to write a history of the years between 220 and 168 B.C., in which Rome rose to dominate the Mediterranean Sea, but he ultimately extended its scope to include the years from 264 to 146 B.C. He believed that the reader and statesman could learn by examining political and military events, especially from the perspective of universal history (as opposed to that of a single people or city-state). Although he consulted a wide variety of Greek and Latin sources, he seldom identified them. A harsh critic of other historians, he had a very high, even austere, conception of the historian's obligations, especially to accuracy. In book 6, from

From *The Histories of Polybius*, vol. 1, translated by Evelyn S. Shuckburgh (London: Macmillan, 1889), pp. 1–3, 458–74, 494–507.

which most of the following sections are taken, Polybius describes Roman institutions as forming a mixed constitution, with checks on the various parts of government to slow the normal cycle of change. His analysis is really an idealization, not an empirical description of Roman government, yet it greatly influenced subsequent political theory. As an educated foreigner with much political and military experience, he wrote in Greek in order to explain Rome to his fellow Greeks. His writings greatly influenced subsequent Greek attitudes toward Rome and contributed to the long process through which Greek interests became identified with those of Rome, and through his participation in the influential Scipionic circle, he was also an important representative of Greek culture to the Roman elite.

Book 1

1. Had the praise of History been passed over by former Chroniclers it would perhaps have been incumbent upon me to urge the choice and special study of records of this sort, as the readiest means men can have of correcting their knowledge of the past. But my predecessors have not been sparing in this respect. They have all begun and ended, so to speak, by enlarging on this theme: asserting again and again that the study of History is in the truest sense an education, and a training for political life; and that the most instructive, or rather the only, method of learning to bear with dignity the vicissitudes of fortune is to recall the catastrophes of others. It is evident, therefore, that no one need think it his duty to repeat what has been said by many, and said well. Least of all myself: for the surprising nature of the events which I have undertaken to relate is in itself sufficient to challenge and stimulate the attention of every one, old or young, to the study of my work. Can any one be so indifferent or idle as not to care to know by what means, and under what kind of polity, almost the whole inhabited world was conquered and brought under the dominion of the single city of Rome, and that too within a period of not quite fifty-three years? [219–167 B.C.] Or who again can be so completely absorbed in other subjects of contemplation or study, as to think any of them superior in importance to the accurate understanding of an event for which the past affords no precedent.

2. We shall best show how marvellous and vast our subject is by comparing the most famous Empires which preceded, and which have been the favourite themes of historians, and measuring them with the superior greatness of Rome. There are but three that deserve even to be so compared and measured: and they are these. The Persians for a certain length of time were possessed of a great empire and dominion. But every time they ven-

tured beyond the limits of Asia, they found not only their empire, but their own existence also in danger. The Lacedaemonians, after contending for supremacy in Greece for many generations, when they did get it, held it without dispute for barely twelve years [405–394 B.C.]. The Macedonians obtained dominion in Europe from the lands bordering on the Adriatic to the Danube,—which after all is but a small fraction of this continent,—and, by the destruction of the Persian Empire, they afterwards added to that the dominion of Asia. And yet, though they had the credit of having made themselves masters of a larger number of countries and states than any people had ever done, they still left the greater half of the inhabited world in the hands of others. They never so much as thought of attempting Sicily, Sardinia, or Libya: and as to Europe, to speak the plain truth, they never even knew of the most warlike tribes of the West. The Roman conquest, on the other hand, was not partial. Nearly the whole inhabited world was reduced by them to obedience: and they left behind them an empire not to be paralleled in the past or rivalled in the future. Students will gain from my narrative a clearer view of the whole story, and of the numerous and important advantages which such exact record of events offers.

3. My History begins in the 140th Olympiad [220–217 B.C.]. The events from which it starts are these. In Greece, what is called the Social war: the first waged by Philip, son of Demetrius and father of Perseus, in league with the Achaeans against the Aetolians. In Asia, the war for the possession of Coele-Syria which Antiochus and Ptolemy Philopator carried on against each other. In Italy, Libya, and their neighbourhood, the conflict between Rome and Carthage, generally called the Hannibalian war. My work thus begins where that of Aratus of Sicyon leaves off. Now up to this time the world's history had been, so to speak, a series of disconnected transactions, as widely separated in their origin and results as in their localities. But from this time forth History becomes a connected whole: the affairs of Italy and Libya are involved with those of Asia and Greece, and the tendency of all is to unity. This is why I have fixed upon this era as the starting-point of my work. For it was their victory over the Carthaginians in this war, and their conviction that thereby the most difficult and most essential step towards universal empire had been taken, which encouraged the Romans for the first time to stretch out their hands upon the rest, and to cross with an army into Greece and Asia.

Now, had the states that were rivals for universal empire been familiarly known to us, no reference perhaps to their previous history would have been necessary, to show the purpose and the forces with which they approached an undertaking of this nature and magnitude. But the fact is that the majority of the Greeks have no knowledge of the previous constitution, power, or achievements either of Rome or Carthage. I therefore concluded that it was necessary to prefix this and the next book to my History. I was anxious that no one, when fairly embarked upon my actual narrative, should feel at a loss, and have to ask what were the designs entertained by the Romans, or the forces and means at their disposal, that they entered upon those undertakings, which did in fact lead to their becoming masters of land and sea everywhere in our part of the world. I wished, on the contrary, that these books of mine, and the prefatory sketch which they contained, might make it clear that the resources they started with justified their original idea, and sufficiently explained their final success in grasping universal empire and dominion.

Book 6

1. I am aware that some will be at a loss to account for my interrupting the course of my narrative for the sake of entering upon the following disquisition on the Roman constitution. But I think that I have already in many passages made it fully evident that this particular branch of my work was one of the necessities imposed on me by the nature of my original design; and I pointed this out with special clearness in the preface which explained the scope of my history. I there stated that the feature of my work which was at once the best in itself, and the most instructive to the students of it, was that it would enable them to know and fully realise in what manner, and under what kind of constitution, it came about that nearly the whole world fell under the power of Rome in somewhat less than fifty-three years,—an event certainly without precedent. This being my settled purpose, I could see no more fitting period than the present for making a pause, and examining the truth of the remarks about to be made on this constitution. In private life if you wish to satisfy yourself as to the badness or goodness of particular persons, you would not, if you wish to get a genuine test, examine their conduct at a time of uneventful repose, but in the hour of brilliant success or conspicuous reverse. For the true test of a perfect man is the power of bearing with spirit and dignity violent changes of fortune. An examination of a constitution should be conducted in the same way: and therefore being unable to find in our day a more rapid or more signal change than that which has happened to Rome, I reserved my disquisition on its constitution for this place. . . .

What is really educational and beneficial to students of history is the clear view of the causes of events, and the consequent power of choosing the better policy in a particular case. Now in every practical undertaking by a state we must regard as the most powerful agent for success or failure the form of its constitution; for from this as from a fountain-head all conceptions and plans of action not only proceed, but attain their consummation. . . .

3. Of the Greek republics, which have again and again risen to greatness and fallen into insignificance, it is not difficult to speak, whether we recount their past history or venture an opinion on their future. For to report what is already known is an easy task, nor is it hard to guess what is to come from our knowledge of what has been. But in regard to the Romans it is neither an easy matter to describe their present state, owing to the complexity of their constitution; nor to speak with confidence of their future, from our inadequate acquaintance with their peculiar institutions in the past whether affecting their public or their private life. It will require then no ordinary attention and study to get a clear and comprehensive conception of the distinctive features of this constitution.

Now, it is undoubtedly the case that most of those who profess to give us authoritative instruction on this subject distinguish three constitutions, which they designate *kingship*, *aristocracy*, *democracy*. But in my opinion the question might fairly be put to them, whether they name these as being the *only* ones, or as the *best*. In either case I think they are wrong. For it is plain that we must regard as the *best* constitution that which partakes of all these three elements. And this is no mere assertion, but has been proved by the example of Lycurgus, who was the first to construct a constitution—that of Sparta—on this principle. Nor can we admit that these are the *only* forms: for we have had before now examples of absolute and tyrannical forms of government, which, while differing as widely as possible from kingship, yet appear to have some points of resemblance to it; on which account all absolute rulers falsely assume and use, as far as they can, the title of king. Again there have been many instances of oligarchical governments having in appearance some analogy to aristocracies, which are, if I may say so, as different from them as it is possible to be. The same also holds good about democracy.

4. I will illustrate the truth of what I say. We cannot hold every absolute government to be a kingship, but only that which is accepted voluntarily, and is directed by an appeal to reason rather than to fear and force. Nor again is every oligarchy to be regarded as an aristocracy; the latter exists only where the power is wielded by the justest and wisest men selected on their merits. Similarly, it is not enough to constitute a democracy that the whole crowd of citizens should have the right to do whatever they wish or propose. But where reverence to the gods, succour of parents, respect to elders, obedience to laws, are traditional and habitual, in such communities, if the will of the majority prevail, we may speak of the form of government as a democracy. So then we enumerate six forms of government, —the three commonly spoken of which I have just mentioned, and three

more allied forms, I mean *despotism*, *oligarchy* and *mob-rule*. The first of these arises without artificial aid and in the natural order of events. Next to this, and produced from it by the aid of art and adjustment, comes *kingship*; which degenerating into the evil form allied to it, by which I mean *tyranny*, both are once more destroyed and aristocracy produced. Again the latter being in the course of nature perverted to *oligarchy*, and the people passionately avenging the unjust acts of their rulers, *democracy* comes into existence; which again by its violence and contempt of law becomes sheer *mob-rule*. No clearer proof of the truth of what I say could be obtained than by a careful observation of the natural origin, genesis, and decadence of these several forms of government. For it is only by seeing distinctly how each of them is produced that a distinct view can also be obtained of its growth, zenith, and decadence, and the time, circumstance, and place in which each of these may be expected to recur. This method I have assumed to be especially applicable to the Roman constitution, because its origin and growth have from the first followed natural causes.

5. Now the natural laws which regulate the merging of one form of government into another are perhaps discussed with greater accuracy by Plato and some other philosophers. But their treatment, from its intricacy and exhaustiveness, is only within the capacity of a few. I will therefore endeavour to give a summary of the subject, just so far as I suppose it to fall within the scope of a practical history and the intelligence of ordinary people. For if my exposition appear in any way inadequate, owing to the general terms in which it is expressed, the details contained in what is immediately to follow will amply atone for what is left for the present unsolved.

What is the origin then of a constitution, and whence is it produced? Suppose that from floods, pestilences, failure of crops, or some such causes the race of man is reduced almost to extinction. Such things we are told have happened, and it is reasonable to think will happen again. Suppose accordingly all knowledge of social habits and arts to have been lost. Suppose that from the survivors, as from seeds, the race of man to have again multiplied. In that case I presume they would, like the animals, herd together; for it is but reasonable to suppose that bodily weakness would induce them to seek those of their own kind to herd with. And in that case too, as with the animals, he who was superior to the rest in strength of body or courage of soul would lead and rule them. For what we see happen in the case of animals that are without the faculty of reason, such as bulls, goats, and cocks,—among whom there can be no dispute that the strongest take the lead,—that we must regard as in the truest sense the teaching of nature. Originally then it is probable that the condition of life among men was this,—herding together like animals and following the strongest and bravest as leaders. The limit of this authority would be physical strength, and the name we should give it would be despotism. But as soon as the idea of family ties and social relation has arisen amongst such agglomerations of men, then is born also the idea of kingship, and then for the first time mankind conceives the notion of goodness and justice and their reverse.

6. The way in which such conceptions originate and come into existence is this. The intercourse of the sexes is an instinct of nature, and the result is the birth of children. Now, if any one of these children, who have been brought up, when arrived at maturity, is ungrateful and makes no return to those by whom he was nurtured, but on the contrary presumes to injure them by word and deed, it is plain that he will probably offend and annoy such as are present, and have seen the care and trouble bestowed by the parents on the nurture and bringing up of their children. For seeing that men differ from the other animals in being the only creatures possessed of reasoning powers, it is clear that such a difference of conduct is not likely to escape their observation; but that they will remark it when it occurs, and express their displeasure on the spot: because they will have an eye to the future, and will reason on the likelihood of the same occurring to each of themselves. Again, if a man has been rescued or helped in an hour of danger, and, instead of showing gratitude to his preserver, seeks to do him harm, it is clearly probable that the rest will be displeased and offended with him, when they know it: sympathising with their neighbour and imagining themselves in his case. Hence arises a notion in every breast of the meaning and theory of duty, which is in fact the beginning and end of justice. Similarly, again, when any one man stands out as the champion of all in a time of danger, and braves with firm courage the onslaught of the most powerful wild beasts, it is probable that such a man would meet with marks of favour and pre-eminence from the common people; while he who acted in a contrary way would fall under their contempt and dislike. From this, once more, it is reasonable to suppose that there would arise in the minds of the multitude a theory of the disgraceful and the honourable, and of the difference between them; and that one should be sought and imitated for its advantages, the other shunned. When, therefore, the leading and most powerful man among his people ever encourages such persons in accordance with the popular sentiment, and thereby assumes in the eyes of his subjects the appearance of being the distributor to each man according to his deserts, they no longer obey him and support his rule from fear of violence, but rather from conviction of its utility, however old he may be, rallying round him with one heart and soul, and fighting against all who form designs against his government. In this way he becomes a *king* instead of a *despot* by imperceptible degrees, reason having ousted brute courage and bodily strength from their supremacy.

7. This then is the natural process of formation among mankind of the notion of goodness and justice, and their opposites; and this is the origin and genesis of genuine kingship: for people do not only keep up the government of such men personally, but for their descendants also for many generations; from the conviction that those who are born from and educated by men of this kind will have principles also like theirs. But if they subsequently become displeased with their descendants, they do not any longer decide their choice of rulers and kings by their physical strength or brute courage; but by the differences of their intellectual and reasoning faculties, from practical experience of the decisive importance of such a distinction. In old times, then, those who were once thus selected, and obtained this office, grew old in their royal functions, making magnificent strongholds and surrounding them with walls and extending their frontiers, partly for the security of their subjects, and partly to provide them with abundance of the necessaries of life; and while engaged in these works they were exempt from all vituperation or jealousy; because they did not make their distinctive dress, food, or drink, at all conspicuous, but lived very much like the rest, and joined in the everyday employments of the common people. But when their royal power became hereditary in their family, and they found every necessary for security ready to their hands, as well as more than was necessary for their personal support, then they gave the rein to their appetites; imagined that rulers must needs wear different clothes from those of subjects; have different and elaborate luxuries of the table; and must even seek sensual indulgence, however unlawful the source, without fear of denial. These things having given rise in the one case to jealousy and offence, in the other to outburst of hatred and passionate resentment, the kingship became a tyranny: the first step in disintegration was taken; and plots began to be formed against the government, which did not now proceed from the worst men but from the noblest, most high-minded, and most courageous, because these are the men who can least submit to the tyrannical acts of their rulers.

8. But as soon as the people got leaders, they cooperated with them against the dynasty for the reasons I have mentioned; and then *kingship* and *despotism* were alike entirely abolished, and *aristocracy* once more began to revive and start afresh. For in their immediate gratitude to those who had deposed the despots, the people employed them as leaders, and entrusted their interests to them; who, looking upon this charge at first as a great privilege, made the public advantage their chief concern, and conducted all kinds of business, public or private, with diligence and caution. But when the sons of these men received the same position of authority from their fathers,—having had no experience of misfortunes, and none at all of civil equality and freedom of speech, but having been bred up from the first

under the shadow of their fathers' authority and lofty position,—some of them gave themselves up with passion to avarice and unscrupulous love of money, others to drinking and the boundless debaucheries which accompanies it, and others to the violation of women or the forcible appropriation of boys; and so they turned an *aristocracy* into an *oligarchy*. But it was not long before they roused in the minds of the people the same feelings as before; and their fall therefore was very like the disaster which befell the tyrants.

9. For no sooner had the knowledge of the jealousy and hatred existing in the citizens against them emboldened some one to oppose the government by word or deed, than he was sure to find the whole people ready and prepared to take his side. Having then got rid of these rulers by assassination or exile, they do not venture to set up a king again, being still in terror of the injustice to which this led before; nor dare they intrust the common interests again to more than one, considering the recent example of their misconduct: and therefore, as the only sound hope left them is that which depends on themselves, they are driven to take refuge in that; and so changed the constitution from an oligarchy to a *democracy*, and took upon themselves the superintendence and charge of the state. And as long as any survive who have had experience of oligarchical supremacy and domination, they regard their present constitution as a blessing, and hold equality and freedom as of the utmost value. But as soon as a new generation has arisen, and the democracy has descended to their children's children, long association weakens their value for equality and freedom, and some seek to become more powerful than the ordinary citizens; and the most liable to this temptation are the rich. So when they begin to be fond of office, and find themselves unable to obtain it by their own unassisted efforts and their own merits, they ruin their estates, while enticing and corrupting the common people in every possible way. By which means when, in their senseless mania for reputation, they have made the populace ready and greedy to receive bribes, the virtue of democracy is destroyed, and it is transformed into a government of violence and the strong hand. For the mob, habituated to feed at the expense of others, and to have its hopes of a livelihood in the property of its neighbours, as soon as it has got a leader sufficiently ambitious and daring, being excluded by poverty from the sweets of civil honours, produces a reign of mere violence. Then come tumultuous assemblies, massacres, banishments, redivisions of land; until, after losing all trace of civilisation, it has once more found a master and a despot.

This is the regular cycle of constitutional revolutions, and the natural order in which constitutions change, are transformed, and return again to their original stage. If a man have a clear grasp of these principles he may perhaps make a mistake as to the dates at which this or that will happen to a particular constitution; but he will rarely be entirely mistaken as to the stage of growth or decay at which it has arrived, or as to the point at which it will undergo some revolutionary change. However, it is in the case of the Roman constitution that this method of inquiry will most fully teach us its formation, its growth, and zenith, as well as the changes awaiting it in the future; for this, if any constitution ever did, owed, as I said just now, its original foundation and growth to natural causes, and to natural causes will owe its decay. My subsequent narrative will be the best illustration of what I say.

10. For the present I will make a brief reference to the legislation of Lycurgus: for such a discussion is not at all alien to my subject. That statesman was fully aware that all those changes which I have enumerated come about by an undeviating law of nature; and reflected that every form of government that was unmixed, and rested on one species of power, was unstable; because it was swiftly perverted into that particular form of evil peculiar to it and inherent in its nature. For just as rust is the natural dissolvent of iron, wood-worms and grubs to timber, by which they are destroyed without any external injury, but by that which is engendered in themselves; so in each constitution there is naturally engendered a particular vice inseparable from it: in kingship it is absolutism; in aristocracy it is oligarchy; in democracy lawless ferocity and violence; and to these vicious states all these forms of government are, as I have lately shown, inevitably transformed. Lycurgus, I say, saw all this, and accordingly combined together all the excellences and distinctive features of the best constitutions, that no part should become unduly predominant, and be perverted into its kindred vice; and that, each power being checked by the others, no one part should turn the scale or decisively out-balance the others; but that, by being accurately adjusted and in exact equilibrium, the whole might remain long steady like a ship sailing close to the wind. The royal power was prevented from growing insolent by fear of the people, which had also assigned to it an adequate share in the constitution. The people in their turn were restrained from a bold contempt of the kings by fear of the Gerusia: the members of which, being selected on grounds of merit, were certain to throw their influence on the side of justice in every question that arose; and thus the party placed at a disadvantage by its conservative tendency was always strengthened and supported by the weight and influence of the Gerusia. The result of this combination has been that the Lacedaemonians retained their freedom for the longest period of any people with which we are acquainted.

Lycurgus however established his constitution without the discipline of adversity, because he was able to foresee by the light of reason the course which events naturally take and the source from which they come. But though the Romans have arrived at the same result in framing their commonwealth, they have not done so by means of abstract reasoning, but through many struggles and difficulties, and by continually adopting reforms from knowledge gained in disaster. The result has been a constitution like that of Lycurgus, and the best of any existing in my time. . . .

11. I have given an account of the constitution of Lycurgus, I will now endeavour to describe that of Rome at the period of their disastrous defeat at Cannae. [216 B.C.]

I am fully conscious that to those who actually live under this constitution I shall appear to give an inadequate account of it by the omission of certain details. Knowing accurately every portion of it from personal experience, and from having been bred up in its customs and laws from childhood, they will not be struck so much by the accuracy of the description, as annoyed by its omissions; nor will they believe that the historian has purposely omitted unimportant distinctions, but will attribute his silence upon the origin of existing institutions or other important facts to ignorance. What is told they depreciate as insignificant or beside the purpose; what is omitted they desiderate as vital to the question: their object being to appear to know more than the writers. But a good critic should not judge a writer by what he leaves unsaid, but from what he says: if he detects misstatements in the latter, he may then feel certain that ignorance accounts for the former; but if what he says is accurate, his omissions ought to be attributed to deliberate judgment and not to ignorance. So much for those whose criticisms are prompted by personal ambition rather than by justice. . . .

Another requisite for obtaining a judicious approval for an historical disquisition, is that it should be germane to the matter in hand; if this is not observed, though its style may be excellent and its matter irreproachable, it will seem out of place, and disgust rather than please. . . .

As for the Roman constitution, it had three elements, each of them possessing sovereign powers: and their respective share of power in the whole state had been regulated with such a scrupulous regard to equality and equilibrium, that no one could say for certain, not even a native, whether the constitution as a whole were an aristocracy or democracy or despotism. And no wonder: for if we confine our observation to the power of the Consuls we should be inclined to regard it as despotic; if on that of the Senate, as aristocratic; and if finally one looks at the power possessed by the people it would seem a clear case of a democracy. What the exact powers of these several parts were, and still, with slight modifications, are, I will now state.

12. The Consuls, before leading out the legions, remain in Rome and are supreme masters of the administration. All other magistrates, except

the Tribunes, are under them and take their orders. They introduce foreign ambassadors to the Senate; bring matters requiring deliberation before it; and see to the execution of its decrees. If, again, there are any matters of state which require the authorisation of the people, it is their business to see to them, to summon the popular meetings, to bring the proposals before them, and to carry out the decrees of the majority. In the preparations for war also, and in a word in the entire administration of a campaign, they have all but absolute power. It is competent to them to impose on the allies such levies as they think good, to appoint the Military Tribunes, to make up the roll for soldiers and select those that are suitable. Besides they have absolute power of inflicting punishment on all who are under their command while on active service: and they have authority to expend as much of the public money as they choose, being accompanied by a quaestor who is entirely at their orders. A survey of these powers would in fact justify our describing the constitution as despotic,—a clear case of royal government. Nor will it affect the truth of my description, if any of the institutions I have described are changed in our time, or in that of our posterity: and the same remarks apply to what follows.

13. The Senate has first of all the control of the treasury, and regulates the receipts and disbursements alike. For the Quaestors cannot issue any public money for the various departments of the state without a decree of the Senate, except for the service of the Consuls. The Senate controls also what is by far the largest and most important expenditure, that, namely, which is made by the censors every purificatory ceremony [*lustrum*] for the repair or construction of public buildings; this money cannot be obtained by the censors except by the grant of the Senate. Similarly all crimes committed in Italy requiring a public investigation, such as treason, conspiracy, poisoning, or wilful murder, are in the hands of the Senate. Besides, if any individual or state among the Italian allies requires a controversy to be settled, a penalty to be assessed, help or protection to be afforded,—all this is the province of the Senate. Or again, outside Italy, if it is necessary to send an embassy to reconcile warring communities, or to remind them of their duty, or sometimes to impose requisitions upon them, or to receive their submission, or finally to proclaim war against them,—this too is the business of the Senate. In like manner the reception to be given to foreign ambassadors in Rome, and the answers to be returned to them, are decided by the Senate. With such business the people have nothing to do. Consequently, if one were staying at Rome when the Consuls were not in town, one would imagine the constitution to be a complete aristocracy: and this has been the idea entertained by many Greeks, and by many kings as well, from the fact that nearly all the business they had with Rome was settled by the Senate.

14. After this one would naturally be inclined to ask what part is left for the people in the constitution, when the Senate has these various functions, especially the control of the receipts and expenditure of the exchequer; and when the Consuls, again, have absolute power over the details of military preparation, and an absolute authority in the field? There is, however, a part left the people, and it is a most important one. For the people is the sole fountain of honour and of punishment; and it is by these two things and these alone that dynasties and constitutions and, in a word, human society are held together: for where the distinction between them is not sharply drawn both in theory and practice, there no undertaking can be properly administered,—as indeed we might expect when good and bad are held in exactly the same honour. The people then are the only court to decide matters of life and death; and even in cases where the penalty is money, if the sum to be assessed is sufficiently serious, and especially when the accused have held the higher magistracies. And in regard to this arrangement there is one point deserving especial commendation and record. Men who are on trial for their lives at Rome, while sentence is in process of being voted,—if even only one of the tribes whose votes are needed to ratify the sentence has not voted,—have the privilege at Rome of openly departing and condemning themselves to a voluntary exile. Such men are safe at Naples or Praeneste or at Tibur, and at other towns with which this arrangement has been duly ratified on oath.

Again, it is the people who bestow offices on the deserving, which are the most honourable rewards of virtue. It has also the absolute power of passing or repealing laws; and, most important of all, it is the people who deliberate on the question of peace or war. And when provisional terms are made for alliance, suspension of hostilities, or treaties, it is the people who ratify them or the reverse.

These considerations again would lead one to say that the chief power in the state was the people's, and that the constitution was a democracy.

15. Such, then, is the distribution of power between the several parts of the state. I must now show how each of these several parts can, when they choose, oppose or support each other.

The Consul, then, when he has started on an expedition with the powers I have described, is to all appearance absolute in the administration of the business in hand; still he has need of the support both of people and Senate, and, without them, is quite unable to bring the matter to a successful conclusion. For it is plain that he must have supplies sent to his legions from time to time; but without a decree of the Senate they can be supplied neither with corn, nor clothes, nor pay, so that all the plans of a commander must be futile, if the Senate is resolved either to shrink from danger or hamper his plans. And again, whether a Consul shall bring any undertaking to a conclusion or no depends entirely upon the Senate: for it has absolute authority at the end of a year to send another Consul to supersede him, or to continue the existing one in his command. Again, even to the successes of the generals the Senate has the power to add distinction and glory, and on the other hand to obscure their merits and lower their credit. For these high achievements are brought in tangible form before the eyes of the citizens by what are called "triumphs." But these triumphs the commanders cannot celebrate with proper pomp, or in some cases celebrate at all, unless the Senate concurs and grants the necessary money. As for the people, the Consuls are pre-eminently obliged to court their favour, however distant from home may be the field of their operations; for it is the people, as I have said before, that ratifies, or refuses to ratify, terms of peace and treaties; but most of all because when laying down their office they have to give an account of their administration before it. Therefore in no case is it safe for the Consuls to neglect either the Senate or the goodwill of the people.

16. As for the Senate, which possesses the immense power I have described, in the first place it is obliged in public affairs to take the multitude into account, and respect the wishes of the people; and it cannot put into execution the penalty for offences against the republic, which are punishable with death, unless the people first ratify its decrees. Similarly even in matters which directly affect the senators,—for instance, in the case of a law diminishing the Senate's traditional authority, or depriving senators of certain dignities and offices, or even actually cutting down their property,—even in such cases the people have the sole power of passing or rejecting the law. But most important of all is the fact that, if the Tribunes interpose their veto, the Senate not only are unable to pass a decree, but cannot even hold a meeting at all, whether formal or informal. Now, the Tribunes are always bound to carry out the decree of the people, and above all things to have regard to their wishes: therefore, for all these reasons the Senate stands in awe of the multitude, and cannot neglect the feelings of the people.

17. In like manner the people on its part is far from being independent of the Senate, and is bound to take its wishes into account both collectively and individually. For contracts, too numerous to count, are given out by the censors in all parts of Italy for the repairs or construction of public buildings; there is also the collection of revenue from many rivers, harbours, gardens, mines, and land—everything, in a word, that comes under the control of the Roman government: and in all these the people at large are engaged; so that there is scarcely a man, so to speak, who is not interested either as a contractor or as being employed in the works. For some purchase the contracts from the censors for themselves; and others go partners

with them; while others again go security for these contractors, or actually pledge their property to the treasury for them. Now over all these transactions the Senate has absolute control. It can grant an extension of time; and in case of unforeseen accident can relieve the contractors from a portion of their obligation, or release them from it altogether, if they are absolutely unable to fulfil it. And there are many details in which the Senate can inflict great hardships, or, on the other hand, grant great indulgences to the contractors: for in every case the appeal is to it. But the most important point of all is that the judges are taken from its members in the majority of trials, whether public or private, in which the charges are heavy. Consequently, all citizens are much at its mercy; and being alarmed at the uncertainty as to when they may need its aid, are cautious about resisting or actively opposing its will. And for a similar reason men do not rashly resist the wishes of the Consuls, because one and all may become subject to their absolute authority on a campaign.

18. The result of this power of the several estates for mutual help or harm is a union sufficiently firm for all emergencies, and a constitution than which it is impossible to find a better. For whenever any danger from without compels them to unite and work together, the strength which is developed by the State is so extraordinary, that everything required is unfailingly carried out by the eager rivalry shown by all classes to devote their whole minds to the need of the hour, and to secure that any determination come to should not fail for want of promptitude; while each individual works, privately and publicly alike, for the accomplishment of the business in hand. Accordingly, the peculiar constitution of the State makes it irresistible, and certain of obtaining whatever it determines to attempt. Nay, even when these external alarms are past, and the people are enjoying their good fortune and the fruits of their victories, and, as usually happens, growing corrupted by flattery and idleness, show a tendency to violence and arrogance,—it is in these circumstances, more than ever, that the constitution is seen to possess within itself the power of correcting abuses. For when any one of the three classes becomes puffed up, and manifests an inclination to be contentious and unduly encroaching, the mutual interdependency of all the three, and the possibility of the pretensions of any one being checked and thwarted by the others, must plainly check this tendency: and so the proper equilibrium is maintained by the impulsiveness of the one part being checked by its fear of the other. . . .

The Roman Republic Compared with Others

43. Nearly all historians have recorded as constitutions of eminent excellence those of Lacedaemonia, Crete, Mantinea, and Carthage. Some have also mentioned those of Athens and Thebes. The former I may allow to

pass; but I am convinced that little need be said of the Athenian and Theban constitutions: their growth was abnormal, the period of their zenith brief, and the changes they experienced unusually violent. Their glory was a sudden and fortuitous flash, so to speak; and while they still thought themselves prosperous, and likely to remain so, they found themselves involved in circumstances completely the reverse. The Thebans got their reputation for valour among the Greeks, by taking advantage of the senseless policy of the Lacedaemonians, and the hatred of the allies towards them, owing to the valour of one, or at most two, men who were wise enough to appreciate the situation. Since fortune quickly made it evident that it was not the peculiarity of their constitution, but the valour of their leaders, which gave the Thebans their success. For the great power of Thebes notoriously took its rise, attained its zenith, and fell to the ground with the lives of Epaminondas and Pelopidas. We must therefore conclude that it was not its constitution, but its men, that caused the high fortune which it then enjoyed.

44. A somewhat similar remark applies to the Athenian constitution also. For though it perhaps had more frequent interludes of excellence, yet its highest perfection was attained during the brilliant career of Themistocles; and having reached that point it quickly declined, owing to its essential instability. For the Athenian demos is always in the position of a ship without a commander. In such a ship, if fear of the enemy, or the occurrence of a storm induce the crew to be of one mind and to obey the helmsman, everything goes well; but if they recover from this fear, and begin to treat their officers with contempt, and to quarrel with each other because they are no longer all of one mind,—one party wishing to continue the voyage, and the other urging the steersman to bring the ship to anchor; some letting out the sheets, and others hauling them in, and ordering the sails to be furled,—their discord and quarrels make a sorry show to lookers on; and the position of affairs is full of risk to those on board engaged on the same voyage: and the result has often been that, after escaping the dangers of the widest seas, and the most violent storms, they wreck their ship in harbour and close to shore. And this is what has often happened to the Athenian constitution. For, after repelling, on various occasions, the greatest and most formidable dangers by the valour of its people and their leaders, there have been times when, in periods of secure tranquillity, it has gratuitously and recklessly encountered disaster. Therefore I need say no more about either it, or the Theban constitution: in both of which a mob manages everything on its own unfettered impulse—a mob in the one city distinguished for headlong outbursts of fiery temper, in the other trained in long habits of violence and ferocity.

45. Passing to the Cretan polity there are two points which deserve our consideration. The first is how such writers as Ephorus, Xenophon, Cal-

listhenes and Plato—who are the most learned of the ancients—could assert that it was like that of Sparta; and secondly how they came to assert that it was at all admirable. I can agree with neither assertion; and I will explain why I say so. And first as to its dissimilarity with the Spartan constitution. The peculiar merit of the latter is said to be its land laws, by which no one possesses more than another, but all citizens have an equal share in the public land. The next distinctive feature regards the possession of money: for as it is utterly discredited among them, the jealous competition which arises from inequality of wealth is entirely removed from the city. A third peculiarity of the Lacedaemonian polity is that, of the officials by whose hands and with whose advice the whole government is conducted, the kings hold an hereditary office, while the members of the Gerusia are elected for life.

46. Among the Cretans the exact reverse of all these arrangements obtains. The laws allow them to possess as much land as they can get with no limitation whatever. Money is so highly valued among them, that its possession is not only thought to be necessary but in the highest degree creditable. And in fact greed and avarice are so native to the soil in Crete, that they are the only people in the world among whom no stigma attaches to any sort of gain whatever. Again all their offices are annual and on a democratical footing. I have therefore often felt at a loss to account for these writers speaking of the two constitutions, which are radically different, as though they were closely united and allied. But, besides overlooking these important differences, these writers have gone out of their way to comment at length on the legislation of Lycurgus: "He was the only legislator," they say, "who saw the important points. For there being two things on which the safety of a commonwealth depends,—courage in the face of the enemy and concord at home,—by abolishing covetousness, he with it removed all motive for civil broil and contest: whence it has been brought about that the Lacedaemonians are the best governed and most united people in Greece." Yet while giving utterance to these sentiments, and though they see that, in contrast to this, the Cretans by their ingrained avarice are engaged in countless public and private seditions, murders and civil wars, they yet regard these facts as not affecting their contention, but are bold enough to speak of the two constitutions as alike. Ephorus, indeed, putting aside names, employs expressions so precisely the same, when discoursing on the two constitutions, that, unless one noticed the proper names, there would be no means whatever of distinguishing which of the two he was describing.

47. In what the difference between them consists I have already stated. I will now address myself to showing that the Cretan constitution deserves neither praise nor imitation.

To my mind, then, there are two things fundamental to every state, in virtue of which its powers and constitution become desirable or objectionable. These are customs and laws. Of these the desirable are those which make men's private lives holy and pure, and the public character of the state civilised and just. The objectionable are those whose effect is the reverse. As, then, when we see good customs and good laws prevailing among certain people, we confidently assume that, in consequence of them, the men and their civil constitution will be good also, so when we see private life full of covetousness, and public policy of injustice, plainly we have reason for asserting their laws, particular customs, and general constitution to be bad. Now, with few exceptions, you could find no habits prevailing in private life more steeped in treachery than those in Crete, and no public policy more inequitable. Holding, then, the Cretan constitution to be neither like the Spartan, nor worthy of choice or imitation, I reject it from the comparison which I have instituted.

Nor again would it be fair to introduce the Republic of Plato, which is also spoken of in high terms by some philosophers. For just as we refuse admission to the athletic contests to those actors or athletes who have not acquired a recognised position or trained for them, so we ought not to admit this Platonic constitution to the contest for the prize of merit unless it can first point to some genuine and practical achievement. Up to this time the notion of bringing it into comparison with the constitutions of Sparta, Rome, and Carthage would be like putting up a statue to compare with living and breathing men. Even if such a statue were faultless in point of art, the comparison of the lifeless with the living would naturally leave an impression of imperfection and incongruity upon the minds of the spectators.

48. I shall therefore omit these, and proceed with my description of the Laconian constitution. Now it seems to me that for securing unity among the citizens, for safe-guarding the Laconian territory, and preserving the liberty of Sparta inviolate, the legislation and provisions of Lycurgus were so excellent, that I am forced to regard his wisdom as something superhuman. For the equality of landed possessions, the simplicity in their food, and the practice of taking it in common, which he established, were well calculated to secure morality in private life and to prevent civil broils in the State; as also their training in the endurance of labours and dangers to make men brave and noble minded: but when both these virtues, courage and high morality, are combined in one soul or in one state, vice will not readily spring from such a soil, nor will such men easily be overcome by their enemies. By constructing his constitution therefore in this spirit, and of these elements, he secured two blessings to the Spartans,—safety for their territory, and a lasting freedom for themselves long after he was gone. He appears however to have made no one provision whatever, particular or

general, for the acquisition of the territory of their neighbours; or for the assertion of their supremacy; or, in a word, for any policy of aggrandisement at all. What he had still to do was to impose such a necessity, or create such a spirit among the citizens, that, as he had succeeded in making their individual lives independent and simple, the public character of the state should also become independent and moral. But the actual fact is, that, though he made them the most disinterested and sober-minded men in the world, as far as their own ways of life and their national institutions were concerned, he left them in regard to the rest of Greece ambitious, eager for supremacy, and encroaching in the highest degree.

49. For in the first place is it not notorious that they were nearly the first Greeks to cast a covetous eye upon the territory of their neighbours, and that accordingly they waged a war of subjugation on the Messenians? [745–724(?), 685–668 B.C.] In the next place is it not related in all histories that in their dogged obstinacy they bound themselves with an oath never to desist from the siege of Messene until they had taken it? And lastly it is known to all that in their efforts for supremacy in Greece they submitted to do the bidding of those whom they had once conquered in war. For when the Persians invaded Greece, they conquered them [479 B.C.], as champions of the liberty of the Greeks; yet when the invaders had retired and fled, they betrayed the cities of Greece into their hands by the peace of Antalcidas [387 B.C.], for the sake of getting money to secure their supremacy over the Greeks. It was then that the defect in their constitution was rendered apparent. For as long as their ambition was confined to governing their immediate neighbours, or even the Peloponnesians only, they were content with the resources and supplies provided by Laconia itself, having all material of war ready to hand, and being able without much expenditure of time to return home or convey provisions with them. But directly they took in hand to despatch naval expeditions, or to go on campaigns by land outside the Peloponnese, it was evident that neither their iron currency, nor their use of crops for payment in kind, would be able to supply them with what they lacked if they abided by the legislation of Lycurgus; for such undertakings required money universally current, and goods from foreign countries. Thus they were compelled to wait humbly at Persian doors, impose tribute on the islanders, and exact contributions from all the Greeks: knowing that, if they abided by the laws of Lycurgus, it was impossible to advance any claims upon any outside power at all, much less upon the supremacy in Greece.

50. My object, then, in this digression is to make it manifest by actual facts that, for guarding their own country with absolute safety, and for preserving their own freedom, the legislation of Lycurgus was entirely sufficient; and for those who are content with these objects we must concede

that there neither exists, nor ever has existed, a constitution and civil order preferable to that of Sparta. But if anyone is seeking aggrandisement, and believes that to be a leader and ruler and despot of numerous subjects, and to have all looking and turning to him, is a finer thing than that,—in this point of view we must acknowledge that the Spartan constitution is deficient, and that of Rome superior and better constituted for obtaining power. And this has been proved by actual facts. For when the Lacedaemonians strove to possess themselves of the supremacy in Greece, it was not long before they brought their own freedom itself into danger. Whereas the Romans, after obtaining supreme power over the Italians themselves, soon brought the whole world under their rule,—in which achievement the abundance and availability of their supplies largely contributed to their success.

51. Now the Carthaginian constitution seems to me originally to have been well contrived in these most distinctively important particulars. For they had kings, and the Gerusia had the powers of an aristocracy, and the multitude were supreme in such things as affected them; and on the whole the adjustment of its several parts was very like that of Rome and Sparta. But about the period of its entering on the Hannibalian war the political state of Carthage was on the decline, that of Rome improving. For whereas there is in every body, or polity, or business a natural stage of growth, zenith, and decay; and whereas everything in them is at its best at the zenith; we may thereby judge of the difference between these two constitutions as they existed at that period. For exactly so far as the strength and prosperity of Carthage preceded that of Rome in point of time, by so much was Carthage then past its prime, while Rome was exactly at its zenith, as far as its political constitution was concerned. In Carthage therefore the influence of the people in the policy of the state had already risen to be supreme, while at Rome the Senate was at the height of its power: and so, as in the one measures were deliberated upon by the many, in the other by the best men, the policy of the Romans in all public undertakings proved the stronger; on which account, though they met with capital disasters, by force of prudent counsels they finally conquered the Carthaginians in the war.

52. If we look however at separate details, for instance at the provisions for carrying on a war, we shall find that whereas for a naval expedition the Carthaginians are the better trained and prepared,—as it is only natural with a people with whom it has been hereditary for many generations to practise this craft, and to follow the seaman's trade above all nations in the world,—yet, in regard to military service on land, the Romans train themselves to a much higher pitch than the Carthaginians. The former bestow their whole attention upon this department: whereas the Carthaginians

wholly neglect their infantry, though they do take some slight interest in the cavalry. The reason of this is that they employ foreign mercenaries, the Romans native and citizen levies. It is in this point that the latter polity is preferable to the former. They have their hopes of freedom ever resting on the courage of mercenary troops: the Romans on the valour of their own citizens and the aid of their allies. The result is that even if the Romans have suffered a defeat at first, they renew the war with undiminished forces, which the Carthaginians cannot do. For, as the Romans are fighting for country and children, it is impossible for them to relax the fury of their struggle; but they persist with obstinate resolution until they have overcome their enemies. What has happened in regard to their navy is an instance in point. In skill the Romans are much behind the Carthaginians, as I have already said; yet the upshot of the whole naval war has been a decided triumph for the Romans, owing to the valour of their men. For although nautical science contributes largely to success in sea-fights, still it is the courage of the marines that turns the scale most decisively in favour of victory. The fact is that Italians as a nation are by nature superior to Phoenicians and Libyans both in physical strength and courage; but still their habits also do much to inspire the youth with enthusiasm for such exploits. One example will be sufficient of the pains taken by the Roman state to turn out men ready to endure anything to win a reputation in their country for valour.

53. Whenever one of their illustrious men dies, in the course of his funeral, the body with all its paraphernalia is carried into the forum to the Rostra, as a raised platform there is called, and sometimes is propped upright upon it so as to be conspicuous, or, more rarely, is laid upon it. Then with all the people standing round, his son, if he has left one of full age and he is there, or, failing him, one of his relations, mounts the Rostra and delivers a speech concerning the virtues of the deceased, and the successful exploits performed by him in his lifetime. By these means the people are reminded of what has been done, and made to see it with their own eyes,—not only such as were engaged in the actual transactions but those also who were not;—and their sympathies are so deeply moved, that the loss appears not to be confined to the actual mourners, but to be a public one affecting the whole people. After the burial and all the usual ceremonies have been performed, they place the likeness of the deceased in the most conspicuous spot in his house, surmounted by a wooden canopy or shrine. This likeness consists of a mask made to represent the deceased with extraordinary fidelity both in shape and colour. These likenesses they display at public sacrifices adorned with much care. And when any illustrious member of the family dies, they carry these masks to the funeral, putting them on men whom they thought as like the originals as possible in

height and other personal peculiarities. And these substitutes assume clothes according to the rank of the person represented: if he was a consul or praetor, a toga with purple stripes; if a censor, whole purple; if he had also celebrated a triumph or performed any exploit of that kind, a toga embroidered with gold. These representatives also ride themselves in chariots, while the fasces and axes, and all the other customary insignia of the particular offices, lead the way, according to the dignity of the rank in the state enjoyed by the deceased in his lifetime; and on arriving at the Rostra they all take their seats on ivory chairs in their order. There could not easily be a more inspiring spectacle than this for a young man of noble ambitions and virtuous aspirations. For can we conceive any one to be unmoved at the sight of all the likenesses collected together of the men who have earned glory, all as it were living and breathing? Or what could be a more glorious spectacle?

54. Besides the speaker over the body about to be buried, after having finished the panegyric of this particular person, starts upon the others whose representatives are present, beginning with the most ancient, and recounts the successes and achievements of each. By this means the glorious memory of brave men is continually renewed; the fame of those who have performed any noble deed is never allowed to die; and the renown of those who have done good service to their country becomes a matter of common knowledge to the multitude, and part of the heritage of posterity. But the chief benefit of the ceremony is that it inspires young men to shrink from no exertion for the general welfare, in the hope of obtaining the glory which awaits the brave. And what I say is confirmed by this fact. Many Romans have volunteered to decide a whole battle by single combat; not a few have deliberately accepted certain death, some in time of war to secure the safety of the rest, some in time of peace to preserve the safety of the commonwealth. There have also been instances of men in office putting their own sons to death, in defiance of every custom and law, because they rated the interests of their country higher than those of natural ties even with their nearest and dearest. There are many stories of this kind, related of many men in Roman history; but one will be enough for our present purpose; and I will give the name as an instance to prove the truth of my words.

55. The story goes that Horatius Cocles, while fighting with two enemies at the head of the bridge over the Tiber, which is the entrance to the city on the north, seeing a large body of men advancing to support his enemies, and fearing that they would force their way into the city, turned round, and shouted to those behind him to hasten back to the other side and break down the bridge. They obeyed him: and whilst they were breaking the bridge, he remained at his post receiving numerous wounds, and

checked the progress of the enemy: his opponents being panic stricken, not so much by his strength as by the audacity with which he held his ground. When the bridge had been broken down, the attack of the enemy was stopped; and Cocles then threw himself into the river with his armour on and deliberately sacrificed his life, because he valued the safety of his country and his own future reputation more highly than his present life, and the years of existence that remained to him. Such is the enthusiasm and emulation for noble deeds that are engendered among the Romans by their customs.

56. Again the Roman customs and principles regarding money transactions are better than those of the Carthaginians. In the view of the latter nothing is disgraceful that makes for gain; with the former nothing is more disgraceful than to receive bribes and to make profit by improper means. For they regard wealth obtained from unlawful transactions to be as much a subject of reproach, as a fair profit from the most unquestioned source is of commendation. A proof of the fact is this. The Carthaginians obtain office by open bribery, but among the Romans the penalty for it is death. With such a radical difference, therefore, between the rewards offered to virtue among the two peoples, it is natural that the ways adopted for obtaining them should be different also.

But the most important difference for the better which the Roman commonwealth appears to me to display is in their religious beliefs. For I conceive that what in other nations is looked upon as a reproach, I mean a scrupulous fear of the gods, is the very thing which keeps the Roman commonwealth together. To such an extraordinary height is this carried among them, both in private and public business, that nothing could exceed it. Many people might think this unaccountable; but in my opinion their object is to use it as a check upon the common people. If it were possible to form a state wholly of philosophers, such a custom would perhaps be unnecessary. But seeing that every multitude is fickle, and full of lawless desires, unreasoning anger, and violent passion, the only resource is to keep them in check by mysterious terrors and scenic effects of this sort. Wherefore, to my mind, the ancients were not acting without purpose or at random, when they brought in among the vulgar those opinions about the gods, and the belief in the punishments in Hades: much rather do I think that men nowadays are acting rashly and foolishly in rejecting them. This is the reason why, apart from anything else, Greek statesmen, if entrusted with a single talent, though protected by ten checking-clerks, as many seals, and twice as many witnesses, yet cannot be induced to keep faith: whereas among the Romans, in the magistracies and embassies, men have the handling of a great amount of money, and yet from pure respect to their oath keep their faith intact. And, again, in other nations it is a rare thing to find a man who keeps his hands out of the public purse, and is entirely pure in such matters: but among the Romans it is a rare thing to detect a man in the act of committing such a crime. . . .

Recapitulation and Conclusion

57. That to all things, then, which exist there is ordained decay and change I think requires no further arguments to show: for the inexorable course of nature is sufficient to convince us of it.

But in all polities we observe two sources of decay existing from natural causes, the one external, the other internal and self-produced. The external admits of no certain or fixed definition, but the internal follows a definite order. What kind of polity, then, comes naturally first, and what second, I have already stated in such a way, that those who are capable of taking in the whole drift of my argument can henceforth draw their own conclusions as to the future of the Roman polity. For it is quite clear, in my opinion. When a commonwealth, after warding off many great dangers, has arrived at a high pitch of prosperity and undisputed power, it is evident that, by the lengthened continuance of great wealth within it, the manner of life of its citizens will become more extravagant; and that the rivalry for office, and in other spheres of activity, will become fiercer than it ought to be. And as this state of things goes on more and more, the desire of office and the shame of losing reputation, as well as the ostentation and extravagance of living, will prove the beginning of a deterioration. And of this change the people will be credited with being the authors, when they become convinced that they are being cheated by some from avarice, and are puffed up with flattery by others from love of office. For when that comes about, in their passionate resentment and acting under the dictates of anger, they will refuse to obey any longer, or to be content with having equal powers with their leaders, but will demand to have all or far the greatest themselves. And when that comes to pass the constitution will receive a new name, which sounds better than any other in the world, liberty or democracy; but, in fact, it will become that worst of all governments, mob-rule.

With this description of the formation, growth, zenith, and present state of the Roman polity, and having discussed also its difference, for better and worse, from other polities, I will now at length bring my essay on it to an end.

2. Quintus Cicero, *Handbook on Canvassing for the Consulship*

Quintus Tullius Cicero, who lived from 102 to 43 B.C., was the younger brother of Marcus Tullius Cicero (see document 4). Educated in Athens in 79 B.C., he held such significant public offices as plebeian aedile (65 B.C.) and praetor (62 B.C.), governor of Rome's richest province, Asia (61–59 B.C.), and legate or deputy in Sardinia (57–56 B.C.), Gaul (54–51 B.C.), and Cilicia (51–50 B.C.). He supported Pompey in his civil war with Julius Caesar and perished in the proscriptions or purges of 43 B.C. that followed the assassination of Julius Caesar.

Scholars debate the authorship (traditionally attributed to Quintus) and date of the *Handbook on Canvassing*, which describes Marcus Cicero's campaign for the consulship in 63 B.C.; it remains a basic source for the institutions and political values of the Late Republic. The consuls were elected by the assembly called the *comitia centuriata* on the Campus Martius (just outside of the city limits of Rome at that time). The vote was not by head, but by *centuriae*, which had originated as military formations. There were 193 *centuriae*, grouped according to age, wealth, and, at the time of Cicero, membership in one of thirty-five *tribus* (tribes) into which Roman citizens had been divided. The word *candidate* comes from the candidate's wearing of a *toga candida*, the plain white toga of the ordinary citizen, rather than the purple-bordered one to which he was entitled as a former magistrate.

I. Although you have all the accomplishments within the reach of human genius, experience, or acuteness, yet I thought it only consistent with my affection to set down in writing what occurred to my mind while thinking, as I do, day and night on your canvass, not with the expectation that you would learn anything new from it, but that the considerations on a subject, which appeared to be disconnected and without system, might be brought under one view by a logical arrangement.

Consider what the state is: what it is you seek: who you are that seek it. Almost every day as you go down to the forum you should say to yourself, "I am a new man," "I am a candidate for the consulship," "This is Rome." For the "newness" of your name you will best compensate by the brilliancy of your oratory. That has ever carried with it very great political distinction. A man who is held worthy of defending consulars cannot be thought unworthy of the consulship. Wherefore, since your reputation in this is

From *The Letters of Cicero*, vol. 1, translated by Evelyn S. Shuckburgh (London: George Bell & Sons, 1908), pp. 367–81.

your starting-point, since whatever you are, you are from this, approach each individual case with the persuasion that on it depends as a whole your entire reputation. See that those aids to natural ability, which I know are your special gifts, are ready for use and always available; and remember what Demetrius[1] wrote about the hard work and practice of Demosthenes; and, finally, take care that both the number and rank of your friends are unmistakable. For you have such as few "new men" have had—all the publicans, nearly the whole equestrian order, many municipal towns specially devoted to you, many persons who have been defended by you, men of every order, many colleges, and, besides these, a large number of the rising generation who have become attached to you in their enthusiasm for rhetoric, and, finally, your friends who visit you daily in large numbers and with such constant regularity. See that you retain these advantages by reminding these persons, by appealing to them, and by using every means to make them understand that this, and this only, is the time for those who are in your debt to shew their gratitude, and for those who wish for your services in the future to place you under an obligation. It also seems possible that a "new man" may be much assisted by the fact that he has the good wishes of men of high rank, and especially of consulars. It is a point in your favour that you should be thought worthy of this position and rank by the very men to whose position and rank you are wishing to attain. All these men must be canvassed with care, agents must be sent to them, and they must be convinced that we have always been at one with the Optimates in our political sentiments, that we have never been demagogues in the very least; that if we seem ever to have said anything in the spirit of that party, we did so with the view of attracting Cn. Pompeius, that we might have the man of the greatest influence either actively on our side in our canvass, or at least not opposed to us. Furthermore, take pains to get on your side the young men of high rank, or retain the affection of those you already have. They will contribute much to your political position. You have very many; make them feel how much you think depends on them: if you induce those to be positively eager who are merely not disinclined, they will be of very great advantage to you.

II. It is also a great set-off to your "newness," that the nobles who are your competitors are of a such a kind that no one can venture to say that their nobility ought to stand them in greater stead than your high character. For instance, who could think of P. Galba and L. Cassius, though by birth of the highest rank, as candidates for the consulship? You see, therefore, that there are men of the noblest families, who from defect of ability are

1. Demetrius of Phaleron, a peripatetic philosopher and statesman, ruled Athens for the king of Macedonia from 317 to 307 B.C.

not your equals. But, you will say, Catiline and Antonius are formidable. Rather I should say that a man of energy, industry, unimpeachable character, great eloquence, and high popularity with those who are the ultimate judges, should wish for such rivals—both from their boyhood stained with blood and lust, both of ruined fortunes. Of one of them we have seen the property put up for sale, and actually heard him declare on oath that at Rome he could not contend with a Greek or obtain an impartial tribunal. We know that he was ejected from the senate by the judgment of genuine censors: in our praetorship we had him as a competitor, with such men as Sabidius and Panthera to back him, because he had no one else to appear for him at the scrutiny. Yet in this office he bought a mistress from the slave market whom he kept openly at his house. Moreover, in his canvass for the consulship, he has preferred to be robbing all the innkeepers, under the disgraceful pretext of a *libera legatio*,[2] rather than to be in town and supplicate the Roman people. But the other! Good heavens! what is his distinction? Is he of equally noble birth? No. Is he richer? No. In manliness, then? How do you make that out? Why, because while the former fears his own shadow, this man does not even fear the laws!—A man born in the house of a bankrupt father, nurtured in the society of an abandoned sister, grown to manhood amidst the massacre of fellow citizens, whose first entrance to public life was made by the slaughter of Roman knights! For Sulla had specially selected Catiline to command that band of Gauls which we remember, who shore off the heads of the Titinii and Nannii and Tanusii: and while with them he killed with his own hands the best man of the day, his own sister's husband, Quintus Caecilius, who was a Roman eques, a man belonging to no party, always quiet by inclination, and then so from age also.

III. Why should I speak of him as a candidate for the consulship, who caused M. Marius, a man most beloved by the Roman people, to be beaten with vine-rods in the sight of that Roman people from one end of the city to the other—forced him up to the tomb—rent his frame with every kind of torture, and while he was still alive and breathing, cut off his head with his sword in his right hand, while he held the hairs on the crown of his head with his left, and carried off his head in his own hand with streams of blood flowing through his fingers? A man who afterwards lived with actors and gladiators on such terms that the former ministered to his lust, the latter to his crimes—who never approached a place so sacred or holy as not to leave there, even if no actual crime were committed, some suspicion of dishonour founded on his abandoned character—a man whose closest friends in

2. The *legatio libera* was the right to travel at public expense for the purpose of personal business, often given by the senate to its members campaigning in the *municipia*, or municipalities, self-governing Italian districts in outlying areas, other than colonies.

the senate were the Curii and the Annii, in the auction rooms the Sapalae and Carvilii, in the equestrian order the Pompilii and Vettii—a man of such consummate impudence, such abandoned profligacy, in fine, such cunning and success in lasciviousness, that he corrupted young boys when almost in the bosoms of their parents? Why should I after this mention Africa to you, or the depositions of the witnesses? They are well known—read them again and again yourself. Nevertheless, I think that I should not omit to mention that he left that court in the first place as needy as some of the jurors were before the trial, and in the second place the object of such hatred, that another prosecution against him is called for every day. His position is such that he is more likely to be nervous even if you do nothing, than contemptuous if you start any proceedings.

What much better fortune in your canvass is yours than that which not long ago fell to the lot of another "new man," Gaius Caelius! He had two men of the highest rank as competitors, but they were of such a character that their rank was the least of their recommendations—genius of the highest order, supreme modesty, very numerous public services, most excellent methods of conducting a canvass, and diligence in carrying them out. And yet Caelius, though much inferior in birth, and superior in hardly anything, beat one of them. Wherefore, if you do what your natural ability and studies, which you have always pursued, enable you to do, what the exigencies of your present position require, what you are capable of doing and are bound to do, you will not have a difficult struggle with competitors who are by no means so conspicuous for their birth as notorious for their vices. For what citizen can there be found so ill-affected as to wish by one vote to draw two daggers against the Republic?

IV. Having thus set forth what advantages you have and might have to set against your "newness," I think I ought now to say a word on the importance of what you are trying for. You are seeking the consulship, an office of which no one thinks you unworthy, but of which there are many who will be jealous. For, while by birth of equestrian rank, you are seeking the highest rank in the state, and yet one which, though the highest, reflects much greater splendour on a man of courage, eloquence, and pure life than on others. Don't suppose that those who have already held that office are blind to the political position you will occupy, when once you have obtained the same. I suspect, however, that those who, though born of consular families, have not attained the position of their ancestors, will, unless they happen to be strongly attached to you, feel some jealousy. Even "new men" who have been praetors I think, unless under great obligations to you, will not like to be surpassed by you in official rank. Lastly, in the populace itself, I am sure it will occur to you how many are envious, how many, from the precedents of recent years, are averse to "new men." It must also needs be that some are angry with you in consequence of the causes which you have pleaded. Nay, carefully consider this also, whether, seeing that you have devoted yourself with such fervour to the promotion of Pompey's glory, you can suppose certain men to be your friends on that account. Wherefore, seeing that you are seeking the highest place in the state, and at the same time that there do exist sentiments opposed to you, you must positively employ every method, and all your vigilance, labour, and attention to business.

V. Again, the canvass for office resolves itself into an activity of two kinds, of which one is concerned with the loyalty of friends, the other with the feelings of the people. The loyalty of friends must be secured by acts of kindness and attention, by length of time, and by an easy and agreeable temper. But this word "friends" has a wider application during a canvass than in other times of our life. For whosoever gives any sign of an inclination to you, or habitually visits at your house, must be put down in the category of friends. But yet the most advantageous thing is to be beloved and pleasant in the eyes of those who are friends on the more regular grounds of relationship by blood or marriage, of membership of the same club, or of some close tie or other. Farther, you must take great pains that, in proportion as a man is most intimate and most closely connected with your household, he should love you and desire your highest honour—as, for instance, your tribesmen, neighbours, clients, and finally your freedmen and even your slaves; for nearly all the talk which forms one's public reputation emanates from domestic sources. In a word, you must secure friends of every class: for show—men conspicuous for their office or name, who, even if they do not give any actual assistance in canvassing, yet add some dignity to the candidate; to maintain your just rights—magistrates, consuls first and then tribunes; to secure the votes of the centuries—men of eminent popularity. Those who either have gained or hope to gain the vote of a tribe or century, or any other advantage, through your influence, take all pains to collect and secure. For during recent years men of ambition have exerted themselves with all their might and main to become sure of getting from their tribesmen what they sought. Do you also your very best, by every means in your power, to make such men attached to you from the bottom of their hearts and with the most complete devotion. If, indeed, men were as grateful as they ought to be, all this should be ready to your hand, as I trust in fact that it is. For within the last two years you have put under an obligation to you four clubs of men who have the very greatest influence in promoting an election, those of C. Fundanius, Q. Gallius, C. Cornelius,[3] C. Orchivius. When they committed the defence of these men to you, I am acquainted with what their clubsmen un-

3. C. Cornelius, tribune in 67 B.C., was accused of *maiestas* (high treason) in 65 B.C. and defended by Marcus Cicero.

dertook and promised you to do, for I was present at the interview. Wherefore you must insist at the present juncture on exacting from them your due by reminding them, appealing to them, solemnly assuring them, and taking care that they thoroughly understand that they will never have any other opportunity of shewing their gratitude. I cannot doubt that these men, from hope of your services in the future as well as from the benefits recently received, will be roused to active exertions. And speaking generally, since your candidature is most strongly supported by that class of friendships which you have gained as a counsel for the defence, take care that to all those, whom you have placed under this obligation to you, their duty should in every case be clearly defined and set forth. And as you have never been in any matter importunate with them, so be careful that they understand that you have reserved for this occasion all that you consider them to owe you.

VI. But since men are principally induced to shew goodwill and zeal at the hustings by three considerations—kindness received, hope of more, personal affection and good feeling—we must take notice how best to take advantage of each of these. By very small favours men are induced to think that they have sufficient reason for giving support at the poll, and surely those you have saved (and their number is very large) cannot fail to understand that, if at this supreme crisis they fail to do what you wish, they will never have anyone's confidence. And though this is so, nevertheless they must be appealed to, and must even be led to think it possible that they, who have hitherto been under an obligation to us, may now put us under an obligation to them. Those, again, who are influenced by hope (a class of people much more apt to be scrupulously attentive) you must take care to convince that your assistance is at their service at any moment, and to make them understand that you are carefully watching the manner in which they perform the duties they owe you, and to allow no mistake to exist as to your clearly perceiving and taking note of the amount of support coming from each one of them. The third class which I mentioned is that of spontaneous and sincere friends, and this class you will have to make more secure by expressions of your gratitude; by making your words tally with the motives which it shall appear to you influenced them in taking up your cause; by shewing that the affection is mutual; and by suggesting that your friendship with them may ripen into intimacy and familiar intercourse. In all these classes alike consider and weigh carefully the amount of influence each possesses, in order to know both the kind of attention to pay to each, and what you are to expect and demand from each. For certain men are popular in their own neighbourhoods and towns; there are others possessed of energy and wealth, who, even if they have not heretofore sought such popularity, can yet easily obtain it at the moment for the sake of one to whom they owe or wish to do a favour. Your attention to such classes of men must be such as to shew them that you clearly understand what is to be expected from each, that you appreciate what you are receiving, and remember what you have received. There are, again, others who either have no influence or are positively disliked by their tribesmen, and have neither the spirit nor the ability to exert themselves on the spur of the moment: be sure you distinguish between such men, that you may not be disappointed in your expectation of support by placing over-much hope on some particular person.

VII. But although you ought to rely on, and be fortified by, friendships already gained and firmly secured, yet in the course of the canvass itself very numerous and useful friendships are acquired. For among its annoyances a candidature has this advantage: you can without loss of dignity, as you cannot in other affairs of life, admit whomsoever you choose to your friendship, to whom if you were at any other time to offer your society, you would be thought guilty of an eccentricity; whereas during a canvass, if you don't do so with many, and take pains about it besides, you would be thought to be no use as a candidate at all. Moreover, I can assure you of this, that there is no one, unless he happens to be bound by some special tie to some one of your rivals, whom you could not induce, if you took pains, to earn your affection by his good services, and to seize the opportunity of putting you under an obligation—let him but fully understand that you value him highly, that you really mean what you say, that he is making a good investment, and that there will accrue from it not only a brief and electioneering friendship, but a firm and lasting one. There will be no one, believe me, if he has anything in him at all, who will let slip this opportunity offered of establishing a friendship with you, especially when by good luck you have competitors whose friendship is one to be neglected or avoided, and who not only are unable to secure what I am urging you to secure, but cannot even make the first step towards it. For how should Antonius make the first step towards attaching people to himself, when he cannot even call them, unaided, by their proper names? I, for one, think that there can be no greater folly than to imagine a man solicitous to serve you whom you don't know by sight. Extraordinary indeed must be the fame, the political position and extent of the public services of that man whom entire strangers, without supporters to back him, would elect to office. That a man without principle or energy, without doing any good service, and without ability, lying under a cloud of discredit, and without friends, should beat a man fortified with the devotion of a numerous circle and by the good opinion of all, cannot possibly occur except from gross negligence.

VIII. Wherefore see that you have the votes of all the centuries secured to you by the number and variety of your friends. The first and most obvious thing is that you should embrace the Roman senators and knights, and the active and popular men of all the other orders. There are many city men of good business habits, there are many freedmen engaged in the forum who are popular and energetic: these men try with all your might both personally and by common friends, as far as you can, to make eager in your behalf; seek them out, send agents to them, shew them that they are putting you under the greatest obligation. After that review the entire city, all colleges, districts, neighbourhoods. If you attach to yourself the leading men of these, you will by their means easily keep a hold upon the multitude. When you have done that, take care to have in your mind a chart of all Italy laid out according to the tribe of each town, and learn it by heart, so that you may not allow any municipality, colony, prefecture, or, in a word, any spot in Italy to exist, in which you have not a sufficient foothold. Inquire also for and trace out individuals in every region, inform yourself about them, seek them out, strengthen their resolution, secure that in their own neighbourhoods they shall canvass for you, and be as it were candidates in your interest. They will wish for you as a friend, if they once see that their friendship is an object with you. Make sure that they *do* understand this by directing your speech specially to this point. Men of country towns, or from the country, think themselves in the position of friends if we of the city know them by name: if, however, they think that they are besides securing some protection for themselves, they do not let slip the opportunity of being obliging. Of such people others in town, and above all your rivals, don't so much as know the existence: you know about them and will easily recognize them, without which friendship is impossible. Nor is such recognition enough (though it is a great thing) unless some hope of material advantage and active friendship follows, for your object is not to be looked upon as a mere "nomenclator," but as a sincere friend also. So when you have both got the favour of these same men in the centuries, who from the means they have taken to secure their personal objects enjoy most popularity among their fellow tribesmen; and have made those all desirous of your success who have influence in any section of their tribe, owing to consideration attaching to their municipality or neighbourhood or college, then you may allow yourself to entertain the highest hopes.

Again, the centuries of the knights appear to me capable of being won over, if you are careful, with considerably more ease. Let your first care be to acquaint yourself with the knights; for they are comparatively few: then make advances to them, for it is much easier to gain the friendship of young men at their time of life. Then again, you have on your side the best of the rising generation, and the most devoted to learning. Moreover, as the equestrian order is yours, they will follow the example of that order, if only you take the trouble to confirm the support of those centuries, not only by the general good affection of the order, but also by the friendships of individuals. Finally, the hearty zeal of the young in canvassing for votes, appearing at various places, bringing intelligence, and being in attendance on you in public are surprisingly important as well as creditable.

IX. And since I have mentioned "attendance," I may add that you should be careful to see large companies every day of every class and order; for from the mere number of these a guess may well be made as to the amount of support you are likely to have in the voting place itself. Such visitors are of three kinds: one consists of morning callers who come to your house, a second of those who escort you to the forum, a third of those who attend you on your canvass. In the case of the morning callers, who are less select and, according to the prevailing fashion, come in greater numbers, you must contrive to make them think that you value even this slight attention very highly. Let those who shall come to your house see that you notice it; shew your gratification to such of their friends as will repeat it to them; frequently mention it to the persons themselves. It often happens that people, when they visit a number of candidates, and observe that there is one who above the rest notices these attentions, devote themselves to him; leave off visiting the others; little by little become devoted to one instead of being neutral, and from sham turn out real supporters. Farthermore, carefully remember this, if you have been told or have discovered that a man who has given you his promise is "dressing for the occasion," as the phrase goes, make as though you had neither heard it nor knew it; if any offers to clear himself to you, because he thinks himself suspected, assert roundly that you have never doubted his sincerity and have no right to doubt it. For the man who thinks that he is not giving satisfaction can never be a friend. You ought, however, to know each man's real feeling, in order to settle how much confidence to place in him.

Secondly, of those who escort you to the forum: since this is a greater attention than a morning call, indicate and make clear that it is still more gratifying to you, and as far as it shall lie in your power go down to the forum at fixed times. The daily escort by its numbers produces a great impression and confers great personal distinction. The third class is that of numbers perpetually attending you on your canvass. See that those who do so spontaneously understand that you regard yourself as for ever obliged by their extreme kindness: from those, on the other hand, who owe you this attention, frankly demand that, as far as their age and business allow, they should constantly be in personal attendance, and that those who are unable to accompany you in person should find relations to take their place in performing this duty. I am very anxious, and think it extremely important, that you should always be surrounded by large numbers. Besides, it confers a great reputation and great distinction to be accompanied by those who by your exertions have been defended, preserved, and acquitted in the law courts. Put this demand fairly before them, that, since by your means and without any payment some have retained their property, others their honour, others their civil existence and entire fortunes, and since there will never be any other time at which they can shew their gratitude, they should remunerate you by this service.

X. And since the point now in discussion is entirely a question of the loyalty of friends, I must not, I think, pass over one caution. Deception, intrigue, and treachery are everywhere. This is not the time for a formal disquisition on the indications by which a true friend may be distinguished from a false: all that is in place now is to give you a hint. Your exalted character has compelled many to pretend to be your friends while really jealous of you. Wherefore remember the saying of Epicharmus, "the muscle and bone of wisdom is to believe nothing rashly." Again, when you have got the feelings of your friends in a sound state, you must then acquaint yourself with the attitude and varieties of your detractors and opponents. There are three: first, those whom you have attacked; second, those who dislike you without definite reason; third, those who are warm friends of your competitors. As to those attacked by you while pleading a friend's cause against them, frankly excuse yourself; remind them of the ties constraining you; give them reason to hope that you will act with equal zeal and loyalty in their cases, if they become your friends. As for those who dislike you without reason, do your best to remove that prejudice either by some actual service, or by holding out hopes of it, or by indicating your kindly feeling towards them. As for those whose wishes are against you owing to friendship for your competitors, gratify them also by the same means as the former, and, if you can get them to believe it, shew that you are kindly disposed to the very men who are standing against you.

XI. Having said enough about securing friendships, I must now speak on another department of a candidate's task, which is concerned with the conciliation of the people. This demands a knack of remembering names, insinuating manners, constant attendance, liberality, the power of setting a report afloat and creating a hopeful feeling in the state. First of all, make the faculty you possess of recognizing people conspicuous, and go on increasing and improving it every day. I don't think there is anything so popular or so conciliatory. Next, if nature has denied you some quality, resolve to assume it, so as to appear to be acting naturally. Although nature has great force, yet in a business lasting only a few months it seems probable that the artificial may be the more effective. For though you are not lacking in the courtesy which good and polite men should have, yet there is great need of a flattering manner which, however faulty and discreditable in other transactions of life, is yet necessary during a candidateship. For when it makes a man worse by truckling, it is wrong; but when only more friendly, it does not deserve so harsh a term; while it is absolutely necessary to a candidate, whose face and expression and style of conversation have to be varied and accommodated to the feelings and tastes of everyone he meets. As for "constant attendance," there is no need of laying down any rule, the phrase speaks for itself. It is, of course, of very great consequence not to go away anywhere: but the real advantage of such constant attendance is not only the being at Rome and in the forum, but the pushing one's canvass assiduously, the addressing oneself again and again to the same persons, the making it impossible (as far as your power goes) for anyone to say that he has not been asked by you, and earnestly and carefully asked. Liberality is, again, of wide application; it is shewn in regard to the management of your private property, which, even if it does not actually reach the multitude, yet, if spoken of with praise by friends, earns the favour of the multitude. It may also be displayed in banquets, which you must take care to attend yourself and to cause your friends to attend, whether open ones or those confined to particular tribes. It may, again, be displayed in giving practical assistance, which I would have you render available far and wide: and be careful therein to be accessible to all by day and night, and not only by the doors of your house, but by your face and countenance, which is the door of the mind; for, if that shews your feelings to be those of reserve and concealment, it is of little good to have your house doors open. For men desire not only to have promises made them, especially in their applications to a candidate, but to have them made in a liberal and complimentary manner. Accordingly, it is an easy rule to make, that you should indicate that whatever you are going to do you will do with heartiness and pleasure; it is somewhat more difficult, and rather a concession to the necessities of the moment than to your inclination, that when you cannot do a thing you should [either promise] or put your refusal pleasantly: the latter is the conduct of a good man, the former of a good candidate. For when a request is made which we cannot grant with honour or without loss to ourselves, for instance, if a man were to ask us to appear in a suit against a friend, a refusal must be given in a gentlemanly way: you must point out to him that your hands are tied, must shew that you are exceedingly sorry, must convince him that you will make up for it in other ways.

XII. I have heard a man say about certain orators, to whom he had offered his case, "that he had been better pleased with the words of the one who declined, than of the one who accepted." So true it is that men are more taken by look and words than by actual services. [This latter course, however, you will readily approve: the former it is somewhat difficult to recommend to a Platonist like you, but yet I will have regard for your present circumstances.] For even those to whom you are forced by any other tie to refuse your advocacy may yet quit you mollified and with friendly feelings. But those to whom you only excuse a refusal by saying that you are hindered by the affairs of closer friends, or by cases more important or previously undertaken, quit you with hostile feelings, and are one and all disposed to prefer an insincere promise to a direct negative from you. C. Cotta, a master in the art of electioneering, used to say that, "so long as the request was not directly contrary to moral duty, he used to promise his assistance to all, to bestow it on those with whom he thought it would be most advantageously invested: he did not refuse anyone, because something often turned up to prevent the person whom he promised from availing himself of it, and it often also occurred that he himself was less engaged than he had thought at the time; nor could anyone's house be full of suitors who only undertook what he saw his way to perform: by some accident or other the unexpected often happens, while business, which you have believed to be actually in hand, from some cause or other does not come off: moreover, the worst that can happen is that the man to whom you have made a false promise is angry." This last risk, supposing you to make the promise, is uncertain, is prospective, and only affects a few; but, if you refuse, the offence given is certain, immediate, and more widely diffused. For many more ask to be allowed to avail themselves of the help of another than actually do so. Wherefore it is better that some of them should at times be angry with you in the forum, than all of them perpetually at your own house: especially as they are more inclined to be angry with those who refuse, than with a man whom they perceive to be prevented by so grave a cause as to be compatible with the desire to fulfil his promise if he possibly could. But that I may not appear to have abandoned my own classification, since the department of a candidate's work on which I am now dilating is that which refers to the populace, I insist on this, that all these observations have reference not so much to the feelings of friends as to popular rumour. Though there is something in what I say which comes under the former head—such as answering with kindness, and giving zealous assistance in the business and the dangers of friends—yet in this part of my argument I am speaking of the things which enable you to win over the populace: for instance, the having your house full of visitors before daybreak, the securing the affection of many by giving them hope of your support, the contriving that men should leave you with more friendly feelings than they came, the filling the ears of as many as possible with the most telling words.

XIII. For my next theme must be popular report, to which very great attention must be paid. But what I have said throughout the foregoing discourse applies also to the diffusion of a favourable report: the reputation for eloquence; the favour of the publicans and equestrian order; the good-will of men of rank; the crowd of young men; the constant attendance of those whom you have defended; the number of those from municipal towns who have notoriously come to Rome on your account; the observations which men make in your favour—that you recognize them, address them politely, are assiduous and earnest in canvassing; that they speak and think of you as kind and liberal; the having your house full of callers long before daybreak; the presence of large numbers of every class; that your look and speech give satisfaction to all, your acts and deeds to many; that everything is done which can be done by hard work, skill, and attention, not to cause the fame arising from all these displays of feeling to reach the people, but to bring the people itself to share them. You have already won the city populace and the affections of those who control the public meetings by your panegyric of Pompey, by undertaking the cause of Manilius,[4] by your defence of Cornelius. We must not let those advantages be forgotten, which hitherto no one has had without possessing at the same time the favour of the great. We must also take care that everyone knows that Cn. Pompeius is strongly in your favour, and that it emphatically suits his purpose that you should win your election. Lastly, take care that your whole candidature is full of *éclat*, brilliant, splendid, suited to the popular taste, presenting a spectacle of the utmost dignity and magnificence. See also, if possible, that some new scandal is started against your competitors for crime or looseness of life or corruption, such as is in harmony with their characters.

Above all in this election you must see that the Republic entertains a good hope and an honourable opinion of you. And yet you must not enter upon political measures in senate-house and public meeting while a candidate: you must hold such things in abeyance, in order that from your life-long conduct the senate may judge you likely to be the supporter of their authority; the Roman knights, along with the loyalists and wealthy, judge you from your past to be eager for peace and quiet times; and the people think of you as not likely to be hostile to their interests from the fact that in your style of speaking in public meetings, and in your declared convictions, you have been on the popular side.

XIV. This is what occurred to me to say on the subject of these two morning reflexions, which I said you ought to turn over in your mind every day as you went down to the forum: "I am a new man," "I am a candidate for the consulship." There remains the third, "This is Rome," a city made

4. Manilius, tribune in 66 B.C., proposed the law appointing Pompey to succeed Lucullus as general in the East. After his year of office, he was accused of *maiestas* and, later, of extortion, but apparently was not found guilty in either case.

up of a combination of nations, in which many snares, much deception, many vices enter into every department of life: in which you have to put up with the arrogant pretensions, the wrong-headedness, the ill-will, the hauteur, the disagreeable temper and offensive manners of many. I well understand that it requires great prudence and skill for a man, living among social vices of every sort, so many and so serious, to avoid giving offence, causing scandal, or falling into traps, and in his single person to adapt himself to such a vast variety of character, speech, and feeling. Wherefore, I say again and again, go on persistently in the path you have begun: put yourself above rivalry in eloquence; it is by this that people at Rome are charmed and attracted, as well as deterred from obstructing a man's career or inflicting an injury upon him. And since the chief plague spot of our state is that it allows the prospect of a bribe to blind it to virtue and worth, be sure that you are fully aware of your own strength, that is, understand that you are the man capable of producing in the minds of your rivals the strongest fear of legal proceeding and legal peril. Let them know that they are watched and scrutinized by you: they will be in terror of your energy, as well as of your influence and power of speech, and above all of the affection of the equestrian order towards you. But though I wish you to hold out this before them, I do not wish you to make it appear that you are already meditating an action, but to use this terror so as to facilitate the gaining of your object: and, in a word, in this contest strain every nerve and use every faculty in such a way as to secure what we seek. I notice that there are no elections so deeply tainted with corruption, but that some centuries return men closely connected with them without receiving money. Therefore, if we are as vigilant as the greatness of our object demands, and rouse our well-wishers to put forth all their energies; and if we allot to men of influence and zeal in our service their several tasks; if we put before our rivals the threat of legal proceedings; if we inspire their agents with fear, and by some means check the distributors, it is possible to secure either that there shall be no bribery or that it shall be ineffectual.

These are the points that I thought, not that I knew better than you, but that I could more easily than you—in the pressing state of your present engagements—collect together and send you written out. And although they are written in such terms as not to apply to all candidates for office, but to your special case and to your particular election, yet I should be glad if you would tell me of anything, that should be corrected or entirely struck out, or that has been omitted. For I wish this little essay "on the duties of a candidate" to be regarded as complete in every respect.

3. Sallust, *The War with Catiline*

Gaius Sallustius Crispus came from the Sabine uplands of central Italy, whose people were renowned for clinging to the rugged virtues that had decayed in cosmopolitan Rome. The clash between virtue and corruption was to be central to Sallust's thinking, and his life. He was born in 86 B.C., and little is known about his first thirty years. Eventually he became involved in the turbulent politics of the capital, and by 52 B.C. he had gained a place in the senate, which he may have been the first member of his family to enter. Newcomers still had difficulty making headway against the old families who monopolized power in the senate, as Cicero had found a generation earlier. Sallust made himself obnoxious to the old guard, both as a vehement anticonservative and as a debauchee, and was expelled in 50 B.C. But the senate's power to govern collapsed during the civil war that broke out almost immediately afterward. When Julius Caesar led his army into Italy in early 49 B.C., Sallust went to join him. Though his services to Caesar's campaign were marginal, he was reinstated in the senate, and at the end of the war he was appointed to govern a newly organized province in North Africa. Sallust used his year as governor to plunder the province. When he returned to Rome in 45 B.C., he narrowly escaped prosecution, which would have meant ejection from the senate for a second time. But his political career was finished. The remaining decade of his life he spent in retirement, during which he produced three works. The first was his monograph *The War with Catiline.* The second, *The War with Jugurtha,* was a monograph twice as long that treated Roman military operations in North Africa toward the end of the second century B.C. and exposed the politics behind them. His last work, of which only fragments remain, was to be a full-dress history of his own times. He began with the year 78 B.C., in which Sulla died shortly after abdicating his dictatorship, and carried the narrative down to 67 B.C., in four and a half books. Sallust died in 35 B.C.

The War with Catiline was probably written between about 43 and 40 B.C., after the assassination of Caesar and perhaps after the murder of Cicero also. As historical writing it has glaring flaws: it is sententious, digressive, careless about chronology, and clumsily proportioned. But Sallust's aim was not so much to reconstruct the circumstances of Catiline's conspiracy as to do justice to the political themes he saw exemplified in it. That is why he moralizes at such length on the conflict between

From *The Catiline of Sallust,* translated by Alfred W. Pollard, 2d ed. (London: Macmillan, 1901), pp. 1–63. Bracketed dates have been added by the editor; other bracketed material is that of the translator.

a reactionary aristocracy and new men (like Sallust himself), on the erosion of civic virtue, and on the effects of unprincipled ambition.

Every man who is anxious to show his superiority over the lower animals may well strive with his utmost power to escape passing his life in obscurity like the cattle whom nature has made to gaze on the ground and serve their belly. With us the sum of our capacity resides jointly in the mind and the body. The mind we use for governance, the body rather for service; sharing the former with the gods, the latter with the beasts. Hence I think it reasonable to seek glory by our powers rather of intellect than of strength, and since the actual life which we enjoy is short, to make the memory of us as abiding as may be. For the glory of wealth and beauty is fleeting and frail, but merit is a possession of eternal honour.

Now it was long hotly contested among men whether military success was more advanced by bodily strength or by mental ability, for what we need is deliberation before we begin, and after deliberation, then well-timed action; either of itself is deficient and lacks the other's help. Thus, at the outset, those who were called "kings"—for that was the first title of dominion known on earth—differed from each other, some employing their intellect, others their bodily powers; for even as late as this men's lives were passed in freedom from avarice, and each was contented with his own possessions. After Cyrus, however, in Asia, and the Lacedaemonians and Athenians in Greece, began the subjugation of towns and nations, and, convinced that the greatest glory was to be found in the greatest empire, held their lust for dominion a fair pretext for war, then at last, by the actual test of results it was proved that it was intellect which was most effective in war. Were then the genius of kings and rulers as potent in peace as in war, there would be more smoothness and consistency in human affairs, nor would you see constant shiftings to and fro, and the whole world subject to change and confusion. For empire is easily retained by the very devices by which it is originally acquired. When diligence, however, has been superseded by sloth, and self-restraint and moderation by lustfulness and pride, a change of fortune accompanies that of character, and thus empire is continually being transferred to the most capable from those who are less so.

Whether they be farmers, sailors, or builders, men find that everything is obedient to merit. Many, however, the slaves of gluttony and sloth, without learning or cultivation, have passed through life as though it were a journey in a foreign land, and thus, in defiance of nature, have actually found their body a pleasure and their real vital powers a burden. Of these, for my own part, I hold the life and death to be alike, since of neither is there any record. To me, indeed, the only man who really seems to live and enjoy his vital powers is he who, in devotion to some task, seeks the fame of a brilliant exploit or virtuous accomplishment. Where the field is so wide, nature points out different paths to different persons.

It is a fine thing to serve the state by action, nor is eloquence despicable. Men may become illustrious alike in peace and war, and many by their own acts, many by their record of the acts of others, win applause. The glory which attends the recorder and the doer of brave deeds is certainly by no means equal. For my own part, however, I count historical narration as one of the hardest of tasks. In the first place, a full equivalent has to be found in words for the deeds narrated, and in the second the historian's censures of crimes are by many thought to be the utterances of ill-will and envy, while his record of the high virtue and glory of the good, tranquilly accepted so long as it deals with what the reader deems to be easily within his own powers, so soon as it passes beyond this is disbelieved as mere invention.

As regards myself, my inclination originally led me, like many others, while still a youth, into public life. There I found many things against me. Modesty, temperance, and merit had departed, and hardihood, corruption, and avarice were flourishing in their stead. My mind, a stranger to bad acquirements, contemned these qualities; nevertheless, with the weakness of youth, I was seized and held amid this throng of vices by my ambition. I presented a contrast to the ill behaviour of my fellows, none the less I was tormented by the same craving for the honours of office, and the same sensitiveness to popularity and unpopularity as the rest. At last, after many miseries and perils, my mind was at peace, and I determined to pass the remainder of my days at a distance from public affairs. It was not, however, my design to waste this honourable leisure in idleness and sloth, nor yet to spend my life in devotion to such slavish employments as agriculture or hunting. I returned to the studies I had once begun, from which my unhappy ambition had held me back, and determined to narrate the history of the Roman people in separate essays, wherever it seemed worthy of record. I was the more inclined to this by the fact that my mind was free alike from the hopes and fears of the political partisan.

I am about, therefore, with the utmost truth I can, briefly to relate the history of the conspiracy of Catiline; for I account this affair as in the highest degree memorable for the novelty both of the crime itself and of the danger it involved. Before I begin my history, a few points concerning this man's character must be made clear.

Lucius Catilina was of noble birth, of great mental and bodily vigour, but of an evil and depraved disposition. From his youth he had delighted in domestic war, murder, rapine, and civil discord, and among these he had passed his early manhood. His body could bear privation, cold, and sleeplessness, to an incredible extent. His mind was bold, crafty, and versatile, skilful alike to feign or conceal whatever he chose. Covetous of his neighbour's substance, a spendthrift of his own, his desires knew no bounds. Not deficient in eloquence, he had little solid wisdom. The ambition of his strange spirit passed all limits, even all belief, so extravagantly high was it pitched. This man, after the tyranny of Lucius Sulla, had been possessed by an overwhelming passion to overpower the government, nor so long as he gained supreme power for himself did he pause to weigh the means by which he should attain it. His headstrong spirit was daily spurred more and more by his want of means and his consciousness of his crimes, each increased by the qualities I have named. Besides this, he was urged on by the corrupt state of public morality, plagued at once by those worst and opposite evils, luxury and avarice.

Since occasion has reminded me of the public morality, I seemed called upon by my subject to go back and briefly explain the civil and military customs of our ancestors, their mode of administering the state, the size at which they left it, and how its beauty and nobility were gradually exchanged for vileness and crime.

The city of Rome, according to the tradition I follow, was originally founded and inhabited by Trojans, who, with Aeneas, their leader, were wandering about as exiles with no settled home. These were aided by Aborigines, a wild race who lived free and unshackled, without laws and without government. It passes belief to tell with what ease these two peoples of unlike race and different language, and each with their own way of life, coalesced after they came within one stronghold. After, however, their state, improved in population, customs, and territory, seemed to have gained some degree of strength and prosperity, as is usual with mortal possessions, their wealth gave rise to ill-will. The neighbouring kings and peoples assailed them, few of their friends came to their aid, the rest, panic-stricken, held aloof from the danger. The Romans, however, active alike at home and in the field, made their preparations in all haste. With mutual exhortations they advanced against the enemy, and shielded with their arms their freedom, country, and kin. When their courage had repelled their own danger, they brought help to their friends and allies, and won themselves friendships by their greater readiness to give than to receive a service.

Their government was according to law, and with the name of "royalty." Chosen men, of bodies enfeebled by age, but of characters strong in wisdom, formed the council of the state. These, either from their age or from a resemblance in their duties, were called "Fathers." The royal power, which had originally conduced to the maintenance of liberty and the increase of the state, was turned at last into mere arrogance and tyranny. They then changed their constitutions, and instituted yearly magistracies and pairs of magistrates, thinking that by this way men's minds would be least able to wax wanton by license. It was at this conjuncture that individuals began more to distinguish themselves, and to display their talents with greater readiness. By kings the good are more liable to be suspected than the bad, and cause for alarm is always found in the merit of others. But as soon as the state had gained its freedom, it is incredible to relate what progress it quickly made; so great was the thirst for glory that had ensued. Now, for the first time, the young men, as soon as they were of age for service, learnt warfare by the experience of hard labour in camp. Handsome arms and warlike steeds now formed their pleasures in preference to women and wine. To men like these no toil was unwonted, no ground rugged or steep, no enemy under arms an object of fear; their courage had subdued all things. But their greatest contests for glory were with one another. Each was eager to strike the foe, to scale the wall, and to be seen so engaged; this they counted wealth, this as good repute and the highest birth. Greedy for fame, they were liberal of money, and wished that their glory might be unbounded, and their wealth honourably won. I could tell of places in which a small Roman force routed huge bodies of the enemy, and of towns naturally strong taken by assault, were it not that this would be too wide a digression.

Fortune, however, is truly everywhere paramount, and she makes known or obscures every event according to her own whim rather than its real value. The performances of the Athenians, as I esteem them, were sufficiently noble and magnificent, and yet somewhat less than fame reports. At Athens, however, there flourished historians of genius, and, consequently, throughout the world the exploits of the Athenians are esteemed as of the highest order. Thus the merits of men of action are valued in proportion to the capabilities of men of genius to extol them in words. But the Roman people have never had any advantage of this kind; among them the most capable men were always the most occupied, no one exercised his mind apart from his body, and the best men preferred action to narration, and to have their own services praised by others rather than themselves to be another's historian.

Thus, as I have said, virtue was practised both at home and on the field. There was the utmost concord and the least possible avarice; the right and the good obtained among them not so much by law as by nature; strife, discord, and enmity, they carried on with their foes; citizens contended with citizens only in merit. In their offerings to the gods they were magnificent, in their domestic expenses sparing, to their friends loyal. Their own and their country's interests they guarded by these two devices—hardihood in war, and generous treatment when peace had ensued. Of this I can adduce a striking proof; in war, punishment was more often inflicted on those who had fought the enemy contrary to orders, or who had too slowly obeyed the signal of recall from battle, than on those who had dared to desert the standard or give way when hard pressed; in peace, they carried on their government rather by kindness than by fear, and when they had received an injury, preferred rather to pardon it than avenge it.

Thus by diligence and fair dealing the state was advanced; great kings were conquered in war, wild races and vast peoples subdued by force; Carthage, the rival of the Roman Empire, perished root and branch; sea and land everywhere lay open before us; when at last fortune began to turn cruel, and throw everything into confusion. Those who had lightly borne toils and dangers, doubtful fortunes and desperate straits, found leisure and wealth, things under other circumstances so desirable, a pitiable burden. At first the lust of money increased, then that of power, and these, it may be said, were the sources of every evil. Avarice subverted loyalty, uprightness, and every other good quality, and in their stead taught men to be proud and cruel, to neglect the gods, and to hold all things venal. Ambition compelled many to become deceitful; they had one thought buried in their breast, another ready on their tongue; their friendships and enmities they valued not at their real worth, but at the advantage they could bring, and they maintained the look rather than the nature of honest men. These evils at first grew gradually, and were occasionally punished; later, when the contagion advanced like some plague, the state was revolutionized, and the government, from being one of the justest and best, became cruel and unbearable. At first it was not so much avarice as ambition which spurred men's minds, a vice, indeed, but one akin to virtue. For glory, distinction, and power in the state are equally desired by good and bad, though the first strives to reach his goal by the path of honour, the second, in the lack of honest arts, uses the weapons of falsehood and deceit. Avarice, on the other hand, implies a zeal for money, an object for which no philosopher ever yearned. Tainting the body and mind of the strong, it weakens them as by some deadly poison; it is always boundless, always insatiable; plenty and want alike fail to lessen it. After Lucius Sulla had seized the government by force of arms, and made a bad end to a good beginning, robbery and plunder became universal; one coveted a house, another an estate, the victors knew neither limit nor sobriety, and citizens became the object of vile and cruel outrage. To make matters worse, Sulla, to secure the loyalty of the army he had led in Asia, in defiance of ancient usage had allowed habits of luxury and far too great freedom. Pleasant and voluptuous quarters in times of quiet had easily enervated the hardy spirit of his men. It was in Asia that a Roman army first gained habits of lustfulness and intemperance, learned to admire statues, paintings, and plate, stole them from their private or public owners, plundered shrines, and polluted everything whether sacred or common. Soldiers like these, when they gained a victory, stripped the conquered bare; for, since even the wise have their temper tried by prosperity, much less could men of this abandoned character use their success with moderation. Riches became a means of distinction and glory, power and influence followed their possession. As a result the edge of virtue was dulled, poverty was accounted a disgrace, and uprightness a kind of ill-nature. Riches made the youth a prey to luxury, avarice, and pride: they plundered and squandered, valued lightly their own property, and coveted that of others; cared neither for modesty nor purity, nor for aught in heaven or earth; and were without principle or moderation. To one acquainted with mansions and villas built on the scale of towns, it is worth while to visit the temples erected by our ancestors, the most godfearing of men. They, indeed, decorated the shrines of the gods with piety, and their own homes with glory, while they deprived their conquered enemies of nothing save the power of doing harm; but in this generation the most worthless of men in the depth of their wickedness have deprived our allies of everything which those brave men in the hour of victory had left them, as if the one and only use of empire were to inflict harm. Why should I tell of things which no one who has not seen them could believe, of how often private individuals have levelled mountains and built over seas? Such men seem to me to have trifled with their riches in the haste with which they ignobly abused what they might honourably have enjoyed. But the passion for defilement, gluttony, and all other kinds of indulgence, kept pace with that for wealth. Each sex alike trampled on their modesty. Sea and land were ransacked to supply the table. Men went to rest before they felt a desire for sleep; they did not wait for hunger or thirst, cold, or weariness, but anticipated them all by luxurious expedients. Such a life, when means had failed, spurred youth into crime. Their minds, tainted with bad accomplishments, could not endure to be deprived of their sensual pleasures, and they abandoned themselves with all the more recklessness to every kind both of gain and expense.

It was in a state of this magnitude and corruption that Catiline, as was indeed easily done, gathered round him, to serve as bodyguard, bands of men stained by every vice and crime. Every gambler, adulterer, and glutton, who, by the gratification of his passion, had cruelly impaired his patrimony, every one whose debts had been swollen to buy indemnity for some deed of crime, all cut-throats from every quarter, all who had committed sacrilege, who had been tried and condemned, or whose deeds made them fear a trial, all who gained a living by polluting their tongues with perjury, or their hands with their countrymen's blood, in fine, all who were harassed by crime, by need, or by the pangs of conscience—it was these who were Catiline's intimate associates; while, did anyone as yet free from guilt chance to become his friend, by daily intercourse and allurement, he was easily made a fit fellow to the rest. It was especially, however, the intimacy of young men that Catiline affected; and their pliable and unformed minds fell an easy prey to his wiles. Complying with the several forms of youthful passion, he helped some to mistresses, bought hounds and horses for others, and, in fine, spared neither his purse nor his honour to make them his faithful creatures. I am aware that there were some who held the belief that the young men who made Catiline's house their resort, behaved with too little regard for decency, but the report obtained credence rather from other considerations than from any direct testimony. At the very outset of his youth Catiline had engaged in many scandalous intrigues; one with a high-born maiden, another with a priestess of Vesta, and others which in like manner set law and morality at defiance. Finally he was seized with a passion for Aurelia Orestilla (a lady in whom no respectable man ever found anything to praise except her beauty), and, on her hesitating to marry him in her dislike of a grown-up stepson, killed the youth,—so it is positively believed,—and thus cleared his house for the unhallowed union. In this deed I trace one of the chief causes of Catiline's bringing his attempt to a point. His impure mind, hostile alike to gods and men, could find rest neither awake nor asleep, so terribly was his frenzied soul ravaged by the pangs of conscience. His countenance grew bloodless, his eyes haggard, his pace now hurried and now slow. Madness was plainly stamped upon his face and expression. The young men whom, as narrated above, he had enticed, he kept instructing in many varieties of crime. It was from their ranks that he provided false witnesses to facts and documents; he bade them think cheaply alike of honour, fortune, and danger, and then, when he had crushed their sense of reputation and decency, he commanded greater crimes. If motives for crime were for the moment wanting, he ensnared or assassinated the inoffensive as though they had offended; he would rather, forsooth, indulge his wickedness and cruelty without a cause than allow hand or brain to become sluggish by disuse. In reliance on friends and associates such as these, and encouraged by the enormous prevalence of debt throughout the world, and by the number of Sulla's soldiers who had squandered their fortunes, and mindful of plunder and ancient victories, were now hoping for civil war, Catiline formed a plan for destroying the constitution. There was no army in Italy; Gnaeus Pompeius was engaged in a war in far distant lands; he had great hopes of success in his own candidature for the consulship; the Senate was unprepared for any emergency; everything was in peace and quietness, and precisely in this Catiline saw his opportunity.

It was about the first of June in the year when Lucius Caesar and Gaius Figulus were consuls [64 B.C.] that he began making overtures, at first to single individuals, encouraging some and sounding others, and expatiating on his own resources, on the lack of preparation in the government, and on the great prizes a conspiracy offered. When he had satisfied himself on the points he desired, he summoned a meeting of all whose needs were the most pressing, and spirit the most daring. To the meeting came Publius Lentulus Sura, Publius Autronius, Lucius Cassius Longinus, Gaius Cethegus, Publius and Servius the two sons of Servius Sulla, Lucius Vargunteius, Quintus Annius, Marcus Porcius Laeca, Lucius Bestia, Quintus Curius; all of senatorial rank; with them were Marcus Fulvius Nobilior, Lucius Statilius, Publius Gabinius Capito, and Gaius Cornelius, from the equestrian order; and in addition to these, many persons from the military colonies and borough towns, men of rank in their own neighbourhood. Many, moreover, of the nobility were associated in this plot, though they kept more in the background. These were spurred on rather by the hope of power than by want or any other necessity. Indeed, great numbers of young men, especially those of noble birth, were favourable to Catiline's attempt, and though, while tranquillity lasted, they had every means of living in splendour or comfort, preferred the doubtful to the certain, and war to peace. There were, too, at that crisis, some who believed that Marcus Licinius Crassus was no stranger to the conspiracy. Gnaeus Pompeius, his personal enemy, was at the head of a large army, and Crassus was thought to be favourable to the growth of any influence that might balance his power, in the confident belief that, should the plot succeed, he would easily secure the chief place among its leaders.

A few conspirators, it must be remarked, of whom Catiline was one, had before this formed a plot against the state, of which I will give the most accurate account I can. In the consulship of Lucius Tullus and Manius Lepidus [66 B.C.], Publius Autronius, and Publius Sulla, the consuls elect, had been put on their trial and punished under the bribery laws. A little after this, Catiline was charged with extortion, and so disqualified as a candidate for the consulship [since he could not give in his name within the legal time]. At the same time a certain Gnaeus Piso, a young man of good birth, but needy, ill-affected and of desperate daring, was being urged by his poverty and evil disposition to embroil the State. With this man, Catiline and Autronius discussed their plot about the end of the first week in December, and planned to murder the consuls [for the year 65 B.C.], Lucius Cotta and Lucius Torquatus, in the Capitol on January 1st, to seize the insignia of office for themselves, and to send Piso with an army to hold the two Spanish provinces. The plot was discovered, and they again postponed their plans of murder to February 5th. On this occasion they plotted the destruction not only of the consuls, but of many of the senators, and had not Catiline, who was stationed in front of the Senate-house, been too hasty in giving the signal to his confederates, on that day would have been accomplished the worst outrage of any since the foundation of Rome. As it was, their armed supporters had not yet mustered in force, and this circumstance ruined the plot. Piso was subsequently sent as quaestor, with the powers of a praetor, to Hither-Spain. This appointment Crassus supported, as he knew Piso for a bitter enemy of Gnaeus Pompeius; nor was the Senate unwilling to grant him a province in their eagerness to remove so abandoned a man from the sphere of politics, while many of the aristocracy looked on him in the light of a bulwark, and the power of Pompeius was already a cause for alarm. Piso, however, was murdered in his province by a troop of Spanish horse at whose head he had placed himself on a march without any other force. Some would make out that the barbarians could not submit to the injustice, arrogance, and cruelty that marked his rule; others, that the horsemen were old and faithful dependents of Gnaeus Pompeius, and attacked Piso with his consent. The Spaniards, they remarked, had never committed such an outrage on other occasions, but had patiently submitted to much previous tyranny. I shall leave this point as an open question, and have now said enough about the earlier conspiracy.

When Catiline saw assembled the men whom I named a little above, although he had held many communications with each of them separately, he yet thought it would serve his purpose to address and encourage them collectively. He conducted them, therefore, to a secluded part of his house, and then, having secured the absence of any witness, spoke somewhat as follows:—

"Had I not myself tested your courage and loyalty, this favourable conjuncture would have offered itself in vain. Our hopes might have been high, and power have lain ready to our hands, but it would have availed nothing. I should not now be abandoning the certain to pursue the doubtful had I only cowardly or frivolous supporters to depend on. As it is, I have learnt your valour and loyalty to myself on many important occasions, and my mind has therefore dared to embark on this greatest and fairest of attempts. I am encouraged, too, by my clear perception that, whether in good or evil fortune, your interests are identical with mine; for in this identity of hopes and fears lies the true bond of friendship.

"The plans which I have been revolving in my mind you have all separately heard ere now. For my own part, however, I find my spirit daily more on fire at the thought of what will be our lot if we fail ourselves to assert our claim to freedom. Ever since the government of the state was merged in the prerogatives and authority of a few influential men, it is to these that kings and princes have been tributary, and peoples and races have paid their dues. We, the remainder of the nation, however energetic and well-disposed, whatever our birth, whether noble or base, have formed an undistinguished crowd without interest or influence, and lie at the mercy of a party to whom, were the state in a sound condition, we should now be a terror. Thus all influence and power, distinction and wealth remain in their own, or their favourites' hand; to us they have left danger and rejections, prosecutions and want. Bravest of men, what is the limit of your endurance? Is it not better to die once for all a brave man's death than to drag out a life of misery and dishonour, as the butts of your enemies' insolence, and lose it shamefully at the end?

"But why speak of this? I call Gods and men to witness that to gain victory depends only on you. Our age is in its prime and our minds at their strongest, our enemies are enfeebled by years and riches. We have only to make a beginning, the course of events will do the rest. And what man, with a temper worthy of that name, can brook their possession of a surplus of wealth to squander on driving back the sea and levelling mountains, while we lack the means to procure even the necessaries of life? That they should join house to house and houses to houses, while we have nowhere a hearth to call our own? They are buying pictures and statuary and plate; are pulling down the work of yesterday to build it anew; in a word, are squandering and abusing their wealth in all possible ways; and yet, though they indulge every passion to the full, they cannot exhaust their riches. We are met by poverty at home and creditors abroad. Our fortunes are bad, our expectations still more forbidding. In fine, what have we left except the breath we draw in misery?

"Must I not then bid you awake? Before you there dawns the freedom for which you have often yearned, and with freedom, wealth, splendour, and glory rise before your eyes. Such, and no less, are the rewards which fortune has decreed to the conquerors. Your dangers and your beggary, the rich spoils which war offers, plead more powerfully with you than any words of mine. Use me as your general or your fellow-soldier; my mind and my body shall ever be at your service. These very plans I hope, with your aid, to carry into execution as consul, unless, haply, my mind deceives me, and you are more ready to serve than to command."

These words were listened to by men who had every evil in abundance, but no good fortune, nor any hope of it. Great, however, as the wages of revolution appeared to them, many yet asked Catiline to explain what would be the object of the war, what the prizes their arms were to seek, what help he counted on or hoped for, and from what quarter. He proceeded to promise them an abolition of debts, a proscription of the rich, together with magistracies, priestly offices, plunder, and all the other accompaniments of war and the licence of victory. In Hither-Spain, he continued, was Piso; in Mauritania, at the head of an army, Publius Sittius Nucerinus; both of them partners in their design. Gaius Antonius, too, was a candidate for the consulship, and he hoped to have him as his colleague, as a man at once intimate with himself and entangled in the greatest difficulties. When himself consul he should join Antonius in making the first move. He then railed and inveighed against the whole aristocratic party; made laudatory mention of each of his own followers; and reminded one of his poverty, another of his desires, many of the danger they stood in or the shame imposed on them by the Censors, and many more of the triumph of Sulla, in which they had found an opportunity for plunder. At last, seeing every mind thoroughly aroused, he bade them be zealous in support of his candidature, and dismissed the meeting. It was asserted by some at the time that Catiline, when, after making a speech, he was preparing to administer an oath to his accomplices, carried round in bowls a mixture of human blood and wine, and only revealed his design after all had tasted of it with an imprecation according to the custom in solemn rites. This [they maintained] he did that their mutual consciousness of such an abomination might make them more loyal to each other. Some, however, were of opinion that this story, together with many others, was invented by people who thought that the unpopularity which Cicero subsequently incurred would be diminished if the crime of his victims were recognised as peculiarly hideous. The evidence I have found for the incident is too slight to support so monstrous a charge.

Among the conspirators was a certain Quintus Curius, a man of no mean station; he was covered, however, with shame and crime, and his infamy had caused the Censors to expel him from the Senate. The man was as frivolous as bold, and could neither keep a secret nor conceal his own crimes; in short, he was heedless alike of his words and deeds. Between him and a certain Fulvia, a woman of birth, there was a long-standing intrigue. He had lately fallen in her good graces owing to his poverty making him less lavish in his presents, when suddenly he began to boast, made her outrageous promises, and threw out at times threats of violence should she fail to be compliant; in fine, his whole behaviour became more haughty than was his wont. On discovering the cause of Curius' strange conduct, Fulvia did not keep secret a danger so threatening to the state, but, while suppressing the name of her informant, told several persons what she had heard in various ways of Catiline's plot. This, more than anything else, roused men's zeal to confer the consulship on Marcus Tullius Cicero. Till that time many of the nobility had been in a ferment of jealousy, and had thought the consulship would be in a manner polluted if obtained by a man of no family, however distinguished. When, however, danger was imminent, jealousy and pride fell into the background.

On the poll being taken, Marcus Tullius and Gaius Antonius were declared elected. Although this at first greatly confounded his partners in the conspiracy, it did not lessen the frenzy of Catiline. On the contrary, his activity increased daily; he stored arms in suitable places throughout Italy, and conveyed money, borrowed on his own or his friends' security, to a certain Manlius at Faesulae, who afterwards was the first to move in the war. He is said also at this period to have gained over many men of every rank, with a number of women, who, though at the outset their beauty had provided them means to support their extravagance, now found their gains, but not their luxury, limited by advancing age, and consequently had contracted huge debts. Through them Catiline hoped to tamper with the slaves of Rome, to fire the city, and either to win over or murder the women's husbands.

Among these women was a certain Sempronia, who had committed many crimes, often worthy of a man's daring. She was well endowed with birth and beauty and fortunate in her husband and children; was well read in Greek and Latin literature, could sing, play, and dance more gracefully than an honest woman need, and had many of the other accomplishments of a riotous life. There was nothing she held less dear than purity and honour; indeed, it would have been hard to determine if she were more careless of her wealth or her repute; so destitute was she of all modesty that, more often than not, she was the first to begin an intrigue. Often ere this she had broken her engagements, forsworn her trust, and been an accomplice in murder; an extravagance which outran her resources had hurried her downwards. Her talents, however, were by no means despicable; she could write verses, bandy jests, and talk modestly, voluptuously, or pertly at will; in short, she was a woman of much pleasantry and wit.

Catiline, though he had made these preparations, was yet a candidate for the next year's consulship [i.e., for the consulship of 62 B.C.], hoping, should he be elected, easily to make a tool of Antonius. In the meantime he was not inactive, but was using every method of intrigue against Cicero. The latter, however, had no lack of craft and adroitness for his own protection. At the very beginning of his consulship, by dint of great promises, he had, through Fulvia, prevailed on the Quintus Curius described above to betray to him Catiline's designs. By an agreement also about the provinces he had constrained his colleague, Antonius, to desist from all disloyalty, while he secretly surrounded his own person with a body-guard of friends and dependents. The day of election came, and Catiline failed alike in his candidature and in the secret attack he had planned against the consuls in the Campus. He determined, therefore, to make open war and to go to every length, since his secret attempt had had so adverse and disgraceful an issue.

Accordingly he despatched Gaius Manlius to Faesulae and that part of Etruria, a certain Septimius of Camerinum to Picenum, Gaius Julius to Apulia, and to other quarters such persons as he thought would in each place be able to advance his ends. Meanwhile at Rome he was working at many plans at the same time, directing secret attacks on the consuls, making arrangements for a conflagration, and occupying suitable points with armed men. He himself went about armed, and bade others do the same, exhorting them always to be ready and on the watch. By day and by night he was active and wakeful, and neither sleeplessness or toil could wear him out. When nothing came of all his activity, at dead of night he again summoned the chiefs of the conspiracy to meet, this time at the house of Marcus Porcius Laeca, and there, after many complaints of their cowardice, informed them that he had despatched Manlius to head the force which he had collected for taking up arms, as well as other agents to other favourable points to begin the war. He was anxious, he said, himself to set out to the army if he could first work the destruction of Cicero, who was a great obstacle to his plans. While all the rest showed fear and hesitation, a Roman knight, named Gaius Cornelius, offered his help, and was joined by a senator, named Lucius Vargunteius. The two determined to proceed, a little later on in the same night, with an armed force to gain entrance to Cicero's house, as though to attend his levee, and then suddenly to take him unprepared and assassinate him in his own home. Curius, on hearing the greatness of the peril which threatened the consul, lost no time in acquainting Cicero, through Fulvia, with the plot laid against him. The assassins were turned away from the gate, and found they had planned their atrocious crime in vain.

Meanwhile, in Etruria, Manlius was tampering with a populace whose poverty, combined with their indignation at the wrong they had suffered in losing, under the tyranny of Sulla, their lands and all their property, now made them eager for revolution. With them were joined robbers of every description who greatly abounded in those parts, besides some veterans from the Sullan colonies, whose lavish indulgence of their passions had left them no remnant of all their immense booty.

Cicero, when informed of this, was distracted by the double nature of his difficulty. On the one hand, he was unable any longer to protect the city from the conspirators' attack by such measures as he could take on his own authority; on the other, he had no certain information as to either the numbers or the designs of the army of Manlius. Under these circumstances he laid the matter before the Senate, which had now for some time been disquieted by the reports prevalent among the people. Following the course usual in dealing with any threatening emergency, the Senate made the decree: "The consuls are to take measures to protect the state from harm." This is the greatest power which the Roman constitution allows the Senate to confer on a magistrate. It authorises him to raise an army, wage war, control in every possible way both citizens and allies, and exercise the highest military and judicial authority at home and in the field. Without this decree the consul has no powers in any of these matters except by command of the people. A few days afterwards, Lucius Saenius, a senator, read before the House a letter which he said had been brought for him from Faesulae. It contained the news that Gaius Manlius, with a large force, had taken up arms on October 23rd. As usual in such cases, some at once began to report signs and wonders; others to assert that people were assembling and arms being transported, and that at Capua and in Apulia the slaves were rising. By a decree of the Senate, Quintus Marcius Rex was despatched to Faesulae, and Quintus Metellus Creticus to Apulia and its neighbourhood. Both these officers were waiting near the city, still retaining their commission as generals. The celebration of their triumphs had been obstructed by the underhand tactics of a clique who were accustomed to set a price on everything whether honourable or the reverse. Besides these, two praetors, Quintus Pompeius Rufus, and Quintus Metellus Celer, were sent to Capua and Picenum respectively, with powers to raise an army adequate to the needs of the time and the danger of the state. Rewards were also offered for any information as to the conspiracy against the state. These rewards were, in the case of a slave, his freedom and one hundred thousand sesterces, and for a free man, a pardon for any share he might have had in the plot and double that sum. A decree was at the same time passed that the gladiatorial schools should be quartered on Capua and the other borough towns according to their means, and that, at Rome, watches should be set throughout the city under the charge of the minor magistrates. By these measures the state was violently excited, and the appearance of the capital quite changed. The life of unrestrained pleasure and indulgence begotten of a long period of tranquillity was suddenly replaced by universal gloom. A state of feverish anxiety ensued. No person or place was thoroughly trusted. There was neither open war nor secured peace, and each man measured the danger only by his own terror. The women, too, to whom the fear of war, now that the limits of the empire were so vast, had come as an unwonted feeling, were in great distress. They raised their hands in prayer to heaven; wept over their little children; were full of questions; and saw danger in everything; throwing aside pride and frivolity, they despaired of themselves and their country.

Despite these preparations for defence, and an accusation by Lucius Paulus under the Plautian law,[1] the ruthless mind of Catiline was busy with all its former plans. At last, either by way of dissembling or to clear himself should he be provoked by taunts from any quarter, he attended the Senate. Thereupon, the consul, Marcus Tullius, either from fear of his pres-

1. This law was one of the measures enacted to control public and private violence.

ence or in a burst of anger, did good service to his country by delivering a brilliant speech, which he afterwards wrote out and published. On his resuming his seat, Catiline, following out his determination to dissemble everything, with downcast look and in tones of entreaty began to beg the senators to form no hasty opinion of him. His birth and his conduct from his youth up justified him in cherishing the highest hopes; it would be wrong of them to imagine that he, a patrician born, whose own and whose ancestors' services to the Roman people had been so numerous, could find it his interest to destroy the state, while Marcus Tullius, a mere citizen-at-will, was engaged in its preservation. He was proceeding to further abuse when a storm of shouts and cries of "Enemy" and "Cutthroat" interrupted him. Furious with rage, he exclaimed, "Since I am beset and driven to destruction by my foes, I will quench in a general ruin the fire that surrounds me."

With these words he flung himself from the Senate-house and hurried to his home. There his brain was soon busy. His treacherous attack on the consul was a failure, and he saw that the city was protected from incendiaries by the watches set. He thought it best, therefore, to increase his army, and to employ the time before the legions could be levied in seizing the numerous positions that might be useful for the war. At dead of night he set out with only a few companions for the camp of Manlius, leaving instructions to Cethegus, Lentulus, and the others whose readiness and daring he had tested, to use every possible means of increasing the strength of their party, of pushing forward the plots against the consul, and of arranging for a massacre, a conflagration, and the other horrors of war. He promised shortly to march against the city in person, with a large army.

While these events were taking place at Rome, Gaius Manlius sent deputies from his force to Marcius Rex with a message to this effect,—"We call gods and men to witness, general, that we took up arms with no designs against our country, nor with any wish to bring others into danger. To ensure the safety of our own persons is our only motive; for, needy wretches as we are, the violence and cruelty of usurers has robbed most of us of our homesteads, and all of fame and fortune. Not one of us was allowed, according to ancient custom, to avail himself of that law, by which, on sacrificing his property, his person would have remained free; so pitiless were the usurers and the judge. Your ancestors often, in compassion for the commons of Rome, relieved their destitution by the decrees they proposed; and, quite recently, within our own recollection, owing to the prevalence of debt, bronze was raised for purposes of repayment to the value of silver, and this with the approval of all honest men. Often, again, the commons themselves, roused either by a lust for power, or by the insolence of magistrates, took up arms, and revolted from the Senate. We, however, ask for neither rule nor riches, though these are the cause of every war and struggle among men; we ask only for that freedom which no brave man ever abandoned while life remained. We adjure you and the Senate to take measures to relieve us, your unhappy fellow-citizens, to restore to us the protection of the law, wrested from us by judicial corruption, and not to force us to seek a course, by which, while perishing ourselves, we may wreak the completest vengeance for our blood." To this, Quintus Marcius replied, "If you have anything to ask of the Senate, throw down your arms, and go to Rome with your petition. Such has ever been the clemency and compassion of the Senate of the Roman people that no one ever asked their help in vain."

To return to Catiline; on his way to join Manlius he sent letters to many men of consular rank, and, besides these, to all persons of any mark, informing them that beset by false accusations, and unable to make head against the cabal of his enemies, he was resigning himself to fortune, and was now on his way to exile at Massilia. This course he was taking, not because his conscience reproached him with the crimes with which he was charged, but to secure the peace of the State and to prevent any dispute about himself giving rise to sedition. To a very different effect was a letter read before the House by Quintus Catulus, which he said had been delivered to him in Catiline's name: of this letter the following is a copy,—

> Lucius Catilina to Quintus Catulus—Your honour, at once so eminent and so practically proved, on which amid my great dangers it pleases me to think, encourages me to commit my affairs into your hands. I have determined, therefore, to enter on no defence as regards the fresh step I have taken, but have made up my mind, since I am conscious of no fault, to lay before you an explanation, of which, I profess, you can easily recognise the truth. Roused by the wrongs and insults I have endured, finding myself robbed of all reward for my toil and energy, and unable to gain the rank which I deserved, I followed my usual bent and undertook the championship of the wretched. This I did, not because my property was insufficient to discharge my personal debts; on the contrary, the generosity of Orestilla was ready to pay off, from her own and her daughter's funds, those contracted as surety for others. No, it was the sight of unworthy men raised to the honours of office that impelled me, and the feeling that I myself was treated as an outcast on false suspicions. For these reasons I have embraced the hope, honourable in my present fortunes, of preserving what position I yet hold. I would write more, but news has just been brought that I am threatened with attack. For the present I commend Orestilla to you, and entrust her to your honour. I implore you, as you love your own children, shield her from harm. Farewell.

Catiline himself abode a few days with Gaius Flaminius at Arretium, and supplied the neighbourhood, with which he had previously tampered, with arms. He then assumed the fasces and other marks of a consular commission, and marched to the camp of Manlius. When this was known at Rome, the Senate pronounced Catiline and Manlius public enemies, and fixed a day, up to which the rest of the conspirators, except those condemned on capital charges, might throw down their arms unharmed. A decree was also passed, ordering the consuls to hold a levy. Antonius was to put himself at the head of an army, and pursue Catiline with all haste; Cicero to remain to protect the capital.

It was at this crisis that the empire of the Roman people, in my opinion, reached its most pitiable condition. From the setting to the rising sun its arms had subdued every land to obedience; at home there was tranquillity and wealth, the first of blessings, as men esteem them, in abundance; and yet there were found citizens with minds hardened, to undertake their own and their country's destruction. Two decrees of the Senate had been passed, but of all that host not one was enticed by the reward offered to betray the conspiracy; not one deserted the camp of Catiline; so virulent was the disease which had settled like a plague on the minds of many citizens. Nor was this mental disorder confined to those who had been admitted to the conspiracy; it may be said that the whole of the common people, in their eagerness for revolution, approved the designs of Catiline. And this seemed but natural, for it always happens in states that the penniless envy the respectable and praise the disaffected, hate the old order and long for the new, and in their disgust at their own fortunes are eager for a general change. Careless of everything, they find in riot and sedition their meat and drink, for poverty is a possession which easily escapes loss. The populace of the capital, however, was especially impetuous, and that for many reasons. In the first place Rome had become a sink into which there poured all who were in any place notorious for crime or vice, others who had shamefully squandered their estates, and, in fine, every one whose disgraceful conduct and actions had made him an exile from his home. Again, there were many whose thoughts dwelt on the triumph of Sulla; they saw some, who had been common soldiers, now senators, and others so rich as to live in a style of regal magnificence; each hoped that, should he take up arms, victory would bring him no less rewards. Besides these, many young men who had starved in the country on the wages of their hands, had been attracted to Rome by public or private bounties, and had learnt to prefer the ease of the capital to thankless toil. These, and all like them, found their profit in disaster to the state, so that we need wonder the less that penniless men of bad character were filled with high hopes, and measured their country's interests by their own. Again, all those whose ancestors had been proscribed during Sulla's triumph, whose property had been confiscated, and their political rights impaired, were awaiting the issue of the struggle with like feelings. To these might be added all who, as being in opposition to the senatorial party, preferred a convulsion in the state to their own exclusion from power. In fine, after many years, just the old disorders had returned to threaten the state. The tribunician power had been restored in the consulship of Pompey and Crassus [70 B.C.], and henceforth young men, of headstrong age and character, possessed themselves of this important office and began to rouse the commons by attacks on the Senate; next by bribery and promises to further kindle their passions; and thus, finally, to attain to distinction and influence. They were strenuously opposed by many of the nobility, who made the defence of the Senate a pretext for advancing their own importance. To put the truth shortly, from the time of Sulla forward, though those who busied themselves with state affairs might allege honourable excuses, in some cases the defence of the people's rights, in others the extension of the authority of the Senate, beneath all this pretext of the public good each was secretly striving to gain power for himself. They showed no moderation, pushed hostility to an extreme, and made a bloody use of victory when won. After the despatch of Pompey to conduct the wars against the Pirates and Mithradates, the power of the commons was broken, and the influence of the oligarchy increased. They held the magistracies, the provincial appointments, and all other patronage, in their own hands; they passed their days in prosperity, free from trouble and anxiety, and by their control of the courts terrified all who while in office treated the commons with great mildness. As soon, however, as, in the perilous condition of the state, a hope of revolution was offered to the commons, the old battle-cry raised their spirits. Had Catiline come off victor, or even on equal terms, from the first battle-field, the state would, no doubt, have been prostrated by massacre and disaster, while the victorious party would only have enjoyed their success till some stronger champion snatched power and freedom from their tired and enfeebled hands. Even as it was, many persons not connected with the conspiracy at the outbreak of the war set out to join Catiline. Among these was a certain Aulus Fulvius, a senator's son, who was dragged back when already on the way, and put to death by his father's order. At Rome, meanwhile, Lentulus was following out the injunction of Catiline, and tampering in person, or through his agents, with all whose character or fortunes made them, he thought, fit instruments of revolution, not confining himself to citizens, but enlisting men of every class, so long as they would be useful in war. In pursuance of this policy, he entrusted a certain Publius Umbrenus with the task of seeking out the ambassadors from the Allobroges, and inducing them, if possible, to join in the war. Their great public and private indebtedness, and the warlike temperament of the Gallic race, led him to hope that they would readily join in such an enterprise. Umbrenus had previously been employed in Gaul, and was acquainted with many of the chief men in the different states. He went to work therefore at once, and on the first occasion of his seeing the ambassadors in the Forum, asked a few questions as to their public affairs, and, as if grieved for their misfortunes, began to inquire what issue they hoped for to so many evils. They complained of the greed of the magistrates, accused the Senate for its failure to help them, and foreboded death as the one cure for their ills. On hearing this, he told them that if they would be men, he would show them a way of escape from the great evils they spoke of. Inspired with extravagant hopes by his words, the Allobroges implored Umbrenus to take pity on them. There was no task so hard or repellent that they would not be most eager to perform it, if it would but free their state from debt. Thereupon Umbrenus took them to the house of Decimus Brutus, which was near the Forum, and was thrown open to the conspirators by the influence of Sempronia; for Brutus at the time was absent from Rome. To lend greater weight to his words, he also summoned Gabinius, and in his presence disclosed the conspiracy, and named his accomplices, including among them, in order to inspire the ambassadors with greater courage, many persons of every rank who were perfectly innocent. At last he procured from the ambassadors a promise of their services, and dismissed them home. The Allobroges, however, wavered for a long time as to what course they should adopt. On the one side was their debt, their love of war, and the great rewards they might expect if victorious; on the other, greater resources, an absence of risk, and a certain and immediate reward instead of uncertain hope. Thus they examined both sides of the question; but the fortune of the republic at last prevailed. They betrayed the whole affair, just as they had heard it, to Quintus Fabius Sanga, whose patronage their state mostly employed. Cicero, informed by Sanga of the plot, instructed the ambassadors to make a great show of zeal for the conspiracy, to visit the rest of the intriguers, make them ample promises, and use every exertion for their complete exposure.

Almost simultaneously, there were risings in Hither and Farther Gaul, as also in Picenum, Bruttium, and Apulia. The agents whom Catiline had previously despatched on every side were, with a rashness that approached insanity, pushing on all their plans at once. Their midnight councils, their transport of arms and weapons, their general hurry and bustle had caused more fear than actual danger. Many of these agents had been brought to trial by the praetor, Quintus Metellus Celer, in accordance with a resolution of the Senate, and by him thrown into prison, and Gaius Murena had pursued the same course in Farther Gaul, where he held command as a legate.

Meanwhile at Rome, Lentulus, with the other heads of the conspiracy, when a large force was, as it seemed to them, in readiness, determined that, on the arrival of Catiline and his army at Faesulae, Lucius Bestia, a tribune of the commons, should hold a public meeting, complain of the steps taken by Cicero, and throw the odium of having caused a most terrible war on that excellent consul. Taking this as their signal, the rank and file of their supporters were on the following night to carry out their respective tasks. Report said that these were distributed in the following manner:—Statilius and Gabinius, with a large force, were to set fire simultaneously to twelve suitable points in the town; the confusion thus caused would gain them easier access to the consul, and to the others at whom they aimed; Cethegus was to beset Cicero's door and attack him by force; others of the conspirators had other victims; and the young men, most of them of noble birth, were to murder their parents, and in the general panic that the simultaneous massacre and fire would occasion, were to sally forth to join Catiline. While these preparations and arrangements were being made, Cethegus was continually complaining of the cowardice of his associates. He declared that by their hesitation and delay they had wasted splendid chances; in such a crisis it was action that was needed, not deliberation, and he himself, he protested, were he joined by only a few others, would attack the Senate house, while the rest played the coward. Naturally bold and impetuous, he was ever ready to strike a blow, and was convinced that prompt action offered the highest advantages.

To return to the Allobroges; in obedience to Cicero's injunction, they procured a meeting through Gabinius with the rest of the conspirators, and demanded from Lentulus, Cethegus, Statilius, and also Cassius, an oath which they might bear, under seal, to their countrymen. Without this it would be a difficult task to make them join in so serious an attempt. The rest did as they were asked without any suspicion, but Cassius promised to go shortly to Gaul in person, and, indeed, left the city on that journey some little time before the ambassadors. On the departure of the latter, Lentulus sent with them a certain Titus Volturcius of Crotona, so that previous to their return home they might strengthen the bonds of their alliance by exchanging assurances with Catiline. He further entrusted Volturcius with a letter to Catiline, of which I give a copy:—"Who I am you will learn from the bearer. Consider the danger of your position, and remember that you are a brave man. Think what your plans demand; seek help from all, even from the lowest." Besides this letter he sent a verbal message asking, now that he had been declared a public enemy by the Senate, what he had to gain by refusing the help of slaves? The preparation he had ordered in the capital had been made; there must be no delay on his part in advancing nearer to Rome. When matters had gone thus far, on the night agreed on for their departure, Cicero, whose emissaries had informed him of everything, gave orders to the praetors, Lucius Valerius Flaccus, and Gaius Pomptinus, to plant an ambush by the Mulvian bridge, and seize the Allobroges, with their retinue. He explained clearly the object on which they were sent, and empowered them to manage the details as need might arise. The praetors, men used to war, quietly stationed their guards, and secretly invested the bridge, according to their instructions. The ambassadors, with Volturcius, had no sooner arrived at the place than a simultaneous shout arose from either side. The Gauls quickly recognised the design, and promptly surrendered to the praetors. Volturcius at first encouraged the rest to resistance, and defended himself with his sword against his numerous assailants; finding, however, that he was deserted by the ambassadors, after many entreaties to Pomptinus on the score of their acquaintance to secure his safety, he at last in great fear and trembling for his life, surrendered to the praetors as though to declared enemies.

On the successful execution of the design a full account was quickly conveyed to the consul, whose mind was filled at once with anxiety and rejoicing, with joy at the news that by the disclosure of the plot, the state was saved from its danger; but, on the other hand, with deep anxiety, in his hesitation as to what must be done with citizens of such rank detected in so great a crime. To punish them, he thought, would bring trouble on himself, while to allow them to escape might ruin the state. Summoning all his resolution, he ordered Lentulus, Cethegus, Statilius, and Gabinius, to be called before him, and with them a certain Caeparius of Tarracina, who was preparing to set out for Apulia, there to rouse the slaves. The rest appeared without delay; Caeparius, who had left his house a little before, had learnt that information of the plot had been given, and escaped from the city. Lentulus, as praetor, the consul himself conducted, holding him by the hand, the rest under guard he ordered to come to the Temple of Concord. Thither he had summoned the Senate, and in a crowded assembly of its members he now introduced Volturcius with the ambassadors, while he ordered the praetor Flaccus to bring the despatch box, with the letters which he had received from the ambassadors. Volturcius was then examined on the subject of his journey, the letter, and finally as to his purpose and motive. At first he made pretences, and tried to conceal all knowledge of the conspiracy; afterwards, when bidden to speak with a guarantee from the state of his safety, he betrayed everything just as it had taken place, and informed the Senate that, as he himself had only been admitted to complicity by Gabinius and Caeparius a few days before, he knew no more than the ambassadors. He could only say that he had been used to hear from Gabinius that Publius Autronius, Servius Sulla, Lucius Vargunteius, and many others were concerned in the conspiracy. The confession of the Gauls was to the same effect, and when Lentulus pretended ignorance, they convicted him not only by the letter but by the words he had often used. "The

Sibylline books," he had said, "prophesied that three Cornelii should rule Rome; Cinna and Sulla had already done so, and he himself was the third to whom fate assigned the government of the city; moreover, this was the twentieth year from that in which the Capitol had been burnt, and augurs had frequently declared on the strength of prodigies that it should be rendered bloody by a civil war." All the prisoners had previously acknowledged their seals; and, accordingly, after the letters had been read, the Senate made a decree that Lentulus on laying down his office, as well as the rest, should be kept in "free" or private custody. Accordingly they were delivered to the following guardians:—Lentulus, to Publius Lentulus Spinther, at that time an aedile; Cethegus, to Quintus Cornificius; Statilius, to Gaius Caesar; Gabinius, to Marcus Crassus; and Caeparius (who had been pursued and just brought back), to a senator named Gnaeus Terentius.

Meanwhile the commons, who, at first, in their eagerness for a revolution, were too favourable to the idea of war, now that the nature of the conspiracy was laid bare, experienced a revulsion of feeling. They cursed the designs of Catiline, exalted Cicero to heaven, and were as full of joy and gladness as though they had escaped from slavery. Any other outrage of war would rather have given them plunder than have done them harm, but a conflagration they thought a ruthless and extravagant measure, and one fraught with misery to themselves, whose whole wealth consisted in articles of daily use and personal clothing.

On the following day there was brought before the Senate a certain Lucius Tarquinius, who was said to have been pursued and captured on his way to join Catiline. He offered, if granted a public guarantee, to give information about the plot, and was ordered by the consul to make a full confession of all he knew. He told the Senate a tale very similar to that of Volturcius, about preparations for firing the city, a massacre of the respectable classes, and the approach of the enemy, but added that he himself had been sent by Marcus Crassus with a message to Catiline "not to let the arrest of Lentulus, Cethegus, and others of the conspirators alarm him, but to make it an additional reason for a rapid advance on Rome, by which the spirits of the rest would be revived and the prisoners more easily rescued from danger." On the mention, however, of Crassus, a man of birth, of enormous wealth, and the very greatest influence, some thought the story unworthy of belief, others again deemed it true, yet were of the opinion that at such a crisis so powerful a man should rather be conciliated than provoked; and as most of the senators were, in their private affairs, at the mercy of Crassus, all united in a cry that the witness was no honest one, and demanded that a motion should be made on the subject. On the motion therefore of Cicero, and in a crowded house, the Senate resolved that, "Whereas the witness of Tarquinius appears dishonest, he is to be kept in custody, and to be granted no further privilege of audience until such time as he confess at whose instigation he fabricated so grievous a charge." It was thought at the time by some that the information was contrived by Publius Autronius, in order that Crassus by the accusation might be made to share the peril of the rest, and these then gain the protection of his power. Others asserted that Tarquinius was set on by Cicero to prevent Crassus, according to his wont, taking the sedition under his patronage, and so embroiling the state. At a later period I personally heard Crassus himself declare that it was Cicero who had put this great insult upon him.

At the same conjuncture Quintus Catulus and Gaius Piso failed, either by bribery or influence, to induce Cicero to have Gaius Caesar dishonestly accused by means of the Allobroges or some other informer. Both these nobles were at bitter enmity with Caesar; Piso he had assailed when on his trial for malversation, on the score of having unjustly punished a certain Transpadane; Catulus hated him on account of their contest for the Pontificate, in that, at the close of his life and after filling the highest offices, he had been beaten by such a youth as Caesar. The state of the latter's affairs also favoured the accusation, as his extraordinary profusion and the splendour of his public entertainments had sunk him heavily in debt. Unable to induce the consul to commit such a crime, they applied themselves to individual intrigues, and, by coining falsehoods, which they declared they had heard from Volturcius or the Allobroges, raised much odium against Caesar. So successful, indeed, were they, that some Roman knights, who were on guard under arms round the Temple of Concord, were carried away either by the greatness of the danger, or their own excitable character, and, on Caesar's leaving the Senate, threatened him with their swords, in order to show their zeal for the constitution.

While the Senate was engaged with this business, and in decreeing rewards to the ambassadors of the Allobroges, and to Titus Volturcius, as informers whose witness had been verified, the freedmen and a few of the dependents of Lentulus went different ways about the city, trying to rouse the artisans and slaves in the streets to rescue him; while others sought out the popular mob captains, who had been wont to sell their services in disturbing the state. Cethegus, moreover, employed messengers to entreat the slaves and freedmen of his household, men picked and trained, to come boldly in an armed body and break into the house where he lay. The consul, on learning of these designs, posted guards wherever occasion demanded, and having summoned the Senate, put the question how they would deal with the men in custody. It should be mentioned that, shortly before this, the Senate in a crowded house had pronounced their conduct treasonable. On the present occasion, Decimus Junius Silanus, who as consul elect was the first called upon to give his opinion as to what was to be done with the actual prisoners, and besides them with Lucius Cassius, Publius Furius, Publius Umbrenus, and Quintus Annius, in the event of their capture, at first gave his vote for their punishment; afterwards, however, he was so influenced by the speech of Gaius Caesar that he declared that on a division he would side with Tiberius Nero, who had proposed that the question should be adjourned till further defensive steps had been taken. The speech of Caesar, when it came to him to be asked his opinion by the consul, was to the following effect:—

"All men, Senators, who deliberate on doubtful matters should be equally free from hate and friendship, from anger and compassion. When these obstruct the view, the mind does not easily discern the truth; nor has any one ever harmonized the dictates of passion and interest. When the intellect is alert it is strong; but if passion gains a footing it becomes a tyrant, and the reason is reduced to impotence. I have no lack of examples of kings and peoples who, under the sway of anger or compassion have erred in their counsels. I prefer, however, to remind you of some occasions on which our own ancestors preserved a due and orderly course of action though it conflicted with their passions. In the Macedonian war, which we carried on with King Perseus, the great and splendid State of Rhodes, which had prospered by the help of the Roman people, proved disloyal and hostile to us. When the war was finished and the conduct of the Rhodians came to be considered, our ancestors, to avoid giving any pretext for an assertion that they went to war not to avenge an injury, but for the sake of wealth, allowed them to go unpunished. Similarly in all our Punic wars, though the Carthaginians often committed many outrages in times both of peace and of truce, our ancestors availed themselves of no opportunity to do the like, but took in consideration rather what was worthy of themselves than what might fairly be inflicted on their enemy.

"A like occasion has now arisen, and you, Senators, must be on your guard lest the crime of Publius Lentulus and his fellows weigh heavier with you than your own dignity, and lead you to a resolution that will better satisfy your wrath than your repute. If, indeed, the object of our search is some penalty adequate to the offence, then I approve of our abandoning all precedent in our measures; but if the enormity of the crime taxes our ingenuity too heavily for this, I am of opinion that we should confine ourselves to such punishments as are by law provided. Most of those who have spoken before me have in studied and noble language bewailed the misfortune of the republic, have dilated on the horrors of war and the fate of the vanquished, and have reminded you of how maids are ravished, children torn from their parents' arms, matrons placed at the mercy of the conquerors' passions, temples and houses plundered, fire and slaughter carried everywhere, and whole towns filled with arms and corpses, blood and mourning. But at what, I ask, was all this eloquence aimed? As if the man whom the horrible reality has not moved could be roused by any eloquence! That is not human nature, nor are men ever wont to underestimate their own injuries; rather, in many cases they have been known to take too serious a view of them. Extravagance of behaviour, Senators, takes a different hue in different stations. Men of low rank pass their life in obscurity, and their faults of passion are known to few, for their notoriety never rises above their fortunes. Those, on the other hand, who are the heirs of a great sovereignty, and live in a high position, have their doings known to all the world. The higher their fortunes the greater the restrictions upon them; they must know nothing of favour or disfavour, and least of all of anger; for what in others is called anger, in rulers receives the name of pride and cruelty. And, though, for my own part, I think any and every punishment inadequate to the crimes of the prisoners, yet most people only remember the end of an incident, and, in the case of the wicked, often forget their misdeeds in talking of their punishment, if that has been somewhat unusually severe.

"I feel sure that the proposal of that brave and active citizen, Decimus Silanus, was made in all zeal for the state, and that in a matter of such importance he would allow himself to be influenced neither by hatred nor partiality. My knowledge of his character and self-restraint convinces me of this. But his motion strikes me, I will not say as cruel—for what proposal could be cruel when aimed at men like these?—but as foreign to the spirit of our state. It must certainly have been either panic or a strong sense of wrong that moved you, Silanus, a consul elect, to propose an unprecedented form of punishment. To speak of terror were needless, especially when, by the activity of our illustrious consul, we have such numerous guards under arms. As to the actual punishment you propose, I might observe, what is indeed the case, that to men in grief and misery death comes as a relief, not as a pain, that it annuls all the ills that flesh is heir to, and that beyond it neither trouble nor joy finds place. But what I wish to ask you is, Why did you not add to your motion that the condemned should first be punished with the scourge? Was it because it is forbidden by the Porcian legislation? If so, there are other laws which forbid condemned citizens to be deprived of life, and offer the alternative of exile. Did you omit it, then, because scourging is a heavier punishment than death? Yet what sentence can be harsh or too severe for men convicted of so atrocious a crime? Again, if you thought scourging the lighter punishment, how is it consistent to fear the law in the smaller matter after neglecting it in the greater?

"It may be asked, Who will take exception to any decree against traitors? I answer, time, the events of a day, and fortune whose caprice rules the world. Whatever the prisoners' fate, it will have been well deserved;

but you, Senators, must consider the precedent which you are establishing. Every bad precedent has arisen out of a measure in itself good; but, when power has fallen to unskilful or less worthy hands, the precedent is no longer applied to fit and deserving subjects, but to unfit and undeserving. The Lacedaemonians, when they had crushed the Athenians, imposed on them an oligarchy of thirty members. This government began by executing, without trial, those whose guilt or unpopularity was greatest; the people rejoiced, and justified their action. As the spirit of license gradually increased, they killed good and bad alike in mere wantonness, while they filled the rest of the citizens with terror. Thus the state paid for its foolish rejoicing the heavy price of slavery. In our own times the victorious Sulla, amid universal approval, ordered the execution of Damasippus and his fellows, who had fattened on the public disasters. The men were stained with crime and treason, their seditious spirit had embroiled the state, and it was agreed that their death was richly deserved. Nevertheless, that action was the inauguration of a great massacre. Did a man covet a house or villa, nay, even a piece of pottery or of raiment, he used all his exertions to include its owner in the list of the proscribed. Those who had rejoiced at the death of Damasippus were soon themselves dragged to execution, and the massacre only ceased when Sulla had glutted all his followers with wealth. I do not fear any such conduct on the part of Marcus Tullius, nor at the present crisis; but a large state contains many and diverse characters. At a future time, and under another consul, entrusted, in his turn, with an army, some false charge may be believed true, and when the consul has followed this precedent, and, at the decree of the Senate, drawn his sword, who will there be to check or restrain him?

"Senators, our ancestors never showed themselves wanting in either wisdom or courage, nor did they allow their pride to prevent them imitating the customs of foreign nations, so long as they were good. Many of their arms and weapons of warfare they adopted from the Samnites, and the emblems of their magistracies from the Etruscans; in fine, they zealously copied in their own administration all that seemed serviceable among their allies or enemies. They preferred, I may say, to imitate rather than to envy the good. Now, it was at this period of imitation that they adopted the Greek custom of scourging citizens and inflicting capital punishment on convicted criminals. With the growth, however, of the state, and the greater violence of party strife, which resulted from the increase of population, it was found that innocent persons were made victims and that other like abuses were becoming common. To meet this danger, the Porcian and other laws were provided, by which convicted persons were allowed to retire into exile. This, Senators, I think a most weighty reason against our adopting any resolution for which there is no precedent. I cannot but think that the men, who, with the small resources at their command, won so great an empire, were endowed with greater courage and wisdom than are we who find a difficulty even in keeping what they so nobly won.

"Am I then in favour of dismissing our prisoners, to swell the army of Catiline? Far from it. My proposal is that their goods be confiscated, and that their persons be imprisoned in such borough towns as are best able to support the charge, and that no one hereafter make any motion with reference to them in the Senate, or bring their case before the people, on pain of the Senate's adjudging his action treasonable and prejudicial to the State."

On the close of Caesar's speech, all the senators merely gave their votes for the different motions, some for the one, some for the other, until it came to Marcus Porcius Cato. He, when asked his opinion, delivered himself as follows:—

"When I turn, Senators, from surveying the dangers of our position, and reflect on the opinions of certain previous speakers, the impression I receive is very different. These speakers appear to have discussed the punishment of the men who have raised war against their country and parents, their altars and hearths. Our position warns us rather to guard against their attack than to consider their sentence. All other crimes you may be content to avenge when they have actually been committed; against this, if you fail to prevent it, you will in vain invoke the law, for when a city is once stormed the conquered have no further resources. I profess, though, I should remember that in you I am appealing to men who ever valued their houses and villas, their statues and paintings more highly than they did the state. If you would keep these cherished possessions, of whatever kind—if you would have leisure to indulge in your pleasures—now at last awake and take an active part in the work of government. This is no question of tribute or of the wrongs done to our allies; it is our liberty and our lives that are at stake.

"Many a time, Senators, have I spoken at length in this house. Often have I complained of the self-indulgence and avarice of our citizens. By so doing I have made many enemies; but as I would never have excused myself or my own inclination for any fault, I could not easily condone actual crimes in the case of the lustfulness of another. You made slight account of this advice, but the stability of the state was not shaken; its resources could bear the strain of your neglect. The question, however, now at stake is not whether our lives shall be moral or immoral, nor as to the size or splendour of the empire of the Roman people; it is whether this empire, just as it is, shall remain our own, or fall, with ourselves, a prey to our enemies. Here some one reminds me of clemency and compassion. Why, long ere this we have ceased to call things by their right names. To be lavish of the goods of others is now called generosity, and to be daring in the commission of crime courage. This fashion has brought the state to the brink of ruin; but even granting, since morality is come to this, that men may be generous with the fortunes of our allies, and compassionate in dealing with plunderers of the exchequer, at least let them hesitate to squander our blood, and, in sparing a few villains, work the ruin of all honest men.

"Gaius Caesar has just addressed to you an eloquent and polished disquisition on life and death. He considers, I suppose, as false those traditions about the dead which assign to the bad a path different from that of the good, leading them to noisome and savage abodes full of horrors and terrors. Holding this opinion, he has moved that the property of the prisoners be confiscated, and they themselves kept in confinement in the borough towns. He evidently fears that, should they remain at Rome, they may be forcibly rescued either by their accomplices or by a hired mob. As if bad and abandoned men were to be found only in the capital, and not throughout Italy, or boldness were not more powerful where the means of repelling it are less! His proposal is thus plainly idle, if he really apprehends danger from the prisoners; while if, amid such general alarm, he alone is fearless, there is the more reason that I should be fearful for you and for myself. In making your decision, then, on Publius Lentulus and his associates, be assured that you are at the same time deciding the fate of the army of Catiline and of all the conspirators. The more vigorous your measures, the more will their courage be shaken. If they see you hesitating, but for a moment, you will have the whole pack marching valiantly against you.

"Think not that it was by arms that our ancestors raised the state from insignificance to grandeur. If that were so, it would now be at its noblest beneath our sway, for our force of allies and citizens, not to mention that of arms and horses, is far greater than was theirs. The sources, however, of their greatness were very different from these, and we have none of them. Such were their energy at home, the justice of their rule abroad, and the unbiassed mind, the slave neither of sin nor of lust, which they brought to their councils. For these we have substituted self-indulgence and avarice, a bankrupt state and private millionaires. Our praise is of riches; idleness our pursuit. Good and bad can no longer be distinguished; intrigue wins all the prizes which merit deserves, and who can wonder at it? Each of you frames his policy to serve his individual ends; in your homes you worship pleasure, in the Senate money or influence; and so, when an attack comes, the state is found with none to defend her.

"However, I will say no more of this. Citizens of the highest rank have conspired to destroy their country; to aid them in the war they summon the Gauls, a people most hostile to the name of Rome; the leader of our enemies with his army is upon us. Can you still be hesitating how to treat enemies caught within your walls? You are to pity them, I suppose. The young men have been led astray by ambition, and you should dismiss them, aye, with arms in their hands. Look to it that this clemency and mercy do not turn to your own misery, when once they have found arms. The state of affairs is indeed unpromising, but perhaps you do not fear it? Say rather that you are in the greatest terror, but that in your sloth and irresolution you hesitate and wait one for another, full, of course, of a pious trust in the eternal gods who have so often upheld this state amid the greatest dangers. I tell you that the help of heaven is not won by vows and womanish prayers; but that by vigilance, by action, by wise counsels, a happy issue is attained. Abandon yourself to sloth and cowardice, and you may invoke the gods, but it will be in vain; they are angered and adverse. In the days of our forefathers, Titus Manlius Torquatus, during the Gallic war, ordered his son to be executed for having fought the enemy against orders. That noble youth atoned by his death for his untempered valour, and are you hesitating as to your sentence on these ruthless traitors? Of course the rest of their lives stands in contrast to this one crime! Respect then the rank of Lentulus, if ever he respected his modesty, his honour, or any god or man. Pardon the youth of Cethegus, if this be not the second time he has made war on his country. What am I to say of Gabinius, of Statilius, of Caeparius? If it had not been for their utter recklessness they could never, I suppose, have entertained such designs upon the state! To conclude, Senators, I profess that, if we could safely make a mistake, I would readily suffer you to be convinced of your error by the course of events, since you despise my words. We are, however, actually beset on every side. Catiline, with his army, is at our throats; we have other enemies within the walls and in the very heart of the city; we can make no preparation and come to no determination without its being known; all these are so many reasons for greater despatch.

"I therefore move that 'inasmuch as the criminal designs of traitorous citizens have placed the state in the greatest danger, and inasmuch as the prisoners by the information of Titus Volturcius and the ambassadors of the Allobroges, and also by their own confessions, stand convicted of having planned a massacre, a conflagration, and other disgraceful and cruel atrocities, against their fellow-citizens and their country; that, therefore, punishment be inflicted according to ancient custom, on those who have confessed their guilt, as though they had been caught in the commission of capital offences.'"

On Cato resuming his seat, all the men of consular rank, together with many other members of the Senate, commended his proposal, and praised his courage to the skies. Reproaching each other for what they now called their timidity, they accounted Cato a great and brilliant statesman, and a decree of the Senate was passed in the words of his resolution.

I have read and heard much of the noble deeds of the Roman people in peace and in war, on land and on sea; and chance has disposed me to consider what circumstance it was that had done most to support it in its gigantic task. I was aware that on many occasions it had confronted large bodies of the enemy with but a handful of troops. I knew of the wars which Rome, with her scanty resources, had waged against wealthy kings. I knew, too, that she had often had to bear the rude attack of fortune; and that in eloquence the Greek, in warlike renown the Gaul, had outstripped her children. After much reflection, however, I arrived at the conclusion that it was the pre-eminent merit of a few of our citizens that had accomplished all; that this was the power that had enabled poverty to subdue wealth, a handful to rout a host. When, however, the state was corrupted by luxury and indolence, the republic, in its turn, by its very greatness, lent strength to its blundering generals and magistrates; while, as if the vigour of their fathers were exhausted, at many periods there was not a single man in Rome of conspicuous merit. In my own time, however, there have been two men of surpassing merit, though different character—Marcus Cato and Gaius Caesar. As my subject has brought them into notice, it is not my design to pass them over without disclosing their respective natures and characters, so far as my ability will allow me.

In birth, age, and eloquence, Caesar and Cato were nearly equal; and they were well matched in the loftiness of their aims, and in the renown which, each in his own way, they attained. Caesar was esteemed for his kind offices and munificence; Cato for the strict uprightness of his life. The former was distinguished by his clemency and compassion; sternness added dignity to the latter. Caesar won renown by his readiness to give, to help, and to pardon; Cato by never offering a bribe. The one was the refuge of the wretched; the other, the destruction of the bad. The former was praised for his affability; the latter for his consistency. In fine Caesar had formed the resolve to work, to be ever on the watch, to promote his friends' interest even to the detriment of his own, and to refuse nothing which was worth the giving. He aimed at a high command, an army, a war in some new field where his talents might be displayed. Cato, on the other hand, made temperance, dignity, and, above all, austerity of behaviour, his pursuit. He did not vie in wealth with the wealthy, nor in intrigue with the intriguer, but in courage with the man of action, in honour with the scrupulous, in self-restraint with the upright. He preferred to be good rather than to seem so; and thus, the less he pursued renown, the more it attended him.

When, as I related, the Senate had passed Cato's resolution, the consul, thinking it better to forestall the coming night, lest the interval should be used for any revolutionary movement, ordered the officers to make the necessary preparations for the execution. After posting guards at various points he personally conducted Lentulus to the prison, while the praetors did the same to the rest. In the prison there is a place, called the Tullianum, which, after a slight ascent to the left, you find sunk about twelve feet in the ground. It is guarded on every side by walls, and above it is an arched roof of stone; desolation, darkness, and stench give it a loathsome and dreadful appearance. Into this place Lentulus was taken down, and there strangled by the appointed executioners. A patrician of the illustrious house of the Cornelii, and a man who had held the office of consul at Rome, he met an end worthy of his character and his crimes. On Cethegus, Statilius, Gabinius, and Caeparius, the same punishment was inflicted.

While this was happening at Rome, Catiline, from the whole force made up of his own contingent and of the original army of Manlius, organized two legions, and filled up the cohorts in proportion to the number of his men. Afterwards, as volunteers or members of the conspiracy arrived in the camp they were drafted in equal numbers into the several divisions; and in a short time he had raised his legions to their proper strength, although at first he had not more than two thousand men. Not more than a quarter, however, of his whole force was equipped with weapons of war. The rest, as chance had armed them, carried hunting spears or javelins, and, in some cases, pointed stakes. On the approach of Antonius with his army, Catiline moved to and fro among the mountains, frequently changed his quarters, turning now towards Rome, now towards Gaul, and offered the enemy no chance of fighting; for he hoped, should his accomplices at Rome succeed in their plans, soon to be at the head of large forces. Meanwhile he rejected the slave bands, which at the outset rallied round him in large numbers. He trusted to the strength of the conspiracy, and at the same time thought it prejudicial to his designs to appear to have made the cause of citizens one with that of runaway slaves. On the arrival at the camp of the news that at Rome the plot was discovered, and that Lentulus, Cethegus, and the others whom I have named above, had been executed, many, who had been enticed to arms by the hope of plunder or desire for revolution, now fell away. The rest Catiline led by forced marches over rugged mountains to the district of Pistoria, intending to retreat secretly by cross roads into Transalpine Gaul. Quintus Metellus Celer, however, was on guard in Picenum with three legions, and surmised that Catiline, in his present difficulty, would be adopting the very course I have described. Learning the latter's route from deserters, he hastily advanced and pitched his camp at the very foot of the mountains which Catiline would have to descend on his hasty march towards Gaul. Antonius also was close upon him; his army was large, but it was aided by the more level character of its road, and he could thus follow in pursuit. Catiline now saw himself hemmed in between the mountains and the forces of the enemy; in the capital he had been defeated; and he had no hope either of escape or refuge. He thought best, therefore, in so perilous a case, to try the fortune of war, and determined to come to an instant engagement with Antonius. Accordingly, he called his troops around him, and spoke as follows:—

"Soldiers, I have long discovered that words cannot inspire courage, and that no speech of a general can give a flagging army energy, or the timid courage. Just so much daring, natural or acquired, as resides in each man's breast, does he display in war. The man insensible to the call of glory and danger you will harangue in vain; his cowardice stops his ears. My motive in calling you together was to give you a few words of advice and at the same time to disclose the motive of my resolution.

"I make certain, soldiers, that you know of the disastrous consequences, to himself and to us, of the cowardice and indolence of Lentulus, and how, while awaiting reinforcements from the capital, I have been prevented from marching towards Gaul. You know, too, as well as I do, our present position. Two hostile armies close our path, the one on the side of Rome, the other of Gaul. Want of corn and other necessaries forbid us to remain longer in our present quarters, desire it though we may. In whatever direction we determine to march, we must cut our way with our swords. I exhort you, therefore, to keep a brave and ready heart, and, when you enter battle, to remember that in your own right hands lie wealth, honour, and fame, as well as your freedom and the possession of your country. If we conquer, our safety will be secured; we shall have provisions in plenty, and the gates of boroughs and colonies will be thrown open to us. If we give way in fear, we shall have all these against us. No place nor friend will protect the man who has failed to protect himself with his own arms. Moreover, soldiers, we and our enemies will be fighting under motives of very different force. For us the contest is for country, for freedom and for life, while our enemies can have little interest in fighting to maintain the supremacy of a narrow class.

"Let these thoughts inspire you with hardihood; advance to the fight, mindful of your ancient valour. You might, though to your deep disgrace, have passed your lives in exile. Some of you might, after the confiscation of your goods, have lingered in Rome, on the watch for a stranger's bounty. Such courses seemed shameful and unbearable to men of spirit, and so you have chosen to follow the one that has led you here. If you would now quit it you must use your daring, for it is at the discretion of the victor that war is changed for peace. To hope for safety in flight, when your backs, unprotected by armour, are turned to the enemy, is indeed folly. In a battle it is always the greatest cowards who run the greatest risks, while courage is as a wall of defence.

"When I look on you, soldiers, and count up your achievements, I am possessed with high hope of victory. Your resolution, your age, and your courage, and above all the inevitable nature of the encounter, which often makes even the timid brave, exhort me to this; and the narrowness of the position prevents our being surrounded by the host of the enemy. If, however, fortune shows herself jealous of your valour, see that you do not fall unavenged, nor prefer by a surrender to be butchered like sheep rather than to fight like men, and leave your enemies a bloody victory that shall cost them dear."

At the end of this speech, after a trifling delay, he ordered the signal to sound, and led his troops, in orderly array, down to the level ground. He then sent away the horses of all who owned them, in order that the soldiers might be encouraged by the sense that their danger was shared by all alike. He himself, on foot, then drew up his army with due regard to the nature of the ground and his own numbers. There was a plain lying between mountains on the left, while on the right the ground was broken with rocks; here he posted eight cohorts to form the front, while the other divisions, with their standards, were stationed in closer order as a reserve. From these cohorts he withdrew the centurions, all of them picked veterans, with the bravest and best armed of the common soldiers, and added them to the front. He ordered Gaius Manlius to take the command on the right, and a certain man of Faesulae on the left. He himself, with his own freed-men and some soldiers' servants, took up his station by the eagle standard which Gaius Marius was said to have used in his army in the Cimbrian war.

On the other side Gaius Antonius was prevented by lameness from taking part in the battle, and entrusted his army to his lieutenant, Marcus Petreius. By him the veteran cohorts which he had levied to suppress the revolt were posted in front, and the rest of the army behind them as a reserve. Petreius himself reviewed his army on horseback, accosting the soldiers by name, encouraging them, and entreating them to remember that they were fighting against half-armed brigands for their country and children, their altars and homes. He was an experienced soldier, and, during a career of more than thirty years in the army, in which he filled the offices of tribune, praefect, legate, and praetor with great distinction, had gained a knowledge of many of his men and their brave deeds; and by reference to these he now kindled their spirits.

When he had satisfied himself on every point, Petreius sounded the signal and ordered the cohorts to advance slowly, and the same movement was made by the enemy. On reaching a distance at which the light troops could engage, the two armies raised a great shout and charged each other, standard to standard. Dropping their javelins, they fought with swords. The veterans, remembering their ancient valour, pressed on to engage at close quarters; their opponents fiercely withstood them, and the conflict raged with the greatest fury. Meanwhile Catiline, with his light troops, was busy in the front. He relieved the hard-pressed, called up fresh men to fill the places of the wounded, had an eye for every need, often fought himself, and often struck down his man. In fine, he played the part at once of an active soldier and a skilful general. Petreius, on seeing Catiline making such vigorous and unexpected exertions, led the cohort of his guards against the enemies' centre. Their ranks were now in confusion, and they could only offer a straggling resistance; he cut them down and proceeded to attack the survivors on either flank. Manlius and the Faesulan fell fighting in the front rank, and Catiline saw that his troops were routed, and only himself and a few others left. He remembered his race and the rank he had once held, and, rushing into the thickest of the foe, fought on till he was pierced with wounds.

It was only after the battle was decided, that it could be fully seen with what daring and resolution Catiline's army had been inspired. Almost the exact position which each had taken up while living he now in death covered with his body. A few of those in the centre, who had been dislodged by the praetor's body guard, had fallen less closely together in the different places where they had made a stand; but all bore their wounds in front. Catiline, however, was found at a distance from his own men among the enemy's dead. He continued to breathe for a short time, and retained on his countenance that savage courage which had marked him in life. I should not forget to mention that out of all that host not a single free-born man was made prisoner, either in the battle or the rout; so unsparing had all been alike of their own and their enemies' lives. Nor was the victory of the national army either happy or bloodless; its bravest soldiers had perished in the fight, or came out of it badly wounded. Many, too, who had come from the camp out of curiosity, or for the sake of plunder, in turning over the bodies of the enemy, found some a friend, others those bound to them by the ties of hospitality or blood, while others recognised the features of an enemy. Thus throughout the whole army grief and gladness, sorrow and rejoicing, held divided sway.

4. Cicero, *Letter to Quintus* (1)

Marcus Tullius Cicero, the eldest son of a wealthy equestrian who nevertheless lacked distinguished lineage, was born at Arpinum on 3 January 106 B.C. He studied philosophy and rhetoric in Rome and Athens, and he pursued a successful legal career from 81 to 66 B.C. Although he was what Romans called a "new man" (not from an established family), he

Ad Quintum fratrem 2.3. From *The Letters of Cicero*, vol. 1, translated by Evelyn S. Shuckburgh (London: George Bell & Sons, 1908), pp. 213–17.

became the most outstanding statesman of the Late Republic. He held a number of public offices before achieving the consulship in 63 B.C. He was a prominent member of the Optimate faction, whose members opposed political and economic reform in defense of the rule of the senate and the established families. He wrote many distinguished moral and philosophical essays. He possessed eight country residences as well as a house in Rome. In 49 B.C., he declined to ally himself with Julius Caesar during the civil war, and finally threw in his lot with Pompey, whose forces he joined in Macedonia. In 44 B.C., after the assassination of Caesar, Cicero was a bitter opponent of Mark Antony, and supported Octavian, whose character he misjudged. He perished at Formiae with his slaves on 7 December 43 B.C., a victim of Mark Antony's purges. Many of the details of the final decades of the Roman Republic are illuminated through his extensive surviving speeches and letters.

Marcus Cicero wrote this letter in Rome, on 12 or 15 February of 56 B.C., to his younger brother Quintus Cicero (see document 2), who then held a post on the island of Sardinia.

It was a troubled time. Rivalry between two ambitious political leaders, Clodius and Milo, contributed to disorder in the city of Rome. Clodius, tribune in 58 B.C., succeeded in exiling Cicero because he had executed Roman citizens, the allies of Catiline, without trial. The tribune Titus Annius Milo was able to secure Cicero's recall to Rome from exile in September of 57 B.C. after an absence of sixteen months. The triumvirate—the alliance of Pompey, Crassus, and Julius Caesar—appeared to be disintegrating. Caesar was in Gaul as military commander, creating a new Roman province and forming an army that was loyal to him. Pompey had received supreme military command in 57 B.C. and therefore could not cross the city limits of Rome. Cicero's brother Quintus, who was stationed on Sardinia, was one of fifteen commissioners who received appointment to support Pompey by attending to the food supply of the people of Rome. Pompey, who sought a new military appointment as an opportunity to offset the power and prestige of Caesar, hoped to lead an army to restore King Ptolemy Auletes of Egypt to his throne after he was overthrown by his subjects. The other contender for this military command was Lentulus, the governor of Cilicia. The tribune Gaius Cato opposed this aim of Pompey.

Cicero's optimism about the probable collapse of the triumvirate was excessive. At a conference in Lucca, northern Etruria, it was agreed that Pompey and Crassus would become consuls in 55 B.C. and that each would receive a strong proconsular army. Pompey was assigned Spain, although he remained in Italy, while Crassus received command in Syria in order to oppose the Parthians, a warlike people who had gained control of much of the former domains of Persia, in what is now Iraq and Iran.

Cicero was forced to submit and to serve the cause of the triumvirate in order to avoid a second exile.

I have already told you the earlier proceedings; now let me describe what was done afterwards. The legations were postponed from the 1st of February to the 13th. On the former day our business was not brought to a settlement. On the 2nd of February Milo appeared for trial. Pompey came to support him. Marcellus spoke on being called upon by me. We came off with flying colours. The case was adjourned to the 7th. Meanwhile (in the senate), the legations having been postponed to the 13th, the business of allotting the quaestors and furnishing the outfit of the praetors was brought before the house. But nothing was done, because many speeches were interposed denouncing the state of the Republic. Gaius Cato published his bill for the recall of Lentulus, whose son thereupon put on mourning. On the 7th Milo appeared. Pompey spoke, or rather wished to speak. For as soon as he got up Clodius's ruffians raised a shout, and throughout his whole speech he was interrupted, not only by hostile cries, but by personal abuse and insulting remarks. However, when he had finished his speech—for he shewed great courage in these circumstances, he was not cowed, he said all he had to say, and at times had by his commanding presence even secured silence for his words—well, when he had finished, up got Clodius. Our party received him with such a shout—for they had determined to pay him out—that he lost all presence of mind, power of speech, or control over his countenance. This went on up to two o'clock—Pompey having finished his speech at noon—and every kind of abuse, and finally epigrams of the most outspoken indecency were uttered against Clodius and Clodia [his sister]. Mad and livid with rage Clodius, in the very midst of the shouting, kept putting questions to his claque: "Who was it who was starving the commons to death?" His ruffians answered, "Pompey." "Who wanted to be sent to Alexandria?" They answered, "Pompey." "Who did they wish to go?" They answered, "Crassus." The latter was present at the time with no friendly feelings to Milo. About three o'clock, as though at a given signal, the Clodians began spitting at our men. There was an outburst of rage. They began a movement for forcing us from our ground. Our men charged: his ruffians turned tail. Clodius was pushed off the rostra: and then we too made our escape for fear of mischief in the riot. The senate was summoned into the Curia: Pompey went home. However, I did not myself enter the senate-house, lest I should be obliged either to refrain from speaking on matters of such gravity, or in defending Pompey (for he was being attacked by Bibulus, Curio, Favonius, and Servilius the younger) should give offence to the loyalists. The business was adjourned to the next day. Clodius fixed the Quirinalia [17th of February] for his prosecution. On the 8th the senate met in the temple of Apollo, that Pompey might attend. Pompey made an impressive speech. That day nothing was concluded. On the 9th in the temple of Apollo a decree passed the senate "that what had taken place on the 7th of February was treasonable." On this day Cato warmly inveighed against Pompey, and throughout his speech arraigned him as though he were at the bar. He said a great deal about me, to my disgust, though it was in very laudatory terms. When he attacked Pompey's perfidy to me, he was listened to in profound silence on the part of my enemies. Pompey answered him boldly with a palpable allusion to Crassus, and said outright that "he would take better precautions to protect his life than Africanus had done, whom C. Carbo had assassinated." Accordingly, important events appear to me to be in the wind. For Pompey understands what is going on, and imparts to me that plots are being formed against his life, that Gaius Cato is being supported by Crassus, that money is being supplied to Clodius, that both are backed by Crassus and Curio, as well as by Bibulus and his other detractors: that he must take extraordinary precautions to prevent being overpowered by that demagogue—with a people all but wholly alienated, a nobility hostile, a senate ill-affected, and the younger men corrupt. So he is making his preparations and summoning men from the country. On his part, Clodius is rallying his gangs: a body of men is being got together for the Quirinalia. For that occasion we are considerably in a majority, owing to the forces brought up by Pompey himself: and a large contingent is expected from Picenum and Gallia, to enable us to throw out Cato's bills also about Milo and Lentulus.

On the 10th of February an indictment was lodged against Sestius for bribery by the informer Cn. Nerius, of the Pupinian tribe, and on the same day by a certain M. Tullius for riot. He was ill. I went at once, as I was bound to do, to his house, and put myself wholly at his service: and that was more than people expected, who thought that I had good cause for being angry with him. The result is that my extreme kindness and grateful disposition are made manifest both to Sestius himself and to all the world, and I shall be as good as my word. But this same informer Nerius also named Cn. Lentulus Vatia and C. Cornelius to the commissioners. On the same day a decree passed the senate "that political clubs and associations should be broken up, and that a law in regard to them should be brought in, enacting that those who did not break off from them should be liable to the same penalty as those convicted of riot."

On the 11th of February I spoke in defence of Bestia on a charge of bribery before the praetor Cn. Domitius, in the middle of the forum and in a very crowded court; and in the course of my speech I came to the incident of Sestius, after receiving many wounds in the temple of Castor, having been preserved by the aid of Bestia. Here I took occasion to pave the way beforehand for a refutation of the charges which are being got up against

Sestius, and I passed a well-deserved encomium upon him with the cordial approval of everybody. He was himself very much delighted with it. I tell you this because you have often advised me in your letters to retain the friendship of Sestius. I am writing this on the 12th of February before daybreak: the day on which I am to dine with Pomponius on the occasion of his wedding.

Our position in other respects is such as you used to cheer my despondency by telling me it would be—one of great dignity and popularity: this is a return to old times for you and me effected, my brother, by your patience, high character, loyalty, and, I may also add, your conciliatory manners. The house of Licinius, near the grove of Piso, has been taken for you. But, as I hope, in a few months' time, after the 1st of July, you will move into your own. Some excellent tenants, the Lamiae, have taken your house in Carinae. I have received no letter from you since the one dated Olbia. I am anxious to hear how you are and what you find to amuse you, but above all to see you yourself as soon as possible. Take care of your health, my dear brother, and though it is winter time, yet reflect that after all it is Sardinia that you are in. . . .

5. Caelius Rufus, *Letter to Cicero*

The Parthians destroyed Crassus' army at Carrhae (Harran, southeastern Turkey) in 53 B.C., and Crassus perished immediately after the battle. His death terminated the triumvirate of Caesar, Crassus, and Pompey. Caesar, whose command was about to expire in Gaul, wished to be elected consul for 48 B.C. and to keep his position as governor of Gaul until then.

Cicero had been compelled to accept the governorship of Cilicia, in southeastern Asia Minor, for 50 B.C. The province faced the menace of a Parthian invasion.

Caelius Rufus, born in 82 B.C., was a well-known orator and writer who was tribune in 52 B.C. He supported Caesar in 50 B.C., but two years later he reversed alignments and supported Pompey, an act that cost him his life. This letter, which he wrote in Rome in September of 50 B.C., provides information on the relations between Caesar and Pompey.

Taking Arsaces [generic term for the Parthian king] prisoner and storming Seleucia [Parthia's capital] was not worth your missing the spectacle of events which have been going on here. Your eyes would never have ached again, if you had only seen Domitius's look when he lost the election. It

Cicero, *Ad familiares* 8.14. From *The Letters of Cicero*, vol. 2, translated by Evelyn S. Shuckburgh (London: George Bell & Sons, 1908), pp. 196–97.

was a very full assembly [*comitia*], and the voting was evidently on party lines: a very few voted from motives of personal connexion or obligation. Accordingly, Domitius is most bitterly angry with me. He never hated any one even of his own friends so much as he does me: and all the more so that he thinks the augurship has been snatched from him unfairly, and that I am at the bottom of it. Now he is furious that people are so much rejoiced at his vexation, and that there was only one man more zealous for Antony than I was. For the young Cn. Domitius himself has given notice of action against the young Cn. Saturninus—who is very unpopular owing to his past life. The trial is now imminent, with good hope, too, of an acquittal, after the acquittal of Sextus Peducaeus. As to high politics—I have often told you in my letters that I see no chance of peace lasting a year; and the nearer the struggle comes, which must come, the clearer does that danger appear. The point, on which the men in power are bound to fight, is this: Cn. Pompeius has made up his mind not to allow C. Caesar to become consul, except on condition of his first handing over his army and provinces: while Caesar is fully persuaded that he cannot be safe if he quits his army. He, however, proposes as a compromise that both should give up their armies. So that mighty love and unpopular union of theirs has not degenerated into mere secret bickering, but is breaking out into open war. Nor can I conceive what line to take in my own conduct—and I feel sure that this doubt will exercise you a good deal also—for between myself and these men there are ties of affection and close connexion, since it is the cause, not the men, that I dislike. I think you are alive to this rule, that men ought in a case of home differences, so long as the contest is carried on constitutionally without an appeal to arms, to follow the party most in the right: when it comes to war and the camp, the stronger party; and to make up one's mind that the safer course is the better. In this quarrel I perceive that Cn. Pompeius has on his side the senate and the judges [*iudices*]:[1] that Caesar will be joined by all whose past life gives them reason to be afraid, or their future no reason to hope: that there is no comparison between their armies. On the whole, there is time enough to weigh the forces of both, and to choose sides.

I almost forgot what above everything else I was bound to write to you. Do you know that the censor Appius is doing marvels? Busying himself about statues, pictures, land-owning, and debt with the greatest vigour? He is persuaded that his censorship is a kind of soap or soda. I think he is wrong: while he is meaning to wash off stains, he is really exposing all his veins and vitals. Hurry home, in the name of gods and men! Come as

1. *Iudices* were judges who heard civil cases, and were usually taken from the higher social classes.

quickly as you can to enjoy a laugh, that a trial under the Scantinian law should be before Drusus, and that Appius should be making regulations about statues and pictures. Believe me, you ought to make haste. Our friend Curio is thought to have acted prudently in his concession as to Pompey's money for his troops. In a word, you want my opinion as to the future. Unless one or the other of these two goes to the Parthian war, I see that a violent quarrel is impending, which the sword and main force will decide. Both are prepared in resolution and forces. If it could only be transacted without extreme danger, fortune is preparing for you a great and enjoyable spectacle.

6. Cicero, *Letter to Paetus*

Cicero returned to Rome after Caesar's victory over Pompey in 48 B.C. He spent most of his time writing at his estates, of which Tusculum, southeast of Rome, was his favorite. In this letter, written in August 46 B.C., he expresses fear that Caesar and Caesar's allies may confiscate his property and that of his friends.

Lucius Papirius Paetus was an educated and wealthy friend, to whom Cicero sent a number of letters about light topics. Balbus, a native of Spain, was Caesar's principal financial adviser.

Aren't you a ridiculous fellow for asking *me* what I think will be done about those municipal towns and lands, when our friend Balbus has been staying with you? As though I were likely to know what he doesn't, and as though, when I do know anything, it is not from him that I always learn it. Nay rather, if you love me, tell me what is going to be done about us: for you have had in your power one from whom you could have learnt it either sober or at any rate drunk. But for myself, I do not ask you for such information: in the first place, because I put it down as so much gain that I have been left alive for the last four years, if gain it is to be called, and if it is life to survive the Republic; and, in the second place, because I think that I myself know what is going to happen. For whatever the stronger chooses will be done, and the stronger will always be the sword. We ought, accordingly, to be content with any concession made to us, whatever it is; the man who was unable to endure this ought to have died.

They are measuring the territory of Veii and Capena. This is not far from my Tusculan property. However, I don't at all alarm myself. I enjoy while I may: I only wish it may last. If that does not turn out to be the case, yet, since I in my courage and philosophy thought that nothing was better

Ad familiares 9.17. From *The Letters of Cicero*, vol. 3, translated by Evelyn S. Shuckburgh (London: George Bell & Sons, 1908), pp. 104–5.

than to remain alive, I cannot but love the man by whose kindness I gained that object. But even if he should desire the continuance of a republic, such as perhaps he wishes and we ought all to pray for, he yet does not know how to do it: so completely has he entangled himself with many other people.

But I am going too far. I forgot that I am writing to you. However, let me assure you of this, that not only I, who am not in his confidence, but even the leader himself is unable to say what is going to happen. For, while we are his slaves, he is a slave to circumstances: and so neither can he possibly be sure of what circumstances will demand, nor we of what he is designing. The reason that I did not send you this answer before was not because I am usually idle, especially in the matter of writing, but because, as I had no certainty about anything, I did not choose to cause you either anxiety from the hesitation, or hope from the confidence of my words. However, I will add this, which is the most absolute truth, that during the present crisis I have not heard a word about the danger you mention. In any case you will be bound, like the man of sense that you are, to hope for the best, prepare yourself for the worst, and bear whatever happens.

7. Horace, *Sixteenth Epode*

Quintus Horatius Flaccus was born in an out-of-the-way town of southeast Italy in 65 B.C. His father, a former slave who made his living by organizing auction sales and taking a commission on them, was just beginning the slow climb up to respectability. He moved to Rome when his son was still young so that Horace could be educated in the capital. Horace grew up among the sons of the aristocracy, and like many of them, he rallied to the side of the "Liberators" who assassinated Julius Caesar in 44 B.C. But in the civil war that followed, the forces led by Mark Antony and Octavian (the future emperor Augustus) defeated the anti-Caesarian party. Horace, with his property forfeited and his prospects ruined, started his life over at the age of twenty-three. He obtained a paid position as a recorder in the small bureaucracy that aided magistrates in Rome, and he began to write poetry. His poems earned him an introduction to and then a friendship with Maecenas, the wealthy dilettante who was also one of Octavian's closest advisers; Octavian was becoming the undisputed master of Rome as his rivals perished in successive rounds of civil war. After the wars ended in 30 B.C., Horace's friendships within the victorious party grew to embrace many of its most

From *Horace for English Readers*, translated by E. C. Wickham (Oxford: Oxford University Press, 1903), pp. 152–54.

prominent men, and even the emperor himself. By the time he died in 8 B.C., he was ensconced as the country's unofficial laureate.

Horace was a lifelong experimenter with poetic forms, and he left a varied collection which includes satires, epistles in verse, and love poems and other lyrics. The *Epodes* are his earliest work: all poems of this book date from the time of civil war between 42 and 31 B.C. The *Sixteenth Epode* may have been roughly contemporaneous with Vergil's *Fourth Eclogue*, which was written in about 40 B.C. Both poems lead into millenarian fantasies, though Horace's view of Rome's future was much gloomier than Vergil's. The standpoint Horace assumed in this poem, as spokesman for his people, was to persist in much of the poetry he wrote after the civil wars were over.

A second age already is wearing away in civil wars, and Rome is tumbling under the strength of her own arms. The city which neither the neighbouring Marsians could destroy, nor the Etruscan bands of threatening Porsena, nor the rival valour of Capua, nor keen Spartacus and the Allobroges faithless to revolution, nor fierce Germany with her blue-eyed sons could tame and Hannibal, the loathing of parents' hearts—that city we shall destroy, an impious age and a doomed race; and the ground it stands on shall be tenanted once more by wild beasts. Ah me, a barbarian conqueror shall stand over its ashes, and trample the city under his horse's ringing hoofs, and scatter in contumely (O sight of horror!) the bones of Quirinus that lie sheltered from winds and suns.

May be you are asking with one voice, or the better part of you, what can help you to get quit of your sad troubles. Let no advice be preferred to this: even as the whole state of the Phocaeans, having sworn an oath, went forth in exile from their lands and the homes of their sires, and left their temples to be the lairs of wild boars and robber wolves, even so to go whithersoever our feet shall carry us, whithersoever over the waters the south wind or the wild south-west shall invite us. Is it your pleasure so? Or has any aught better to advise? Then, since the omens favour, why delay to embark? Only let us swear to this: So soon as stones shall rise from the water's depth and swim on the surface, then let it be no sin for us to come back; no shame to turn our sails and set them for home when the Po shall wash the Matine hill-tops or lofty Mount Apennine shall run out into the sea, when strange loves shall make monstrous unions of unheard-of passion, when tigers choose to mate with stags and the dove with the kite, when cattle grow trustful and fear not the tawny lion, and the goat grows smooth and learns to love the salt seas. Such an oath let us swear, or any other that may cut off for ever all sweet returning, and let us go—the entire state, having sworn our oath, or at least the part better than the wilful crowd—leave softness and despair to hug still their ill-starred bed of sloth. You who have men's hearts, put aside womanish wailing, and spread your sails along the Tuscan shore. For us is waiting the ambient Ocean. Let us look for the land, the happy land, the islands of wealth; where the soil unploughed gives its corn-crop year by year, and the vineyard ever blooms unpruned, and the olive shoot buds and never breaks its promise, and the dark blue fig adorns its own ungrafted tree. Honey drops from the hollow holm-oak, light streams dance down the mountain-side with tinkling foot. There the she-goats come unsummoned to the milkpail, and the flock for love brings home its full udders; no bear of the evening roars around the sheepfold, nor the ground heaves high with vipers. And many another wonder shall our happy eyes see—how neither the watery east wind sweeps the land with floods of rain, nor the fruitful plants are burnt in a dry soil, for that the king of heaven tempers either extreme. Hither nor the sturdy rowers of the Argo brought their pine bark, nor the shameless Colchian set her foot. Hither sailors from Sidon never turned their yard-arms, nor Ulysses' toil-worn crew. No taint of plague destroys their herds, no dog-star's furious rages fever their flocks. These shores Jupiter severed from the world for a people of the good, when he debased with brass the times of gold—with brass and then with iron he made hard the ages, from which now a happy escape is offered to the good through my prophetic mouth.

8. Vergil, *Fourth Eclogue*

Publius Vergilius Maro was born in 70 B.C., of north Italian parents whose means and standing were modest even by local standards. They lived near Mantua in the central Po valley, where trouble descended during the civil wars. After the anti-Caesarian party was defeated at the battle of Philippi in 42 B.C., the victorious commanders, Antony and Octavian, expropriated much of the land around Mantua and reassigned it to their soldiers. Vergil's neighbors and perhaps even his own family were among the dispossessed. But by this time Vergil's talent was beginning to be recognized and he had made a number of important friends in Rome. If he or his family did in fact suffer any loss from the confiscations, it was soon remedied.

His *Eclogues*, which probably appeared in about 39 B.C., are filled with reverberations of recent events—the assassination of Julius Caesar, the civil war, the confiscations, and the political struggles within the triumvirate. Over the next few years, Vergil became identified with the literary circle around Maecenas, Octavian's principal adviser, and through

From Paul Alpers, *The Singer of the Eclogues* (Berkeley and Los Angeles: University of California Press, 1979), pp. 27, 29, 31. Reprinted by permission of the publisher.

Maecenas, he befriended Octavian himself. At the end of the civil wars in 30 B.C. he published his second book, the *Georgics*. These poems celebrate the peace and bounty to be found in working the land, and praise the leader who had restored order. Octavian was now the unrivaled master of the state, a position he marked by taking the name Augustus. Vergil spent the last decade of his life writing an epic about Augustus' legendary ancestor Aeneas, who settled the survivors of Troy in the land where Rome was to rise. The poet died in 19 B.C. as he was preparing to revise and polish what he had written. But he left a more or less complete draft of the *Aeneid*, which Augustus arranged to have published as it was.

The *Fourth Eclogue* is not like the shepherd songs which make up the rest of the book. It is an oracular piece, as Vergil indicates at the outset by recalling a prediction of the Sibyl, an ancient prophetess of Italy whose utterances were preserved in sacred books for the guidance of the Roman state. The poem is addressed to Asinius Pollio, one of Vergil's influential friends, whom it compliments on his consulship in the year 40 B.C. But the identity of the babe whom Vergil glorifies is a mystery. Even in Vergil's own time, interpreters could not decide whether he was talking about a child of Pollio, or of Octavian's sister and Mark Antony (who were married when the two rivals made a temporary peace in the year 40 B.C.), or of Octavian himself. Christians in late antiquity interpreted the poem as a prophecy of Christ's birth. Perhaps no real child was involved at all; Vergil may have had a symbolic birth in mind. Whoever the child is, the poem is a vision of the future, conceived in reaction against present turmoil.

Sicilian muse, let's sing a nobler song:
Low shrubs and orchards do not always please;
Let us sing woods to dignify a consul.
The last great age the Sibyl's song foretold
Rolls round: the centuries are born anew!
The Maid returns,[1] old Saturn's reign returns,
Offspring of heaven, a hero's race descends.
Now as the babe is born, with whom iron men
Shall cease, and golden men spread through the world,
Bless him, chaste goddess: now your Apollo reigns.
This age's glory and the mighty months
Begin their courses, Pollio, with you
As consul, and all traces of our crimes

1. The Maid is the patron goddess of justice, who in the myth of the ages of man withdrew from earth as human society declined from an age of gold into an age of iron.

Annulled release earth from continual fear.
He shall assume a god's life and see gods
Mingling with heroes and be seen by them,
Ruling the world calmed by his father's hand.
But first, child, earth's uncultivated gifts
Will spring up for you—wandering ivy, herbs,
Smiling acanthus and Egyptian beans.
Goats will come home, their udders swollen with milk,
All by themselves; herds will not fear huge lions;
Your crib itself will shower you with flowers.
Serpents shall die and poison-bearing plants
Die, and Assyrian spice grow everywhere.
But when heroic praise, parental deeds
You read and come to know what manhood is,
Plains slowly will turn gold with tender grain,
The crimson grape festoon neglected briers,
And rough-skinned oaks will sweat with honeydew.
Yet lingering traces of our ancient guilt
Will cause men to attempt the sea in ships,
Girdle walled towns, cleave furrows in the earth.
Another Argo, with another Tiphys,
Will carry chosen heroes; other wars
Will send the great Achilles back to Troy.
Later, when strengthening years have made you man,
Traders will leave the sea, no sailing pine
Will barter goods: all lands will grow all things.
Earth will not feel the hoe, nor vines the knife;
The plowman's strength will ease the oxen's yoke.
Wool will not learn to counterfeit its hues,
Since in the fields the ram himself will blush
All purple, or transmute his fleece to gold;
Spontaneous dyes will clothe the feeding lambs.
"O ages such as these, make haste!" declared
The spinners of the steadfast will of Fate.
Advance—now is the time—to triumphs wide,
Dear scion of the gods, Jove's generation.
Behold the trembling of the massy globe,
The lands, the far-flung seas, the depths of sky:
How all rejoices at the coming age!
O that a remnant of long life be mine,
Giving me breath to celebrate your deeds:
Orpheus would not vanquish me in song
Nor Linus, though their parents stand by them,

Calliope and beautiful Apollo.
Even Pan, though Arcady should judge our contest,
Pan would say Arcady judged him the loser.
Come now, sweet boy, with smiling greet your mother
(She carried you ten long and tedious months)
Come now, sweet boy: who smiles not on a parent
Graces no god's carouse nor goddess' bed.

9. Augustus, *Record of His Accomplishments*

Octavian Caesar, Julius Caesar's grandnephew and adoptive son, was born on 23 September 63 B.C., and died on 19 August A.D. 14. In 30 B.C. he emerged victorious from a series of civil wars that had followed the assassination of Julius Caesar in 44 B.C. In January of 27 B.C., he handed back emergency powers to the Roman senate, whose members voted to name him Augustus, by which name he has since been known, and endowed him with certain Roman magisterial powers, which he describes in this text. Many historians have defined this moment as the beginning of the Principate, or era of the Roman emperors (because the emperor was called *princeps*, or "first citizen"). In A.D. 14, shortly before his death, Augustus ordered the erection of two bronze tablets in Rome that contained, in his own words, "a record of his accomplishments." The originals are lost, but copies were placed in many prominent buildings around the empire. The only complete surviving text today is an inscription on the wall of a mosque—which was originally a pagan temple, and then a church—in the city of Ancyra, or Ankara, Turkey, and hence the document is often called the *Monumentum Ancyranum*. One of its purposes was the shaping of public opinion. It is divided into four parts, one each on honors (sections 1–14), expenditures (sections 15–24), and accomplishments (sections 25–33), and a conclusion that describes Augustus's position in the government.

A copy is set out below of "The achievements of the Divine Augustus, by which he brought the world under the empire of the Roman people, and of the expenses which he bore for the state and people of Rome"; the original is engraved on two bronze pillars set up at Rome.

1. At the age of nineteen on my own responsibility and at my own expense I raised an army, with which I successfully championed the liberty of

From P. A. Brunt and J. M. Moore, eds., *Res Gestae Divi Augusti: The Achievements of the Divine Augustus* (London: Oxford University Press, 1967), pp. 19–37 (odd-numbered pages). Reprinted by permission of Oxford University Press.

the republic when it was oppressed by the tyranny of a faction. 2. On that account the senate passed decrees in my honour enrolling me in its order in the consulship of Gaius Pansa and Aulus Hirtius, assigning me the right to give my opinion among the consulars and giving me *imperium*.[1] 3. It ordered me as a propraetor to provide in concert with the consuls that the republic should come to no harm. 4. In the same year, when both consuls had fallen in battle, the people appointed me consul and triumvir for the organization of the republic.

2. I drove into exile the murderers of my father [Julius Caesar], avenging their crime through tribunals established by law; and afterwards, when they made war on the republic, I twice defeated them in battle.

3. I undertook many civil and foreign wars by land and sea throughout the world, and as victor I spared the lives of all citizens who asked for mercy. 2. When foreign peoples could safely be pardoned I preferred to preserve rather than to exterminate them. 3. The Roman citizens who took the soldier's oath of obedience to me numbered about 500,000. I settled rather more than 300,000 of these in colonies or sent them back to their home towns after their period of service; to all these I assigned lands or gave money as rewards for their military service. 4. I captured six hundred ships, not counting ships smaller than triremes.

4. I celebrated two ovations and three curule triumphs and I was twenty-one times saluted as *imperator*. The senate decreed still more triumphs to me, all of which I declined. I laid the bay leaves with which my *fasces* were wreathed in the Capitol after fulfilling all the vows which I had made in each war. 2. On fifty-five occasions the senate decreed that thanksgivings should be offered to the immortal gods on account of the successes on land and sea gained by me or by my legates acting under my auspices. The days on which thanksgivings were offered in accordance with decrees of the senate numbered eight hundred and ninety. 3. In my triumphs nine kings or children of kings were led before my chariot. 4. At the time of writing I have been consul thirteen times and am in the thirty-seventh year of tribunician power.

5. The dictatorship was offered to me by both senate and people in my absence and when I was at Rome in the consulship of Marcus Marcellus and Lucius Arruntius, but I refused it. 2. I did not decline in the great dearth of corn to undertake the charge of the corn-supply, which I so administered that within a few days I delivered the whole city from apprehension and immediate danger at my own cost and by my own efforts. 3. At that time the consulship was also offered to me, to be held each year for the rest of my life, and I refused it.

6. In the consulship of Marcus Vinicius and Quintus Lucretius, and

1. Imperium was the supreme administrative power which belonged to chief officials; it included command in war and interpretation and implementation of law.

afterwards in that of Publius and Gnaeus Lentulus, and thirdly in that of Paullus Fabius Maximus and Quintus Tubero, the senate and people of Rome agreed that I should be appointed supervisor of laws and morals without a colleague and with supreme power, but I would not accept any office inconsistent with the custom of our ancestors. 2. The measures that the senate then desired me to take I carried out in virtue of my tribunician power. On five occasions, of my own initiative, I asked for and received from the senate a colleague in that power.

7. I was triumvir for the organization of the republic for ten consecutive years. 2. Up to the day of writing I have been *princeps senatus* for forty years. 3. I am *pontifex maximus*,[2] *augur*, *quindecimvir sacris faciundis*, *septemvir epulonum*, *frater arvalis*, *sodalis Titius*, *fetialis*.

8. In my fifth consulship I increased the number of patricians on the instructions of the people and the senate. 2. I revised the roll of the senate three times. In my sixth consulship with Marcus Agrippa as colleague, I carried out a census of the people, and I performed a *lustrum* [purificatory ceremony] after a lapse of forty-two years; at that *lustrum* 4,063,000 Roman citizens were registered. 3. Then a second time I performed a *lustrum* with consular *imperium* and without a colleague, in the consulship of Gaius Censorinus and Gaius Asinius; at that *lustrum* 4,233,000 citizens were registered. 4. Thirdly I performed a *lustrum* with consular imperium, with Tiberius Caesar, my son, as colleague, in the consulship of Sextus Pompeius and Sextus Appuleius; at that *lustrum* 4,937,000 citizens were registered. 5. By new laws passed on my proposal I brought back into use many exemplary practices of our ancestors which were disappearing in our time, and in many ways I myself transmitted exemplary practices to posterity for their imitation.

9. The senate decreed that vows should be undertaken every fifth year by the consuls and priests for my health. In fulfilment of these vows games have frequently been celebrated in my lifetime, sometimes by the four most distinguished colleges of priests, sometimes by the consuls. 2. Moreover, all the citizens, individually and on behalf of their towns, have unanimously and continuously offered prayers at all the *pulvinaria* [shrines] for my health.

10. My name was inserted in the hymn of the Salii by a decree of the senate, and it was enacted by law that my person should be inviolable for ever and that I should hold the tribunician power for the duration of my life. 2. I declined to be made *pontifex maximus* in the place of my colleague who was still alive [Marcus Aemilius Lepidus], when the people offered me this priesthood which my father had held. Some years later,

2. The *pontifex maximus* headed the college of priests and controlled public religion, including the priesthoods and religious associations listed here.

after the death of the man who had taken the opportunity of civil disturbance to seize it for himself, I received this priesthood, in the consulship of Publius Sulpicius and Gaius Valgius, and such a concourse poured in from the whole of Italy to my election as has never been recorded at Rome before that time.

11. The senate consecrated the altar of Fortuna Redux before the temples of Honour and Virtue at the Porta Capena in honour of my return, and it ordered that the *pontifices* [high-priests] and Vestal virgins should make an annual sacrifice there on the anniversary of my return to the city from Syria in the consulship of Quintus Lucretius and Marcus Vinicius, and it named the day the Augustalia from my *cognomen* [family or individual surname].

12. In accordance with the will of the senate some of the praetors and tribunes of the plebs with the consul Quintus Lucretius and the leading men were sent to Campania to meet me, an honour that up to the present day has been decreed to no one besides myself. 2. On my return from Spain and Gaul in the consulship of Tiberius Nero and Publius Quintilius after successfully arranging affairs in those provinces, the senate resolved that an altar of the Augustan Peace should be consecrated next to the Campus Martius in honour of my return, and ordered that the magistrates and priests and Vestal virgins should perform an annual sacrifice there.

13. It was the will of our ancestors that the gateway of Janus Quirinus should be shut when victories had secured peace by land and sea throughout the whole empire of the Roman people; from the foundation of the city down to my birth, tradition records that it was shut only twice, but while I was the leading citizen the senate resolved that it should be shut on three occasions.

14. My sons, Gaius and Lucius Caesar, of whom Fortune bereaved me in their youth, were for my honour designated as consuls by the senate and people of Rome when they were fourteen, with the provision that they should enter on that magistracy after the lapse of five years.[3] And the senate decreed that from the day when they were led into the forum they should take part in the councils of state. 2. Furthermore each of them was presented with silver shields and spears by the whole body of *equites Romani* and hailed as *princeps iuventutis*.[4]

15. To each member of the Roman plebs I paid under my father's will 300 sesterces, and in my own name I gave them 400 each from the booty of

3. Gaius and Lucius were the sons of Augustus's daughter Iulia and his friend and commander Marcus Vipsanius Agrippa; Augustus adopted both, but Gaius died in A.D. 4 at age twenty-four, and Lucius in A.D. 2 at age nineteen.

4. The *equites romani* were members of the equestrian order, and the *princeps iuventutis* was their leader.

war in my fifth consulship, and once again in my tenth consulship I paid out 400 sesterces as a largesse to each man from my own patrimony, and in my eleventh consulship I bought grain with my own money and distributed twelve rations apiece, and in the twelfth year of my tribunician power I gave every man 400 sesterces for the third time. These largesses of mine never reached fewer than 250,000 persons. 2. In the eighteenth year of my tribunician power and my twelfth consulship I gave 240 sesterces apiece to 320,000 members of the urban plebs. 3. In my fifth consulship I gave 1,000 sesterces out of booty to every one of the colonists drawn from my soldiers; about 120,000 men in the colonies received this largesse at the time of my triumph. 4. In my thirteenth consulship I gave 60 *denarii*[5] apiece to the plebs who were then in receipt of public grain; they comprised a few more than 200,000 persons.

16. I paid cash to the towns for the lands that I assigned to soldiers in my fourth consulship, and later in the consulship of Marcus Crassus and Gnaeus Lentulus. The sum amounted to about 600,000,000 sesterces paid for lands in Italy, and about 260,000,000 disbursed for provincial lands. Of all those who founded military colonies in Italy or the provinces I was the first and only one to have done this in the recollection of my contemporaries. 2. Later, in the consulships of Tiberius Nero and Gnaeus Piso, of Gaius Antistius and Decimus Laelius, of Gaius Calvisius and Lucius Pasienus, of Lucius Lentulus and Marcus Messalla and of Lucius Caninius and Quintus Fabricius I paid monetary rewards to soldiers whom I settled in their home towns after completion of their service, and on this account I expended about 400,000,000 sesterces.

17. Four times I assisted the treasury with my own money, so that I transferred to the administrators of the treasury 150,000,000 sesterces. 2. In the consulship of Marcus Lepidus and Lucius Arruntius, when the military treasury was founded by my advice for the purpose of paying rewards to soldiers who had served for twenty years or more, I transferred to it from my own patrimony 170,000,000 sesterces.

18. From the consulship of Gnaeus and Publius Lentulus onwards, whenever the taxes did not suffice, I made distributions of grain and money from my own granary and patrimony, sometimes to 100,000 persons, sometimes to many more.

19. I built the Senate House, and the Chalcidicum adjacent to it, the temple of Apollo on the Palatine with its porticoes, the temple of the divine Julius, the Lupercal, the portico at the Flaminian circus, which I permitted to bear the name of the portico of Octavius after the man who erected the

5. At this time, one silver *denarius* was equal to four sesterces, twenty-five *denarii* to one gold *aureus*, and forty-two gold *aurei* to one Roman pound (327.45 grams).

previous portico on the same site, a *pulvinar* at the Circus Maximus, (2) the temples on the Capitol of Jupiter Feretrius and Jupiter the Thunderer, the temple of Quirinus, the temples of Minerva and Queen Juno and Jupiter Libertas on the Aventine, the temple of the Lares at the top of the Sacred Way, the temple of the Di Penates in the Velia, the temple of Youth, and the temple of the Great Mother on the Palatine.

20. I restored the Capitol and the theatre of Pompey, both works at great expense without inscribing my own name on either. 2. I restored the channels of the aqueducts, which in several places were falling into disrepair through age, and I brought water from a new spring into the aqueduct called Marcia, doubling the supply. 3. I completed the Forum Julium and the basilica between the temples of Castor and Saturn, works begun and almost finished by my father, and when that same basilica was destroyed by fire, I began to rebuild it on an enlarged site, to be dedicated in the name of my sons, and in case I do not complete it in my life time, I have given orders that it should be completed by my heirs. 4. In my sixth consulship I restored eighty-two temples of the gods in the city on the authority of the senate, neglecting none that required restoration at that time. 5. In my seventh consulship I restored the Via Flaminia[6] from the city as far as Rimini, together with all bridges except the Mulvian and the Minucian.

21. I built the temple of Mars the Avenger[7] and the Forum Augustum on private ground from the proceeds of booty. I built the theatre adjacent to the temple of Apollo on ground in large part bought from private owners, and provided that it should be called after Marcus Marcellus, my son-in-law. 2. From the proceeds of booty I dedicated gifts in the Capitol and in the temples of the divine Julius, of Apollo, of Vesta and of Mars the Avenger; this cost me about 100,000,000 sesterces. 3. In my fifth consulship I remitted 35,000 lb. of *aurum coronarium* [crown gold] contributed by the *municipia* and colonies of Italy to my triumphs, and later, whenever I was acclaimed imperator, I refused the *aurum coronarium* which the *municipia* and colonies continued to vote with the same good will as before.

22. I gave three gladiatorial games in my own name and five in that of my sons or grandsons; at these games some 10,000 men took part in combat. Twice in my own name and a third time in that of my grandson I presented to the people displays by athletes summoned from all parts. 2. I produced shows in my own name four times and in place of other magis-

6. The Via Flaminia, or Flaminian Road, runs from Rome north to Ariminum on the Adriatic coast.

7. The temple of Mars the Avenger, or Mars Ultor, had been built by Augustus in memory of the destruction of Julius Caesar's murderers in the battle of Philippi (42 B.C.).

trates twenty-three times. On behalf of the college of *quindecimviri* [board of fifteen priests], as its president, with Marcus Agrippa as colleague, I produced the Secular Games in the consulship of Gaius Furnius and Gaius Silanus. In my thirteenth consulship I was the first to produce the games of Mars, which thereafter in each succeeding year have been produced by the consuls in accordance with a decree of the senate and by statute. 3. I gave beast-hunts of African beasts in my own name or in that of my sons and grandsons in the circus or forum or amphitheatre on twenty-six occasions, on which about 3,500 beasts were destroyed.

23. I produced a naval battle as a show for the people at the place across the Tiber now occupied by the grove of the Caesars, where a site 1,800 feet long and 1,200 broad was excavated. There thirty beaked triremes or biremes and still more smaller vessels were joined in battle. About 3,000 men, besides the rowers, fought in these fleets.

24. After my victory, I replaced in the temples of all the cities of the province of Asia the ornaments which my late adversary, after despoiling the temples, had taken into his private possession. 2. Some eighty silver statues of me, on foot, on horse and in chariots, had been set up in Rome; I myself removed them, and with the money that they realized I set golden offerings in the temple of Apollo, in my own name and in the names of those who had honoured me with the statues.

25. I made the sea peaceful and freed it of pirates. In that war I captured about 30,000 slaves who had escaped from their masters and taken up arms against the republic, and I handed them over to their masters for punishment. 2. The whole of Italy of its own free will swore allegiance to me and demanded me as the leader in the war in which I was victorious at Actium.[8] The Gallic and Spanish provinces, Africa, Sicily and Sardinia swore the same oath of allegiance. 3. More than seven hundred senators served under my standards at that time, including eighty-three who previously or subsequently (down to the time of writing) were appointed consuls, and about one hundred and seventy who were appointed priests.

26. I extended the territory of all those provinces of the Roman people on whose borders lay peoples not subject to our government. 2. I brought peace to the Gallic and Spanish provinces as well as to Germany, throughout the area bordering on the Ocean from Cadiz to the mouth of the Elbe. 3. I secured the pacification of the Alps from the district nearest the Adriatic to the Tuscan sea, yet without waging an unjust war on any people. 4. My fleet sailed through the Ocean eastwards from the mouth of the Rhine to the territory of the Cimbri, a country which no Roman had

8. Actium, the site of the decisive battle in 31 B.C., is a promontory in Greece just opposite the island of Leucas.

visited before either by land or sea, and the Cimbri, Charydes, Semnones and other German peoples of that region sent ambassadors and sought my friendship and that of the Roman people. 5. At my command and under my auspices two armies were led almost at the same time into Ethiopia and Arabia Felix; vast enemy forces of both peoples were cut down in battle and many towns captured. Ethiopia was penetrated as far as the town of Nabata, which adjoins Meroe; in Arabia the army advanced into the territory of the Sabaeans to the town of Mariba.

27. I added Egypt to the empire of the Roman people. 2. Greater Armenia I might have made a province after its king, Artaxes, had been killed, but I preferred, following the model set by our ancestors, to hand over that kingdom to Tigranes, son of King Artavasdes and grandson of King Tigranes; Tiberius Nero, who was then my stepson, carried this out. When the same people later rebelled and went to war, I subdued them through the agency of my son Gaius and handed them over to be ruled by King Ariobarzanes, son of Artabazus King of the Medes, and after his death to his son Artavasdes. When he was killed, I sent Tigranes, a scion of the royal Armenian house, to that kingdom. 3. I recovered all the provinces beyond the Adriatic sea towards the east, together with Cyrene, the greater part of them being then occupied by kings. I had previously recovered Sicily and Sardinia which had been seized in the slave war.

28. I founded colonies of soldiers in Africa, Sicily, Macedonia, both Spanish provinces, Achaea, Asia, Syria, Gallia Narbonensis and Pisidia. 2. Italy too has twenty-eight colonies founded by my authority, which were densely populated in my lifetime.

29. By victories over enemies I recovered in Spain and in Gaul, and from the Dalmatians several standards lost by other commanders. 2. I compelled the Parthians to restore to me the spoils and standards of three Roman armies and to ask as suppliants for the friendship of the Roman people. Those standards I deposited in the innermost shrine of the temple of Mars the Avenger.

30. The Pannonian peoples, whom the army of the Roman people never approached before I was the leading citizen, were conquered through the agency of Tiberius Nero, who was then my stepson and legate; I brought them into the empire of the Roman people, and extended the frontier of Illyricum to the banks of the Danube. 2. When an army of Dacians crossed the Danube, it was defeated and routed under my auspices, and later my army crossed the Danube and compelled the Dacian peoples to submit to the commands of the Roman people.

31. Embassies from kings in India were frequently sent to me; never before had they been seen with any Roman commander. 2. The Bastarnae, Scythians and the kings of the Sarmatians on either side of the river Don,

and the kings of the Albanians and the Iberians and the Medes sent embassies to seek our friendship.

32. The following kings sought refuge with me as suppliants: Tiridates, King of Parthia, and later Phraates son of King Phraates; Artavasdes, King of the Medes; Artaxares, King of the Adiabeni; Dumnobellaunus and Tincommius, Kings of the Britons; Maelo, King of the Sugambri; . . .rus, King of the Marcomanni and Suebi. 2. Phraates, son of Orodes, King of Parthia, sent all his sons and grandsons to me in Italy, not that he had been overcome in war, but because he sought our friendship by pledging his children. 3. While I was the leading citizen very many other peoples have experienced the good faith of the Roman people which had never previously exchanged embassies or had friendly relations with the Roman people.

33. The Parthian and Median peoples sent to me ambassadors of their nobility who sought and received kings from me, for the Parthians Vonones, son of King Phraates, grandson of King Orodes, and for the Medes Ariobarzanes, son of King Artavasdes, grandson of King Ariobarzanes.

34. In my sixth and seventh consulships, after I had extinguished civil wars, and at a time when with universal consent I was in complete control of affairs, I transferred the republic from my power to the dominion of the senate and people of Rome. 2. For this service of mine I was named Augustus by decree of the senate, and the door-posts of my house were publicly wreathed with bay leaves and a civic crown was fixed over my door and a golden shield was set in the Curia Julia, which, as attested by the inscription thereon, was given me by the senate and people of Rome on account of my courage, clemency, justice and piety. 3. After this time I excelled all in influence, although I possessed no more official power than others who were my colleagues in the several magistracies.

35. In my thirteenth consulship the senate, the equestrian order and the whole people of Rome gave me the title of Father of my Country, and resolved that this should be inscribed in the porch of my house and in the Curia Julia and in the Forum Augustum below the chariot which had been set there in my honour by decree of the senate. 2. At the time of writing I am in my seventy-sixth year.

Appendix

1. The amount of money that he gave to the treasury or to the Roman *plebs* or to discharged soldiers was 2,400,000,000 sesterces.

2. His new buildings were: the temples of Mars, of Jupiter the Thunderer and Feretrius, of Apollo, of the divine Julius, of Quirinus, of Minerva, of Queen Juno, of Jupiter Libertas, of the Lares, of the Di Penates, of Youth, of the Great Mother, the Lupercal, the shrine at the Circus,

the Senate House with the Chalcidicum, the Forum Augustum, the Basilica Julia, the theatre of Marcellus, the Octavian portico, the grove of the Caesars beyond the Tiber.

3. He restored the Capitol and sacred buildings to the number of eighty-two, the theatre of Pompey, the aqueducts and the Via Flaminia.

4. The expenditure that he devoted to dramatic shows, to gladiatorial exhibitions and athletes and hunts and the sea battle, and the money granted to colonies, *municipia*, towns destroyed by earthquake and fire or to individual friends and senators whose property qualification he made up, was beyond counting.

10. Tacitus, *Annals* (Selection)

Little is known about the life of Publius Cornelius Tacitus, although his personality is stamped on every page of his writings. He was born between A.D. 55 and 60. His family probably came either from north Italy or from that part of Gaul along the Mediterranean which was among the first regions outside Italy to become Romanized; his wife belonged to a Roman family which had settled there. Tacitus held his first public offices under the emperors Vespasian and Titus, to whose favor he owed his entry into the senate. But the crucial years of his career fell during the oppressive and sanguinary reign of Domitian (A.D. 81–96). The degradation of serving under Domitian in the senate blackened everything that Tacitus later wrote about the Principate. He reached the consulate a year or two after the tyrant was assassinated, and in about A.D. 112 he became governor in Asia Minor, a prestigious assignment reserved for senior senators. That is the last fact known about him.

During the years of his ascent through the hierarchy of the senate, Tacitus set about establishing a reputation as an orator. But as soon as Domitian was dead, he turned to historical writing. He began with a trio of short works devoted to more or less contemporary topics: a monograph about the national character and tribal organization of the Germans, a dialogue on the decline of modern oratory, and a biography of his father-in-law, whom he portrayed as a capable general spited by Domitian. From his own day Tacitus worked progressively backward toward the founding of the Principate by Augustus. His first major work was the *Histories*, which covered the period from the civil war of A.D. 69–70 to the death of Domitian. His last work, the *Annals*, ran from the death of Augustus to the overthrow of Nero, last member of the family dynasty which Augustus founded. Tacitus' great strength as a writer was that he

Annales 1.1–15. From *The Annals of Tacitus*, translated by Alfred John Church and William Jackson Brodribb (London: Macmillan, 1869), pp. 1–10.

never lost focus: in every area of public life, he could detect (sometimes because he strained to detect) the vicious effects of the emperor's unlimited power.

The short excerpt which follows opens book 1 of the *Annals*. Tacitus begins with the succession to Augustus because it was a decisive moment in the history of the Principate. Although Augustus held a number of extraordinary powers and was acknowledged as Rome's foremost citizen, his position in the state had developed as a position of honor invented for him personally. It was not a public office, like the consulship or tribunate, and therefore there was no constitutional mechanism for transferring it to anyone else. Nevertheless, after he died, Tiberius moved into the very same position. At that point, it became apparent to all that the Principate would be a continuing institution.

---

1. Rome at the beginning was ruled by kings. Freedom and the consulship were established by Lucius Brutus. Dictatorships were held for a temporary crisis. The power of the decemvirs did not last beyond two years, nor was the consular jurisdiction of the military tribunes of long duration. The despotisms of Cinna and Sulla were brief; the rule of Pompeius and of Crassus soon yielded before Caesar; the arms of Lepidus and Antonius before Augustus; who, when the world was wearied by civil strife, subjected it to empire under the title of "Prince." But the successes and reverses of the old Roman people have been recorded by famous historians; and fine intellects were not wanting to describe the times of Augustus, till growing sycophancy scared them away. The histories of Tiberius, Gaius, Claudius, and Nero, while they were in power, were falsified through terror, and after their death were written under the irritation of a recent hatred. Hence my purpose is to relate a few facts about Augustus—more particularly his last acts, then the reign of Tiberius, and all which follows, without either bitterness or partiality, from any motives to which I am far removed.

2. When after the destruction of Brutus and Cassius there was no longer any army of the Commonwealth, when Pompeius was crushed in Sicily, and when, with Lepidus pushed aside and Antonius slain, even the Julian faction had only Caesar left to lead it, then, dropping the title of triumvir, and giving out that he was a Consul, and was satisfied with a tribune's authority for the protection of the people, Augustus won over the soldiers with gifts, the populace with cheap corn, and all men with the sweets of repose, and so grew greater by degrees, while he concentrated in himself the functions of the Senate, the magistrates, and the laws. He was wholly unopposed, for the boldest spirits had fallen in battle, or in the proscription, while the remaining nobles, the readier they were to be slaves, were raised the higher by wealth and promotion, so that, aggrandised by revolu-

tion, they preferred the safety of the present to the dangerous past. Nor did the provinces dislike that condition of affairs, for they distrusted the government of the Senate and the people, because of the rivalries between the leading men and the rapacity of the officials, while the protection of the laws was unavailing, as they were continually deranged by violence, intrigue, and finally by corruption.

3. Augustus meanwhile, as supports to his despotism, raised to the pontificate and curule aedileship Claudius Marcellus, his sister's son, while a mere stripling, and Marcus Agrippa, of humble birth, a good soldier, and one who had shared his victory, to two consecutive consulships, and as Marcellus soon afterwards died, he also accepted him as his son-in-law. Tiberius Nero and Claudius Drusus, his stepsons, he honoured with imperial titles, although his own family was as yet undiminished. For he had admitted the children of Agrippa, Gaius and Lucius, into the house of the Caesars; and before they had yet laid aside the dress of boyhood he had most fervently desired, with an outward show of reluctance, that they should be entitled "princes of the youth," and be consuls-elect. When Agrippa died, and Lucius Caesar as he was on his way to our armies in Spain, and Gaius while returning from Armenia, still suffering from a wound, were prematurely cut off by destiny, or by their step-mother Livia's treachery, Drusus too having long been dead, Nero remained alone of the stepsons, and in him everything tended to centre. He was adopted as a son, as a colleague in empire and a partner in the tribunician power, and paraded through all the armies, no longer through his mother's secret intrigues, but at her open suggestion. For she had gained such a hold on the aged Augustus that he drove out as an exile into the island of Planasia, his only grandson, Agrippa Postumus, who, though devoid of worthy qualities, and having only the brute courage of physical strength, had not been convicted of any gross offence. And yet Augustus had appointed Germanicus, Drusus's offspring, to the command of eight legions on the Rhine, and required Tiberius to adopt him, although Tiberius had a son, now a young man, in his house; but he did it that he might have several safeguards to rest on. He had no war at the time on his hands except against the Germans, which was rather to wipe out the disgrace of the loss of Quintilius Varus and his army than out of an ambition to extend the empire, or for any adequate recompense. At home all was tranquil, and there were magistrates with the same titles; there was a younger generation, sprung up since the victory of Actium, and even many of the older men had been born during the civil wars. How few were left who had seen the republic!

4. Thus the State had been revolutionised, and there was not a vestige left of the old sound morality. Stripped of equality, all looked up to the commands of a sovereign without the least apprehension for the present,

while Augustus in the vigour of life, could maintain his own position, that of his house, and the general tranquillity. When in advanced old age, he was worn out by a sickly frame, and the end was near and new prospects opened, a few spoke in vain of the blessings of freedom, but most people dreaded and some longed for war. The popular gossip of the large majority fastened itself variously on their future masters. "Agrippa was savage, and had been exasperated by insult, and neither from age nor experience in affairs was equal to so great a burden. Tiberius Nero was of mature years, and had established his fame in war, but he had the old arrogance inbred in the Claudian family, and many symptoms of a cruel temper, though they were repressed, now and then broke out. He had also from earliest infancy been reared in an imperial house; consulships and triumphs had been heaped on him in his younger days; even in the years which, on the pretext of seclusion he spent in exile at Rhodes, he had had no thoughts but of wrath, hypocrisy, and secret sensuality. There was his mother too with a woman's caprice. They must, it seemed, be subject to a female and to two striplings besides, who for a while would burden, and some day rend asunder the State."

5. While these and like topics were discussed, the infirmities of Augustus increased, and some suspected guilt on his wife's part. For a rumour had gone abroad that a few months before he had sailed to Planasia on a visit to Agrippa, with the knowledge of some chosen friends, and with one companion, Fabius Maximus; that many tears were shed on both sides, with expressions of affection, and that thus there was a hope of the young man being restored to the home of his grandfather. This, it was said, Maximus had divulged to his wife Marcia, she again to Livia. All was known to Caesar, and when Maximus soon afterwards died, by a death some thought to be self-inflicted, there were heard at his funeral wailings from Marcia, in which she reproached herself for having been the cause of her husband's destruction. Whatever the fact was, Tiberius as he was just entering Illyria was summoned home by an urgent letter from his mother, and it has not been thoroughly ascertained whether at the city of Nola he found Augustus still breathing or quite lifeless. For Livia had surrounded the house and its approaches with a strict watch, and favourable bulletins were published from time to time, till, provision having been made for the demands of the crisis, one and the same report told men that Augustus was dead and that Tiberius Nero was master of the State.

6. The first crime of the new reign was the murder of Postumus Agrippa. Though he was surprised and unarmed, a centurion of the firmest resolution despatched him with difficulty. Tiberius gave no explanation of the matter to the Senate; he pretended that there were directions from his father ordering the tribune in charge of the prisoner not to delay the slaughter of

Agrippa, whenever he should himself have breathed his last. Beyond a doubt, Augustus had often complained of the young man's character, and had thus succeeded in obtaining the sanction of a decree of the Senate for his banishment. But he never was hard-hearted enough to destroy any of his kinsfolk, nor was it credible that death was to be the sentence of the grandson in order that the stepson might feel secure. It was more probable that Tiberius and Livia, the one from fear, the other from a stepmother's enmity, hurried on the destruction of a youth whom they suspected and hated. When the centurion reported, according to military custom, that he had executed the command, Tiberius replied that he had not given the command, and that the act must be justified to the Senate.

As soon as Sallustius Crispus who shared the secret (he had, in fact, sent the written order to the tribune) knew this, fearing that the charge would be shifted on himself, and that his peril would be the same whether he uttered fiction or truth, he advised Livia not to divulge the secrets of her house or the counsels of friends, or any services performed by the soldiers, nor to let Tiberius weaken the strength of imperial power by referring everything to the Senate, for "the condition," he said, "of holding empire is that an account cannot be balanced unless it be rendered to one person."

7. Meanwhile at Rome people plunged into slavery—consuls, senators, knights. The higher a man's rank, the more eager his hypocrisy, and his looks the more carefully studied, so as neither to betray joy at the decease of one emperor nor sorrow at the rise of another, while he mingled delight and lamentations with his flattery. Sextus Pompeius and Sextus Appuleius, the consuls, were the first to swear allegiance to Tiberius Caesar, and in their presence the oath was taken by Seius Strabo and Gaius Turranius, respectively the commander of the praetorian cohorts and the superintendent of the corn supplies. Then the Senate, the soldiers and the people did the same. For Tiberius would inaugurate everything with the consuls, as though the ancient constitution remained, and he hesitated about being emperor. Even the proclamation by which he summoned the senators to their chamber, he issued merely with the title of Tribune, which he had received under Augustus. The wording of the proclamation was brief, and in a very modest tone. "He would," it said, "provide for the honours due to his father, and not leave the lifeless body, and this was the only public duty he now claimed."

As soon, however, as Augustus was dead, he had given the watchword to the praetorian cohorts, as commander-in-chief. He had the guard under arms, with all the other adjuncts of a court; soldiers attended him to the forum; soldiers went with him to the Senate House. He sent letters to the different armies, as though supreme power was now his, and showed hesitation only when he spoke in the Senate. His chief motive was fear that

Germanicus, who had at his disposal so many legions, such vast auxiliary forces of the allies, and such wonderful popularity, might prefer the possession to the expectation of empire. He looked also at public opinion, wishing to have the credit of having been called and elected by the State rather than of having crept into power through the intrigues of a wife and a dotard's adoption. It was subsequently understood that he assumed a wavering attitude, to test likewise the temper of the nobles. For he would twist a word or a look into a crime and treasure it up in his memory.

8. On the first day of the Senate he allowed nothing to be discussed but the funeral of Augustus, whose will, which was brought in by the Vestal Virgins, named as his heirs Tiberius and Livia. The latter was to be admitted into the Julian family with the name of Augusta; next in expectation were the grand and great-grandchildren. In the third place, he had named the chief men of the State, most of whom he hated, simply out of ostentation and to win credit with posterity. His legacies were not beyond the scale of a private citizen, except a bequest of forty-three million five hundred thousand sesterces "to the people and populace of Rome," of one thousand to every praetorian soldier, and of three hundred to every man in the legionary cohorts composed of Roman citizens.

Next followed a deliberation about funeral honours. Of these the most imposing were thought fitting. The procession was to be conducted through "the gate of triumph," on the motion of Gallus Asinius; the titles of the laws passed, the names of the nations conquered by Augustus were to be borne in front, on that of Lucius Arruntius. Messala Valerius further proposed that the oath of allegiance to Tiberius should be yearly renewed, and when Tiberius asked him whether it was at *his* bidding that he had brought forward this motion, he replied that he had proposed it spontaneously, and that in whatever concerned the State he would use only his own discretion, even at the risk of offending. This was the only style of adulation which yet remained. The Senators unanimously exclaimed that the body ought to be borne on their shoulders to the funeral pyre. The emperor left the point to them with disdainful moderation, and he then admonished the people by a proclamation not to indulge in that tumultuous enthusiasm which had distracted the funeral of the Divine Julius, or express a wish that Augustus should be burnt in the Forum instead of in his appointed resting-place in the Campus Martius.

On the day of the funeral soldiers stood round as a guard, amid much ridicule from those who had either themselves witnessed or who had heard from their parents of the famous day when slavery was still something fresh, and freedom had been resought in vain, when the slaying of Caesar, the Dictator, seemed to some the vilest, to others, the most glorious of deeds. "Now," they said, "an aged sovereign, whose power had lasted long, who had provided his heirs with abundant means to coerce the State, requires forsooth the defence of soldiers that his burial may be undisturbed."

9. Then followed much talk about Augustus himself, and many expressed an idle wonder that the same day marked the beginning of his assumption of empire and the close of his life, and, again, that he had ended his days at Nola in the same house and room as his father Octavius. People extolled too the number of his consulships, in which he had equalled Valerius Corvus and Gaius Marius combined, the continuance for thirty-seven years of the tribunician power, the title of Imperator twenty-one times earned, and his other honours which had been either frequently repeated or were wholly new. Sensible men, however, spoke variously of his life with praise and censure. Some said "that dutiful feeling towards a father, and the necessities of the State in which laws had then no place, drove him into civil war, which can neither be planned nor conducted on any right principles. He had often yielded to Antonius, while he was taking vengeance on his father's murderers, often also to Lepidus. When the latter sank into feeble dotage and the former had been ruined by his profligacy, the only remedy for his distracted country was the rule of a single man. Yet the State had been organized under the name neither of a kingdom nor a dictatorship, but under that of a prince. The ocean and remote rivers were the boundaries of the empire; the legions, provinces, fleets, all things were linked together; there was law for the citizens; there was respect shown to the allies. The capital had been embellished on a grand scale; only in a few instances had he resorted to force, simply to secure general tranquillity."

10. It was said, on the other hand, "that filial duty and State necessity were merely assumed as a mask. It was really from a lust of sovereignty that he had excited the veterans by bribery, had, when a young man and a subject, raised an army, tampered with the Consul's legions, and feigned an attachment to the faction of Pompeius. Then, when by a decree of the Senate he had usurped the high functions and authority of Praetor, when Hirtius and Pansa were slain—whether they were destroyed by the enemy, or Pansa by poison infused into a wound, Hirtius by his own soldiers and Caesar's treacherous machinations—he at once possessed himself of both their armies, wrested the consulate from a reluctant Senate, and turned against the State the arms with which he had been intrusted against Antonius. Citizens were proscribed, lands divided, without so much as the approval of those who executed these deeds. Even granting that the deaths of Cassius and of the Bruti were sacrifices to a hereditary enmity (though duty requires us to waive private feuds for the sake of the public welfare), still Pompeius had been deluded by the phantom of peace, and Lepidus by the mask of friendship. Subsequently, Antonius had been lured on by the

treaties of Tarentum and Brundisium, and by his marriage with the sister, and paid by his death the penalty of a treacherous alliance. No doubt, there was peace after all this, but it was a peace stained with blood; there were the disasters of Lollius and Varus, the murders at Rome of the Varros, Egnatii, and Julii."

The domestic life too of Augustus was not spared. "Nero's wife had been taken from him, and there had been the farce of consulting the pontiffs, whether, with a child conceived and not yet born, she could properly marry. There were the excesses of Quintus Tedius and Vedius Pollio; last of all, there was Livia, terrible to the State as a mother, terrible to the house of the Caesars as a stepmother. No honour was left for the gods, when Augustus chose to be himself worshipped with temples and statues, like those of the deities, and with flamens and priests. He had not even adopted Tiberius as his successor out of affection or any regard to the State, but, having thoroughly seen his arrogant and savage temper, he had sought glory for himself by a contrast of extreme wickedness." For, in fact, Augustus, a few years before, when he was a second time asking from the Senate the tribunician power for Tiberius, though his speech was complimentary, had thrown out certain hints as to his manners, style, and habits of life, which he meant as reproaches, while he seemed to excuse. However, when his obsequies had been duly performed, a temple with a religious ritual was decreed him.

11. After this all prayers were addressed to Tiberius. He, on his part, urged various considerations, the greatness of the empire, his distrust of himself. "Only," he said, "the intellect of the Divine Augustus was equal to such a burden. Called as he had been by him to share his anxieties, he had learnt by experience how exposed to fortune's caprices was the task of universal rule. Consequently, in a state which had the support of so many great men, they should not put everything on one man, as many, by uniting their efforts would more easily discharge public functions." There was more grand sentiment than good faith in such words. Tiberius's language even in matters which he did not care to conceal, either from nature or habit, was always hesitating and obscure, and now that he was struggling to hide his feelings completely, it was all the more involved in uncertainty and doubt. The Senators, however, whose only fear was lest they might seem to understand him, burst into complaints, tears, and prayers. They raised their hands to the gods, to the statue of Augustus, and to the knees of Tiberius, when he ordered a document to be produced and read. This contained a description of the resources of the State, of the number of citizens and allies under arms, of the fleets, subject kingdoms, provinces, taxes, direct and indirect, necessary expenses and customary bounties. All these details

Augustus had written with his own hand, and had added a counsel, that the empire should be confined to its present limits, either from fear or out of jealousy.

12. Meantime, while the Senate stooped to the most abject supplication, Tiberius happened to say that although he was not equal to the whole burden of the State, yet he would undertake the charge of whatever part of it might be intrusted to him. Thereupon Asinius Gallus said, "I ask you, Caesar, what part of the State you wish to have intrusted to you?" Confounded by the sudden inquiry he was silent for a few moments; then, recovering his presence of mind, he replied that it would by no means become his modesty to choose or to avoid in a case where he would prefer to be wholly excused. Then Gallus again, who had inferred anger from his looks, said that the question had not been asked with the intention of dividing what could not be separated, but to convince him by his own admission that the body of the State was one, and must be directed by a single mind. He further spoke in praise of Augustus, and reminded Tiberius himself of his victories, and of his admirable deeds for many years as a civilian. Still, he did not thereby soften the emperor's resentment, for he had long been detested from an impression that, as he had married Vipsania, daughter of Marcus Agrippa, who had once been the wife of Tiberius, he aspired to be more than a citizen, and kept up the arrogant tone of his father Asinius Pollio.

13. Next, Lucius Arruntius, who differed but little from the speech of Gallus, gave like offence, though Tiberius had no old grudge against him, but simply mistrusted him, because he was rich and daring, had brilliant accomplishments, and corresponding popularity. For Augustus, when in his last conversations he was discussing who would refuse the highest place, though sufficiently capable, who would aspire to it without being equal to it, and who would unite both the ability and ambition, had described Marcus Lepidus as able but contemptuously indifferent, Gallus Asinius as ambitious and incapable, Lucius Arruntius as not unworthy of it, and, should the chance be given him, sure to make the venture. About the two first there is a general agreement, but instead of Arruntius some have mentioned Gnaeus Piso, and all these men, except Lepidus, were soon afterwards destroyed by various charges through the contrivance of Tiberius. Quintus Haterius too and Mamercus Scaurus ruffled his suspicious temper, Haterius by having said—"How long, Caesar, will you suffer the State to be without a head?" Scaurus by the remark that there was a hope that the Senate's prayers would not be fruitless, seeing that he had not used his right as Tribune to negative the motion of the Consuls. Tiberius instantly broke out into invective against Haterius; Scaurus, with whom he was far more deeply displeased, he passed over in silence. Wearied at last

by the assembly's clamorous importunity and the urgent demands of individual Senators, he gave way by degrees, not admitting that he undertook empire, but yet ceasing to refuse it and to be entreated. It is known that Haterius having entered the palace to ask pardon, and thrown himself at the knees of Tiberius as he was walking, was almost killed by the soldiers, because Tiberius fell forward, accidentally or from being entangled by the suppliant's hands. Yet the peril of so great a man did not make him relent, till Haterius went with entreaties to Augusta, and was saved by her very earnest intercessions.

14. Great too was the Senate's sycophancy to Augusta. Some would have her styled "parent;" others "mother of the country," and a majority proposed that to the name of Caesar should be added "son of Julia." The emperor repeatedly asserted that there must be a limit to the honours paid to women, and that he would observe similar moderation in those bestowed on himself, but annoyed at the invidious proposal, and indeed regarding a woman's elevation as a slight to himself, he would not allow so much as a lictor to be assigned her, and forbade the erection of an altar in memory of her adoption, and any like distinction. But for Germanicus Caesar he asked pro-consular powers, and envoys were despatched to confer them on him, and also to express sympathy with his grief at the death of Augustus. The same request was not made for Drusus, because he was consul elect and present at Rome. Twelve candidates were named for the praetorship, the number which Augustus had handed down, and when the Senate urged Tiberius to increase it, he bound himself by an oath not to exceed it.

15. It was then for the first time that the elections were transferred from the Campus Martius to the Senate. For up to that day, though the most important rested with the emperor's choice, some were settled by the partialities of the tribes. Nor did the people complain of having the right taken from them, except in mere idle talk, and the Senate, being now released from the necessity of bribery and of degrading solicitations, gladly upheld the change, Tiberius confining himself to the recommendation of only four candidates who were to be nominated without rejection or canvass. Meanwhile the tribunes of the people asked leave to exhibit at their own expense games to be named after Augustus and added to the Calendar as the Augustales. Money was, however, voted from the exchequer, and though the use of the triumphal robe in the circus was prescribed, it was not allowed them to ride in a chariot. Soon the annual celebration was transferred to the praetor, to whose lot fell the administration of justice between citizens and foreigners.

11. Tacitus, *Histories* (Selection)

Four books and part of a fifth are all that remain of Tacitus's *Histories*, which originally comprised at least twelve books. The surviving portion covers A.D. 69, the "year of the four emperors" (Galba, Otho, Vitellius, and Vespasian), and some of A.D. 70. It is a complicated account of conspiracies and rebellions ultimately set in motion by the fall of the emperor Nero in the previous year. In the spring of A.D. 68 many of the tribes of Gaul had risen in revolt at the call of Julius Vindex, an assimilated Gaul who was governing his native country in the name of Rome. Soon afterwards, Galba, one of Nero's governors in Spain, renounced his allegiance and began a march on Rome. When the news about Galba was followed by the defection of the senate and of the guard commander Nymphidius Sabinus, Nero was frightened into suicide. Picking up the story several months after Galba arrived in Rome and organized his government, Tacitus relates only the last two weeks of his reign. But he begins by surveying political factors which would remain in play throughout the struggle over the succession. The army was one of the most important factors. The Principate had evolved from a military dictatorship born of civil war; in the chaos of A.D. 69 and 70, it reverted to its origins.

1. I begin my work with the time when Servius Galba was consul for the second time with Titus Vinius for his colleague. Of the former period, the 820 years dating from the founding of the city, many authors have treated; and while they had to record the transactions of the Roman people, they wrote with equal eloquence and freeedom. After the conflict at Actium, and when it became essential to peace, that all power should be centered in one man, these great intellects passed away. Then too the truthfulness of history was impaired in many ways; at first, through men's ignorance of public affairs, which were now wholly strange to them, then, through their passion for flattery, or, on the other hand, their hatred of their masters. And so between the enmity of the one and the servility of the other, neither had any regard for posterity. But while we instinctively shrink from a writer's adulation, we lend a ready ear to detraction and spite, because flattery involves the shameful imputation of servility, whereas malignity wears the false appearance of honesty. I myself knew nothing of Galba, of Otho, or of Vitellius, either from benefits or from injuries. I would not deny that my elevation was begun by Vespasian, augmented by Titus, and still further advanced by Domitian; but those who profess inviolable truthfulness must

Historiae 1.1–50. From *The Histories of Tacitus*, translated by Alfred John Church and William Jackson Brodribb (London: Macmillan, 1872), pp. 1–25.

speak of all without partiality and without hatred. I have reserved as an employment for my old age, should my life be long enough, a subject at once more fruitful and less anxious in the reign of the Divine Nerva and the empire of Trajan, enjoying the rare happiness of times, when we may think what we please, and express what we think.

2. I am entering on the history of a period rich in disasters, frightful in its wars, torn by civil strife, and even in peace full of horrors. Four emperors perished by the sword. There were three civil wars; there were often wars that had both characters at once. There were disturbances in Illyricum; Gaul wavered in its allegiance; Britain was thoroughly subdued and immediately abandoned; the tribes of the Suevi and the Sarmatae rose in concert against us; the Dacians had the glory of inflicting as well as suffering defeat; the armies of Parthia were all but set in motion by the cheat of a counterfeit Nero. Now too Italy was prostrated by disasters either entirely novel, or that recurred only after a long succession of ages; cities in Campania's richest plains were swallowed up and overwhelmed; Rome was wasted by conflagrations, its oldest temples consumed, and the Capitol itself fired by the hands of citizens. Sacred rites were profaned; there was profligacy in the highest ranks; the sea was crowded with exiles, and its rocks polluted with bloody deeds. In the capital there were yet worse horrors. Nobility, wealth, the refusal or the acceptance of office, were grounds for accusation, and virtue ensured destruction. The rewards of the informers were no less odious than their crimes; for while some seized on consulships and priestly offices, as their share of the spoil, others on procuratorships, and posts of more confidential authority, they robbed and ruined in every direction amid universal hatred and terror. Slaves were bribed to turn against their masters, and freedmen to betray their patrons; and those who had not an enemy were destroyed by friends.

3. Yet the age was not so barren in noble qualities, as not also to exhibit examples of virtue. Mothers accompanied the flight of their sons; wives followed their husbands into exile; there were brave kinsmen and faithful sons-in-law; there were slaves whose fidelity defied even torture; there were illustrious men driven to the last necessity, and enduring it with fortitude; there were closing scenes that equalled the famous deaths of antiquity. Besides the manifold vicissitudes of human affairs, there were prodigies in heaven and earth, the warning voices of the thunder, and other intimations of the future, auspicious or gloomy, doubtful or not to be mistaken. Never surely did more terrible calamities of the Roman people, or evidence more conclusive, prove that the Gods take no thought for our happiness, but only for our punishment.

4. I think it proper, however, before I commence my purposed work, to pass under review the condition of the capital, the temper of the armies, the attitude of the provinces, and the elements of weakness and strength which

existed throughout the whole empire, that so we may become acquainted, not only with the vicissitudes and the issues of events, which are often matters of chance, but also with their relations and their causes. Welcome as the death of Nero had been in the first burst of joy, yet it had not only roused various emotions in Rome, among the Senators, the people, or the soldiery of the capital, it had also excited all the legions and their generals; for now had been divulged that secret of the empire, that emperors could be made elsewhere than at Rome. The Senators enjoyed the first exercise of freedom with the less restraint, because the Emperor was new to power, and absent from the capital. The leading men of the Equestrian order sympathised most closely with the joy of the Senators. The respectable portion of the people, which was connected with the great families, as well as the dependants and freedmen of condemned and banished persons, were high in hope. The degraded populace, frequenters of the arena and the theatre, the most worthless of the slaves, and those who having wasted their property were supported by the infamous excesses of Nero, caught eagerly in their dejection at every rumour.

5. The soldiery of the capital, who were imbued with the spirit of an old allegiance to the Caesars, and who had been led to desert Nero by intrigues and influences from without rather than by their own feelings, were inclined for change, when they found that the donative promised in Galba's name was withheld, and reflected that for great services and great rewards there was not the same room in peace as in war, and that the favour of an emperor created by the legions must be already preoccupied. They were further excited by the treason of Nymphidius Sabinus, their prefect, who himself aimed at the throne. Nymphidius indeed perished in the attempt, but, though the head of the mutiny was thus removed, there yet remained in many of the soldiers the consciousness of guilt. There were even men who talked in angry terms of the feebleness and avarice of Galba. The strictness once so commended, and celebrated in the praises of the army, was galling to troops who rebelled against the old discipline, and who had been accustomed by fourteen years' service under Nero to love the vices of their emperors, as much as they had once respected their virtues. To all this was added Galba's own expression, "I choose my soldiers, I do not buy them," noble words for the commonwealth, but fraught with peril for himself. His other acts were not after this pattern.

6. Titus Vinius and Cornelius Laco, one the most worthless, the other the most spiritless of mankind, were ruining the weak old Emperor, who had to bear the odium of such crimes and the scorn felt for such cowardice. Galba's progress had been slow and blood-stained. Cingonius Varro, consul elect, and Petronius Turpilianus, a man of consular rank, were put to death; the former as an accomplice of Nymphidius, the latter as one of Nero's

generals. Both had perished without hearing or defence, like innocent men. His entry into the capital, made after the slaughter of thousands of unarmed soldiers, was most ill-omened, and was terrible even to the executioners. As he brought into the city his Spanish legion, while that which Nero had levied from the fleet still remained, Rome was full of strange troops. There were also many detachments from Germany, Britain, and Illyria, selected by Nero, and sent on by him to the Caspian passes, for service in the expedition which he was preparing against the Albani, but afterwards recalled to crush the insurrection of Vindex. Here there were vast materials for a revolution, without indeed a decided bias towards any one man, but ready to a daring hand.

7. In this conjuncture it happened that tidings of the deaths of Fonteius Capito and Clodius Macer reached the capital. Macer was executed in Africa, where he was undoubtedly fomenting sedition, by Trebonius Garutianus the procurator, who acted on Galba's authority; Capito fell in Germany, while he was making similar attempts, by the hands of Cornelius Aquinus and Fabius Valens, legates of legions, who did not wait for an order. There were however some who believed that Capito, though foully stained with avarice and profligacy, had yet abstained from all thought of revolution, that this was a treacherous accusation invented by the commanders themselves, who had urged him to take up arms, when they found themselves unable to prevail, and that Galba had approved of the deed, either from weakness of character, or to avoid investigation into the circumstances of acts which could not be altered. Both executions, however, were unfavourably regarded; indeed, when a ruler once becomes unpopular, all his acts, be they good or bad, tell against him. The freedmen in their excessive power were now putting up everything for sale; the slaves caught with greedy hands at immediate gain, and, reflecting on their master's age, hastened to be rich. The new court had the same abuses as the old, abuses as grievous as ever, but not so readily excused. Even the age of Galba caused ridicule and disgust among those whose associations were with the youth of Nero, and who were accustomed, as is the fashion of the vulgar, to value their emperors by the beauty and grace of their persons.

8. Such, as far as one can speak of so vast a multitude, was the state of feeling at Rome. Among the provinces, Spain was under the government of Cluvius Rufus, an eloquent man, who had all the accomplishments of civil life, but who was without experience in war. Gaul, besides remembering Vindex, was bound to Galba by the recently conceded privileges of citizenship, and by the diminution of its future tribute. Those Gallic states, however, which were nearest to the armies of Germany, had not been treated with the same respect, and had even in some cases been deprived of their territory; and these were reckoning the gains of others and their own

losses with equal indignation. The armies of Germany were at once alarmed and angry, a most dangerous temper when allied with such strength; while elated by their recent victory, they feared because they might seem to have supported an unsuccessful party. They had been slow to revolt from Nero, and Verginius had not immediately declared for Galba; it was doubtful whether he had himself wished to be emperor, but all agreed that the empire had been offered to him by the soldiery. Again, the execution of Capito was a subject of indignation, even with those who could not complain of its injustice. They had no leader, for Verginius had been withdrawn on the pretext of his friendship with the Emperor. That he was not sent back, and that he was even impeached, they regarded as an accusation against themselves.

9. The army of Upper Germany despised their legate, Hordeonius Flaccus, who, disabled by age and lameness, had no strength of character and no authority; even when the soldiery were quiet, he could not control them, much more in their fits of frenzy were they irritated by the very feebleness of his restraint. The legions of Lower Germany had long been without any general of consular rank, until, by the appointment of Galba, Aulus Vitellius took the command. He was son of that Vitellius who was censor and three times consul; this was thought sufficient recommendation. In the army of Britain there was no angry feeling; indeed no troops behaved more blamelessly throughout all the troubles of these civil wars, either because they were far away and separated by the ocean from the rest of the empire, or because continual warfare had taught them to concentrate their hatred on the enemy. Illyricum too was quiet, though the legions drawn from that province by Nero had, while lingering in Italy, sent deputations to Verginius. But separated as these armies were by long distances, a thing of all others the most favourable for keeping troops to their duty, they could neither communicate their vices, nor combine their strength.

10. In the East there was as yet no movement. Syria and its four legions were under the command of Licinius Mucianus, a man whose good and bad fortune were equally famous. In his youth he had cultivated with many intrigues the friendship of the great. His resources soon failed, and his position became precarious, and as he also suspected that Claudius had taken some offence, he withdrew into a retired part of Asia, and was as like an exile, as he was afterwards like an emperor. He was a compound of dissipation and energy, of arrogance and courtesy, of good and bad qualities. His self-indulgence was excessive, when he had leisure, yet whenever he had served, he had shown great qualities. In his public capacity he might be praised; his private life was in bad repute. Yet over subjects, friends, and colleagues, he exercised the influence of many fascinations.

He was a man who would find it easier to transfer the imperial power to another, than to hold it for himself. Flavius Vespasian, a general of Nero's appointment, was carrying on the war in Judaea with three legions, and he had no wish or feeling adverse to Galba. He had in fact sent his son Titus to acknowledge his authority and bespeak his favour, as in its proper place I shall relate. As for the hidden decrees of fate, the omens and the oracles that marked out Vespasian and his sons for imperial power, we believed in them only after his success.

11. Ever since the time of the Divine Augustus Roman Knights have ruled Egypt as kings, and the forces by which it has to be kept in subjection. It has been thought expedient thus to keep under home control a province so difficult of access, so productive of corn, ever distracted, excitable, and restless through the superstition and licentiousness of its inhabitants, knowing nothing of laws, and unused to civil rule. Its governor was at this time Tiberius Alexander, a native of the country. Africa and its legions, now that Clodius Macer was dead, were disposed to be content with any emperor, after having experienced the rule of a smaller tyrant. The two divisions of Mauritania, Rhaetia, Noricum and Thrace and the other provinces governed by procurators, as they were near this or that army, were driven by the presence of such powerful neighbours into friendship or hostility. The unarmed provinces with Italy at their head were exposed to any kind of slavery, and were ready to become the prize of victory. Such was the state of the Roman world, when Servius Galba, consul for the second time, with Titus Vinius for his colleague, entered upon a year, which was to be the last of their lives, and which well nigh brought the commonwealth to an end.

12. A few days after the 1st of January, there arrived from Belgica despatches of Pompeius Propinquus, the Procurator, to this effect; that the legions of Upper Germany had broken through the obligation of their military oath, and were demanding another emperor, but conceded the power of choice to the Senate and people of Rome, in the hope that a more lenient view might be taken of their revolt. These tidings hastened the plans of Galba, who had been long debating the subject of adoption with himself and with his intimate friends. There was indeed no more frequent subject of conversation during these months, at first because men had liberty and inclination to talk of such matters, afterwards because the feebleness of Galba was notorious. Few had any discrimination or patriotism, many had foolish hopes for themselves, and spread interested reports, in which they named this or that person to whom they might be related as friend or dependant. They were also moved by hatred of Titus Vinius, who grew daily more powerful, and in the same proportion more unpopular. The very easi-

ness of Galba's temper stimulated the greedy cupidity which great advancement had excited in his friends, because with one so weak and so credulous wrong might be done with less risk and greater gain.

13. The real power of the Empire was divided between Vinius, the consul, and Cornelius Laco, prefect of the Praetorian Guard. Icelus, a freedman of Galba, was in equal favour; he had been presented with the rings of knighthood, and bore the Equestrian name of Martianus. These men, being at variance, and in smaller matters pursuing their own aims, were divided in the affair of choosing a successor, into two opposing factions. Vinius was for Marcus Otho, Laco and Icelus agreed, not indeed in supporting any particular individual, but in striving for some one else. Galba indeed was aware of the friendship between Vinius and Otho; the gossip of those who allow nothing to pass in silence had named them as father-in-law and son-in-law, for Vinius had a widowed daughter, and Otho was unmarried. I believe that he had also at heart some care for the commonwealth, in vain, he would think, rescued from Nero, if it was to be left with Otho. For Otho's had been a neglected boyhood and a riotous youth, and he had made himself agreeable to Nero by emulating his profligacy. For this reason the Emperor had entrusted to him, as being the confidant of his amours, Poppaea Sabina, the imperial favourite, until he could rid himself of his wife Octavia. Soon suspecting him with regard to this same Poppaea, he sent him out of the way to the province of Lusitania, ostensibly to be its governor. Otho ruled the province with mildness, and, as he was the first to join Galba's party, was not without energy, and, while the war lasted, was the most conspicuous of the Emperor's followers, he was led to cherish more and more passionately every day those hopes of adoption which he had entertained from the first. Many of the soldiers favoured him, and the court was biassed in his favour, because he resembled Nero.

14. When Galba heard of the mutiny in Germany, though nothing was as yet known about Vitellius, he felt anxious as to the direction which the violence of the legions might take, while he could not trust even the soldiery of the capital. He therefore resorted to what he supposed to be the only remedy, and held a council for the election of an emperor. To this he summoned, besides Vinius and Laco, Marius Celsus, consul elect, and Ducennius Geminus, prefect of the city. Having first said a few words about his advanced years, he ordered Piso Licinianus to be summoned. It is uncertain whether he acted on his own free choice, or, as believed by some, under the influence of Laco, who through Rubellius Plautus had cultivated the friendship of Piso. But, cunningly enough, it was as a stranger that Laco supported him, and the high character of Piso gave weight to his advice. Piso, who was the son of M. Crassus and Scribonia, and thus of noble descent on both sides, was in look and manner a man of the old type.

Rightly judged, he seemed a stern man, morose to those who estimated him less favourably. This point in his character pleased his adopted father in proportion as it raised the anxious suspicions of others.

15. We are told that Galba, taking hold of Piso's hand, spoke to this effect: "If I were a private man, and were now adopting you by the Act of the Curiae before the Pontiffs, as our custom is, it would be a high honour to me to introduce into my family a descendant of Cn. Pompeius and M. Crassus; it would be a distinction to you to add to the nobility of your race the honours of the Sulpician and Lutatian houses. As it is, I, who have been called to the throne by the unanimous consent of gods and men, am moved by your splendid endowments and by my own patriotism to offer to you, a man of peace, that power, for which our ancestors fought, and which I myself obtained by war. I am following the precedent of the Divine Augustus, who placed on an eminence next to his own, first his nephew Marcellus, then his son-in-law Agrippa, afterwards his grandsons, and finally Tiberius Nero, his step-son. But Augustus looked for a successor in his own family, I look for one in the state, not because I have no relatives or companions of my campaigns, but because it was not by any private favour that I myself received the imperial power. Let the principle of my choice be shewn not only by my connections which I have set aside for you, but by your own. You have a brother, noble as yourself, and older, who would be well worthy of this dignity, were you not worthier. Your age is such as to be now free from the passions of youth, and such your life that in the past you have nothing to excuse. Hitherto, you have only borne adversity; prosperity tries the heart with keener temptations; for hardships may be endured, whereas we are spoiled by success. You indeed will cling with the same constancy to honour, freedom, friendship, the best possessions of the human spirit, but others will seek to weaken them with their servility. You will be fiercely assailed by adulation, by flattery, that worst poison of the true heart, and by the selfish interests of individuals. You and I speak together with perfect frankness, but others will be more ready to address us as emperors than as men. For to urge his duty upon a prince is indeed a hard matter; to flatter him, whatever his character, is a mere routine gone through without any heart.

16. "Could the vast frame of this empire have stood and preserved its balance without a directing spirit, I was not unworthy of inaugurating a republic. As it is, we have been long reduced to a position, in which my age can confer no greater boon on the Roman people than a good successor, your youth no greater than a good emperor. Under Tiberius, Gaius, and Claudius, we were, so to speak, the inheritance of a single family. The choice which begins with us will be a substitute for freedom. Now that the family of the Julii and the Claudii has come to an end, adoption will dis-

cover the worthiest successor. To be begotten and born of a princely race is a mere accident, and is only valued as such. In adoption there is nothing that need bias the judgment, and if you wish to make a choice, an unanimous opinion points out the man. Let Nero be ever before your eyes, swollen with the pride of a long line of Caesars; it was not Vindex with his unarmed province, it was not myself with my single legion, that shook his yoke from our necks. It was his own profligacy, his own brutality, and that, though there had been before no precedent of an emperor condemned by his own people. We, who have been called to power by the issues of war, and by the deliberate judgment of others, shall incur unpopularity, however illustrious our character. Do not however be alarmed, if, after a movement which has shaken the world, two legions are not yet quiet. I did not myself succeed to a throne without anxiety; and when men shall hear of your adoption I shall no longer be thought old, and this is the only objection which is now made against me. Nero will always be regretted by the thoroughly depraved; it is for you and me to take care, that he be not regretted also by the good. To prolong such advice, suits not this occasion, and all my purpose is fulfilled if I have made a good choice in you. The most practical and the shortest method of distinguishing between good and bad measures, is to think what you yourself would or would not like under another emperor. It is not here, as it is among nations despotically ruled, that there is a distinct governing family, while all the rest are slaves. You have to reign over men who cannot bear either absolute slavery or absolute freedom." This, with more to the same effect, was said by Galba; he spoke to Piso as if he were creating an emperor; the others addressed him as if he were an emperor already.

17. It is said of Piso that he betrayed no discomposure or excessive joy, either to the gaze to which he was immediately subjected, or afterwards when all eyes were turned upon him. His language to the Emperor, his father, was reverential; his language about himself was modest. He shewed no change in look or manner; he seemed like one who had the power rather than the wish to rule. It was next discussed whether the adoption should be publicly pronounced in front of the Rostra, in the Senate, or in the camp. It was thought best to go to the camp. This would be a compliment to the soldiery, and their favour, base as it was to purchase it by bribery or intrigue, was not to be despised if it could be obtained by honourable means. Meanwhile the expectant people had surrounded the palace, impatient to learn the great secret, and those who sought to stifle the ill-concealed rumour did but spread it the more.

18. The 10th of January was a gloomy, stormy day, unusually disturbed by thunder, lightning, and all bad omens from heaven. Though this had from ancient time been made a reason for dissolving an assembly, it did not

deter Galba from proceeding to the camp; either because he despised such things as being mere matters of chance, or because the decrees of fate, though they be foreshewn, are not escaped. Addressing a crowded assembly of the soldiers he announced, with imperial brevity, that he adopted Piso, following the precedent of the Divine Augustus, and the military custom by which a soldier chooses his comrade. Fearing that to conceal the mutiny would be to make them think it greater than it really was, he spontaneously declared that the 4th and 18th legions, led by a few factious persons, had been insubordinate, but had not gone beyond certain words and cries, and that they would soon return to their duty. To this speech he added no word of flattery, no hint of a bribe. Yet the tribunes, the centurions, and such of the soldiers as stood near, made an encouraging response. A gloomy silence prevailed among the rest, who seemed to think that they had lost by war that right to a donative which they had made good even in peace. It is certain that their feelings might have been conciliated by the very smallest liberality on the part of the parsimonious old man. He was ruined by his old-fashioned inflexibility, and by an excessive sternness which we are no longer able to endure.

19. Then followed Galba's speech in the Senate, which was as plain and brief as his speech to the soldiery. Piso delivered a graceful oration and was supported by the feeling of the Senate. Many who wished him well, spoke with enthusiasm; those who had opposed him, in moderate terms; the majority met him with an officious homage, having aims of their own and no thought for the state. Piso neither said nor did anything else in public in the following four days which intervened between his adoption and his death. As tidings of the mutiny in Germany were arriving with daily increasing frequency, while the country was ready to receive and to credit all intelligence that had an unfavourable character, the Senate came to a resolution to send deputies to the German armies. It was privately discussed whether Piso should go with them to give them a more imposing appearance; they, it was said, would bring with them the authority of the Senate, he the majesty of the Caesar. It was thought expedient to send with them Cornelius Laco, prefect of the Praetorian Guard, but he thwarted the design. In nominating, excusing, and changing the deputies, the Senate having entrusted the selection to Galba, the Emperor shewed a disgraceful want of firmness, yielding to individuals, who made interest to stay or to go, as their fears or their hopes prompted.

20. Next came the question of money. On a general inquiry it seemed the fairest course to demand restitution from those who had caused the public poverty. Nero had squandered in presents two thousand two hundred million sesterces. It was ordered that each recipient should be sued, but should be permitted to retain a tenth part of the bounty. They had however

barely a tenth part left, having wasted the property of others in the same extravagances in which they had squandered their own, till the most rapacious and profligate among them had neither capital nor land remaining, nothing in fact but the appliances of their vices. Thirty Roman Knights were appointed to conduct the process of recovery, a novel office, and made burdensome by the number and intriguing practices of those with whom it had to deal. Everywhere were sales and brokers, and Rome was in an uproar with auctions. Yet great was the joy to think that the men whom Nero had enriched would be as poor as those whom he had robbed. About this time were cashiered two tribunes of the Praetorian Guard, Antonius Taurus and Antonius Naso, an officer of the City cohorts, Aemilius Pacensis, and one of the watch, Julius Fronto. This led to no amendment with the rest, but only started the apprehension, that a crafty and timid policy was getting rid of individuals, while all were suspected.

21. Otho, meanwhile, who had nothing to hope while the State was tranquil, and whose whole plans depended on revolution, was being roused to action by a combination of many motives, by a luxury that would have embarrassed even an emperor, by a poverty that a subject could hardly endure, by his rage against Galba, by his envy of Piso. He even pretended to fear to make himself keener in desire. "I was," said he, "too formidable to Nero, and I must not look for another Lusitania, another honourable exile. Rulers always suspect and hate the man who has been named for the succession. This has injured me with the aged Emperor, and will injure me yet more with a young man whose temper, naturally savage, has been rendered ferocious by prolonged exile. How easy to put Otho to death! I must therefore do and dare now while Galba's authority is still unsettled, and before that of Piso is consolidated. Periods of transition suit great attempts, and delay is useless where inaction is more hurtful than temerity. Death, which nature ordains for all alike, yet admits of the distinction of being either forgotten, or remembered with honour by posterity; and, if the same lot awaits the innocent and the guilty, the man of spirit will at least deserve his fate."

22. The soul of Otho was not effeminate like his person. His confidential freedmen and slaves, who enjoyed a license unknown in private families, brought the debaucheries of Nero's court, its intrigues, its easy marriages, and the other indulgences of despotic power, before a mind passionately fond of such things, dwelt upon them as his if he dared to seize them, and reproached the inaction that would leave them to others. The astrologers also urged him to action, predicting from their observation of the heavens revolutions, and a year of glory for Otho. This is a class of men, whom the powerful cannot trust, and who deceive the aspiring, a class which will always be proscribed in this country, and yet always re-

tained. Many of these men were attached to the secret councils of Poppaea and were the vilest tools in the employ of the imperial household. One of them, Ptolemaeus, had attended Otho in Spain, and had there foretold that his patron would survive Nero. Gaining credit by the result, and arguing from his own conjectures and from the common talk of those who compared Galba's age with Otho's youth, he had persuaded the latter that he would be called to the throne. Otho however received the prediction as the words of wisdom and the intimation of destiny, with that inclination so natural to the human mind readily to believe in the mysterious.

23. Nor did Ptolemaeus fail to play his part; he now even prompted to crime, to which from such wishes it is easy to pass. Whether indeed these thoughts of crime were suddenly conceived, is doubtful. Otho had long been courting the affections of the soldiery, either in the hope of succeeding to the throne, or in preparation for some desperate act. On the march, on parade, and in their quarters, he would address all the oldest soldiers by name, and in allusion to the progresses of Nero would call them his messmates. Some he would recognise, he would inquire after others, and would help them with his money and interest. He would often intersperse his conversation with complaints and insinuations against Galba and anything else that might excite the vulgar mind. Laborious marches, a scanty commissariat, and the rigour of military discipline, were especially distasteful, when men, accustomed to sail to the lakes of Campania and the cities of Greece, had painfully to struggle under the weight of their arms over the Pyrenees, the Alps, and vast distances of road.

24. The minds of the soldiery were already on fire, when Maevius Pudens, a near relative of Tigellinus, added, so to speak, fuel to the flames. In his endeavour to win over all who were particularly weak in character, or who wanted money and were ready to plunge into revolution, he gradually went so far as to distribute, whenever Galba dined with Otho, one hundred sesterces to each soldier of the cohort on duty, under pretext of treating them. This, which we may almost call a public bounty, Otho followed up by presents more privately bestowed on individuals; nay he bribed with such spirit, that, finding there was a dispute between Cocceius Proculus, a soldier of the bodyguard, and one of his neighbours, about some part of their boundaries, he purchased with his own money the neighbour's entire estate, and made a present of it to the soldier. He took advantage of the lazy indifference of the Prefect, who overlooked alike notorious facts and secret practices.

25. He then entrusted the conduct of his meditated treason to Onomastus, one of his freedmen, who brought over to his views Barbius Proculus, officer of the watchword to the bodyguard, and Veturius, a deputy centurion in the same force. Having assured himself by various conversations

with these men that they were cunning and bold, he loaded them with presents and promises, and furnished them with money with which to tempt the cupidity of others. Thus two soldiers from the ranks undertook to transfer the Empire of Rome, and actually transferred it. Only a few were admitted to be accomplices in the plot, but they worked by various devices on the wavering minds of the remainder; on the more distinguished soldiers, by hinting that the favours of Nymphidius had subjected them to suspicion; on the vulgar herd, by the anger and despair with which the repeated postponement of the donative had inspired them. Some were fired by their recollections of Nero and their longing regrets for their old license. All felt a common alarm at the idea of having to serve elsewhere.

26. The contagion spread to the legions and the auxiliary troops, already excited by the news of the wavering loyalty of the army of Germany. So ripe were the disaffected for mutiny and so close the secrecy preserved by the loyal, that they would actually have seized Otho on the 14th of January, as he was returning from dinner, had they not been deterred by the risks of darkness, the inconvenient dispersion of the troops over the whole city, and the difficulty of concerted action among a half-intoxicated crowd. It was no care for the state, which they deliberately meditated polluting with the blood of their Emperor; it was a fear lest in the darkness of night any one who presented himself to the soldiers of the Pannonian or German army might be fixed on instead of Otho, whom few of them knew. Many symptoms of the approaching outburst were repressed by those who were in the secret. Some hints, which had reached Galba's ears, were turned into ridicule by Laco the prefect, who knew nothing of the temper of the soldiery, and who, inimical to all measures, however excellent, which he did not originate, obstinately thwarted men wiser than himself.

27. On the 15th of January, as Galba was sacrificing in front of the temple of Apollo, the Haruspex Umbricius announced to him that the entrails had a sinister aspect, that treachery threatened him, that he had an enemy at home. Otho heard, for he had taken his place close by, and interpreted it by contraries in a favourable sense, as promising success to his designs. Not long after his freedman Onomastus informed him that the architect and the contractors were waiting for him. It had been arranged thus to indicate that the soldiers were assembling, and that the preparations of the conspiracy were complete. To those who inquired the reason of his departure, Otho pretended that he was purchasing certain farm-buildings, which from their age he suspected to be unsound, and which had therefore to be first surveyed. Leaning on his freedman's arm, he proceeded through the palace of Tiberius to the Velabrum, and thence to the golden milestone near the temple of Saturn. There three and twenty soldiers of the bodyguard saluted him as Emperor, and, while he trembled at their scanty num-

ber, put him hastily into a chair, drew their swords, and hurried him onwards. About as many more soldiers joined them on their way, some because they were in the plot, many from mere surprise; some shouted and brandished their swords, others proceeded in silence, intending to let the issue determine their sentiments.

28. Julius Martialis was the tribune on guard in the camp. Appalled by the enormity and suddenness of the crime, or perhaps fearing that the troops were very extensively corrupted and that it would be destruction to oppose them, he made many suspect him of complicity. The rest of the tribunes and centurions preferred immediate safety to danger and duty. Such was the temper of men's minds, that while there were few to venture on so atrocious a treason, many wished it done, and all were ready to acquiesce.

29. Meanwhile the unconscious Galba, busy with his sacrifice, was importuning the gods of an empire that was now another's. A rumour reached him, that some senator unknown was being hurried into the camp; before long it was affirmed that this senator was Otho. At the same time came messengers from all parts of the city, where they had chanced to meet the procession, some exaggerating the danger, some, who could not even then forget to flatter, representing it as less than the reality. On deliberation it was determined to sound the feeling of the cohort on guard in the palace, but not through Galba in person, whose authority was to be kept unimpaired to meet greater emergencies. They were accordingly collected before the steps of the palace, and Piso addressed them as follows:—"Comrades, this is the sixth day since I became a Caesar by adoption, not knowing what was to happen, whether this title was to be desired, or dreaded. It rests with you to determine what will be the result to my family and to the state. It is not that I dread on my own account the gloomier issue; for I have known adversity, and I am learning at this very moment that prosperity is fully as dangerous. It is the lot of my father, of the Senate, of the Empire itself, that I deplore, if we have either to fall this day, or to do what is equally abhorrent to the good, to put others to death. In the late troubles we had this consolation, a capital unstained by bloodshed, and power transferred without strife. It was thought that by my adoption provision was made against the possibility of war, even after Galba's death.

30. "I will lay no claim to nobleness, or moderation, for indeed, to count up virtues in comparing oneself with Otho is needless. The vices, of which alone he boasts, overthrew the Empire, even when he was but the Emperor's friend. Shall he earn that Empire now by his manner and his gait, or by those womanish adornments? They are deceived, on whom luxury imposes by its false show of liberality; he will know how to squander, he will not know how to give. Already he is thinking of debaucheries, of

revels, of tribes of mistresses. These things he holds to be the prizes of princely power, things, in which the wanton enjoyment will be for him alone, the shame and the disgrace for all. Never yet has any one exercised for good ends the power obtained by crime. The unanimous will of mankind gave to Galba the title of Caesar, and you consented when he gave it to me. Were the Senate, the Country, the People, but empty names, yet, comrades, it is your interest that the most worthless of men should not create an Emperor. We have occasionally heard of legions mutinying against their generals, but your loyalty, your character, stand unimpeached up to this time. Even with Nero, it was he that deserted you, not you that deserted him. Shall less than thirty runaways and deserters whom no one would allow to choose a tribune or centurion for themselves, assign the Empire at their pleasure? Do you tolerate the precedent? Do you by your inaction make the crime your own? This lawless spirit will pass into the provinces, and though we shall suffer from this treason, you will suffer from the wars that will follow. Again, no more is offered you for murdering your prince, than you will have if you shun such guilt. We shall give you a donative for loyalty, as surely as others can give it for your treason."

31. The soldiers of the body-guard dispersed, but the rest of the cohort, who shewed no disrespect to the speaker, displayed their standards, acting, as often happens in a disturbance, on mere impulse and without any settled plan, rather than, as was afterwards believed, with treachery and an intention to deceive. Celsus Marius was sent to the picked troops from the army of Illyricum, then encamped in the Portico of Vipsanius. Instructions were also given to Amulius Serenus and Quintius Sabinus, centurions of the first rank, to bring up the German soldiers from the Hall of Liberty. No confidence was placed in the legion levied from the fleet, which had been enraged by the massacre of their comrades, whom Galba had slaughtered immediately on his entry into the capital.[1] Meanwhile Cetrius Severus, Subrius Dexter, and Pompeius Longinus, all three military tribunes, proceeded to the Praetorian camp, in the hope that a sedition, which was but just commencing, and not yet fully matured, might be swayed by better counsels. Two of the tribunes, Subrius and Cetrius, the soldiers assailed with menaces; Longinus they seized and disarmed; it was not his rank as an officer, but his friendship with Galba, that bound him to that Prince, and roused a stronger suspicion in the mutineers. The legion levied from the fleet joined the Praetorians without any hesitation. The Illyrian detachments drove Celsus away with a shower of javelins. The German veterans

1. When Galba reached Rome, he was met by irregular troops whom Nero had recruited for an expedition overseas, and who now demanded recognition as a permanent unit. Galba used force to quell the demonstration.

wavered long. Their frames were still enfeebled by sickness, and their minds were favourably disposed towards Galba, who, finding them exhausted by their long return voyage from Alexandria, whither they had been sent on by Nero, had supplied their wants with a most unsparing attention.

32. The whole populace and the slaves with them were now crowding the palace, clamouring with discordant shouts for the death of Otho and the destruction of the conspirators, just as if they were demanding some spectacle in the circus or amphitheatre. They had not indeed any discrimination or sincerity, for on that same day they would raise with equal zeal a wholly different cry. It was their traditional custom to flatter any ruler with reckless applause and meaningless zeal. Meanwhile two suggestions were keeping Galba in doubt. Titus Vinius thought that he should remain within the palace, array the slaves against the foe, secure the approaches, and not go out to the enraged soldiers. "You should," he said, "give the disaffected time to repent, the loyal time to unite. Crimes gain by hasty action, better counsels by delay. At all events, you will still have the same facilities of going out, if need be, whereas, your retreat, should you repent of having gone, will be in the power of another."

33. The rest were for speedy action, "before," they said, "the yet feeble treason of this handful of men can gather strength. Otho himself will be alarmed, Otho, who stole away to be introduced to a few strangers, but who now, thanks to the hesitation and inaction in which we waste our time, is learning how to play the Prince. We must not wait till, having arranged matters in the camp, he bursts into the Forum, and under Galba's very eyes makes his way to the Capitol, while our noble Emperor with his brave friends barricades the doors of his palace. We are to stand a siege forsooth, and truly we shall have an admirable resource in the slaves, if the unanimous feeling of this vast multitude, and that which can do so much, the first burst of indignation, be suffered to subside. Moreover that cannot be safe which is not honourable. If we must fall, let us go to meet the danger. This will bring more odium upon Otho, and will be more becoming to ourselves." Vinius opposing this advice, Laco assailed him with threats, encouraged by Icelus, who persisted in his private animosities to the public ruin.

34. Without further delay Galba sided with these more plausible advisers. Piso was sent on into the camp, as being a young man of noble name, whose popularity was of recent date, and who was a bitter enemy to Titus Vinius, that is, either he was so in reality, or these angry partisans would have it so, and belief in hatred is but too ready. Piso had hardly gone forth when there came a rumour, at first vague and wanting confirmation, that Otho had been slain in the camp; soon, as happens with these great

fictions, men asserted that they had been present, and had seen the deed; and, between the delight of some and the indifference of others, the report was easily believed. Many thought the rumour had been invented and circulated by the Othonianists, who were now mingling with the crowd, and who disseminated these false tidings of success to draw Galba out of the palace.

35. Upon this not only did the people and the ignorant rabble break out into applause and vehement expressions of zeal, but many of the Knights and Senators, losing their caution as they laid aside their fear, burst open the doors of the palace, rushed in, and displayed themselves to Galba, complaining that their revenge had been snatched from them. The most arrant coward, the man, who, as the event proved, would dare nothing in the moment of danger, was the most voluble and fierce of speech. No one knew anything, yet all were confident in assertion, till at length Galba in the dearth of all true intelligence, and overborne by the universal delusion, assumed his cuirass, and as, from age and bodily weakness, he could not stand up against the crowd that was still rushing in, he was elevated on a chair. He was met in the palace by Julius Atticus, a soldier of the bodyguard, who, displaying a bloody sword, cried "I have slain Otho." "Comrade," replied Galba, "who gave the order?" So singularly resolute was his spirit in curbing the license of the soldiery; threats did not dismay him, nor flatteries seduce.

36. There was now no doubt about the feeling of all the troops in the camp. So great was their zeal, that, not content with surrounding Otho with their persons in close array, they elevated him to the pedestal, on which a short time before had stood the gilt statue of Galba, and there, amid the standards, encircled him with their colours. Neither tribunes nor centurions could approach. The common soldiers even insisted that all the officers should be watched. Everything was in an uproar with their tumultuous cries and their appeals to each other, which were not, like those of a popular assembly or a mob, the discordant expressions of an idle flattery; on the contrary, as soon as they caught sight of any of the soldiers who were flocking in, they seized him, gave him the military embrace, placed him close to Otho, dictated to him the oath of allegiance, commending sometimes the Emperor to his soldiers, sometimes the soldiers to their Emperor. Otho did not fail to play his part; he stretched out his arms, and bowed to the crowd, and kissed his hands, and altogether acted the slave, to make himself the master. It was when the whole legion from the fleet had taken the oath to him, that feeling confidence in his strength, and thinking that the men, on whose individual feeling he had been working, should be roused by a general appeal, he stood before the rampart of the camp, and spoke as follows:

37. "Comrades, I cannot say in what character I have presented myself to you; I refuse to call myself a subject, now that you have named me Prince, or Prince, while another reigns. Your title also will be equally uncertain, so long as it shall be a question, whether it is the Emperor of the Roman people, or a public enemy, whom you have in your camp. Mark you, how in one breath they cry for my punishment and for your execution. So evident it is, that we can neither perish, nor be saved, except together. Perhaps, with his usual clemency, Galba has already promised that we should die, like the man, who, though no one demanded it, massacred so many thousands of perfectly guiltless soldiers. A shudder comes over my soul, whenever I call to mind that ghastly entry, Galba's solitary victory, when, before the eyes of the capital he gave orders to decimate the prisoners, the suppliants, whom he had admitted to surrender. These were the auspices with which he entered the city. What is the glory that he has brought to the throne? None but that he has murdered Obultronius Sabinus and Cornelius Marcellus in Spain, Betuus Chilo in Gaul, Fonteius Capito in Germany, Clodius Macer in Africa, Cingonius on the high road, Turpilianus in the city, Nymphidius in the camp. What province, what camp in the world, but is stained with blood and foul with crime, or, as he expresses it himself, purified and chastened? For what others call crimes he calls reforms, and, by similar misnomers, he speaks of strictness instead of barbarity, of economy instead of avarice, while the cruelties and affronts inflicted upon you he calls discipline. Seven months only have passed since Nero fell, and already Icelus has seized more than the Polycleti, the Vatinii, and the Elii amassed. Vinius would not have gone so far with his rapacity and lawlessness had he been Emperor himself; as it is, he has lorded it over us as if we had been his own subjects, has held us as cheap as if we had been another's. That one house would furnish the donative, which is never given you, but with which you are daily upbraided.

38. "Again, that we might have nothing to hope even from his successor, Galba fetches out of exile the man in whose ill-humour and avarice he considers that he has found the best resemblance to himself. You witnessed, comrades, how by a remarkable storm even the Gods discountenanced that ill-starred adoption; and the feeling of the Senate, of the people of Rome, is the same. It is to your valour that they look, in you these better counsels find all their support, without you, noble as they may be, they are powerless. It is not to war or to danger that I invite you; the swords of all Roman soldiers are with us. At this moment Galba has but one half-armed cohort, which is detaining, not defending him. Let it once behold you, let it receive my signal, and the only strife will be, who shall oblige me most. There is no room for delay in a business which can only be approved when it is done." He then ordered the armoury to be opened. The soldiers imme-

diately seized the arms without regard to rule or military order, no distinction being observed between Praetorians and legionaries, both of whom again indiscriminately assumed the shields and helmets of the auxiliary troops. No tribune or centurion encouraged them, every man acted on his own impulse and guidance, and the vilest found their chief incitement in the dejection of the good.

39. Meanwhile, appalled by the roar of the increasing sedition and by the shouts which reached the city, Piso had overtaken Galba, who in the interval had quitted the palace, and was approaching the Forum. Already Marius Celsus had brought back discouraging tidings. And now some advised that the Emperor should return to the palace, others that he should make for the Capitol, many again that he should occupy the Rostra, though most did but oppose the opinions of others, while, as ever happens in these ill-starred counsels, plans for which the opportunity had slipped away seemed the best. It is said that Laco, without Galba's knowledge, meditated the death of Vinius, either hoping by this execution to appease the fury of the soldiers, or believing him to be an accomplice of Otho, or, it may be, out of mere hatred. The time and the place however made him hesitate; he knew that a massacre once begun is not easily checked. His plan too was disconcerted by a succession of alarming tidings, and the desertion of immediate adherents. So languid was now the zeal of those who had at first been eager to display their fidelity and courage.

40. Galba was hurried to and fro with every movement of the surging crowd; the halls and temples all around were thronged with spectators of this mournful sight. Not a voice was heard from the people or even from the rabble. Everywhere were terror-stricken countenances, and ears turned to catch every sound. It was a scene neither of agitation nor of repose, but there reigned the silence of profound alarm and profound indignation. Otho however was told that they were arming the mob. He ordered his men to hurry on at full speed, and to anticipate the danger. Then did Roman soldiers rush forward like men who had to drive a Vologeses or Pacorus from the ancestral throne of the Arsacidae,[2] not as though they were hastening to murder their aged and defenceless Emperor. In all the terror of their arms, and at the full speed of their horses, they burst into the Forum, thrusting aside the crowd and trampling on the Senate. Neither the sight of the Capitol, nor the sanctity of the overhanging temples, nor the thought of rulers past or future, could deter them from committing a crime, which any one succeeding to power must avenge.

2. The Arsacidae were the ruling dynasty of Parthia, an empire which the Romans considered barbarous, despotic, and unstable.

41. When this armed array was seen to approach, the standard-bearer of the cohort that escorted Galba (he is said to have been one Atilius Vergilio) tore off and dashed upon the ground Galba's effigy. At this signal the feeling of all the troops declared itself plainly for Otho. The Forum was deserted by the flying populace. Weapons were pointed against all who hesitated. Near the Lake of Curtius, Galba was thrown out of his litter and fell to the ground, through the alarm of his bearers. His last words have been variously reported according as men hated or admired him. Some have said that he asked in a tone of entreaty what wrong he had done, and begged a few days for the payment of the donative. The more general account is, that he voluntarily offered his neck to the murderers, and bade them haste and strike, if it seemed to be for the good of the Commonwealth. To those who slew him it mattered not what he said. About the actual murderer nothing is clearly known. Some have recorded the name of Terentius, an enrolled pensioner, others that of Lecanius; but it is the current report that one Camurius, a soldier of the 15th legion, completely severed his throat by treading his sword down upon it. The rest of the soldiers foully mutilated his arms and legs, for his breast was protected, and in their savage ferocity inflicted many wounds even on the headless trunk.

42. They next fell on Titus Vinius; and in his case also it is not known whether the fear of instant death choked his utterance, or whether he cried out that Otho had not given orders to slay him. Either he invented this in his terror, or he thus confessed his share in the conspiracy. His life and character incline us rather to believe that he was an accomplice in the crime which he certainly caused. He fell in front of the temple of the Divine Julius, and at the first blow, which struck him on the back of the knee; immediately afterwards Julius Carus, a legionary, ran him through the body.

43. A noble example of manhood was on that day witnessed by our age in Sempronius Densus. He was a centurion in a cohort of the Praetorian Guard, and had been appointed by Galba to escort Piso. Rushing, dagger in hand, to meet the armed men, and upbraiding them with their crime, he drew the attention of the murderers on himself by his exclamations and gestures, and thus gave Piso, wounded as he was, an opportunity of escape. Piso made his way to the temple of Vesta, where he was admitted by the compassion of one of the public slaves, who concealed him in his chamber. There, not indeed through the sanctity of the place or its worship, but through the obscurity of his hiding-place, he obtained a respite from instant destruction, till there came, by Otho's direction and specially eager to slay him, Sulpicius Florus, of the British auxiliary infantry, to whom Galba had lately given the citizenship, and Statius Murcus, one of the body-guard. Piso was dragged out by these men and slaughtered in the entrance of the temple.

44. There was, we are told, no death of which Otho heard with greater joy, no head which he surveyed with so insatiable a gaze. Perhaps it was, that his mind was then for the first time relieved from all anxiety, and so had leisure to rejoice; perhaps there was with Galba something to recall departed majesty, with Vinius some thought of old friendship, which troubled with mournful images even that ruthless heart; Piso's death, as that of an enemy and a rival, he felt to be a right and lawful subject of rejoicing. The heads were fixed upon poles and carried about among the standards of the cohorts, close to the eagle of the legion, while those who had struck the blow, those who had been present, those who whether truly or falsely boasted of the act, as of some great and memorable achievement, vied in displaying their bloodstained hands. Vitellius afterwards found more than 120 memorials from persons who claimed a reward for some notable service on that day. All these persons he ordered to be sought out and slain, not to honour Galba, but to comply with the traditional policy of rulers, who thus provide protection for the present and vengeance for the future.

45. One would have thought it a different Senate, a different people. All rushed to the camp, outran those who were close to them, and struggled with those who were before, inveighed against Galba, praised the wisdom of the soldiers, covered the hand of Otho with kisses; the more insincere their demonstrations, the more they multiplied them. Nor did Otho repulse the advances of individuals, while he checked the greed and ferocity of the soldiers by word and look. They demanded that Marius Celsus, consul elect, Galba's faithful friend to the very last moment, should be led to execution, loathing his energy and integrity as if they were vices. It was evident that they were seeking to begin massacre and plunder, and the proscription of all the most virtuous citizens, and Otho had not yet sufficient authority to prevent crime, though he could command it. He feigned anger, and ordered him to be loaded with chains, declaring that he was to suffer more signal punishment, and thus he rescued him from immediate destruction.

46. Every thing was then ordered according to the will of the soldiery. The Praetorians chose their own prefects. One was Plotius Firmus, who had once been in the ranks, had afterwards commanded the watch, and who, while Galba was yet alive, had embraced the cause of Otho. With him was associated Licinius Proculus, Otho's intimate friend, and consequently suspected of having encouraged his schemes. Flavius Sabinus they appointed prefect of the city, thus adopting Nero's choice, in whose reign he had held the same office, though many in choosing him had an eye to his brother Vespasian. A demand was then made, that the fees for furloughs usually paid to the centurions should be abolished. These the common soldiers paid as a kind of annual tribute. A fourth part of every company

might be scattered on furlough, or even loiter about the camp, provided that they paid the fees to the centurions. No one cared about the amount of the tax, or the way in which it was raised. It was by robbery, plunder, or the most servile occupations that the soldiers' holiday was purchased. The man with the fullest purse was worn out with toil and cruel usage till he bought his furlough. His means exhausted by this outlay, and his energies utterly relaxed by idleness, the once rich and vigorous soldier returned to his company a poor and spiritless man. One after another was ruined by the same poverty and license, and rushed into mutiny and dissension, and finally into civil war. Otho, however, not to alienate the affections of the centurions by an act of bounty to the ranks, promised that his own purse should pay these annual sums. It was undoubtedly a salutary reform, and was afterwards under good emperors established as a permanent rule of the service. Laco, prefect of the city, who had been ostensibly banished to an island, was assassinated by an enrolled pensioner, sent on by Otho to do the deed. Martianus Icelus, being but a freedman, was publicly executed.

47. A day spent in crime found its last horror in the rejoicings that concluded it. The Praetor of the city summoned the Senate; the rest of the Magistrates vied with each other in their flatteries. The Senators hastily assembled and conferred by decree upon Otho the tribunician office, the name of Augustus, and every imperial honour. All strove to extinguish the remembrance of those taunts and invectives, which had been thrown out at random, and which no one supposed were rankling in his heart. Whether he had forgotten, or only postponed his resentment, the shortness of his reign left undecided. The Forum yet streamed with blood, when he was borne in a litter over heaps of dead to the Capitol, and thence to the palace. He suffered the bodies to be given up for burial, and to be burnt. For Piso, the last rites were performed by his wife Verania and his brother Scribonianus; for Vinius, by his daughter Crispina, their heads having been discovered and purchased from the murderers, who had reserved them for sale.

48. Piso, who was then completing his thirty-first year, had enjoyed more fame than good fortune. His brothers, Magnus and Crassus, had been put to death by Claudius and Nero respectively. He was himself for many years an exile, for four days a Caesar, and Galba's hurried adoption of him only gave him this privilege over his elder brother, that he perished first. Vinius had lived to the age of fifty-seven, with many changes of character. His father was of a praetorian family, his maternal grandfather was one of the proscribed. He had disgraced himself in his first campaign when he served under the legate Calvisius Sabinus. That officer's wife, urged by a perverse curiosity to view the camp, entered it by night in the disguise of a soldier, and after extending the insulting frolic to the watches and the gen-

eral arrangements of the army, actually dared to commit the act of adultery in the head-quarters. Vinius was charged with having participated in her guilt, and by order of Gaius was loaded with irons. The altered times soon restored him to liberty. He then enjoyed an uninterrupted succession of honours, first filling the praetorship, and then commanding a legion with general satisfaction, but he subsequently incurred the degrading imputation of having pilfered a gold cup at the table of Claudius, who the next day directed that he alone should be served on earthenware. Yet as proconsul of Gallia Narbonensis he administered the government with strict integrity. When forced by his friendship with Galba to a dangerous elevation, he shewed himself bold, crafty, and enterprising; and whether he applied his powers to vice or virtue, was always equally energetic. His will was made void by his vast wealth; that of Piso owed its validity to his poverty.

49. The body of Galba lay for a long time neglected, and subjected, through the license which the darkness permitted, to a thousand indignities, till Argius his steward, who had been one of his slaves, gave it a humble burial in his master's private gardens. His head, which the sutlers and camp-followers had fixed on a pole and mangled, was found only the next day in front of the tomb of Patrobius, a freedman of Nero's, whom Galba had executed. It was put with the body, which had by that time been reduced to ashes. Such was the end of Servius Galba, who in his seventy-three years had lived prosperously through the reigns of five Emperors, and had been more fortunate under the rule of others than he was in his own. His family could boast an ancient nobility, his wealth was great. His character was of an average kind, rather free from vices, than distinguished by virtues. He was not regardless of fame, nor yet vainly fond of it. Other men's money he did not covet, with his own he was parsimonious, with that of the State avaricious. To his freedmen and friends he shewed a forbearance, which, when he had fallen into worthy hands, could not be blamed; when, however, these persons were worthless, he was even culpably blind. The nobility of his birth and the perils of the times made what was really indolence pass for wisdom. While in the vigour of life, he enjoyed a high military reputation in Germany; as proconsul he ruled Africa with moderation, and when advanced in years shewed the same integrity in Eastern Spain. He seemed greater than a subject while he was yet in a subject's rank, and by common consent would have been pronounced equal to empire, had he never been emperor.

50. The alarm of the capital, which trembled to see the atrocity of these recent crimes, and to think of the old character of Otho, was heightened into terror by fresh news about Vitellius, news which had been suppressed before the murder of Galba, in order to make it appear that only the army of Upper Germany had revolted. That two men, who for shamelessness, indolence, and profligacy, were the most worthless of mortals, had been

selected, it would seem, by some fatality to ruin the Empire, became the open complaint, not only of the Senate and the Knights, who had some stake and interest in the country, but even of the common people. It was no longer to the late horrors of a dreadful peace, but to the recollections of the civil wars, that men recurred, speaking of how the capital had been taken by Roman armies, how Italy had been wasted and the provinces spoiled, of Pharsalia, Philippi, Perusia, and Mutina, and all the familiar names of great public disasters. "The world," they said, "was well-nigh turned upside down when the struggle for empire was between worthy competitors, yet the Empire continued to exist after the victories of Gaius Julius and Caesar Augustus; the Republic would have continued to exist under Pompey and Brutus. And is it for Otho or for Vitellius that we are now to repair to the temples? Prayers for either would be impious, vows for either a blasphemy, when from their conflict you can only learn that the conqueror must be the worse of the two." Some were speculating on Vespasian and the armies of the East. Vespasian was indeed preferable to either, yet they shuddered at the idea of another war, of other massacres. Even about Vespasian there were doubtful rumours, and he, unlike any of his predecessors, was changed for the better by power.

12. Pliny the Younger, *Panegyric to Trajan* (Selections)

Gaius Plinius Caecilius Secundus, or Pliny the Younger, lived from approximately A.D. 61 to 112. He was one of the wealthiest private persons in the empire, with extensive property in Rome and in the north Italian countryside where his family originated. He was an accomplished and prolific writer, and many of his letters have survived. He had a distinguished legal career during which he held many public posts, including that of praetor (a type of judge) in A.D. 93 or 95, administrator of various public treasuries at Rome, and governor of the rich province of Bithynia in Asia Minor during about 110–12.

In A.D. 100 he received the highest honor open to a private person, the consulship. The speech which follows is an expanded version of the one that he actually delivered in the senate on the assumption of that office. His purpose is to thank and praise the emperor Trajan (A.D. 98–117), through whose support he obtained the consulate. He alludes to the tyrannical reign of the assassinated Emperor Domitian (A.D. 81–96), which he contrasts unfavorably with the benefits and promise of that of Trajan. Despite its panegyrical character, this speech reveals something of what

From *Plinius Secundus: Letters and Panegyricus*, vol. 2, translated by Betty Radice (Cambridge, Mass.: Harvard University Press, 1959), pp. 323–35, 351–55, 369–77, 427–29, 475–85, 511, 517–19, 543–47 (odd-numbered pages). Reprinted by permission of the publishers and the Loeb Classical Library.

the Roman upper class expected of an emperor, what they admired in Trajan, and what they thought about their past as well as about their contemporary senate.

---

1. Our ancestors in their wisdom, Conscript Fathers, laid down the excellent rule that a speech no less than a course of action should take its start from prayers: thinking that nothing could be properly and prudently begun by mortal men without the aid and counsel of the immortal gods and the honour due to them. Who should duly observe this custom if not the consul? And what occasion could be more appropriate for doing so than the day when by the Senate's command we are called on to express thanks in the name of our country to the best of emperors? For what gift of the gods could be greater and more glorious than a prince whose purity and virtue make him their own equal? If it were still in doubt whether the rulers of the earth were given us by the hazards of chance or by some heavenly power, it would be evident that our emperor at least was divinely chosen for his task; for it was no blind act of fate but Jupiter himself who chose and revealed him in the sight and hearing of us all, among the many altars of the Capitol, in the very place where the god makes his presence as clearly felt as in the heavens and stars. Wherefore, mighty Jupiter, once the founder and now the preserver of our realm, it is my right and proper duty to address my prayers to you: grant, I pray you, that my speech prove worthy of consul, Senate and prince, that independence, truth, and sincerity mark my every word, and my vote of thanks be as far removed from a semblance of flattery as it is from constraint.

2. It is my view that not only the consul but every citizen alike should endeavour to say nothing about our ruler which could have been said of any of his predecessors. Away, then, with expressions formerly prompted by fear: I will have none of them. The sufferings of the past are over: let us then have done with the words which belong to them. An open tribute to our Emperor demands a new form, now that the wording of our private talk has changed. Times are different, and our speeches must show this; from the very nature of our thanks both the recipient and the occasion must be made clear to all. Nowhere should we flatter him as a divinity and a god; we are talking of a fellow-citizen, not a tyrant, one who is our father not our over-lord. He is one of us—and his special virtue lies in his thinking so, as also in his never forgetting that he is a man himself while a ruler of men. Let us then appreciate our good fortune and prove our worth by our use of it, and at the same time remember that there can be no merit if greater deference is paid to rulers who delight in the servitude of their subjects than to those who value their liberty. The people must have their own

ways of distinguishing between their rulers. They all give the same acclamation now to one for his valour as another had a short time ago for his good looks, and the cries which greeted the voice and attitudes of one of his predecessors now serve to praise their present emperor's devotion to duty, his clemency and restraint. What about us? Is it the divine nature of our prince or his humanity, his moderation and his courtesy which joy and affection prompt us to celebrate in a single voice? Surely nothing could reveal him as citizen and senator more appropriately than the title bestowed on him of *Optimus*, Best, one which by contrast with the insolence of some of his predecessors he can claim as his individual right. One and all and all alike we acclaim his good fortune, and with it our own, and beg him to "continue thus" or again, "to hear our prayers," as if forming our requests in the sure knowledge that he will grant these. For his part, he listens with tears in his eyes, and his blushes show his awareness that he is addressed not as the holder of his title of prince but as himself.

3. This moderation, then, which we have all maintained in the sudden surge of our affection, we must individually try to keep in our more studied tributes, remembering that there is no more sincere nor welcome kind of thanks than that which most resembles the spontaneous acclamation which has no time for artifice. For my own part, I shall strive to make my speech conform with the modesty and moderation of my prince, and while paying due tribute to his merits shall remind myself of what his ears can endure to hear. And indeed it does him honour of no ordinary kind if in thanking him my fears are not that he will think I say too little in his praise but that I say too much. This is my sole anxiety, the only difficulty in my path; for it is easy, Conscript Fathers, to render thanks where they are due. There is no danger that in my references to his humanity he will see a reproach for arrogance; that he will suppose I mean extravagance by modest expenditure, and cruelty by forbearance; that I think him covetous and capricious when I call him generous and kind, profligate and idle instead of self-controlled and active, or that I judge him a coward when I speak of him as a brave man. I do not even fear that my gratitude or lack of it will be judged in accordance with the adequacy of my words, for I have noted that the gods themselves delight in the innocence and purity of their worshippers rather than in the elaborate preparation of the prayers they offer, and prefer the man who brings a chaste and sinless heart to their shrines to one who comes with a studied invocation.

4\. . . . I often used to wonder, Conscript Fathers, what great gifts should be proper to the man whose word or gesture of command could rule land and sea and determine peace or war; but when I tried to picture to myself a ruler worthy of power equalling that of the immortal gods, even in my fondest hopes I never conceived the like of him whom we see before us today. One man may have shone in war, but his glory has grown dim in time of peace, while another has distinguished himself in civil life but not in arms. Some have won respect through men's fear, while others in courting popularity have sunk low. Sometimes the honour gained at home has been thrown away outside it, while at others a public reputation has been lost in private life. In fact there has been no one up till now whose virtues have remained unsullied by the close proximity of his faults. Contrast our prince, in whose person all the merits which win our admiration are found in complete and happy harmony! His essential seriousness and authority lose nothing through his candour and good humour; he can show humanity but remain a sovereign power. In addition, his splendid bearing and tall stature, his fine head and noble countenance, to say nothing of the firm strength of his maturity and the premature signs of advancing age with which the gods have seen fit to mark his hair and so enhance his look of majesty—are these not sufficient signs to proclaim him far and wide for what he is: our prince?

5. And rightly so: for he was not created for us by civil wars and a country racked by the arms of battle, but in peace, through adoption, by heavenly powers in our lands at long last moved by prayer. How could any man-made emperor ever be permitted to rank equal with the chosen of the gods? Indeed, their choice of you, Caesar Augustus, and their divine favour were made manifest at the very moment of your setting out to join your army by an omen without precedent. The names of all your predecessors were revealed to those who sought the oracles either by a gush of blood from the victims or a flight of birds on the left; but in your case, as you mounted the Capitol, following due precedent, the citizens gathered there for other reasons hailed you with a shout as if you were already emperor: for when the doors of the temple opened for your entry, the entire crowd assembled at the threshold cried *Imperator*! At the time it was thought that they were addressing Jupiter, but events have proved that the title was intended for you, and the omen was thus interpreted by all. You alone were unwilling to accept it, for you were reluctant to assume imperial power, a sure sign that you would use it well. So then you had to be pressed. Even then you could only be persuaded because you saw your country in peril and the whole realm tottering to a fall; for you were resolved only to take up the burden of supreme power when it was threatened with destruction. This, I fancy, explains the rioting and mutiny which had broken out in the army; it was to provide the widespread violence and terror which were needed to overcome your diffidence. Just as a period of calm in sky and sea is welcomed by contrast with storm and tempest, similarly, I think, that earlier season of unrest was designed to increase our appreciation of the peace we owe to you. Such are the vicissitudes of our mortal lot: misfortune is born of prosperity, and good fortune of ill-luck. God conceals their

origins in both cases, and the causes of good and evil are hidden for the most part, each behind the other's mask. . . .

12. Now once more terror is in their midst; our enemies are afraid, and crave permission to obey commands. They see that Rome has a leader who ranks with her heroes of old, whose title of *Imperator* was on seas stained with the bloodshed of victory and on battlefields piled high with the bodies of the dead. Today, therefore, we are receiving hostages, not paying for them; huge losses and vast sums of money are no longer needed to buy terms of peace which shall name us as the conquerors. The prayers and entreaties are on the other side, for us to grant or refuse at will, so long as we promise our country's sovereign power. They show their gratitude when we will listen, but if we are deaf to their pleas, dare not complain—how could they, when they know how you encamped confronting a dangerous enemy at the very time which was best for them and least favourable to us: when the Danube is bridged by ice from bank to bank and can carry vast preparations for war across its frozen surface, so that its savage peoples can enjoy the double protection of their own arms and the winter weather of their native climate? Once you were on the spot, the seasons might have been reversed; the enemy were stopped up inside their lairs, while our armies were eager to cross the river and, if you permitted, adopt the enemy's tactics and launch a winter campaign on them unprovoked.

13. Thus your enemies bowed before your reputation. What shall I say now of the admiration which you won from your own men? They saw how you shared their hunger and thirst on field manoeuvres and how their commander's sweat and dust was mingled with their own; with nothing to mark you out save your height and physique, in open battle you launched your spears at close quarters or received those aimed at you; you delighted in the courage of your soldiers and rejoiced whenever a heavier blow struck you on shield or helmet, praising your assailants and urging them on to greater deeds of daring—which they at once performed. Nothing escaped your direction or your observant eye; it was you who assigned the men their arms before the start of operations, and tested the spears so that when one seemed too heavy for a man you could wield it yourself. Again, it was you who comforted the weary and attended to the sick, for it was your habit to inspect your comrades' tents before you retired to your own; the last man must go off duty before you would take a rest yourself. Such were the great generals of the past, bred in the homes of Fabricius, Scipio, and Camillus; if they have a lesser claim upon my admiration it is because in their day a man could be inspired by keen rivalry with his betters. But now that interest in arms is displayed in spectacle instead of personal skill, and has become an amusement instead of a discipline, when exercises are no longer directed by a veteran crowned by the mural or civic crown, but by some petty Greek trainer, it is good to find one single man to delight in the tradi-

tions and the valour of our fathers, who can strive with none but himself for rival, press on with only his own example before him, and since he is to wield authority alone, will prove that he alone is worthy! . . .

16. But nurtured though you were on the glories of war, you have remained a lover of peace, and for this your moderation commands our greater praise. Your own father had been granted triumphal honours, and on the day of your adoption laurels were dedicated to Capitoline Jupiter, but you did not seek opportunity for triumphs of your own. You have neither fear of war, nor any desire to cause one. How magnificent it was, august Emperor, to stand on the Danube's bank knowing that a triumph was certain did you but cross, and yet have no urge to press on against a foe who refused battle, proof alike of valour and of moderation, the one denying battle to the enemy wanting it, the other denying battle to yourself. And so the day will come when the Capitol shall see no masquerade of triumph, the chariots and sham trappings of false victory, but an emperor coming home with true and genuine honour, bringing peace and the end of strife, and the submission of his enemies so evident that none shall be left to conquer. Here is an achievement which is nobler than any triumph! For hitherto our victories have been won only after our sovereignty has been slighted; but now, if some native king shall presume so far in his folly as to call down your just wrath and indignation on his head, though he be defended by the seas between, the mighty rivers or sheer mountains, he will surely find that all these barriers yield and fall away before your prowess, and will fancy that the mountains have subsided, the rivers dried up and the sea drained off, while his country falls a victim not only to our fleets but to the natural forces of the earth! . . .

21. Although your many outstanding merits surely called for you to assume some new title and honour, you refused the title of Father of your country, and it was only after a prolonged struggle between us and your modesty that in the end you were persuaded. Others accepted that title from the start along with that of Emperor and Caesar, on the first day of their principate, but you waved it away until even in your own grudging estimate of your services, you had to admit it was your due. Thus you alone have been Father of the country in fact before you were in name. In our hearts, in our minds we knew you as this; the title made no difference to the devotion of your people, except for our feeling of ingratitude if we addressed you only as Emperor and Caesar when we felt we had a Father in you. And now that you bear the name, how kind and considerate you show yourself, living with your subjects as a father with his children! You left us as an ordinary citizen, you return as emperor, knowing your subjects as you are known to them; in your thoughts we have not changed, nor in ours have you; you are one among us all, the greatest of us simply because you are the best.

22. Now first of all, think of the day when you entered your city, so long awaited and so much desired! The very method of your entry won delight and surprise, for your predecessors chose to be borne, or carried in, not satisfied even to be drawn by four white horses in a triumphal carriage, but lifted up on human shoulders in their overbearing pride. You towered above us only because of your own splendid physique; your triumph did not rest on our humiliation, won as it was over imperial arrogance. Thus neither age, health nor sex held your subjects back from feasting their eyes on this unexpected sight: small children learned who you were, young people pointed you out, old men admired: even the sick disregarded their doctors' orders and dragged themselves out for a glimpse of you as if this could restore their health. There were some who cried that they had lived long enough now they had seen and welcomed you, others that this was a reason for longer life. Women rejoiced as never before to bear children now that they knew they had brought forth citizens and soldiers to live and serve under your rule and command. Roofs could be seen sagging under the crowds they bore, not a vacant inch of ground was visible except under a foot poised to step, streets were packed on both sides leaving only a narrow passage for you, on every side the excited populace, cheers and rejoicing everywhere. All felt the same joy at your coming, when you were coming to be the same for all, joy which could still grow as you moved forward, and (one might say) swell with every step.

23. There was general delight when you embraced the members of the Senate, as they had embraced you when you went away, when you singled out the leading knights for the honour of being greeted by name without an official intermediary, when you not only took the first step in greeting your clients but added some touches of friendliness, and still greater delight when you moved slowly and quietly forward where the crowds of spectators fell back, letting yourself be jostled as one of the people, though in fact the crowds pressed thickest where you were. On that very first day you made yourself accessible to all, for no party of satellites attended you; you moved in the midst of the elite of the senators or knights, as the numbers of either party prevailed as they gathered round you, and your lictors quietly and courteously cleared your path. As for the soldiers present, they differed from the civilians in neither dress, propriety, nor discipline. But when you proceeded to mount the Capitol, how gladly everyone remembered your adoption, and what special joy it was for those who had first hailed you as *Imperator* in that very place! But the greatest pleasure of all, I fancy, was that of the god who was your father in his own creation. Above all, as you trod in the same steps as your father when he prepared to reveal the mighty secret of the gods, how the crowd rejoiced with fresh outbursts of cheering, as this day recalled that other which had brought it into being! Everywhere there were altars, but still not enough for their victims; every-

one's prayers were for your safety alone, since each man knew they would be answered for himself and his children if they were granted for you. Then you walked to the palace, with the same modest demeanour as if it had been a private house, and everyone returned home to repeat the sincere expression of a happiness which was wholly spontaneous.

24. Such an entry would have overwhelmed another; but you became daily more admirable, more perfect, such a prince in fact as others can only promise to be. You alone have gained and grown in reputation through passage of time, for you have two extremes combined and blended in your person, a beginner's modesty and the assurance of one long accustomed to command. You do not direct your subjects to grovel at your feet, returning a kiss with no more than a proffered hand; your lips keep their old courtesy now you are emperor, your hand respects its proper use. You used to go on foot before, you still do now; you delighted in hard work, and still delight; though fortune has changed all around you, she changed nothing in yourself. When the prince moves among his subjects they are free to stand still or approach him, to accompany him or pass ahead, for you do not walk in our midst to confer a benefit by your presence, nor put us in your debt if we enjoy your company. Anyone who approaches you can stay at your side, and conversation lasts till it is ended by his discretion, not by any loftiness of yours. We are ruled by you and subject to you, but no more than we are to the laws, for these too must regulate our desires and passions, always with us and among us. You shine out in splendour like Honour, like Sovereignty, for these are always above mortal men and yet inseparable from them. Previous rulers in their scorn for us, and, it may be, through fear of being brought down to our level, had lost the use of their legs; carried on the shoulders and bowed backs of slaves they rose above our heads. But you are borne aloft by your own renown and glory, by freedom and your subjects' love, far above those self-same rulers; you are lifted to the heavens by the very ground we all tread, where your imperial footsteps are mingled with our own. . . .

44. What an advantage it is to have attained success through adversity! You shared our lives, our dangers, our fears, the common lot at that time of all innocent men. You know from experience how bad rulers come to be hated even by those who have corrupted them. You can remember how you joined in our prayers and protests—witness the fact that your sentiments have remained those of a citizen since you became prince, while your merits have proved greater than anything you could have hoped for in another. You have inspired us not to be satisfied with less than perfection in our ruler, whereas hitherto we prayed only for someone who would prove better than the worst. Consequently everyone knows you—and himself—too well to covet your position after you; a willing successor might even be harder to find than a capable one, for who would voluntarily shoulder your

burden of responsibility or readily stand comparison with you? Experience has taught you how difficult it is to succeed a good emperor—and you could plead the fact of your adoption. No one could imagine it easy for any comer to repeat a situation where no one need purchase security by disgrace, where everyone's life is safe and safe with honour, where foresight and prudence no longer prompt men to spend a lifetime keeping out of sight. The rewards of virtue are now the same under an emperor as they were in times of liberty, and good deeds win more solid recognition than the mere consciousness of having performed them. You value enterprise in your subjects, you foster and encourage signs of character and spirit, instead of forcing them into subjection as your predecessors did. People find that honesty pays, now that they are convinced that it does them no harm—indeed, it brings them honours, priesthoods, provinces from your hands, and they flourish in your friendship and favour. This payment for application and integrity spurs on others like them, while encouraging men of different character to mend their ways; for it is the rewards for vice and virtue which make men bad or good. Not many people have a strong enough character to pursue or shun good or evil with no thought of advantage; for the rest, when they see the reward for effort, activity and thrift going to idleness, torpor and extravagance, set about gaining similar advantages by the same devices as they see others use. Their one wish is to resemble such men, be one of them, until their wishing makes them so.

45. Previous emperors, with the exception of your father and one or two more (and that is saying too much), did in fact take more pleasure in the vices of their subjects than in their virtues, first because everyone likes a man after his own heart, then because they supposed that slavery would be more acceptable to people unfitted to be anything but slaves. Such men gathered up all the favours, open-armed; while honest citizens who were forced to bury themselves in retirement were neglected and only saw the light of day at their trials for treason. By contrast, you choose your friends from the best of your subjects, and quite rightly, the affection of a good prince lit on the very men most hated by a bad one. Tyranny and the principate are diametrically opposed; knowing this, you realize how a true prince is most welcome to those who can least endure a tyrant. These then are the men you promote and show as a typical example of the way of life and kind of man you prefer; and if you have not yet assumed the censorship and superintendence of our morals, it is because you would rather test our character by benefits than correctives. Besides, I fancy that a ruler may do more for the morals of his country by permitting good conduct than by compelling it. We are easily led wherever he takes us, following (as it were) in his steps; now we see before us one whose affection and approval we all seek to win, in a way those unlike him can never hope to do; so that by the firmness of our allegiance we are reaching the point when we shall all con-

form with the ways of a single man. (We are surely not so wrong-headed that we can only copy a bad ruler and not a good one.) You need only continue as you are, Caesar, and the principles of your conduct will have the same effective power as a censorship. Indeed, an emperor's life *is* a censorship, and a true perpetual one; this is what guides and directs us, for example is what we need more than command. Fear is unreliable as a teacher of morals. Men learn better from examples, which have the great merit of proving that their advice is practicable. . . .

47. As for the lives and characters of the young—how you are forming them in true princely fashion! And the teachers of rhetoric and professors of philosophy—how you hold them in honour! Under you the liberal arts are restored, to breathe and live in their own country—the learning which the barbarity of the past punished with exile, when an emperor acquainted with all the vices sought to banish everything hostile to vice, motivated less by hatred for learning as by fear for its authority. But you embrace these very arts, opening arms, eyes and ears to them, a living example of their precepts, as much their lover as the subject of their regard. Every lover of culture must applaud all your actions, while reserving his highest praise for your readiness to give audiences. Your father had shown his magnanimity by giving the title of "open house" to what (before your time or his) had been a stronghold of tyranny—yet this would have been an empty formula had he not adopted a son capable of living in the public eye. Between your habits and that inscription there is perfect accord; every action of yours suggests you might have set it there yourself. No forum, no temple is so free of access: not even the Capitol and the very site of your adoption are more public and open to all. There are no obstacles, no grades of entry to cause humiliation, nor a thousand doors to be opened only to find still more obstacles barring the way. No, everything is peaceful before reaching you and on leaving you and above all, in your presence; such deep silence, such great reverence, that from the prince's house an example of calm and moderation returns to every humble hearth and modest home. . . .

65. In the Forum, too, you mounted the platform of your own accord and were equally scrupulous to submit yourself to the laws. No one had intended these laws to apply to the Emperor, Caesar, but you were unwilling for your privileges to extend beyond our own. The result is that we are all the more willing for them to do so. There is a new turn of phrase which I hear and understand for the first time—not "the prince is above the law" but "the law is above the prince"; Caesar bows to the same restrictions as any other consul. He takes the oath of obedience to the law with the gods as witness (for who if not Caesar can command their attention?)—he takes it under the watchful eye of those who must take it too, well aware that no one must be more scrupulous about keeping to his oath than the man most concerned that there should be no perjury.

Then, at the moment of laying down your consulship, you swore a similar oath that you had done nothing contrary to the law; and this, as a statement of achievement, was even finer than your earlier promise. To appear on the platform so often, to frequent a place shunned by the pride of princes, there to assume and there to lay down your offices: how this conduct becomes you, and how it contrasts with the conduct of those who took up a consulship for a day or two—or, rather, failed to take it up—only to issue a proclamation that they had flung it aside! That was what took the place of the assembly, the platform and their oath, doubtless to make their consulship end as it had begun, and to provide the only indication that they had been elected at all: namely, the absence of any other consul.

66. I have not left out our prince's consulship, Conscript Fathers, but I wanted all I had to say about oaths to be dealt with at once, for this is no barren, empty subject in which a single facet of his glory must be broken up into fragments and handled several times. The first day of your consulship had hardly dawned before you entered the Senate-house and exhorted us, individually and collectively, to resume our freedom, to take up the responsibilities of the power we might be thought to share, to watch over the interests of the people, and to take action. All your predecessors had said the same, but none had been believed. In our mind's eye were the shipwrecks of the many who had advanced in a hazardous period of calm, only to be sunk by an unforeseen storm; for no sea could be more treacherous than the flattery of those emperors whose instability and guile made it more difficult to be on guard against their favour than their wrath. But in your case, we have no fears, and are all eagerness to follow your lead. You bid us be free, and we shall be free; you tell us to express ourselves openly, and we shall do so, for our previous hesitation was due to no cowardice or natural inertia, but to fear and apprehension, and the lamentable caution born of our perils which bade us turn eyes and ears and minds from our country, from that republic which was utterly destroyed. Today we can place our trust and reliance on your promises and sworn oath, and open our lips long sealed by servitude, loosen our tongues which were bound to silence by so many evils: for you truly wish us to be what you bid us, and your exhortations are free from all overtones of deception. In short, no traps are laid today for the trustful, bringing their own dangers for those who set them—for no prince has ever been deceived unless he led the way in deception.

67. For my part, I believe I have formed this impression of the Father of us all as much from the manner of his delivery as from the words he has said. Only consider the seriousness of his sentiments, the unaffected candour of his words, the assurance in his voice and decision in his countenance, and the complete sincerity of his gaze, his pose and gestures, in fact of his entire person! So, we may be sure, he will always remember the

advice he gave us, and will always understand that in making use of the freedom he granted we are acting only in obedience to him. We need have no fears that he will think us improvident if we show no hesitation in profiting by the security of the times, since he remembers how differently we lived under a wicked emperor. We were accustomed to offering vows to ensure the eternity of the empire and the safety of the emperors, or, rather, the safety of the emperors and thereby the eternity of the empire. But in the case of our present emperor, it is worth noting the wording of these vows, and the clause "if he has ruled the State well and in the interests of all." Such vows are indeed worthy of being always renewed and always discharged. At your instigation, Caesar, the State has struck a bargain with the gods that they shall preserve your health and safety as long as you do the same for everyone else; otherwise they are to turn their attention from protecting your life, and to abandon you to such vows as are taken in secret. Others used to wish to outlive the State, and took steps to do so; but for you, the thought of personal safety is hateful unless it be bound up with the safety of us all. You permit no prayers on your behalf unless they benefit their authors, and every year you set the gods to reconsider you, insisting that they must revise their opinion if you have changed since the time of your election. But you act with full knowledge, Caesar, in your pact with the gods to preserve you if you deserve it; you are well aware that no one can judge this better than the gods themselves. Can you not imagine, Conscript Fathers, how his thoughts run, night and day: "I have put arms to be used against me, if public interest demands, in the hands of my own prefect; but when it comes to the gods, I will never seek to avert either their wrath or their indifference, rather will I beg and pray that my country shall never have to offer vows on my behalf against its will, or if it has already done so, that they shall not be binding."

68. Thus, Caesar, from your agreement with the gods you have a glorious reward in your continued safety. For by stipulating that the gods shall preserve you only "if you have ruled the State well and in the interests of all" you can be confident that you are ruling well, as long as they are preserving you. And so you can be carefree and happy all through that day which was fraught with fear and anxiety for the other emperors, who spent it racked by suspense, uncertain how far to try our patience, awaiting from all quarters the messages of our common servitude. And if perchance some of these were delayed by rivers, snow, or adverse winds, they jumped to the conclusion that they would get their just deserts. Their apprehensions were always the same; for a bad ruler fears anyone worthier than himself as a likely successor, so when all are worthier, all are feared. Your own tranquillity is not interrupted either by belated messages or slow delivery of letters; you can be sure that everywhere the oath is being taken for you, as

you have taken it for us all, for no one would deny himself this pleasure. The fact is, we love you as you deserve—but in our own self-interest rather than in yours. The day will never dawn when we offer vows on your behalf only from a sense of duty, with no benefit to ourselves. (There is no virtue in supporting a prince who can claim the credit for our support.) We may well complain that it is only the rulers we hate who violate our privacy, for if good and bad were equally inquisitive, what universal admiration for yourself you would find, what delight and rejoicing, what conversations you would hear everywhere between us and our wives and children, and even before the hearths and altars of our homes! You would then understand how we are sparing those sensitive ears of yours. But however different love and hatred may be, they have one close resemblance: we give our love more unrestrainedly to good princes in this very place where we have freely hated bad ones. . . .

80. Now let me turn to judicial matters, where you showed how strictness need not be cruel nor mercy weak. You did not mount the tribunal for the purpose of enriching your private exchequer, and the only reward you sought in passing sentence was the knowledge that justice had been done. Before you stood the litigants, concerned more for your opinion of them than for their fortunes, fearful of your judgement on their character rather than on their case. This is indeed the true care of a prince, or even that of a god, to settle rivalry between cities, to soothe the passions of angry peoples less by exercise of power than by reason: to intervene where there has been official injustice, to undo what should never have been done: finally, like a swift-moving star, to see all, hear all, and be present at once with aid wherever your help is sought. It is thus, I fancy, that the great Father of the universe rules all with a nod of the head, if he ever looks down on earth and deigns to consider mortal destinies among his divine affairs. Now he is rid of this part of his duties, free to devote himself to heaven's concerns, since he has given you to us to fill his role with regard to the entire human race. And you are filling it, worthy of his trust in you: since every passing day brings every advantage for us and the greatest glory for you. . . .

83. One of the chief features of high estate is that it permits no privacy, no concealment, and in the case of princes, it flings open the door not only to their homes but to their private apartments and deepest retreats; every secret is exposed and revealed to rumour's listening ear. But in your case, Caesar, nothing could better redound to your credit than a searching inspection of this kind. Your public conduct is indeed remarkable, but no less so your private life. Splendid though it is to keep yourself thus unspotted by any form of vice, it is even more so to do the same for the members of your family, for the more difficult it is to vouch for others rather than oneself, the more honour is due to you for combining your own excellence with

making all those around you reach the same high standard. Many distinguished men have been dishonoured by an ill-considered choice of a wife or weakness in not getting rid of her; thus their fame abroad was damaged by their loss of reputation at home, and their relative failure as husbands denied them complete success as citizens. But your own wife contributes to your honour and glory, as a supreme model of the ancient virtues; the Chief Pontiff himself, had he to take a wife, would choose her, or one like her—if one exists. From your position she claims nothing for herself but the pleasure it gives her, unswerving in her devotion not to your power but to yourself. You are just the same to each other as you have always been, and your mutual appreciation is unchanged; success has brought you nothing but a new understanding of your joint ability to live in its shadow. How modest she is in her attire, how unassuming when she walks abroad! This is the work of her husband who has fashioned and formed her habits; there is glory enough for a wife in obedience. When she sees her husband unaccompanied by pomp and intimidation, she also goes about in silence, and as far as her sex permits, she follows his example of walking on foot. This would win her praise even if you did the opposite, but with a husband so moderate in his habits, how much respect she owes him as his wife, and herself as a woman! . . .

94. To end my speech, I call on the gods, the guardians and defenders of our empire, speaking as consul on behalf of all humanity: and to you in particular, Capitoline Jupiter, I address my prayer that you shall continue your benefits, and augment the great gifts you have bestowed by making them perpetual. You heard our prayers under a bad prince; now give ear to our wishes on behalf of his opposite. We are not burdening you with vows—we do not pray for peace, concord, and serenity, nor for wealth and honours: our desire is simple, all-embracing, and unanimous: the safety of our prince. This is no new concern we ask of you, for it was you who took him under your protection when you snatched him from the jaws of that monster of rapacity; for at the time when all the peaks were tottering to their fall, no one could have stood high above them all and remained untouched except by your intervention. So he escaped the notice of the worst of emperors, though he could not remain unnoticed by the best. It was you too who gave him clear signs of your interest as he set out to join his army, when you yielded to him your own name and glory; and you who spoke your opinion through the voice of the Emperor, when you chose a son for him, a father for us, a Chief Pontiff for yourself. It is therefore with increased confidence, using the same form of vow that he asked to be made on his behalf, that I make this my earnest prayer: "If he rules the State well and in the interests of all," first preserve him for our grandsons and great-grandsons, then grant him one day a successor born of him and formed by

him in the image of the adopted son he is, or if fate denies him this, guide and direct his choice to someone worthy to be adopted in your temple on the Capitol.

95. To you, Conscript Fathers, my debt is great, and this is published in the official records. You it was who paid me tribute according to the best traditions, for my orderly conduct as tribune, my moderation as praetor, my integrity and determination in carrying out the requests you made of my professional services for the protection of our allies. More recently, you hailed my designation as future consul with such acclamation that I am well aware that I must redouble my efforts if I am to receive your continued approval, and retain and increase it day by day; I do not forget that the truest judgement on whether a man merits an office or not is passed at the moment of his assuming it. All I ask is your support in my present undertaking and your belief in what I say. If then it is true that I advanced in my career under that most treacherous of emperors before he admitted his hatred for honest men, but was halted in it once he did so, preferring a longer route when I saw what the short cuts were which opened the way to office; that in bad times I was one of those who lived with grief and fear, and can be counted among the serene and happy now that better days have come; that, finally, I love the best of princes as much as I was hated by the worst: then I shall act not as if I consider myself consul to day and ex-consul tomorrow, but as if I were still a candidate for the consulate, and in this way shall minister at all times to the reverence which is due to you all.

2
Rome and Its Subjects

13. Cicero, *Letter to Quintus* (2)

Marcus Tullius Cicero wrote this letter to his younger brother Quintus in December of 60 B.C. or early 59 B.C., just after the Roman senate had extended Quintus's term as governor of the rich Roman province of Asia (not the continent but part of westernmost Anatolia) for one more year. Although this province included some of the empire's richest lands and self-governing cities, it was virtually bankrupt because of the extortions of the tax farmers who bid for the right to collect taxes. Also burdensome were the demands of the aediles, who were responsible for the expensive games celebrated at Rome; they solicited "voluntary" contributions from provincials to reimburse themselves for their heavy expenses. Cicero used this letter to discuss the duties of and some of the challenges that confronted a Roman provincial governor.

I. Though I have no doubt that many messengers, and even common rumour, with its usual speed, will anticipate this letter, and that you will already have heard from others that a third year has been added to my loss and your labour, yet I thought you ought to receive from me also the news of this tiresome circumstance. For not in one, but in several of my previous letters, in spite of others having given up the idea in despair, I gave you hope of being able at an early date to quit your province, not only that I might as long as possible cheer you with a pleasurable belief, but also because I and the praetors took such pains in the matter, that I felt no misgiving as to the possibility of its being arranged. As it is, since matters have so turned out that neither the praetors by the weight of their influence, nor I by my earnest efforts, have been able to prevail, it is certainly difficult not

Ad Quintum fratrem 1.1. From *The Letters of Cicero*, vol. 1, translated by Evelyn S. Shuckburgh (London: George Bell & Sons, 1908), pp. 70–87.

to be annoyed; yet our minds, practised as they are in conducting and supporting business of the utmost gravity, ought not to be crushed or weakened by vexation. And since men ought to feel most vexed at what has been brought upon them by their own fault, it is I who ought in this matter to be more vexed than you. For it is the result of a fault on my part, against which you had protested both in conversation at the moment of your departure, and in letters since, that your successor was not named last year. In this, while consulting for the interests of our allies, and resisting the shameless conduct of some merchants, and while seeking the increase of our reputation by your virtues, I acted unwisely, especially as I made it possible for that second year to entail a third. And as I confess the mistake to have been mine, it lies with your wisdom and kindness to remedy it, and to see that my imprudence is turned to advantage by your careful performance of your duties. And truly, if you exert yourself in every direction to earn men's good word, not with a view to rival others, but henceforth to surpass yourself, if you rouse your whole mind and your every thought and care to the ambition of gaining a superior reputation in all respects, believe me, one year added to your labour will bring us, nay, our posterity also, a joy of many years' duration. Wherefore I begin by entreating you not to let your soul shrink and be cast down, nor to allow yourself to be overpowered by the magnitude of the business as though by a wave; but, on the contrary, to stand upright and keep your footing, or even advance to meet the flood of affairs. For you are not administering a department of the state, in which fortune reigns supreme, but one in which a well-considered policy and an attention to business are the most important things. But if I had seen you receiving the prolongation of a command in a great and dangerous war, I should have trembled in spirit, because I should have known that the dominion of fortune over us had been at the same time prolonged. As it is, however, a department of the state has been intrusted to you in which fortune occupies no part, or, at any rate, an insignificant one, and which appears to me to depend entirely on your virtue and self-control. We have no reason to fear, as far as I know, any designs of our enemies, any actual fighting in the field, any revolts of allies, any default in the tribute or in the supply of corn, any mutiny in the army: things which have very often befallen the wisest of men in such a way, that they have been no more able to get the better of the assault of fortune, than the best of pilots a violent tempest. You have been granted profound peace, a dead calm: yet if the pilot falls asleep, it may even so overwhelm him, though if he keeps awake it may give him positive pleasure. For your province consists, in the first place, of allies of a race which, of all the world, is the most civilized; and, in the second place, of citizens, who, either as being publicans [*publicani*, or tax collectors], are very closely connected with me, or, as being traders who have made money, think that they owe the security of their property to my consulship.

II. But it may be said that among even such men as these there occur serious disputes, many wrongful acts are committed, and hotly contested litigation is the result. As though I ever thought that you had no trouble to contend with! I know that the trouble is exceedingly great, and such as demands the very greatest prudence; but remember that it is prudence much more than fortune on which, in my opinion, the result of your trouble depends. For what trouble is it to govern those over whom you are set, if you do but govern yourself? That may be a great and difficult task to others, and indeed it is most difficult: to you it has always been the easiest thing in the world, and indeed ought to be so, for your natural disposition is such that, even without discipline, it appears capable of self-control; whereas a discipline has, in fact, been applied that might educate the most faulty of characters. But while you resist, as you do, money, pleasure, and every kind of desire yourself, there will, I am to be told, be a risk of your not being able to suppress some fraudulent banker or some rather over-extortionate tax-collector! For as to the Greeks, they will think, as they behold the innocence of your life, that one of the heroes of their history, or a demigod from heaven, has come down into the province. And this I say, not to induce you to act thus, but to make you glad that you are acting or have acted so. It is a splendid thing to have been three years in supreme power in Asia without allowing statue, picture, plate, napery, slave, anyone's good looks, or any offer of money—all of which are plentiful in your province—to cause you to swerve from the most absolute honesty and purity of life. What can be imagined so striking or so desirable as that a virtue, a command over the passions, a self-control such as yours, are not remaining in darkness and obscurity, but have been set in the broad daylight of Asia, before the eyes of a famous province, and in the hearing of all nations and peoples? That the inhabitants are not being ruined by your progresses, drained by your charges, agitated by your approach? That there is the liveliest joy, public and private, wheresoever you come, the city regarding you as a protector and not a tyrant, the private house as a guest and not a plunderer?

III. But in these matters I am sure that mere experience has by this time taught you that it is by no means sufficient to have these virtues yourself, but that you must keep your eyes open and vigilant, in order that in the guardianship of your province you may be considered to vouch to the allies, the citizens, and the state, not for yourself alone, but for all the subordinates of your government. However, you have in the persons of your legates [*legati*] men likely to have a regard for their own reputation. Of these in rank, position, and age Tubero is first; who, I think, particularly as he is a writer of history, could select from his own Annals many whom he would like and would be able to imitate. Allienus, again, is ours, as well in heart and affection, as in his conformity to our principles. I need not speak of Gratidius: I am sure that, while taking pains to preserve his own reputation, his fraternal affection for us makes him take pains for ours also. Your quaestor is not of your own selection, but the one assigned you by lot. He is bound both to act with propriety of his own accord, and to conform to the policy and principles which you lay down. But should any one of these adopt a lower standard of conduct, you should tolerate such behaviour, if it goes no farther than a breach, in his private capacity, of the rules by which he was bound, but not if it goes to the extent of employing for gain the authority which you granted him as a promotion. For I am far from thinking, especially since the moral sentiments of the day are so much inclined to excessive laxity and self-seeking, that you should investigate every case of petty misconduct, and thoroughly examine every one of these persons; but that you should regulate your confidence by the trustworthiness of its recipient. And among such persons you will have to vouch for those whom the Republic has itself given you as companions and assistants in public affairs, at least within the limits which I have before laid down.

IV. In the case, however, of those of your personal staff or official attendants whom you have yourself selected to be about you—who are usually spoken of as a kind of praetor's cohort—we must vouch, not only for their acts, but even for their words. But those you have with you are the sort of men of whom you may easily be fond when they are acting rightly, and whom you may very easily check when they shew insufficient regard for your reputation. By these, when you were raw to the work, your frank disposition might possibly have been deceived—for the better a man is the less easily does he suspect others of being bad—now, however, let this third year witness an integrity as perfect as the two former, but still more wary and vigilant. Listen to that only which you are supposed to listen to; don't let your ears be open to whispered falsehoods and interested suggestions. Don't let your signet ring be a mere implement, but, as it were, your second self: not the minister of another's will, but a witness of your own. Let your marshal hold the rank which our ancestors wished him to hold, who, looking upon this place as not one of profit, but of labour and duty, scarcely ever conferred it upon any but their freedmen, whom they indeed controlled almost as absolutely as their slaves.[1] Let the lictor be the dispenser of your clemency, not of his own; and let the fasces and axes which they carry before you constitute ensigns rather of rank than of power.[2] Let it, in fact, be known to the whole province that the life, children, fame, and

1. The marshal, or *accensus*, was the confidential secretary of the *propraetor*.

2. The lictors accompanied the governor, carrying the *fasces* (ceremonial rods) that were the symbol of his authority.

fortunes of all over whom you preside are exceedingly dear to you. Finally, let it be believed that you will, if you detect it, be hostile not only to those who have accepted a bribe, but to those also who have given it. And, indeed, no one will give anything, if it is made quite clear that nothing is usually obtained from you through those who pretend to be very influential with you. Not, however, that the object of this discourse is to make you over-harsh or suspicious towards your staff. For if any of them in the course of the last two years has never fallen under suspicion of rapacity, as I am told about Caesius and Chaerippus and Labeo—and think it true, because I know them—there is no authority, I think, which may not be intrusted to them, and no confidence which may not be placed in them with the utmost propriety, and in anyone else like them. But if there is anyone of whom you have already had reason to doubt, or concerning whom you have made some discovery, in such a man place no confidence, intrust him with no particle of your reputation.

V. If, however, you have found in the province itself anyone, hitherto unknown to us, who has made his way into intimacy with you, take care how much confidence you repose in him; not that there may not be many good provincials, but, though we may hope so, it is risky to be positive. For everyone's real character is covered by many wrappings of pretence and is concealed by a kind of veil: face, eyes, expression very often lie, speech most often of all. Wherefore, how can you expect to find in that class any who, while foregoing for the sake of money all from which we can scarcely tear ourselves away, will yet love you sincerely and not merely pretend to do so from interested motives? I think, indeed, it is a hard task to find such men, especially if we notice that the same persons care nothing for almost any man out of office, yet always with one consent shew affection for the praetors. But of this class, if by chance you have discovered any to be fonder of you—for it may so happen—than of your office, such a man indeed gladly admit upon your list of friends: but if you fail to perceive that, there is no class of people you must be more on your guard against admitting to intimacy, just because they are acquainted with all the ways of making money, do everything for the sake of it, and have no consideration for the reputation of a man with whom they are not destined to pass their lives. And even among the Greeks themselves you must be on your guard against admitting close intimacies, except in the case of the very few, if such are to be found, who are worthy of ancient Greece. As things now stand, indeed, too many of them are untrustworthy, false, and schooled by long servitude in the arts of extravagant adulation. My advice is that these men should all be entertained with courtesy, but that close ties of hospitality or friendship should only be formed with the best of them: excessive intimacies with them are not very trustworthy—for they do not venture to oppose our wishes—and they are not only jealous of our countrymen, but of their own as well.

VI. And now, considering the caution and care that I would shew in matters of this kind—in which I fear I may be somewhat over-severe—what do you suppose my sentiments are in regard to slaves? Upon these we ought to keep a hold in all places, but especially in the provinces. On this head many rules may be laid down, but this is at once the shortest and most easily maintained—that they should behave during your progresses in Asia as though you were travelling on the Appian way, and not suppose that it makes any difference whether they have arrived at Tralles or Formiae. But if, again, any one of your slaves is conspicuously trustworthy, employ him in your domestic and private affairs; but in affairs pertaining to your office as governor, or in any department of the state, do not let him lay a finger. For many things which may, with perfect propriety, be intrusted to slaves, must yet not be so intrusted, for the sake of avoiding talk and hostile remark. But my discourse, I know not how, has slipped into the didactic vein, though that is not what I proposed to myself originally. For what right have I to be laying down rules for one who, I am fully aware, in this subject especially, is not my inferior in wisdom, while in experience he is even my superior? Yet, after all, if your actions had the additional weight of my approval, I thought that they would seem more satisfactory to yourself. Wherefore, let these be the foundation on which your public character rests: first and foremost your own honesty and self-control, then the scrupulous conduct of all your staff, the exceedingly cautious and careful selection in regard to intimacies with provincials and Greeks, the strict and unbending government of your slaves. These are creditable even in the conduct of our private and everyday business: in such an important government, where morals are so debased and the province has such a corrupting influence, they must needs seem divine. Such principles and conduct on your part are sufficient to justify the strictness which you have displayed in some acts of administration, owing to which I have encountered certain personal disputes with great satisfaction, unless, indeed, you suppose me to be annoyed by the complaints of a fellow like Paconius—who is not even a Greek, but in reality a Mysian or Phrygian—or by the words of Tuscenius, a madman and a knave, from whose abominable jaws you snatched the fruits of a most infamous piece of extortion with the most complete justice.

VII. These and similar instances of your strict administration in your province we shall find difficulty in justifying, unless they are accompanied by the most perfect integrity: wherefore let there be the greatest strictness in your administration of justice, provided only that it is never varied from favour, but is kept up with impartiality. But it is of little avail that justice is administered by yourself with impartiality and care, unless the same is done by those to whom you have intrusted any portion of this duty. And, indeed, in my view there is no very great variety of business in the government of Asia: the entire province mainly depends on the administration of justice. In it we have the whole theory of government, especially of provincial government, clearly displayed: all that a governor has to do is to shew consistency and firmness enough, not only to resist favouritism, but even the suspicion of it. To this also must be added courtesy in listening to pleaders, consideration in pronouncing a decision, and painstaking efforts to convince suitors of its justice, and to answer their arguments. It is by such habits that C. Octavius has recently made himself very popular; in whose court, for the first time, the lictor did not interfere, and the marshal kept silence, while every suitor spoke as often and as long as he chose. In which conduct he would perhaps have been thought over-lax, had it not been that this laxity enabled him to maintain the following instance of severity. The partisans of Sulla were forced to restore what they had taken by violence and terrorism. Those who had made inequitable decrees, while in office, were now as private citizens forced to submit to the principles they had established. The strictness on his part would have been thought harsh, had it not been rendered palatable by many sweetening influences of courtesy. But if this gentleness was sufficient to make him popular at Rome, where there is such haughtiness of spirit, such unrestrained liberty, such unlimited licence of individuals, and, in fine, so many magistrates, so many means of obtaining protection, such vast power in the hands of the popular assembly, and such influence exercised by the senate, how welcome must a praetor's courtesy be in Asia, in which there is such a numerous body of citizens and allies, so many cities, so many communities, all hanging on one man's nod, and in which there are no means of protection, no one to whom to make a complaint, no senate, no popular assembly! Wherefore it requires an exalted character, a man who is not only equitable from natural impulse, but who has also been trained by study and the refinements of a liberal education, so to conduct himself while in the possession of such immense power, that those over whom he rules should not feel the want of any other power.

VIII. Take the case of the famous Cyrus, portrayed by Xenophon, not as an historical character, but as a model of righteous government, the serious dignity of whose character is represented by that philosopher as combined with a peculiar courtesy. And, indeed, it is not without reason that our hero Africanus used perpetually to have those books in his hands, for there is no duty pertaining to a careful and equitable governor which is not to be found in them.[3] Well, if *he* [Cyrus] cultivated those qualities, though never

3. The work referred to is Xenophon's treatise *Cyropaideia* (written ca. 360 B.C.); Africanus was the younger Publius Cornelius Scipio, the Aemilianus, who destroyed Carthage in 146 B.C.

destined to be in a private station, how carefully ought those to maintain them to whom power is given with the understanding that it must be surrendered, and given by laws under whose authority they must once more come? In my opinion all who govern others are bound to regard as the object of all their actions the greatest happiness of the governed. That this is your highest object, and has been so since you first landed in Asia, has been published abroad by consistent rumour and the conversation of all. It is, let me add, not only the duty of one who governs allies and citizens, but even of one who governs slaves and dumb animals, to serve the interests and advantage of those under him. In this point I notice that everyone agrees that you take the greatest pains: no new debt is being contracted by the states, while many have been relieved by you from a heavy and longstanding one. Several cities that had become dilapidated and almost deserted—of which one was the most famous state in Ionia, the other in Caria, Samus and Halicarnassus—have been given a new life by you: there is no party fighting, no civil strife in the towns: you take care that the government of the states is administered by the best class of citizens: brigandage is abolished in Mysia; murder suppressed in many districts; peace is established throughout the province; and not only the robberies usual on highways and in country places, but those more numerous and more serious ones in towns and temples, have been completely stopped: the fame, fortunes, and repose of the rich have been relieved of that most oppressive instrument of praetorial rapacity—vexatious prosecution; the expenses and tribute of the states are made to fall with equal weight on all who live in the territories of those states: access to you is as easy as possible: your ears are open to the complaints of all: no man's want of means or want of friends excludes him, I don't say from access to you in public and on the tribunal, but even from your house and chamber: in a word, throughout your government there is no harshness or cruelty—everywhere clemency, mildness, and kindness [*humanitas*][4] reign supreme.

IX. What an immense benefit, again, have you done in having liberated Asia from the tribute exacted by the aediles, a measure which cost me some violent controversies! For if one of our nobles complains openly that by your edict, "No moneys shall be voted for the games," you have robbed him of 200,000 sesterces, what a vast sum of money would have been paid, had a grant been made to the credit of every magistrate who held games, as had become the regular custom! However, I stopped these complaints by taking up this position—what they think of it in Asia I don't know, in Rome it meets with no little approval and praise—I refused to accept a sum of money which the states had decreed for a temple and monument in our

4. *Humanitas*—"kindness" or "love of mankind"—was a Greco-Roman virtue that was often invoked as an ideal quality of a ruler.

honour, though they had done so with the greatest enthusiasm in view both of my services and of your most valuable benefactions; and though the law contained a special and distinct exception in these words, "that it was lawful to receive for temple or monument"; and though again the money was not going to be thrown away, but would be employed on decorating a temple, and would thus appear to have been given to the Roman people and the immortal Gods rather than to myself—yet, in spite of its having desert, law, and the wishes of those who offered the gift in its favour, I determined that I must not accept it, for this reason among others, namely, to prevent those, to whom such an honour was neither due nor legal, from being jealous. Wherefore adhere with all your heart and soul to the policy which you have hitherto adopted—that of being devoted to those whom the senate and people of Rome have committed and intrusted to your honour and authority, of doing your best to protect them, and of desiring their greatest happiness. Even if the lot had made you governor of Africans, or Spaniards, or Gauls—uncivilized and barbarous nations—it would still have been your duty as a man of feeling to consult for their interests and advantage, and to have contributed to their safety. But when we rule over a race of men in which civilization [*humanitas*] not only exists, but from which it is believed to have spread to others, we are bound to repay them, above all things, what we received from them. For I shall not be ashamed to go so far—especially as my life and achievements have been such as to exclude any suspicion of sloth or frivolity—as to confess that, whatever I have accomplished, I have accomplished by means of those studies and principles which have been transmitted to us in Greek literature and schools of thought. Wherefore, over and above the general good faith which is due to all men, I think we are in a special sense under an obligation to that nation, to put in practice what it has taught us among the very men by whose maxims we have been brought out of barbarism.

X. And indeed Plato, the fountain-head of genius and learning, thought that states would only be happy when scholars and philosophers began being their rulers, or when those who were their rulers had devoted all their attention to learning and philosophy. It was plainly this union of power and philosophy that in his opinion might prove the salvation of states. And this perhaps has at length fallen to the fortune of the whole empire: certainly it has in the present instance to your province, to have a man in supreme power in it, who has from boyhood spent the chief part of his zeal and time in imbibing the principles of philosophy, virtue, and humanity. Wherefore be careful that this third year, which has been added to your labour, may be thought a prolongation of prosperity to Asia. And since Asia was more fortunate in retaining you than I was in my endeavour to bring you back, see that my regret is softened by the exultation of the province. For if you have displayed the very greatest activity in earning honours such as, I think, have never been paid to anyone else, much greater ought your activity to be in preserving these honours. What I for my part think of honours of that kind I have told you in previous letters. I have always regarded them, if given indiscriminately, as of little value, if paid from interested motives, as worthless: if, however, as in this case, they are tributes to solid services on your part, I hold you bound to take much pains in preserving them. Since, then, you are exercising supreme power and official authority in cities, in which you have before your eyes the consecration and apotheosis of your virtues, in all decisions, decrees, and official acts consider what you owe to those warm opinions entertained of you, to those verdicts on your character, to those honours which have been rendered you. And what you owe will be to consult for the interests of all, to remedy men's misfortunes, to provide for their safety, to resolve that you will be both called and believed to be the "father of Asia."

XI. However, to such a resolution and deliberate policy on your part the great obstacle are the publicans: for, if we oppose them, we shall alienate from ourselves and from the Republic an order which has done us most excellent service, and which has been brought into sympathy with the Republic by our means; if, on the other hand, we comply with them in every case, we shall allow the complete ruin of those whose interests, to say nothing of their preservation, we are bound to consult. This is the one difficulty, if we look the thing fairly in the face, in your whole government. For disinterested conduct on one's own part, the suppression of all inordinate desires, the keeping a check upon one's staff, courtesy in hearing causes, in listening to and admitting suitors—all this is rather a question of credit than of difficulty: for it does not depend on any special exertion, but rather on a mental resolve and inclination. But how much bitterness of feeling is caused to allies by that question of the publicans we have had reason to know in the case of citizens who, when recently urging the removal of the port-dues in Italy, did not complain so much of the dues themselves, as of certain extortionate conduct on the part of the collectors. Wherefore, after hearing the grievances of citizens in Italy, I can comprehend what happens to allies in distant lands. To conduct oneself in this matter in such a way as to satisfy the publicans, especially when contracts have been undertaken at a loss, and yet to preserve the allies from ruin, seems to demand a virtue with something divine in it, I mean a virtue like yours. To begin with, that they are subject to tax at all, which is their greatest grievance, ought not to be thought so by the Greeks, because they were so subject by their own laws without the Roman government. Again, they cannot despise the word publican, for they have been unable to pay the assessment according to Sulla's poll-tax without the aid of the publican. But that Greek publicans are not more considerate in exacting the payment of taxes than our own may be gathered from the fact that the Caunii, and all the islands assigned to the Rhodians by Sulla, recently appealed to the protection of the senate, and petitioned to be allowed to pay their tax to us rather than to the Rhodians. Wherefore neither ought those to revolt at the name of a publican who have always been subject to tax, nor those to despise it who have been unable to make up the tribute by themselves, nor those to refuse his services who have asked for them. At the same time let Asia reflect on this, that if she were not under our government, there is no calamity of foreign war or internal strife from which she would be free. And since that government cannot possibly be maintained without taxes, she should be content to purchase perpetual peace and tranquility at the price of a certain proportion of her products.

XII. But if they will fairly reconcile themselves to the existence and name of publican, all the rest may be made to appear to them in a less offensive light by your skill and prudence. They may, in making their bargains with the publicans, not have regard so much to the exact conditions laid down by the censors as to the convenience of settling the business and freeing themselves from farther trouble. You also may do, what you have done splendidly and are still doing, namely, dwell on the high position of the publicans, and on your obligations to that order, in such a way as—putting out of the question all considerations of your power and the power of your official authority and dignity—to reconcile the Greeks with the publicans, and to beg of those, whom you have served eminently well, and who owe you everything, to suffer you by their compliance to maintain and preserve the bonds which unite us with the publicans. But why do I address these exhortations to you, who are not only capable of carrying them out of your own accord without anyone's instruction, but have already to a great extent thoroughly done so? For the most respectable and important companies do not cease offering me thanks daily, and this is all the more gratifying to me because the Greeks do the same. Now it is an achievement of great difficulty to unite in feeling things which are opposite in interests, aims, and, I had almost said, in their very nature. But I have not written all this to instruct you—for your wisdom requires no man's instruction—but it has been a pleasure to me while writing to set down your virtues, though I have run to greater length in this letter than I could have wished, or than I thought I should.

XIII. There is one thing on which I shall not cease from giving you advice, nor will I, as far as in me lies, allow your praise to be spoken of with a reservation. For all who come from your province do make one reservation in the extremely high praise which they bestow on your virtue, integrity, and kindness—it is that of sharpness of temper. That is a fault which, even in our private and everyday life, seems to indicate want of solidity and strength of mind; but nothing, surely, can be more improper than to combine harshness of temper with the exercise of supreme power. Wherefore I will not undertake to lay before you now what the greatest philosophers say about anger, for I should not wish to be tedious, and you can easily ascertain it yourself from the writings of many of them: but I don't think I ought to pass over what is the essence of a letter, namely, that the recipient should be informed of what he does not know. Well, what nearly everybody reports to me is this: they usually say that, as long as you are not out of temper, nothing can be pleasanter than you are, but that when some instance of dishonesty or wrong-headedness has stirred you, your temper rises to such a height that no one can discover any trace of your usual kindness. Wherefore, since no mere desire for glory, but circumstances and fortune have brought us upon a path of life which makes it inevitable that men will always talk about us, let us be on our guard, to the utmost of our means and ability, that no glaring fault may be alleged to have existed in us. And I am not now urging, what is perhaps difficult in human nature generally, and at our time of life especially, that you should change your disposition and suddenly pluck out a deeply-rooted habit, but I give you this hint: if you cannot completely avoid this failing, because your mind is surprised by anger before cool calculation has been able to prevent it, deliberately prepare yourself beforehand, and daily reflect on the duty of resisting anger, and that, when it moves your heart most violently, it is just the time for being most careful to restrain your tongue. And that sometimes seems to me to be a greater virtue than not being angry at all. For the latter is not always a mark of superiority to weakness, it is sometimes the result of dullness; but to govern temper and speech, however angry you may be, or even to hold your tongue and keep your indignant feelings and resentment under control, although it may not be a proof of perfect wisdom, yet requires no ordinary force of character. And, indeed, in this respect they tell me that you are now much more gentle and less irritable. No violent outbursts of indignation on your part, no abusive words, no insulting language are reported to me: which, while quite alien to culture and refinement, are specially unsuited to high power and place. For if your anger is implacable, it amounts to extreme harshness; if easily appeased, to extreme weakness. The latter, however, as a choice of evils, is, after all, preferable to harshness.

XIV. But since your first year gave rise to most talk in regard to this particular complaint—I believe because the wrong-doing, the covetousness, and the arrogance of men came upon you as a surprise, and seemed to you unbearable—while your second year was much milder, because habit and reflexion, and, as I think, my letters also, rendered you more tolerant and gentle, the third ought to be so completely reformed, as not to give even the smallest ground for anyone to find fault. And here I go on to urge upon you, not by way of exhortation or admonition, but by brotherly entreaties, that you would set your whole heart, care, and thought on the gaining of praise from everybody and from every quarter. If, indeed, our achievements were only the subject of a moderate amount of talk and commendation, nothing eminent, nothing beyond the practice of others, would have been demanded of you. As it is, however, owing to the brilliancy and magnitude of the affairs in which we have been engaged, if we do not obtain the very highest reputation from your province, it seems scarcely possible for us to avoid the most violent abuse. Our position is such that all loyalists support us, but demand also and expect from us every kind of activity and virtue, while all the disloyal, seeing that we have entered upon a lasting war with them, appear contented with the very smallest excuse for attacking us. Wherefore, since fortune has allotted to you such a theatre as Asia, completely packed with an audience, of immense size, of the most refined judgment, and moreover, naturally so capable of conveying sound, that its expressions of opinion and its remarks reach Rome, put out all your power, I beseech you, exert all your energies to appear not only to have been worthy of the part we played here, but to have surpassed everything done there by your high qualities.

XV. And since chance has assigned to me among the magistracies the conduct of public business in the city, to you that in a province, if my share is inferior to no one's, take care that yours surpasses others. At the same time think of this: we are not now working for a future and prospective glory, but are fighting in defence of what has been already gained; which indeed it was not so much an object to gain as it is now our duty to defend. And if anything in me could be apart from you, I should desire nothing more than the position which I have already gained. The actual fact, however, is that unless all your acts and deeds in your province correspond to my achievements, I shall think that I have gained nothing by those great labours and dangers, in all of which you have shared. But if it was you who, above all others, assisted me to gain a most splendid reputation, you will certainly also labour more than others to enable me to retain it. You must not be guided by the opinions and judgments of the present generation only, but of those to come also: and yet the latter will be a more candid judgment, for it will not be influenced by detraction and malice. Finally, you should think of this—that you are not seeking glory for yourself alone (and even if that were the case, you still ought not to be careless of it, especially as you had determined to consecrate the memory of your name by the most splendid monuments), but you have to share it with me, and to hand it down to our children. In regard to which you must be on your guard lest by any excess of carelessness you should seem not only to have neglected your own interests, but to have begrudged those of your family also.

XVI. And these observations are not made with the idea of any speech of mine appearing to have roused you from your sleep, but to have rather "added speed to the runner." For you will continue to compel all in the future, as you have compelled them in the past, to praise your equity, self-control, strictness, and honesty. But from my extreme affection I am possessed with a certain insatiable greed for glory for you. However, I am convinced that, as Asia should now be as well-known to you as each man's own house is to himself, and since to your supreme good sense such great experience has now been added, there is nothing that affects reputation which you do not know as well as possible yourself, and which does not daily occur to your mind without anybody's exhortation. But I, who when I read your writing seem to hear your voice, and when I write to you seem to be talking to you, am therefore always best pleased with your longest letter, and in writing am often somewhat prolix myself. My last prayer and advice to you is that, as good poets and painstaking actors always do, so you should be most attentive in the last scenes and conclusion of your function and business, so that this third year of your government, like a third act in a play, may appear to have been the most elaborated and most highly finished. You will do that with more ease if you will think that I, whom you always wished to please more than all the world besides, am always at your side, and am taking part in everything you say and do. It remains only to beg you to take the greatest care of your health, if you wish me and all your friends to be well also. Farewell.

14. Two Trials for Provincial Misgovernment

When the Romans began to improvise a system of provincial administration, they thought of the governor as a held-over Roman magistrate who exercised his powers abroad. Throughout the Late Republic and most of the Principate, Roman governors were, with rare exceptions, former consuls or praetors taken from the ranks of the senate. But unlike a consul or a praetor in Rome, a governor in his province had no colleague who could check his actions. In practice, his power was absolute. The Romans attempted to remedy the corruption for which they had opened so much opportunity. Increasingly elaborate laws defined and prohibited most abuses which a governor might be tempted to commit. The laws also established procedures by which subjects in the provinces could obtain restitution of money or property extorted from them.

The Trial of Marius Priscus: Pliny, *Letters* 2.11. The Trial of Julius Bassus: Pliny, *Letters* 4.9. Translated for this volume by Peter White.

The courts that enforced the laws were in Rome. Under the Republic, there was an extortion court set up to deal exclusively with provincial misconduct; the jury was made up solely of senators during some periods and included knights and other affluent citizens during others. Under the Principate, accusations against governors were usually heard either by the full senate, which convened as a jury, or by the emperor and his council.

In the following letters, Pliny (see the introduction to document 12) describes two extortion trials in which he had a part, in A.D. 100 and 103; at the first he argued for the prosecution, at the second for the defense. He tends to dwell more on the orgy of fine speeches in which the trials culminated than on the deeds which came to light. But through incidental comments he provides a glimpse of relationships—between governors and provincial moguls, and between defendants and their fellow-senators—that could compromise the justice dispensed in senatorial courts.

The Trial of Marius Priscus

Gaius Pliny to Arrianus: Though the love of peace and quiet has led you out of public life, you still care deeply about issues of national import, and you are always pleased when the senate takes up some business that is worthy of it. Well then, here is an account of a case just concluded which starred a distinguished personality, set a salutary standard of judicial toughness, and turned on an issue of unforgettable importance. Charges were brought against Marius Priscus from the province of Africa, where he had been governor. Priscus waived trial and asked to have a review board assess damages under the accelerated procedure. Cornelius Tacitus[1] and I, who had been appointed by the senate to represent the provincials, felt honor-bound to inform the house that Priscus had committed atrocities far exceeding the kind of charges which the accelerated procedure was set up to handle: he had taken bribes for sentencing and even executing innocent persons. At that point Catius Fronto rose to urge that the trial be limited to charges under the extortion law. Fronto has a rare talent for drawing tears, and he filled all the sails of his oratory with gusts of pathos. His speech prompted a hot dispute with loud outcries from both sides. Some insisted that a trial conducted in the senate had to follow the procedure specified by the law. Others said that the procedure was up to the house, and that the charges brought should be commensurate with the defendant's misdeeds. Finally Julius Ferox, the consul-elect, gave proof of his scrupulous integ-

1. Cornelius Tacitus later became famous as a historian (see document 10).

rity by proposing that we appoint a review board for Priscus, but also subpoena the persons from whom he was supposed to have taken money for condemning the innocent. This proposal not only carried, but after all our wrangling was the only one to attract significant support. The lesson to be learned is that sympathy and personal liking have an overwhelming impact at first, but they are cooled and gradually dissipated by rational discussion. That is why, when a hush descends on a group of people, no one cares to take the line that any number support while everyone is babbling. The confused view of problems which you have in the midst of a crowd clears up when you get away from the crowd.

The persons summoned to appear, Vitellius Honoratus and Flavius Marcianus, duly presented themselves. Honoratus was accused of procuring the banishment of a Roman knight and the execution of seven of his friends for 300,000 sesterces. Marcianus was accused of paying 700,000 sesterces to have a series of punishments inflicted on one Roman knight: the man was cudgeled, condemned to the mines, and strangled in prison. As for Honoratus, his timely demise removed him from the senate's jurisdiction. Marcianus did come up for trial, but with Priscus not present. The ex-consul Tuccius Cerialis therefore claimed his right to address the house, and requested that Priscus be party to the proceedings. I don't know whether the idea was that Priscus would appear in a more woeful light if he were there, or in a blacker light—though I really think that Cerialis's idea was that a charge applicable to two men should properly be defended by both, and if it could not be refuted, then both should be punished for it.

The trial was postponed to the next sitting of the house, which presented a very grand spectacle before a word was spoken. The emperor was presiding in his capacity as consul, and anyway, January always brings crowds of people, especially senators, to Rome. Over and above that, the significance of the case, the spread of rumor and speculation after the adjournment, and people's natural curiosity about great and rare events had brought everyone out. You can imagine our trepidation at having to speak on such an important matter in that assembly, before the emperor. Though I have addressed the house time and time again, and have nowhere found a more receptive audience, on that day everything seemed new, and filled me with new dread. I was also conscious of the difficulty of my case. In the dock stood a man who until recently had been an elder statesman and a state priest, but was now neither. I had the handicap of prosecuting a defendant who had been convicted once already; the feeling that his conviction was over and done with earned him sympathy, and that counterbalanced the brutality of his offence. Well, summoning my nerve and my thoughts as best I could, I began to speak and, for all my fears, found a good response from the audience. I spoke for nearly five hours (I started with twelve water clocks filled right to the top, and then I obtained four more). Even the parts of the case that I expected would be hard to deal with fell into line as I spoke. The emperor showed such attentive concern for me (it would be too much to say nervousness) that several times he passed a message to my freedman, who was standing behind me, and warned me to go easy on my voice and lungs. He was afraid I was putting too much strain on my slight physique. I was followed by Claudius Marcellinus, who spoke in defence of Marcianus. Then the senate adjourned, to reconvene on the next day. By this time it was so late that nightfall would have cut short any further pleading.

On the next day Salvius Liberalis took up the defense of Priscus. He is shrewd, well organized, forceful, and eloquent, and he unfolded all his arts in that case. Cornelius Tacitus responded in a ringing oration with the distinctive Tacitean stateliness. Catius Fronto then made an outstanding second speech on behalf of Priscus. It consisted more of appeals for mercy than answers to the charges, which was the appropriate strategy at that point. Dusk came on as he was speaking, but he was able to finish. The presentation of evidence thus fell on the third day. It was a wonderful reenactment of old times: sessions adjourned at nightfall, called to order on three successive mornings, and kept going for three days. The consul-elect Cornutus Tertullus, who is the very model of unflinching honesty, urged that the 700,000 sesterces which Priscus took should be forfeited to the state treasury; that Priscus should be banished from Rome and Italy; and that Marcianus should be banished from Africa as well as Rome and Italy. He wound up his motion by voicing the sense of the senate that Tacitus and I had worthily discharged our duty because we conducted the case assigned to us conscientiously and courageously. His motion was endorsed by the other consuls-elect and all the ex-consuls up to Pompeius Collega. Collega recommended that the 700,000 sesterces be forfeited to the treasury; that Marcianus be interned for a period of five years; and that Priscus pay only the penalty for extortion, which had already been inflicted. Both motions found numerous backers, with perhaps a majority favoring the more lenient (or more lax) sentence—even some of the people who had appeared to side with Cornutus began shifting their support to Collega after he spoke. But when the senators dispersed to right and left at the division of the house, those who had been standing near the consuls' seats started to line up with Cornutus. At that point the individuals who had thrown in with Collega crossed over to the other side, and Collega was left with just a handful. Later he complained intensely about Regulus and the others who had put him up to saying what he said: Regulus had dictated the very words of the motion, and then left him in the lurch. That is just like Regulus: always oscillating between the ultimate in gall and the ultimate in caution.

That was the end of the major proceeding. But an obligation of some importance still remains to be discharged. Priscus's deputy, Hostilius Firminus, got drawn into the case and was heavily incriminated. On the evidence of Marcianus's account books, and of a speech which he uttered before the town council of Lepcis, Firminus was convicted of having lent himself to the degrading business of arranging a payment of 200,000 sesterces from Marcianus to Priscus. He was also convicted of having taken 10,000 for himself (entered in Marcianus's books under the ignominious heading "Paid to Perfumer"—which fits the swish and depilated recipient). In the absence of Firminus, who had either missed the session or purposely stayed away, the senate resolved to discuss his case at the next meeting, as Cornutus recommended.

That's the city news; now you give me the country news. How are your trees and vines and crops and ever-sensitive sheep coming along? Unless you reciprocate with a letter just as long, you can't look forward to anything but the briefest note next time. Goodbye.

The Trial of Julius Bassus

Gaius Pliny to Cornelius Ursus: Julius Bassus, that hapless soul whose tribulations have made him a legend, has been on trial for the last few days. Under Vespasian he was indicted by two persons (not officials) and the case was remanded to the senate, where it languished for some time until Bassus was finally cleared and acquitted. His friendship with Domitian then made him leery of Titus; Domitian banished him, and Nerva recalled him. He obtained the governorship of Bithynia, but came back under indictment. He was aggressively prosecuted, and as stoutly defended. Reaction was mixed, but most voted for some form of clemency.

Pomponius Rufus led off the prosecution with a well-organized and powerful speech. He was followed by Theophanes, one of the Bithynian representatives, who had instigated the whole business. I delivered the reply, as Bassus had asked me to lay the groundwork for his whole defense. It was my job to highlight the personal distinctions which he owed in no small part to his adversities as well as to his lineage, to bring out the mercenary motives of the informers plotting against him, and to explain what accounted for the enmity of agitators like Theophanes. He also wanted me to deal with the charge that weighed most heavily against him. As far as the other things went, though they may have sounded worse, he deserved acquittal and even commendation. But naive and shortsighted as he was, he had accepted from people of the province some things he assumed were being offered out of friendship, because he had been quaestor there before. That was what hurt him. What he called gifts, his accusers called thefts and plunder. Still, the law does forbid accepting even gifts. I asked myself how I was to deal with this problem, what line of defense to take. Should I deny that he took anything? I was afraid that an action I dared not admit might really look like theft. Besides, denial of a manifest fact was bound to aggravate the charge, not diminish it, all the more as the defendant had left his lawyers so little leeway. He had told a number of people, including the emperor, that he had received "just little birthday presents or Saturnalia trinkets, the same sort as he had sent in many instances." Well then, should I have pleaded for clemency? I might as well have cut my client's throat, as admit that his infractions were so great he could only be saved by clemency. Should I have tried to justify his conduct? That would not have done him any good, and would have made me look unscrupulous. In my dilemma I decided to strike a middle course, and I think I succeeded.

Nightfall brought a halt to my oration as it does to battles. I had spoken for three and a half hours, with one and a half still to go. Under the law the prosecution gets six hours and the defense nine; Bassus had divided his allotment between me and the follow-up speaker in such a way that I was to use five hours and the other man was to use the remainder. My speech had gone so well that I was for ending where I had broken off. It is foolhardy not to be content with success. I was also afraid that my stamina might run out if I resumed again, since it is harder to start up after stopping than to press straight on. And there was a risk too that my audience would come cold to another installment of a speech which had previously been shelved, or get bored with more of the same. A speech is like the flame of a torch, which is kept going by constant shaking and is hard to revive if it dies down. In the same way, a speaker's ardor and a listener's concentration need to be steadily kept up; they die away after pauses that break the tension. However, Bassus begged and pleaded with me and was practically in tears that I should use my full time. I submitted, putting consideration for him ahead of consideration for myself. It went well. I found the senators so fresh and alert that they seemed more keyed up than jaded by my previous speech. Lucceius Albinus then took over, so smoothly that people felt our two speeches presented a pleasant contrast of styles but a single overarching design. Herennius Pollio weighed in with a tough response for the prosecution, and then Theophanes spoke again. His impudent insistence on speaking after two fine orators and former consuls was of a piece with his behavior throughout. He demanded extra time, in fact, speaking till dark and on into the night, after the lamps were brought in. On the next day Homullus and Fronto delivered admirable speeches for the defense, and the fourth day was taken up with the presentation of evidence.

The consul-elect Baebius Macer declared his view that Bassus was guilty under the extortion law, while Caepio Hispo urged that a review board should fix restitution, but that Bassus should be allowed to keep his senatorial rank. Both recommendations were justified. "How is that possible," you will ask, "when they were so divergent?" Well, Macer focused on the letter of the law, and was consistent in condemning Bassus for taking gifts contrary to the law. Caepio took the view (certainly valid) that the senate was entitled either to soften or to intensify the law, and so he acted reasonably in recommending clemency for behavior which is admittedly illegal, but not uncommon. Caepio's motion carried the day. Even as he rose to speak, he received the loud applause to which a speaker usually sits down. Since his speech was such a hit in prospect, you can imagine the response when he actually began to speak. Still, opinions are divided, in the community at large as well as in the senate. Those who supported Caepio's motion criticize Macer's as being draconian and rigid. Macer's supporters, on the other hand, claim that the other motion was lax and even muddleheaded, since it is inconsistent to let someone keep his senate seat after you have sentenced him to make restitution.

At the end of the trial there was also a third resolution before the house. Valerius Paulinus endorsed Caepio's motion, but added that there should be an investigation of Theophanes as soon as he finished serving with the Bithynian deputation. Paulinus charged that in the course of the prosecution he had at several points infringed the very law under which he prosecuted Bassus. The consuls failed to call for a vote on this motion, though it was notably well received by most of the senators. But Paulinus gained credit for demonstrating fair-mindedness and principle. After the session was over, people crowded around Bassus and noisily congratulated him. The latest twist in a legend of calamities which had already made him famous stirred up sympathy, as did the spectacle of a gaunt old man looking disheveled and distressed.

This letter is only a stopgap, the precursor of my speech, which will come to you loaded with full details. But you have a while to wait—a speech on a subject so important is going to need more than cursory rewriting. Goodbye.

15. Municipal Charters and Regulations

Greek culture was well entrenched in south Italy, Sicily, and the eastern Mediterranean by the time the Roman empire expanded into these regions. Here the Romans found sophisticated cities and civic institutions,

Selections from the Lex Julia Municipalis, in *Six Roman Laws*, translated by E. G. Hardy (Oxford: Oxford University Press, 1911), pp. 155–61. Selections from Lex Coloniae Genetivae Juliae, Lex Municipalis Salpensana, and Lex Municipalis Malacitana, in *Three Spanish Charters and Other Documents*, translated by E. G. Hardy (Oxford: Oxford University Press, 1912), pp. 31–32, 38–39, 42, 46–47, 58–59, 83, 92–93, 102–7.

which for the most part they allowed to function according to established practice. But in the rest of Italy, and in the western Mediterranean generally, they regularly encountered peoples and tribes less advanced than themselves, and here Rome became the standard of urban organization. Its influence was more than a matter of setting an example. The Romans founded many towns as colonies in which to settle veteran soldiers and their urban poor; many existing towns they reorganized in the course of turning newly conquered territories into provinces. In either case, the towns received detailed charters which were drawn up by commissioners from Rome and engraved on bronze tablets, like other records meant to be permanent.

Remnants of about half a dozen such charters have been found at various sites in Italy and southern Spain. Since none is preserved in its entirety, no town's system of government is fully documented. Chronologically, the charters span a period of two centuries, during which the Romans kept modifying administrative policy; functions in force at the beginning of the first century B.C. were not necessarily in force at the end of the first century A.D. Another complication is that Rome created many gradations of status among towns. The inhabitants of some were Roman citizens and enjoyed all the rights of citizens, while the inhabitants of others possessed more limited rights, which differed from place to place. Some towns were allowed to handle civil and criminal cases according to local custom, while others were subject to the jurisdiction of the Roman governor or officials in Rome. Some were liable to taxation, while others were not. Charters were drawn up on a case-by-case basis, therefore, and not according to a uniform plan. For all these reasons, no one text adequately represents Roman ideas about local government. But certain tendencies emerge when charters are compared. The following excerpts, which deal with elections and the duties of office, show how the Romans fostered a municipal governing class whose economic and social outlook was parallel to their own, and also how they transplanted mechanisms of Roman government to the towns.

The selections are taken from four documents. The Tablet of Heraclea contains regulations which pertain to all the towns of Italy, not to one particular town; it is thought to be a law drafted by Julius Caesar in 46 or 45 B.C. and promulgated after his death. The Charter of Urso was drawn up for a colony of Roman citizens (possibly freedman citizens) which Caesar founded in southern Spain at about the same time. The charters of Salpensa and Malaca (also in southern Spain) were drawn up more than a hundred years later, in A.D. 82 or 83; most inhabitants of these towns, unlike those of Urso, did not possess Roman citizenship.

The elements of an ancient city-state are still visible in these constitutions. The citizen assembly persisted, although its functions were minimal. Each town had a council, usually composed of former magistrates who served for life, as in the Roman senate. But the Romans were reluctant to give the name of "senator" to anyone who sat on an ordinary town council; the charters speak instead of "decurions" or "councillors" (*conscripti*). Administrative posts were organized according to the Roman principle of collegiality: a magistrate had broad powers, but also a colleague with countervailing power in the form of a veto. The *duoviri*—"the Two"—were the town's chief executives. At the next level down stood two aediles, who were responsible for the upkeep of public property and the enforcement of municipal ordinances. (Sometimes the *duoviri* and the aediles were referred to together as the *quattuorviri*—"the Four.") Many towns also had two quaestors who administered municipal finances.

Regulation of Electoral Procedures

No person who is or shall be less than thirty years of age,[1] shall, after the first day of January in the second year from this date, stand for or accept or hold the office of duovir or quattuorvir or any other magistracy in a township [*municipium*] or colony or prefecture, unless he shall have served three campaigns on horseback in a legion, or six campaigns on foot in a legion, such campaigns being served in a camp or a province during the greater part of each several year, or during two consecutive periods of six months, which in any year may be counted as equivalent to two years, or unless he shall be entitled by the laws or plebiscites or by virtue of a treaty to exemption from military duty, whereby he is freed from compulsory service. Furthermore, no person who practises the trade of auctioneer or beadle or undertaker shall, so long as he practises such trade, stand for or accept or have or hold the office of duovir or quattuorvir, or any other magistracy in a township or colony or prefecture, or become a senator or decurion or conscript or declare his vote as such, within such community. . . .

In every township, colony, prefecture, forum, or village [*conciliabulum*] of Roman citizens, it shall be unlawful for all such persons as shall be hereafter mentioned, within such communities, to be in the senate or among the decurions or councillors [*conscripti*], or to vote by speech or voting tablet in the said order; to wit: such persons as shall have been convicted of theft

1. After Augustus, the minimum age was twenty-five.

committed by themselves, or shall have compounded for the theft with the injured party; or those persons who have been or shall be condemned in an action for trust, partnership, guardianship, agency; for injurious conduct or for fraudulent intent, or those persons who have been or shall be condemned under the Lex Plaetoria,[2] or for action committed by them contrary to the said law; or those persons who have been or shall have been bound by oath with a view to fighting as gladiators; or those persons who have or shall have certified their insolvency before the praetor, or certified their solvency to escape assignment for debt; or those persons who have or shall have given notice to their sureties or creditors to the effect that they are unable to pay in full, or have or shall have compounded to that effect with the said sureties or creditors; or those persons in whose behalf such obligations have been or shall be undertaken or incurred; or those persons whose property has been or shall be seized or publicly sold in accordance with the edict of those magistrates invested or to be invested with judicial authority, except in cases where the seizure or public sale took place at the time when the said persons were under legal wardship, or were absent on the public service, provided that such absence was not due to false pretence or wrongful intent; or those persons who have been or shall be condemned by a criminal court in Rome, whereby their residence in Italy is rendered unlawful, and are not or shall not be restored to their former status; or those persons who have been or shall be condemned in a criminal court within the township, colony, prefecture, forum, or village to which they shall belong; or those persons who have been or shall be held to have brought an accusation or done any act for the purpose of making a false charge or from collusion; or those persons who for any dishonourable cause have lost or shall lose their rank in the army; or whom a general for such cause has cashiered or shall cashier; or those persons who have received or shall receive money or any other reward for bringing in the head of a Roman citizen;[3] or who has or shall have prostituted his person; or those persons who shall be trainers of gladiators, or who keep a gladiatorial school; or maintain a public brothel. . . .

It shall not be lawful for any persons who within a township, colony, prefecture, forum, or village are forbidden by this law to be senators or decurions or councillors, to stand for or to hold the office of duovir or quattuorvir or any other magistracy or competence from which he would pass into the said order, nor to sit in the space assigned to senators, decurions, or councillors at the games or gladiatorial contests; nor to be present at a public banquet; nor shall any person, elected or returned contrary to this

2. This law dealt with fraud in legal transactions involving minors.

3. This provision was aimed at persons who had hunted down persons on Sulla's proscription list in 82–81 B.C.

law, rank as duovir or quattuorvir, or hold any magistracy or competence within such communities. (Tablet of Heraclea, sections 89–96, 108–23, 135–40)

No person in the Colonia Genetiva Julia, being a candidate or standing for election to any magistracy within the said colony, shall, after the issue of this law, with a view of seeking such magistracy, or during the year in which he shall be a candidate, or shall stand for or intend to stand for such magistracy, knowingly and of wrongful intent provide entertainments, or invite any person to dinner, or hold or provide a banquet, or, knowingly and with wrongful intent, cause another person to hold a banquet or invite any person to dinner with a view to his candidature, but, nevertheless, the said candidate himself, who shall be seeking a magistracy, may, if he so desire, in all good faith, invite during the said year daily any persons not exceeding nine.

No candidate seeking office shall knowingly and with wrongful intent give or make largess of any gift or present or any other thing with a view to his candidature. Nor shall any person, with a view to the candidature of another, provide entertainments, or invite any person to dinner, or hold a banquet, or, knowingly and with wrongful intent, give or make largess of any gift or present or any other thing. Any person acting in contravention of this shall be condemned to pay to the colonists of the Colonia Genetiva Julia 5,000 sesterces, and may be sued or prosecuted in accordance with this law for that amount through assessors [*recuperatores*] before a duovir or prefect by any person at will. (Charter of Urso, chapter 132)

The person holding the electoral assembly [*comitia*] in accordance with this law shall summon the citizens to register their votes according to their wards [*curiae*], calling all the wards to the vote by a single summons, in such manner that the said wards, each in a separate voting booth, may register their votes by means of tablets. He shall likewise see that three of the citizens of the said township are placed at the voting box of each ward, not themselves belonging to that ward, with intent to guard and count the votes, and that before performing such duty, each of the said three citizens shall take oath that he will deal with the counting of the votes and make report thereon with all good faith. Furthermore, he shall not hinder candidates for an office from placing each one guard at every several voting box. And the said guards, both those placed by the person holding the electoral assembly and those placed by candidates for office, shall each register his vote in that ward, at whose voting box he shall be placed as guard, and the votes of the said guards shall be as lawful and valid as if each had registered his vote in his own ward.

Of the candidates who shall have secured more votes than others in any ward, the person holding the said electoral assembly shall return that candidate who has more votes than the rest, as elected and created by that ward, and then the next in order, until the number proper to be elected is made up. If in any ward two or more candidates shall have secured the same number of votes, he shall prefer a married man or one with the rights of a married man to an unmarried man without children and without the rights of married men, a man with children to a man without children, and a man with more children to a man with fewer children, and shall return the former as having a majority of votes.[4] In such matter, two children lost after the ceremony of naming, or one boy or girl lost after puberty or marriageable age, shall be counted as equivalent to one surviving child. If two or more candidates shall have secured the same number of votes, and shall possess the same claims, he shall subject their names to the lot, and shall return that person before the rest, whose name is first drawn by the lot.

The person holding the electoral assembly in accordance with this law shall, when the voting lists of all the wards have been brought in, subject the names of the wards to the lot, and draw out one by one the names of the several wards by lot, and as the name of each ward is drawn, he shall order those candidates elected by the said ward to be declared in the order in which the several candidates shall have secured a majority of the wards; he shall, after they have in accordance with this law taken oath and given security for public money, return the same as appointed and created, until the number of magistrates proper to be created by this law is made up. If two or more persons shall have the same number of wards, he shall take the same course concerning such persons, as has already been set forth concerning those who obtained an equal number of votes, and shall return the several candidates in order of election by the same method.

No person shall use his veto or perform any other act to prevent the electoral assembly from being held and completed in accordance with this law in the said township. Any person knowingly and of wrongful intent acting contrary to this shall for every such act be condemned to pay 10,000 sesterces to the citizens of the Municipium Flavium Malacitanum [Malaca], and in respect to the said money, the right to take legal action, to sue and to prosecute, shall belong to every citizen of the said township, and to any other person specified by this law.

As each of the candidates for the duovirate or aedileship or quaestorship shall have obtained a majority of the wards, the person holding the said

4. This and the following provisions mirror legislation enacted under the emperor Augustus to encourage marriage and the rearing of children. When competing for public office, husbands and fathers had certain advantages over bachelors and married men without children. Sometimes those advantages were conferred by imperial fiat on persons who did not qualify in the ordinary way.

electoral assembly shall, before returning the candidate as appointed and created, administer an oath openly in public, by Jupiter and by the divine Augustus and the divine Claudius and the divine Vespasian Augustus and the divine Titus Augustus and by the spirit of the emperor Caesar Domitian Augustus and by the tutelary gods, that he will perform all acts required by this law, and that knowingly and of wrongful intent he neither has performed nor will perform any act contrary to the same.

As respecting persons in the said township, who are candidates for the duovirate or quaestorship, or who, owing to fewer than the proper number of names having been announced, are put into the position of having votes registered in their behalf in accordance with this law, each of the said persons on the day when the electoral assembly is held shall, before the votes are registered, at the discretion of the person holding the assembly, furnish sureties to the corporate body of citizens that the public money, handled by him in the course of his magistracy, shall be secured to the said citizens. If in such matter the guarantee of the said sureties shall appear insufficient, the candidate shall, at the discretion of the aforesaid person, make registration of securities, and the said person shall without prejudice and in all good faith accept sureties and securities from the same until the guarantee is sufficient. If any of the persons, for whom votes may be properly registered at the elections of duovirs or quaestors, shall be the cause whereby insufficient security is furnished, then the person holding the electoral assembly shall not accept the candidature of such person. (Charter of Malaca, chapters 55–60)

Some Responsibilities of Magistrates

All duoviri, except those first appointed after this law, shall during their magistracy at the discretion of the decurions celebrate a gladiatorial show or dramatic spectacles to Jupiter, Juno, and Minerva, and to the gods and goddesses, or such part of the said shows as shall be possible, during four days, for the greater part of each day, and on the said spectacles and the said shows each of the said persons shall expend of his own money not less than 2,000 sesterces, and out of the public money it shall be lawful for each several duovir to expend a sum not exceeding 2,000 sesterces, and it shall be lawful for the said persons so to do with impunity. Always provided that no person shall expend or make assignment of any portion of the money, which in accordance with this law shall be properly given or assigned for those sacrifices which are publicly performed in the colony or in any other place.

All aediles during their magistracy shall celebrate a gladiatorial show or dramatic spectacles to Jupiter, Juno, and Minerva, or whatever portion of such shows shall be possible, during three days for the greater part of each day, and during one day games in the circus or forum to Venus, and on the said spectacles or shows each of the said aediles shall expend out of his own money not less than 2,000 sesterces, and from the public funds it shall be lawful to expend for each several aedile 1,000 sesterces, and a duovir or prefect shall see that the said money is given and assigned, and it shall be lawful for the aediles to receive the same without prejudice. . . .

No duovir, appointed or created after the establishment of the colony, and no prefect, left in charge by a duovir in accordance with the charter of the colony, shall, concerning public ground or for public ground, receive or accept from a contractor or leaseholder or surety any gift or present or remuneration or any other favour; nor shall he cause any such favour to be bestowed upon himself or upon any of his staff.

Any person acting in contravention of this shall be condemned to pay to the colonists of the Colonia Genetiva Julia 20,000 sesterces, and may be sued or prosecuted by any person at will for that amount.

No person in this colony shall adjudicate or have jurisdiction, save the duoviri, or a prefect left in charge by a duovir, or an aedile, as provided for in this law. Nor shall any one by virtue of such authorization or power cause any person to adjudicate in the said colony, save those empowered so to do by this law. . . .

If any decurion of the said colony shall make demand of a duovir or prefect that a proposal be made to the decurions concerning public money or fines or penalties, or concerning public grounds, lands, or buildings, necessitating a judicial inquiry and adjudication; then shall the duovir or other person charged with jurisdiction, on the first available day, consult the decurions on the said matter, and cause a decree of the decurions to be made, provided that a majority of the decurions are present, when such matter is discussed. Whatever a majority of the decurions then present shall have determined shall be lawful and valid. . . .

No duovir, holding a judicial inquiry or conducting a trial in accordance with this law, shall, unless such trial is by this law bound to be concluded in one day, hold the said inquiry or conduct the said trial before the first or after the eleventh hour of the day. The said duovir shall also, in respect to the several accusers, give to the chief accuser the privilege of making his accusation for four hours, and to every subordinate accuser for two hours. In the case of an accuser conceding a portion of his time to another person, he shall give to the said person, to whom such time is conceded, by so much the longer time for speaking. He shall likewise give to the person, who shall have conceded a portion of his time to another, by so much the shorter time for speaking. For whatsoever number of hours in all the whole number of accusers shall have the privilege of speaking in each several action, he shall give to the defendant or the person pleading for the defendant the privilege of speaking for twice the said number of hours in each action. (Charter of Urso, chapters 70–71, 93–94, 96, 102)

As respecting the duovirs or aediles or quaestors of the said township, there shall belong the right and power of veto by the said duovirs, both against each other, and in cases where some person shall appeal either to one or both of them against an aedile or aediles, or against a quaestor or quaestors; the same right and power shall also belong to the aediles, against one another [and likewise to the quaestors against one another]; such veto shall be within the three days next following the date of appeal and the possibility of such action; always provided that nothing be done contrary to this law, and that appeal be made to none of the said magistrates more than once in the same matter; nor shall any person, when a veto has been cast, act contrary thereto. (Charter of Salpensa, chapter 27)

In all townships, colonies, or prefectures of Roman citizens, such as are or shall be within Italy, those persons who shall hold the highest magistracy or competence within such communities shall, at the time when the censor or any other magistrate at Rome shall take a census of the people, and within the sixty days next following upon his knowledge of such census being taken at Rome, proceed to take a census of all those persons belonging to their respective townships, colonies, or prefectures who shall be Roman citizens; from all such persons, duly sworn, they shall receive their gentile names, their first names, their fathers or patrons, their tribes, their surnames, their age, and a statement of their property, in accordance with the schedule set forth by the magistrate about to take the census of the people at Rome; all such particulars they shall cause to be entered in the public records of their respective communities, and shall despatch the said papers to the officials then taking the census at Rome by the hands of delegates, selected for that purpose by a majority of the decurions or councillors present at a meeting convened for such selection; they shall further see that, within sixty days of the date on which the aforesaid magistrates shall have completed the census of the people at Rome, the said delegates shall reach the said magistrates, and deliver the papers of their respective townships, colonies, or prefectures. (Tablet of Heraclea, sections 142–52)

A Perquisite of Ex-magistrates

All persons created duoviri, aediles, or quaestors in accordance with this law shall be Roman citizens, on laying down the magistracy at the end of the year, together with their parents and wives, and children born in lawful wedlock, and subject to patriarchal authority, and in like manner grandsons and granddaughters being the children of a son, and subject to patriarchal authority, always provided that no more Roman citizens be created than the number of magistrates proper to be elected in accordance with this law. (Charter of Salpensa, chapter 21)

16. Oversight of Municipal Affairs in Bithynia

Until the civil wars of the first century B.C., all provinces of the empire were administered by the Roman senate. When Augustus came to power, responsibility for the provinces was divided. Those regions which were sensitive or unruly, and required a large army presence, were administered by the emperor through governors whom he selected and who reported directly to him; they usually served for a term of three or more years. The senate retained authority only over the more stable provinces. Its governors were chosen by a random process which combined seniority and the drawing of lots, and they usually served for only a single year.

From time to time an emergency caused a senatorial province to be put under the emperor's care. The province of Bithynia (in what is northwest Turkey today) was transferred from the senate to the emperor Trajan in about A.D. 110. What provoked this intervention was not a military emergency, but the widespread mismanagement of town finances, over which local authorities had generally been permitted full control. The stability of the towns was crucial because the central government delegated many of its administrative responsibilities to local bodies. Trajan was so concerned about good fiscal management that he appointed supervisors even for towns in Italy, though Italy was not a province. In Bithynia, his troubleshooter was Pliny (see the introduction to document 12), who had previously served as a treasury official in Rome. Among Pliny's published letters there are more than a hundred items of official correspondence concerning Bithynia, including letters Pliny received from Trajan as well as the ones he wrote. From that series the following exchanges are taken.

Gaius Pliny to the Emperor Trajan: I enjoyed a most invigorating voyage as far as Ephesus, Sir. But after I began traveling by coach, a bad heat spell plus a bit of fever gave me some trouble, which caused me to stop at Pergamum. Then I transferred to boats of the coastal line and was held back

Pliny, *Letters* 10.17a, 10.23–24, 10.33–34, 10.37–42, 10.52–53. Translated for this volume by Peter White.

by adverse winds. I entered Bithynia some days later than I had hoped, on the 17th of September. Still, I can't complain about the delay, since I did have the auspicious opportunity of celebrating your birthday in the province. Now I am examining the disbursements, revenues, and debtor lists of the municipality of Prusa. The closer my involvement becomes, the more I realize how necessary it is. In a number of cases, funds are being detained by private individuals for various reasons, and besides that, money is being paid out for expenses that are by no means legitimate. That is what I have to tell you, Sir, fresh upon my arrival. (10.17a)

Gaius Pliny to the Emperor Trajan: Sir, the citizens of Prusa have a public bath. It is dingy and old. Naturally they set a high priority on building a new one, and I think you can acquiesce in their aim. There will be the money to do it—first of all, those sums in private hands which I have begun to call in and collect. And second, the townspeople are prepared to apply toward construction the money which has always gone to subsidize the dole of olive oil. But money aside, the prestige of the town and the magnificence of your reign are tied up in this project. (10.23)

Trajan to Pliny: If the construction of a new bath will not overtax the resources of Prusa, then we can acquiesce in their aim—provided that no assessment is levied for it, and that it does not force them to curtail basic operations later on. (10.24)

Gaius Pliny to the Emperor Trajan: While I was touring the other end of the province, a tremendous fire at Nicomedia destroyed many private homes and two public buildings on opposite sides of the same street, the temple of Isis and the civic boosters' center. The fire spread as far as it did thanks both to a high wind and to the shiftlessness of bystanders who chose to stand stock-still contemplating the disaster. But apart from that, the town had no pumps or buckets, or any kind of fire-fighting apparatus at all. Well, the equipment will be procured: I have already given instructions on that score. But please consider, Sir, whether you think a corps of professionals should be formed, limited to 150 persons. I will undertake to make sure that none but actual firemen are enrolled, and that they do not misuse the right of association granted them. It will not be difficult to ride herd on so few. (10.33)

Trajan to Pliny: Your idea that a corps of firemen could be formed at Nicomedia has many precedents in its favor. But we need to keep in mind that your province and particularly the cities in that area have had trouble with just such outfits. Whatever name, for whatever purpose, we give to people who band together, they will turn into political groups in no time at all. Therefore it is better to provide equipment which will be of use in fighting fires, and to put property owners on notice that they should take action themselves, and call on the services of bystanders if circumstances require. (10.34)

Gaius Pliny to the Emperor Trajan: Sir, the citizens of Nicomedia have spent 3,318,000 sesterces on an aqueduct which was halted before it was finished, and finally torn down. They then committed 200,000 sesterces to a second aqueduct, but since this one was also abandoned, they face further expense on top of all the money they have already thrown away, if they are to have any water. I have personally inspected the spring, which is crystal-clear. I think the water should be carried by elevated conduit, according to the original plan, so that the supply will reach more than just the lower levels of the town. A few arches are still in place; some new ones could be built with dressed stone taken from the second project, and I think a fair stretch should be constructed of brick, which is cheaper and more convenient. But it is critically important that you send out a hydraulic engineer or an architect so that past experience here does not repeat itself. I can only assure you that in terms of utility and beauty, this project is fully worthy of your reign. (10.37)

Trajan to Pliny: Arrangements should be made to supply water to the town of Nicomedia. I have every confidence that you will set to work with the diligence that is called for. But, good lord, part of that diligence should be to find out whose fault it was that the Nicomedians wasted so much money up till now. We don't want them just scratching each other's backs with this starting and stopping of aqueducts. Therefore bring to my attention whatever you find out. (10.38)

Gaius Pliny to the Emperor Trajan: Sir, at Nicaea a theater which is well into the construction phase but not finished has already cost more than 10,000,000 sesterces (at any rate, that is what I am told; I have not gone over the books). All wasted, I am afraid. The structure has settled and developed huge cracks, possibly because it was built on soft, wet ground, or because the stone used was weak and porous. The question is to decide whether to continue work, or to stop, or even to demolish the building—the foundations and lower tiers that support the rest look a lot more grandiose than solid to me. With the interruption of work on the main part, some complementary structures which were promised by private citizens (halls outside, and a colonnade around the top of the auditorium) are now in limbo.

Before I arrived here, the citizens of Nicaea also began to restore their gymnasium, which had been destroyed by fire. The plans called for a more spacious complex with more buildings than before. They have already invested a fair amount, but to no practical purpose I fear: the layout is poorly designed and the buildings are too far apart. Furthermore an architect (admittedly a rival of the man who began the job) tells me that though the walls are twenty-two feet thick, they will not take the weight put on them: that is because the core consists of loose stone, and there is no outer girdle of brick.

At Claudiopolis, too, building is underway (if it should not be called excavation) for an enormous public bath sited in a hollow at the foot of a mountain. The funds in this case come from entrance fees which have either been paid already by the new members you graciously added to the town council, or which will be paid when I move to collect.

I am very anxious that good use be made of the public funds at Nicaea, and of your kind involvement (more precious than money) at Claudiopolis. And so I feel obliged to ask that you send out an architect to have a look at the baths as well as the theater. We need to know whether it makes more sense, after all the money that has been spent, to finish the projects as best we can according to plan, or whether to rebuild what needs rebuilding or move what needs moving so that we do not throw good money after bad. (10.39)

Trajan to Pliny: Since you are on the spot, you are in the best position to resolve what should be done about the theater under construction at Nicaea. I will be content to have some note of your decision. Wait till the theater is finished before pressing members of the community to follow through on projects meant to accompany it. These Greeks are in love with gymnasiums, which is probably why the Nicaeans were too ambitious when they started building. They should be content with something that meets their needs. Decide for yourself what to tell the citizens of Claudiopolis about their ill-located bath. It is not possible that you have no architects; there are men with experience and talent in every province. At least you shouldn't imagine that it saves time to have them sent from Rome, as we usually get them from Greece ourselves. (10.40)

Gaius Pliny to the Emperor Trajan: As I contemplate the scope of your imagination and the grandeur of your position, it strikes me as appropriate to indicate projects which combine practicality and style in such a way as to ensure your glory now and in ages to come. In the territory of Nicomedia there is a large lake. Over it marble, produce, firewood, and lumber are shipped cheaply and easily by boat as far as the highway, and from there with great effort and still greater expense by wagon as far as the coast. The engineering needed to improve the situation would entail a lot of manpower, but that is available. The countryside is densely populated and the city even more so, and there is reason to expect that all the inhabitants will cooperate enthusiastically in a project which will benefit all. The only thing needed on your side, if you don't mind, is to send a surveyor or architect who will measure carefully whether the lake is above sea level; the local builders maintain that it is sixty feet higher. I have discovered a cutting in the vicinity that dates from the royal period. But since it was never finished, I cannot tell whether it was meant to drain the adjacent fields or to connect the lake and the river; nor is it clear whether the king simply died in the midst of things, or whether he despaired of realizing his plan. But (you must pardon my zeal for your glory) that just increases my eagerness for you to carry through what kings could do no more than begin. (10.41)

Trajan to Pliny: We might be interested in your project of connecting the lake to the sea. But there must be careful study of its sources and volume of intake, to make sure that it will not drain away completely if given an outlet to the sea. You can borrow a surveyor from [the governor of Moesia,] Calpurnius Macer, and I will send an engineer with the appropriate background from Rome. (10.42)

Gaius Pliny to the Emperor Trajan: That day on which you saved the realm by taking it under your care, Sir, we commemorated with all the joy the thought inspires in us. We prayed that the gods would bless and protect you for the good of all mankind, because our security is linked to your well-being. I administered the oath of allegiance to the soldiers at the traditional ceremony, and the people of the province manifested their devotion by chiming in. (10.52)

Trajan to Pliny: My dear Pliny, I am grateful for your letter about the fealty and joy which soldiers and civilians alike showed during the ceremonies you organized on the anniversary of my accession. (10.53)

17. Aristides, *To Rome* (Selections)

Aelius Aristides was born to a Greek landowning family in either A.D. 117 or 129, and died in 181, in the province of Mysia in western Asia Minor.

From James H. Oliver, "The Ruling Power: A Study of the Roman Empire in the Second Century after Christ through the Roman Oration of Aelius Aristides," *Transactions of the American Philosophical Society*, n.s. 43 (1953), pt. 4, pp. 895–907. Reprinted by permission of the American Philosophical Society. Paragraph numbering follows that of James H. Oliver.

Although he studied rhetoric in Pergamum and Athens (in Athens under the famous rhetorician Herodes Atticus) and visited Rome at twenty-six years of age, he spent most of his life in Asia Minor, especially in the major port of Smyrna (Izmir, Turkey).

He composed and probably delivered this famous speech in praise of Rome in A.D. 144 or 156, during the exceptionally peaceful and prosperous reign of Emperor Antoninus Pius. Rhetoric was one of the forms of Greek literature that flourished most spectacularly under Roman dominion, and one of its most popular categories was the panegyric, or praise, of cities. Although it is not an objective or critical evaluation of Rome and conditions within the empire, it reveals what qualities of Roman rule appealed to the urban, educated elite among Rome's Greek subjects. It is also a significant expression of the successful identification of many Greeks with the interests and goals of the Roman leadership, although the elegant and learned Greek in which Aristides wrote is a reminder that educated Greeks never abandoned their own language for Latin. Concepts such as "the civilized world" also point to Rome's great intellectual debt to the Hellenistic thought-world. The scarcity of other kinds of literary sources for the second half of the second century makes this speech, despite the need for critical caution, an important source on contemporary perceptions of Rome and her empire.

---

1. It is a time-honored custom of travellers setting forth by land or sea to make a prayer pledging the performance of some vow—whatever they have in mind—on safe arrival at their destination. I recall a poet who playfully parodied the custom by pledging "a grain of incense—with gilded horns!" As for me the vow that I made as I journeyed hither was not of the usual stupid and irrelevant kind, nor one unrelated to the art of my profession: merely that if I came through safely I would salute your city with a public address.

2. But since it was quite impossible to pledge words commensurate with your city, it became evident that I had need of a second prayer. It is perhaps really presumptuous to dare undertake an oration to equal such majesty in a city. However, I have promised to address you, and I can speak only as I can. Yet even so it may not be unacceptable, for I could name others too who hold that if they do the very best they can, it will seem good enough to the gods.

3. But, sirs, you who are at home in the great city, if you share the hope that I prove not false to my vow, join your prayers to mine for the success of my boldness. Suffer me to say at once, before I come to the praise of your city, that here I found men—in a phrase of Euripides—"able to inspire

one, though he were speechless before, to eloquence and skill," to discourse on things quite beyond his natural gifts.

4. Praise of your city all men sing and will continue to sing. Yet their words accomplish less than if they had never been spoken. Their silence would not have magnified or diminished her in the least, nor changed your knowledge of her. But their encomiums accomplish quite the opposite of what they intend, for their words do not show precisely what is truly admirable. If an artist should make a botch of it after undertaking to portray in a painting a body of famous beauty, probably everyone would say it would have been better not to paint it at all; to have let them see the body itself, or at least not to show them a caricature. 5. And so I think it is with your city. Their speeches take away from her most of her wonders. It is like some effort to describe the marvelous size of an army such as Xerxes'. The man tells of seeing 10,000 infantry here, and 20,000 there, and so and so many cavalry, without reporting in what excites his wonder even a mere fraction of the whole.

6. For it is she who first proved that oratory cannot reach every goal. About her not only is it impossible to speak properly, but it is impossible even to see her properly. In truth it requires some all-seeing Argos—rather, the all-seeing god who dwells in the city. For beholding so many hills occupied by buildings, or on plains so many meadows completely urbanized, or so much land brought under the name of the city, who could survey her accurately? And from what point of observation?

7. Homer says of snow that as it falls, it covers "the crest of the range and the mountain peaks and the flowering fields and the rich acres of men, and," he says, "it is poured out over the white sea, the harbors and the shores." So also of this city. Like the snow, she covers mountain peaks, she covers the land intervening, and she goes down to the sea, where the commerce of all mankind has its common exchange and all the produce of the earth has its common market. Wherever one may go in Rome, there is no vacancy to keep one from being, there also, in mid-city.

8. And indeed she is poured out, not just over the level ground, but in a manner with which the simile cannot begin to keep pace, she rises great distances into the air, so that her height is not to be compared to a covering of snow but rather to the peaks themselves. And as a man who far surpasses others in size and strength likes to show his strength by carrying others on his back, so this city, which is built over so much land, is not satisfied with her extent, but raising upon her shoulders others of equal size, one over the other, she carries them. It is from this that she gets her name, and strength [*rōmē*] is the mark of all that is hers. Therefore, if one chose to unfold, as it were, and lay flat on the ground the cities which now

she carries high in air, and place them side by side, all that part of Italy which intervenes would, I think, be filled and become one continuous city stretching to the Strait of Otranto.

9. Though she is so vast as perhaps even now I have not sufficiently shown, but as the eye attests more clearly, it is not possible to say of her as of other cities, "There she stands." Again it has been said of the capital cities of the Athenians and the Lacedaemonians—and may no ill omen attend the comparison—that the first would in size appear twice as great as in its intrinsic power, the second far inferior in size to its intrinsic power. But of this city, great in every respect, no one could say that she has not created power in keeping with her magnitude. No, if one looks at the whole empire and reflects how small a fraction rules the whole world, he may be amazed at the city, but when he has beheld the city herself and the boundaries of the city, he can no longer be amazed that the entire civilized world is ruled by one so great.

10. Some chronicler, speaking of Asia, asserted that one man ruled as much land as the sun passed, and his statement was not true because he placed all Africa and Europe outside the limits where the sun rises in the East and sets in the West. It has now however turned out to be true. Your possession is equal to what the sun can pass, and the sun passes over your land. Neither the Chelidonean nor the Cyanean promontories limit your empire, nor does the distance from which a horseman can reach the sea in one day, nor do you reign within fixed boundaries, nor does another dictate to what point your control reaches; but the sea like a girdle lies extended at once in the middle of the civilized world and of your hegemony.

11. Around it lie the great continents greatly sloping, ever offering to you in full measure something of their own. Whatever the seasons make grow and whatever countries and rivers and lakes and arts of Hellenes and non-Hellenes produce are brought from every land and sea, so that if one would look at all these things, he must needs behold them either by visiting the entire civilized world or by coming to this city. For whatever is grown and made among each people cannot fail to be here at all times and in abundance. And here the merchant vessels come carrying these many products from all regions in every season and even at every equinox, so that the city appears a kind of common emporium of the world.

12. Cargoes from India and, if you will, even from Arabia the Blest one can see in such numbers as to surmise that in those lands the trees will have been stripped bare and that the inhabitants of these lands, if they need anything, must come here and beg for a share of their own. Again one can see Babylonian garments and ornaments from the barbarian country beyond arriving in greater quantity and with more ease than if shippers from Naxos

or from Cythnos, bearing something from those islands, had but to enter the port of Athens. Your farms are Egypt, Sicily and the civilized part of Africa.

13. Arrivals and departures by sea never cease, so that the wonder is, not that the harbor has insufficient space for merchant vessels, but that even the sea has enough, [if] it really does.

And just as Hesiod said about the ends of the Ocean, that there is a common channel where all waters have one source and destination, so there is a common channel to Rome and all meet here, trade, shipping, agriculture, metallurgy, all the arts and crafts that are or ever have been, all the things that are engendered or grow from the earth. And whatever one does not see here neither did nor does exist. And so it is not easy to decide which is greater, the superiority of this city in respect to the cities that now are or the superiority of this empire in respect to the empires that ever were.

14. I blush now: after such great and impressive matters have been mentioned, my argument reaches a point where it is without great and impressive material; I shall distinguish myself ingloriously by recalling some barbarian empire or Hellenic power and it will seem that I intend to do the opposite of what the Aeolic poets did. For they, when they wished to disparage any work of their contemporaries, compared it with something great and famous among the ancients, thinking in this way best to expose its deficiency. Yet having no other way to show the degree of your empire's superiority, I shall compare it with petty ancient ones. For you have made all the greatest achievements appear very small by your success in surpassing them. Selecting the most important, I shall discuss them, though you perhaps will laugh at them then.

15. On the one hand, let us look at the Persian Empire, which in its day had indeed reputation among the Hellenes and gave to the king who ruled it the epithet "great"—for I shall omit the preceding empires which were even less ideal—and let us see all in succession, both its size and the things which were done in its time. Therefore we must examine in conjunction how they themselves enjoyed what they had acquired and how they affected their subjects.

16. First then, what the Atlantic now means to you, the Mediterranean was to the "King" in that day. Here his empire stopped, so that the Ionians and Aeolians were at the end of his world. Once when he, "the King of those from the Sunrise to the Sunset," tried to cross into Greece, he evoked wonder less for his own greatness than for the greatness of his defeat, and he exhibited his splendour in the enormity of his losses. He who failed by so much to win control over Hellas, and who held Ionia as his most remote possession, is, I think, left behind by your empire not by a mere discus

throw or an arrow's flight, but by a good half of the civilized world and by the sea in addition.

17. Moreover, even within these boundaries he was not always king with full authority, but as the power of Athens or the fortunes of Lacedaemon varied, now king as far as Ionia, Aeolis and the sea, and then again no longer down to Ionia and the sea, but as far as Lydia without seeing the sea west of the Cyanean Islands, being a king while he stayed upcountry just like a king in a game of children, coming down again with the consent of those who would let him be king. This the army of Agesilaus revealed, and before him that of the Ten Thousand with Clearchus, the one marching as through its own country, all the way to Phrygia, the other penetrating, as through a solitude, beyond the Euphrates.

18. What enjoyments they derived from their empire are illustrated in the shrewd and neat remark of Oebaras. It is said that he first told Cyrus, who was grieved at his much wandering, that if he wished to be king, he ought—ay, there was necessity—to go marching around to every part of his empire, will he nill he, for he saw what happened to the leather bag: the parts on which he set foot became depressed and touched, while the parts off which he stepped rose up again and were depressed once more only with another trampling. They were a kind of vagrant kings and were superior to the nomadic Scythians only in so far as they went around in carriages instead of carts,—a kind of nomadic kings and wanderers who, on account of their distrust and fear of settling in one place, crushed down their country, really like some leather bag, and, by this, controlling now Babylon, again Susa, then Ecbatana, not understanding how to hold it [all] at all times nor tending it as shepherds.

19. In truth such were deeds of men who, as it were, dared not trust that the empire was their own. They did not mind it as their own, nor did they raise either the urban or the rural areas to beauty and full size, but like those who have laid violent hands on property not their own they consumed it without conscience or honor, seeking to keep their subjects as weak as possible, and as if, in the feat of the five exercises, vying with each other in murders, the second ever tried to outdo the man before. It was a contest to slaughter as many people, to expel as many families and villages, and to break as many oaths as possible.

20. Those then are the enjoyments they derived from their famous power. The consequences of these enjoyments were what a law of nature ordained, hatreds and plots from those who were so used, and defections and civil wars and constant strife and ceaseless rivalries.

21. They themselves harvested these rewards, as if ruling as the result of a curse rather than in answer to a prayer, while the subjects received all that

those who are ruled by men like that must of necessity receive, and of which some mention has already been made, more or less. A child's beauty was a terror to its parents, a wife's beauty a terror to her husband. Not he who committed the most crimes but he who acquired the most property was doomed to destruction. It could almost be said that more cities then were being destroyed and demolished than are being founded today.

22. It was easier to be preserved when fighting against the Persians than when obeying them. For in battle they were easily defeated, but where they had power their insolence knew no bounds. And those who served them they despised as slaves, while those who were free they punished as enemies. Consequently they passed their lives in giving and receiving hatred. And so in war, which was their way of settling disputes in the majority of cases, they often feared their subjects more than their enemies.

23. Fundamentally two things were wrong. The Persians did not know how to rule and their subjects did not co-operate, since it is impossible to be good subjects if the rulers are bad rulers. Government and slave-management were not yet differentiated, but king and master were equivalent terms. They certainly did not proceed in a reasonable manner and with great objectives. For the word "master" [*despōtēs*] applies properly within the circle of a private household; when it extends to cities and nations, the role is hard to keep up.

24. Again Alexander, who acquired the great empire—so it looked until yours arose—by overrunning the earth, to tell the truth, more closely resembled one who acquired a kingdom than one who showed himself a king. For what happened to him, I think, is as if some ordinary person were to acquire much good land but were to die before receiving the yield of it.

25. He advanced over most of the earth and reduced all who opposed him; and he had absolutely all the hardships. But he could not establish the empire nor place the crown upon the labors he had endured, but died midway in the course of his affairs. So one might say that he won very many battles but, as a king, he did very little, and that he became a great contender for kingship, but never received any enjoyable result worthy of his genius and skill. What happened to him was much as if a man, while contending in an Olympic contest, defeated his opponents, then died immediately after the victory before rightly adjusting the crown upon his head.

26. After all, what laws did he ordain for each of his peoples? Or what contributions in taxes, men or ships did he put on a permanent basis? Or by what routine administration with automatic progress and fixed periods of time did he conduct his affairs? In civil administration what successes did he achieve among the people under his rule? He left only one real memorial of his endowment as a statesman, the city by Egypt which bears his name; he did well in founding this for you, the greatest city after yours, for

you to have and to control. Thus he abolished the rule of the Persians, yet he himself all but never ruled.

27. Now, when he died, the empire of the Macedonians immediately broke up into innumerable pieces, and the Macedonians showed by what they did that the rule of an empire was beyond their capabilities. They could not even hold their own country any longer, but came to that point of fortune where they were compelled to abandon their own country in order to rule over alien territory, more like men who had been deported than like men with a capacity for command. And it was a riddle: Macedonians, each reigning not in Macedon but wherever he could, who garrisoned rather than governed their cities and districts, men driven from home, appointed as kings not by the great king but by themselves, and if the expression be permitted, satraps without king. With which term shall we describe a condition such as theirs, for were they not more like robber chieftains than like kings?

28. Now, however, the present empire has been extended to boundaries of no mean distance, to such, in fact, that one cannot even measure the area within them. On the contrary, for one who begins a journey westward from the point where at that period the empire of the Persian found its limit, the rest is far more than the entirety of his domain, and there are no sections which you have omitted, neither city nor tribe nor harbor nor district, except possibly some that you condemned as worthless. The Red Sea and the Cataracts of the Nile and Lake Maeotis, which formerly were said to lie on the boundaries of the earth, are like the courtyard walls to the house which is this city of yours. On the other hand, you have explored Ocean. Some writers did not believe that Ocean existed at all, or did not believe that it flowed around the earth; they thought that poets had invented the name and had introduced it into literature for the sake of entertainment. But you have explored it so thoroughly that not even the island therein has escaped you.

29. Vast and comprehensive as is the size of it, your empire is much greater for its perfection than for the area which its boundaries encircle. There are no pockets of the empire held by Mysians, Sacae, Pisidians, or others, land which some have occupied by force, others have detached by revolt, who cannot be captured. Nor is it merely called the land of the *King*, while really the land of all who are able to hold it. Nor do satraps fight one another as if they had no king; nor are cities at variance, some fighting against these and some against those, with garrisons being dispatched to some cities and being expelled from others. But for the eternal duration of this empire the whole civilized world prays all together, emitting, like a flute after a thorough cleaning, one note with more perfect precision than a chorus; so beautifully is it harmonized by the leader in command.

30. The keynote is taken by all, everywhere, in the same way. And those who have settled in the mountains are, in their avoidance of discord, lower in pride than those who dwell in the least elevated plains, while those in the rich plains, both men who have cleruchic holdings and men who have your colonial land, are engaged in agriculture. Conditions no longer differ from island to mainland, but all, as one continuous country and one people, heed quietly.

31. All directions are carried out by the chorus of the civilized world at a word or gesture of guidance more easily than at some plucking of a chord; and if anything need be done, it suffices to decide and there it is already done.

The governors sent out to the city-states and ethnic groups are each of them rulers of those under them, but in what concerns themselves and their relations to each other they are all equally among the ruled, and in particular they differ from those under their rule in that it is they—one might assert—who first show how to be the right kind of subject. So much respect has been instilled in all men for him who is the great governor, who obtains for them their all.

32. They think that he knows what they are doing better than they do themselves. Accordingly they fear his displeasure and stand in greater awe of him than one would of a despot, a master who was present and watching and uttering commands. No one is so proud that he can fail to be moved upon hearing even the mere mention of the Ruler's name, but, rising, he praises and worships him and breathes two prayers in a single breath, one to the gods on the Ruler's behalf, one for his own affairs to the Ruler himself. And if the governors should have even some slight doubt whether certain claims are valid in connection with either public or private lawsuits and petitions from the governed, they straightway send to him with a request for instructions what to do, and they wait until he renders a reply, like a chorus waiting for its trainer.

33. Therefore, he has no need to wear himself out traveling around the whole empire nor, by appearing personally, now among some, then among others, to make sure of each point when he has the time to tread their soil. It is very easy for him to stay where he is and manage the entire civilized world by letters, which arrive almost as soon as they are written, as if they were carried by winged messengers.

34. But that which deserves as much wonder and admiration as all the rest together, and constant expression of gratitude both in word and action, shall now be mentioned. You who hold so vast an empire and rule it with such a firm hand and with so much unlimited power have very decidedly won a great success, which is completely your own.

36. For of all who have ever gained empire you alone rule over men who

are free. Caria has not been given to Tissaphernes, nor Phrygia to Pharnabazus, nor Egypt to someone else; nor is the country said to be enslaved, as household of so-and-so, to whomsoever it has been turned over, a man himself not free. But just as those in states of one city appoint the magistrates to protect and care for the governed, so you, who conduct public business in the whole civilized world exactly as if it were one city state, appoint the governors, as is natural after elections, to protect and care for the governed, not to be slave masters over them. Therefore governor makes way for governor unobtrusively, when his time is up, and far from staying too long and disputing the land with his successor, he might easily not stay long enough even to meet him.

37. Appeals to a higher court are made with the ease of an appeal from deme to dicastery, with no greater menace for those who make them than for those who have accepted the local verdict. Therefore one might say that the men of today are ruled by the governors who are sent out, only in so far as they are content to be ruled.

38. Are not these advantages beyond the old "Free Republic" of every people? For under Government by the People it is not possible to go outside after the verdict has been given in the city's court, not even to other jurors, but, except in a city so small that it has to have jurors from out of town, one must ever be content with the local verdict . . . [deprived] undeservedly, or, as plaintiff, not getting possession even after a favorable verdict.

But now in the last instance there is another judge, a mighty one, whose comprehension no just claim ever escapes. 39. There is an abundant and beautiful equality of the humble with the great and of the obscure with the illustrious, and, above all, of the poor man with the rich and of the commoner with the noble, and the word of Hesiod comes to pass, "For he easily exalts, and the exalted he easily checks," namely this judge and princeps as the justice of the claim may lead, like a breeze in the sails of a ship, favoring and accompanying, not the rich man more, the poor man less, but benefiting equally whomsoever it meets.

40. I shall treat also the records of Hellenic states, since I have come to that part of my speech, but I feel shame and fear lest my argument sound too trivial. Nevertheless, treat them I shall, but as I just said, not as comparing equal with equal. In the absence of other parallels, I am compelled to use those at hand, because in such a case it is absurd to keep asserting with enthusiasm that it is impossible to find other achievements even remotely equal to yours but that all are overshadowed by these, yet to keep waiting for a time to make comparisons when we may have equal achievements to recall. It is inappropriate, I think, because even similar achievements, if we had any to report, would not be similarly astonishing.

41. Again I am by no means unaware that these Hellenic records, in

proud extent of territory and grand scale of operations, are still poorer than the Persian record which I just now examined. But to surpass the Hellenes in wisdom and restraint, while outdoing the Barbarians in riches and in might, seems to me a great achievement and one fulfilling the ideal and more glorious than every other.

42. My next subject, then, is what kind of international organizations the Hellenic states created and how they fared therewith. If it appear that they were unable to preserve much smaller organizations, obviously this will decide the issue.

43. The Athenians and the Lacedaemonians did all they could to get control and hegemony, and theirs was the power to sail the sea and to rule over the Cyclades and hold the Thraceward regions and Thermopylae and the Hellespont and Coryphasion. That was the extent of their power. Their experience was as if a man who wished to obtain possession of a body received some claws and extremities instead of the whole body and with these in his possession thought that he had just what he wanted. So they too, after striving for hegemony, brought home small islands and headlands and havens and such places, and they wore themselves out around the sea, in pursuit of an hegemony which existed more in their dreams than within their powers of acquisition.

44. Nevertheless, at times as if their turn had come around in the allotment, each city became chairman of the Hellenes without keeping the office even for a single, say, generation. So there was no clear supremacy, but in the struggle for hegemony they inflicted upon each other the so-called Cadmean victory. It was as if each city always demanded that the others be not the only ones to get a chance at being hated, but that they themselves might have a share.

45. For just one Lacedaemonian leader so disposed the Hellenes that they willingly got rid of the Lacedaemonians and [gladly] sought other rulers for themselves. After they had given themselves to the Athenians, in a little while they repented, not liking the disproportion of the tributes imposed nor those who used the tributes as a pretext for graft, and being dragged to Athens every year to render an account concerning their own local affairs, while cleruchs were being dispatched into their country and ships to collect extra funds beyond the tribute, if perhaps another need prevailed.

46. Moreover they were unable to maintain the freedom of their citadels and were in the power of the politicians whom the Athenians installed, both those with good intentions and equally those with bad. They were obliged to undertake unnecessary campaigns, often in holidays and festivals, and in brief, from the Athenian leadership they derived no benefit great enough to make it worth their while to perform these heavy services.

47. As a result of these conditions the majority were disgusted with the Athenians, and turning again from them to the Lacedaemonians, just as formerly from the latter to the Athenians, they were deceived again by the Lacedaemonians. The latter first proclaimed that they would fight the Athenians in behalf of the liberty of the Hellenes, and in this way they attracted many. When they had destroyed the walls of Athens and had secured control of the Greek world and could do anything, they so far outdid the Athenians that they established in all the Greek cities tyrannies, which they euphemistically called decarchies.

48. And destroying one arbitrary government, that of the Athenians, in its place they introduced many from themselves which incessantly harassed the governed, not from a seat at Athens nor from one at Sparta but from positions permanently located in the very lands of the governed and interwoven, as it were, in the local institutions. So if, as they started the war, they had announced to the Hellenes that they would fight the Athenians in order to do them greater and more frequent injuries than the Athenians did and to make what the Hellenes had from the Athenians look like freedom, there would have been no better way to make good their promise. 49. And in consequence they soon gave way to one fugitive and were abandoned by the Thebans and were hated by the Corinthians; the sea was made full of their "harmonizers" who were being expelled because they were disharmonious and because, when installed as governors, they held the cities in a way which belied the very name of harmost [one who arranges, governor].

50. From the misdoings of those men and the hatred which the Hellenes for that reason felt for the Lacedaemonians, the Thebans gathered strength and defeated the latter in the Battle of Leuctra; but as soon as the Lacedaemonians were out of the way, then no one could endure the Thebans, who had succeeded in one battle. On the contrary, it became clear that it was yet more to the advantage of the Hellenes that the Cadmeia (i.e., Thebes) be occupied by, than victorious over, the Lacedaemonians. Thus the Thebans now received their hate.

51. These examples I have collected, certainly not to denounce the Hellenes generally like the extraordinary author [Anaxamines of Lampsachus] of the "Three-headed Creature"—may it never be so necessary—, but wishing to show thereby that the knowledge how to rule did not yet exist before your time. For if it did exist, it would be among the Hellenes, who distinguished themselves for skill, I venture to say, very greatly, at least in the other arts. But this knowledge is both a discovery of your own and to other men an importation from you. For it might well be true if one were to say about the Hellenes as a whole what has already been said in the case of the Athenians, that they were good at resisting foreign rule and defeating the Persians and at expending their wealth in public service and enduring

hardships, but were themselves still untrained to rule, and in the attempt they failed.

52. First they used to send into the cities garrisons which of course were not always less numerous than the able-bodied natives in the countries to which they were being sent. Secondly they aroused suspicion among those who were not yet garrisoned that they were conducting all business by force and violence. So there were two results, an insecure grip on the object of their encroachment, yet a powerful reputation for encroachment: they were failing to hold the cities securely, and besides they were earning hatred and were reaping the hardships instead of the blessings of empire.

53. Then, what followed? Ever widely dispersed and separated they became too weak at home and were unable to preserve their own land, through seeking to hold that of others. So neither were they able to outnumber, in the troops they sent elsewhere, those whom they strove to rule, nor was it possible to maintain an adequate defence with those they left behind for their own protection. They were too few abroad, too few at home. Without the ultimate means to hold the empire, its expansion posed for them an insoluble problem. Thus the aims which they pursued were in opposition to their needs. The success of their plans became an embarrassment, almost a curse, while the failure was less a burden for them and less terrifying. Instead of rulers they seemed no different from a fallen city's scattered remnants, toiling for the sake of toil. For as the poets say (of Sisyphus), the crowning effort would unaccountably weaken at the moment the end was reached, and back (the stone) would roll to where it had been.

54. It was no longer to their interest that the governed should be either strong or weak: they did not want them strong because of possible treachery, nor weak because of the menace of wars from outside, and in order to have some advantage from the league of allies. Toward them the Athenians had come to feel much like those who, in a game of draughts, advance their pieces to one position and pull them back to another, without knowing what use they will make of them. But wishing, as they did, both to have their allies, and not to have them, the Athenians would take them in hand and move them without being able to say whither they were going in earnest.

55. And the strangest and most absurd thing of all: they would make the rest, who had rebellion in mind themselves, go to war against those who were rebelling. It was much as if in doing so they were asking the very rebels to take the field against their own rebellion. They were unreasonably leading against the rebels men who were on the rebels' side, and to whom it was surely inexpedient to reveal the help that in serious effort could be given to the others against the Athenians. 56. So in this also they were ac-

complishing the very opposite of their wish and of their interest, because, in their desire for the recovery of those in revolt, they were causing the revolt even of those allies who were with them. For they showed them that if they remained they would be available to the Athenians for use against each other, but that leagued together in revolt, they would all be securely free, because at the end the Athenians would have none left through whom the rebels might be taken. Therefore, they did themselves more harm than their faithless allies did, in that the latter seceded individually, while they themselves introduced a universal defection as a result of their activity.

57. Thus in that period there was still no orderly system of imperial rule and they did not go after it with knowledge of what an orderly system was. Although their holdings were small and, as it were, marginal lands and military allotments, nevertheless they were unable to retain even these because of their own inexperience and weakness. For they did not lead the cities with kindness nor did they have the power to hold them firmly, being simultaneously oppressive and weak. So at last they were stripped of their plumage like Aesop's jackdaw, and were fighting alone against all.

58. Well, this which, in a word, escaped all previous men was reserved for you alone to discover and perfect. And no wonder! Just as in other spheres the skills come to the fore when the material is there, so when a great empire of surpassing power arose, the skill too accumulated and entered into its composition, and both were mutually reinforced. On account of the size of the empire the experience necessarily accrued, while on account of the knowledge how to rule with justice and with reason the empire flourished and increased.

59. But there is that which very decidedly deserves as much attention and admiration now as all the rest together. I mean your magnificent citizenship with its grand conception, because there is nothing like it in the records of all mankind. Dividing into two groups all those in your empire—and with this word I have indicated the entire civilized world—you have everywhere appointed to your citizenship, or even to kinship with you, the better part of the world's talent, courage, and leadership, while the rest you recognized as a league under your hegemony.

60. Neither sea nor intervening continent are bars to citizenship, nor are Asia and Europe divided in their treatment here. In your empire all paths are open to all. No one worthy of rule or trust remains an alien, but a civil community of the World has been established as a Free Republic under one, the best, ruler and teacher of order; and all come together as into a common civic center, in order to receive each man his due.

61. What another city is to its own boundaries and territory, this city is to the boundaries and territory of the entire civilized world, as if the latter

were a country district and she had been appointed common town. It might be said that this one citadel is the refuge and assembly place of all neighbors or of all who dwell in outside demes.

62. She has never failed them, but like the soil of the earth, she supports all men; and as the sea, which receives with its gulfs all the many rivers, hides them and holds them all and still, with what goes in and out, is and seems ever the same, so actually this city receives those who flow in from all the earth and has even sameness in common with the sea. The latter is not made greater by the influx of rivers, for it has been ordained by fate that with the waters flowing in, the sea maintain its volume; here no change is visible because the city is so great.

63. Let this passing comment, which the subject suggested, suffice. As we were saying, you who are "great greatly" distributed your citizenship. It was not because you stood off and refused to give a share in it to any of the others that you made your citizenship an object of wonder. On the contrary, you sought its expansion as a worthy aim, and you have caused the word Roman to be the label, not of membership in a city, but of some common nationality, and this not just one among all, but one balancing all the rest. For the categories into which you now divide the world are not Hellenes and Barbarians, and it is not absurd, the distinction which you made, because you show them a citizenry more numerous, so to speak, than the entire Hellenic race. The division which you substituted is one into Romans and non-Romans. To such a degree have you expanded the name of your city.

64. Since these are the lines along which the distinction has been made, many in every city are fellow-citizens of yours no less than of their own kinsmen, though some of them have not yet seen this city. There is no need of garrisons to hold their citadels, but the men of greatest standing and influence in every city guard their own fatherlands for you. And you have a double hold upon the cities, both from here and from your fellow citizens in each.

65. No envy sets foot in the empire, for you yourselves were the first to disown envy, when you placed all opportunities in view of all and offered those who were able a chance to be not governed more than they governed in turn. Nor does hatred either steal in from those who are not chosen. For since the constitution is a universal one and, as it were, of one state, naturally your governors rule not as over the property of others but as over their own. Besides, all the masses have as a share in it the permission to [take refuge with you] from the power of the local magnates, [but there is] the indignation and punishment from you which will come upon them immediately, if they themselves dare to make any unlawful change.

66. Thus the present regime naturally suits and serves both rich and

poor. No other way of life is left. There has developed in your constitution a single harmonious, all-embracing union; and what formerly seemed to be impossible has come to pass in your time: [maintenance] of control over an empire, over a vast one at that, and at the same time firmness of rule [without] unkindness.

67a. Thus the cities can be clear of garrisons. Mere detachments of horse and foot suffice for the protection of whole countries, and even these are not concentrated in the cities with billets [in] every household, but are dispersed throughout the rural area within bounds and orbits of [their own]. Hence many nations do not know where at any time their guardians are. But if anywhere a city through excess of growth had passed beyond the ability to maintain order by itself, you did not begrudge to these in their turn the men to stand by and guard them carefully.

68. It is not safe for those to rule who have not power. The second best way to sail, they say, is to be governed by one's betters, but by you now it has been shown to be actually the first best way. Accordingly, all are held fast and would not ask to secede any more than those at sea from the helmsman. As bats in caves cling fast to each other and to the rocks, so all from you depend with much concern not to fall from this cluster of cities, and would sooner conceive fear of being abandoned by you, than abandon you themselves. 67b. And as a result all send their tribute to you with more pleasure than some would actually receive it from others: they have good reason.

69. They no longer dispute over the right to rule and to have first honors, which caused the outbreak of all the wars of the past. Instead, the rulers of yore do not even recall with certainty what domain they once had, while the others, like water in silent flow, are most delightfully at rest. They have gladly ceased from toil and trouble, for they have come to realize that in the other case they were fighting vainly over shadows. As in the myth of a Pamphylian, or if not so, then Plato's myth, the cities, already being laid, as it were, upon the funeral pyre by their mutual strife and disorder, merely received the right leadership all at once and suddenly revived. How they reached this point they have no explanation and can only wonder at the present. They have come to feel like men aroused from sleep: instead of the dreams they but recently had, they awakened to the sudden vision and presence of these genuine blessings.

70. Wars, even if they once occurred, no longer seem to have been real; on the contrary, stories about them are interpreted more as myth by the many who hear them. If anywhere an actual clash occurs along the border, as is only natural in the immensity of a great empire, because of the madness of Getae or the misfortune of Libyans or the wickedness of those around the Red Sea, who are unable to enjoy the blessings they have, then

simply like myths they themselves quickly pass and the stories about them. 71a. So great is your peace, though war was traditional among you.

72a. In regard to the civil administration of the whole empire it has been stated in what way you thought of it and what kind you established. Now it is time to speak about the army and military affairs, how you contrived in this matter and what organization you gave it. 71b. Yes, for the shoemakers and masons of yesterday are not the hoplites and cavalry of today. On the stage a farmer appears as a soldier after a quick change of costume, and in poor homes the same person cooks the meal, keeps the house, makes the bed. But you were not so undiscriminating. You did not expect that those engaged in other occupations would be made into soldiers by the need, nor did you leave it to your enemies to call you together. 72b. Rather in this too it is amazing how wise you were, and there is no precedent to serve as a parallel all the way.

73. For the Egyptians also progressed to the point of segregating the military, and it was deemed a very clever invention of theirs to have those who defended their country settled in special areas away from the rest. As in so many other respects, when compared to others, they were, it seemed, "clever Egyptians," as the saying goes. But when you visualized the same thing, you did not execute it in the same way. Instead you made a more equitable and more skillful segregation. In the former system it was not possible for each of the two groups to have equality of citizenship; the soldiers, who alone and forever bore the hardships, were in an inferior status to those who did not fight. Therefore the system was neither fair, nor agreeable to them. With you, on the other hand, since all have equality, a separate establishment for the military is successful.

74. Thus a courage like that of Hellenes and Egyptians and any others one might mention is surpassed by yours, and all, far as they are behind you in actual arms, trail still further in the conception. On the one hand you deemed it unworthy of your rule for those from this city to be subject to the levy and to the hardships and to enjoy no advantage from the present felicity; on the other hand you did not put your faith in alien mercenaries. Still you needed soldiers before the hour of crisis. So what did you do? You found an army of your own for which the citizens were undisturbed. This possibility was provided for you by that plan for all the empire, according to which you count no one an alien when you accept him for any employment where he can do well and is then needed.

75. Who then have been assembled and how? Going over the entire league, you looked about carefully for those who would perform this liturgy, and when you found them, you released them from the fatherland and gave them your own city, so that they became reluctant henceforth to call themselves by their original ethnics. Having made them fellow-citizens,

you made them also soldiers, so that the men from this city would not be subject to the levy, and those performing military service would none the less be citizens, who together with their enrollment in the army had lost their own cities but from that very day had become your fellow-citizens and defenders.

76. Under your hegemony this is the contribution which all make to the armed forces, and no city is disaffected. You asked from each only as many as would cause no inconvenience to the givers and would not be enough by themselves to provide the individual city with a full quota of an army of its own. Therefore all cities are well pleased with the dispatch of these men to be their own representatives in the union army, while locally each city has no militia of its own men whatsoever, and [for military protection] they look nowhere but to you, because it is for this sole purpose that those who went out from the cities have been marshalled in good order.

77. And again, after you selected from everywhere the most competent men, you had a very profitable idea. It was this. You thought that when even those picked out for their excellent physiques and bodily superiority train for the festivals and the prize contests, then those who would be the contenders in the greatest engagements of real war, and victors in as many victories as one might chance to win in behalf of such an empire, ought not to come together merely in a crisis. You thought that the latter, selected from all as the strongest and, especially, most competent, ought to train for a long while ahead of time so as to be superior the minute they took their stand.

78. So these men, once you eliminated the morally and the socially base, you [introduced into] the community of the ruling nation, not without the privileges I mentioned nor in such a way that they would envy those who stay in the city because they themselves were not of equal rights at the start, but in such a way that they would consider their share of citizenship as an honor. Having found and treated them thus, you led them to the boundaries of the empire. There you stationed them at intervals, and you assigned areas to guard, some to some, others to others.

79. They account also for the plan which you devised and evolved in regard to the walls which is worth comment now. One could call this city neither unwalled in the reckless manner of the Lacedaemonians nor again fortified with the splendor of Babylon or of any other city which before or after may have been walled in a more impressive style. On the contrary, you have made the fortification of Babylon seem frivolity and a woman's work indeed. 80. To place the walls around the city itself as if you were hiding her or fleeing from your subjects you considered ignoble and inconsistent with the rest of your concept, as if a master were to show fear of his own slaves. Nevertheless, you did not forget walls, but these you placed

around the empire, not the city. And you erected walls splendid and worthy of you, as far away as possible, visible to those within the circuit, but, for one starting from the city, an outward journey of months and years if he wished to see them.

81. Beyond the outermost ring of the civilized world, you drew a second line, quite as one does in walling in a town, another circle, more widely curved and more easily guarded. Here you built the walls to defend you and then erected towns bordering upon them, some in some parts, others elsewhere, filling them with colonists, giving these the comfort of arts and crafts, and in general establishing beautiful order.

82. An encamped army like a rampart encloses the civilized world in a ring. The perimeter of this enclosure, if a survey were made, would not be ten parasangs, nor twenty, nor a little more, nor a distance that one could say offhand, but as far as from the settled area of Aethiopia to the Phasis and from the Euphrates in the interior to the great outermost island toward the West; all this one can call a ring and circuit of the walls. 83. They have not been built with asphalt and baked brick nor do they stand there gleaming with stucco. Oh, but these ordinary works too exist at their individual places—yes, in very great number, and, as Homer says of the palace wall, "fitted close and accurately with stones, and boundless in size and gleaming more brilliantly than bronze."

84. But the ring, much greater and more impressive, in every way altogether unbreachable and indestructible, outshines them all, and in all time there has never been a wall so firm. For it is a barrier of men who have not acquired the habit of flight. It is they who defend these ordinary walls. They have perfected in the employment of all the tools of war exercises which bind them to one another in that union of the Myrmidons which Homer in the passage cited compared to the wall: a formation of helmets so close that an arrow cannot pass; a platform of shields raised overhead which would support in mid-air racetracks so much firmer than those constructible in town that even horsemen could race upon them, "a bronze plain," as one will then truthfully claim to see, for it is this in particular which deserves the phrase of Euripides; a line of breastplates so clinging to one another that if one ordered the man between two others to take his place with only light arms, the shields on either side would come half way and meet to cover him; and a shower of javelins, as it were, falling from heaven in a solid mass. Such are the parallel harmonies or systems of defence which curve around you, that circle of the fortifications at individual points, and that ring of those who keep watch over the whole world.

85. Once long ago Darius, with Artaphernes and Datis, succeeded in destroying one city on one island by dragging a net over its territory to catch the citizens. In a manner of speaking you too used a net; you dragged

it over the whole civilized world. But having done so, you now preserve all the cities by means of the very citizens you caught, the strangers whom they share with you. When you selected them, as I said, from all, you led them out, providing the men who showed quality with expectations that they would have no regret. The man who at any time might hold the first rank would not be from the nobility, and the man of second rank would not be from the second class and so on throughout the rest of the order. Each man would hold the post that was his due in the sense that not words but deeds would here distinguish the men of quality. And of these things you gave illustrious examples. Consequently they all consider unemployment a disaster and think that engagements are occasions for the fulfillment of their prayers, and against the enemy they are of one mind but in relation to each other they are perpetual rivals for preference, and they alone of mankind pray to meet with enemies.

86. Accordingly, upon seeing the training and organization of the military, one will think that the opponents in the words of Homer, "were they ten [or twenty times] as many," would soon be completely routed and in single combats overcome. And one who looks into the system of recruitment and replacement will express and feel what the king of Egypt meant when Cambyses was plundering the country and pillaging the sanctuaries. Standing upon the walls of Thebes, the Egyptian held out to him a clod of earth and a cup of water from the Nile; therewith he signified that as long as Cambyses was unable to carry away Egypt itself with the river Nile and to drag it off as plunder, he had not yet received the wealth of the Egyptians, but while river and land remained the Egyptians would soon have just as much again and the wealth of Egypt would never run out. So also concerning your military system one is justified in thinking and stating that as long as none can move the land itself from its foundation and leave a vacuum on departure, as long as the civilized world itself must remain in place, there is no way to make the wealth in your multitude of soldiers run out, for you have as many as you want arriving from all the civilized world.

87. In respect to military science, furthermore, you have made all men look like children. For you did not prescribe exercises for soldiers and officers to train for victory over the enemy only, but for victory over themselves first. Therefore, every day the soldier lives in discipline and no one ever leaves the post assigned to him, but as in some permanent chorus he knows and keeps his position and the subordinate does not on that account envy him who has a higher rank, but he himself rules with precision those whose superior he is.

88. It seems a pity that others have already said it first about the Lacedaemonians that, but for a few, their army consisted in commanders of commanders. It was a proper phrase to have been kept for you and to have

been applied to your case first, whereas the right occasion had not yet come when the author brought it forth. However, the Lacedaemonian army may well have been so small that there was nothing incredible in even all of them being commanders. But merely to name the branches and nationalities of your armed forces would not be easy. In these many units your soldiers, beginning with one who examines everything and looks after all—nations, cities, armies, are themselves leaders, through all the intermediate grades I could not mention, down to one in command of four or even two men. Like a spinning of thread which is continuously drawn from many filaments into fewer and fewer strands, the many individuals of your forces are always drawn together into fewer and fewer formations; and so they reach their complete integration through those who are at each point placed in command, one over others, each of these over others still, and so on. Does this not rise above Man's power of organization?

89. An impulse comes over me to change the Homeric line a little at the end and say, "Such within, I ween, is of Olympian Zeus the" empire. For when one ruler rules so many, and when his agents and envoys, much inferior to him but much superior to those over whom they watch, perform all commands quietly without noise and confusion, and envy is absent, and all actions everywhere are full of justice and respect, and the reward of virtue escapes no one, does not this epic tone seem right, this version of the line?

90. It appears to me that in this state you have established a constitution not at all like any of those among the rest of mankind. Formerly there seemed to be three constitutions in human society. Two were tyranny and oligarchy, or kingship and aristocracy, since they were known under two names each according to the view one took in interpreting the character of the men in control. A third category was known as democracy whether the leadership was good or bad. The cities had received one or the other constitution as choice or chance prevailed for each. Your state, on the other hand, is quite dissimilar; it is such a form of government as if it were a mixture of all the constitutions without the bad aspects of any one. That is why precisely this form of constitution has prevailed. So when one looks at the strength of the People and sees how easily they get all that they want and ask, he will deem it a complete democracy except for the faults of democracy. When he looks at the Senate sitting as a council and keeping the magistracies, he will think that there is no aristocracy more perfect than this. When he looks at the Ephor and Prytanis, who presides over all of these, him from whom it is possible for the People to get what they want and for the Few to have the magistracies and power, he will see in this one, the One who holds the most perfect monarchic rule, One without a share in the vices of a tyrant and One elevated above even kingly dignity.

91. It is not strange that you alone made these distinctions and discoveries how to govern both in the world and in the city itself. For you alone are rulers, so to speak, according to nature. Those others who preceded you established an arbitrary, tyrannical rule. They became masters and slaves of each other in turn, and as rulers they were a spurious crew. They succeeded each other as if advancing to the position in a ball game. Macedonians had a period of enslavement to Persians, Persians to Medes, Medes to Assyrians, but as long as men have known you, all have known you as rulers. Since you were free right from the start and had begun the game as it were in the rulers' position, you equipped yourselves with all that was helpful for the position of rulers, and you invented a new constitution such as no one ever had before, and you prescribed for all things fixed rules and fixed periods.

92. I should not perhaps be bringing it up at the wrong moment if I now expressed a thought which for a long time has occurred to me, and, rising to my very lips, has often forced itself upon me, but so far has always been pushed aside by the argument. How far you surpass all in total extent of your empire and in firmness of grip and plan of civil administration is set forth in what has already been said; but now, it seems to me that one would not miss the mark if he said the following: all those of the past who ruled over a very large part of the earth ruled, as it were, naked bodies by themselves, mere persons composing the ethnic groups or nations. 93. For when were there so many cities both inland and on the coast, or when have they been so beautifully equipped with everything? Did ever a man of those who lived then travel across country as we do, counting the cities by days and sometimes riding on the same day through two or three cities as if passing through sections of merely one? Hence the inferiority of those who lived in former times appears, because the past is so much surpassed, not only in the element at the head of the empire, but also in cases where identical groups have been ruled by others and by you. Those whom the others ruled did not as individuals have the equality of civil rights and privileges, but against the primitive organization of an ethnic group in that time one can set the municipal organization of the same group's city of today. It might very well be said that while the others have been kings, as it were, of open country and strongholds, you alone are rulers of civilized communities.

94. Now all the Greek cities rise up under your leadership, and the monuments which are dedicated in them and all their embellishments and comforts redound to your honor like beautiful suburbs. The coasts and interiors have been filled with cities, some newly founded, others increased under and by you.

95. Ionia, the much contested, freed of garrisons and of satraps, is visible to all, first in beauty. She has now advanced beyond herself by as

much as she formerly seemed to surpass the other lands in elegance and grace. Alexander's great and noble city by Egypt has become a glory of your hegemony, like a necklace or armlet among a wealthy lady's other possessions.

96. Taking good care of the Hellenes as of your foster parents, you constantly hold your hand over them, and when they are prostrate, you raise them up. You release free and autonomous those of them who were the noblest and the leaders of yore, and you guide the others moderately with much consideration and forethought. The barbarians you educate, rather mildly or sternly according to the nature that each has because it is right that those who are rulers of men be not inferior to those who are trainers of horses, and that they have tested their natures and guide them accordingly.

97. As on holiday the whole civilized world lays down the arms which were its ancient burden and has turned to adornment and all glad thoughts with power to realize them. All the other rivalries have left the [cities], and this one contention holds them all, how each city may appear most beautiful and attractive. All localities are full of gymnasia, fountains, monumental approaches, temples, workshops, schools, (98) and one can say that the civilized world, which had been sick from the beginning, as it were, has been brought by the right knowledge to a state of health. Gifts never cease from you to the cities, and it is not possible to determine who the major beneficiaries have been, because your kindness is the same to all.

99. Cities gleam with radiance and charm, and the whole earth has been beautified like a garden. Smoke rising from plains and fire signals for friend and foe have disappeared, as if a breath had blown them away, beyond land and sea. Every charming spectacle and an infinite number of festal games have been introduced instead. Thus like an ever-burning sacred fire the celebration never ends, but moves around from time to time and people to people, always somewhere, a demonstration justified by the way all men have fared. Thus it is right to pity only those outside your hegemony, if indeed there are any, because they lose such blessings.

100. It is you again who have best proved the general assertion, that Earth is mother of all and common fatherland. Now indeed it is possible for Hellene or non-Hellene, with or without his property, to travel wherever he will, easily, just as if passing from fatherland to fatherland. Neither Cilician Gates nor narrow sandy approaches to Egypt through Arab country, nor inaccessible mountains, nor immense stretches of river, nor inhospitable tribes of barbarians cause terror, but for security it suffices to be a Roman citizen, or rather to be one of those united under your hegemony.

101. Homer said, "Earth common of all," and you have made it come true. You have measured and recorded the land of the entire civilized world; you have spanned the rivers with all kinds of bridges and hewn highways through the mountains and filled the barren stretches with posting stations;

you have accustomed all areas to a settled and orderly way of life. Therefore, I see on reflection that what is held to be the life before Triptolemus is really the life before your time,—a hard and boorish life, not far removed from that of the wild mountains. Though the citizens of Athens began the civilized life of today, this life in its turn has been firmly established by you, who came later but who, men say, are better.

102. There is no need whatsoever now to write a book of travels and to enumerate the laws which each country uses. Rather you yourselves have become universal guides for all; you threw wide all the gates of the civilized world and gave those who so wished the opportunity to see for themselves; you assigned common laws for all and you put an end to the previous conditions which were amusing to describe but which, if one looked at them from the standpoint of reason, were intolerable; you made it possible to marry anywhere, and you organized all the civilized world, as it were, into one family.

103. Before the rule of Zeus, as the poets say, the universe was full of strife, confusion and disorder, but when Zeus came to the rule he settled everything, and the Titans, forced back by Zeus and the gods who supported him, departed to the lowest caverns of the earth. Thus one who reflects about the world before your time and about the condition of affairs in your period would come to the opinion that before your empire there had been confusion everywhere and things were taking a random course, but when you assumed the presidency, confusion and strife ceased, and universal order entered as a brilliant light over the private and public affairs of man, laws appeared and altars of gods received man's confidence.

104. For formerly they used to lay waste the world as if (like Cronos) they were mutilating their parents, and though they did not swallow their children (like Cronos), they destroyed each other's children and their own in their strife even at sanctuaries. But now a clear and universal freedom from all fear has been granted both to the world and to those who live in it. And it seems to me that they are wholly rid of evil treatment and have accepted the many incentives toward following good leadership, while the gods, beholding, seem to lend a friendly hand to your empire in its achievement and to confirm to you its possession, (105)—Zeus, because you tend for him nobly his noble creation, the civilized world; Hera, who is honored because of marriage rites properly performed; Athena and Hephaestus, because of the esteem in which the crafts are held; Dionysus and Demeter, because their crops are not outraged; Poseidon, because the sea has been cleansed for him of naval battles and has received merchant vessels instead of triremes. The chorus of Apollo, Artemis and the Muses never ceases to behold its servants in the theatres; for Hermes there are both international games and embassies. And when did Aphrodite ever have a better chance to plant the seed and enhance the beauty of the offspring, or when did the

cities ever have a greater share in her blessings? It is now that the gracious favors of Asclepius and the Egyptian gods have been most generously bestowed upon mankind. Ares certainly has never been slighted by you. There is no fear that he will cause a general disturbance as when overlooked at the banquet of the Lapiths. On the contrary, he dances the ceaseless dance along the banks of the outermost rivers and keeps the weapons clean of blood. The all-seeing Helius, moreover, casting his light, saw no violence or injustice in your case and marked the absence of woes such as were frequent in former times. Accordingly, there is good reason why he looks and shines with most delight upon your empire.

106. Just as Homer did not fail to realize that your empire was to be, but foresaw it and made a prophecy of it in his epic, so Hesiod, were he as complete a poet and as prophetic, would not, I think, in listing the Generations of Men have begun with the Golden Race as he actually does. And having once made this beginning, he would not at least, in treating of the last, the Iron Race, have named as the time for its ruin to occur the hour "when those born with hoary temples come into being," but rather when your protectorate and empire come. That is the hour he would have named for the Iron tribe to perish on the earth. To Justice and Respect in that period he would have assigned a return amongst men. And he would have pitied those born before your time.

107. Your ways and institutions, which were really introduced by you, are ever held in honor and have become ever more firmly established. The present great governor like a champion in the games clearly excels to such an extent his own ancestors that it is not easy to declare by how much he excels men of a different stock. One would say that justice and law are in truth whatever he decrees. This too [one can see] clearly before all else, that the partners whom he has to help him rule, men [like] sons of his own, similar unto him, are more than had any of his predecessors.

108. But the trial which we undertook at the beginning of our speech is beyond any man's power, namely to compose the oration which would equal the majesty of your empire, for it would require just about as much time as time alloted to the empire, and that would be all eternity. Therefore it is best to do like those poets who compose dithyrambs and paeans, namely to add a prayer and so close the oration.

109. Let all the gods and the children of the gods be invoked to grant that this empire and this city flourish forever and never cease until stones [float] upon the sea and trees cease to put forth shoots in spring, and that the great governor and his sons be preserved and obtain blessings for all.

My bold attempt is finished. Now is the time to register your decision whether for better or for worse.

3
Legal Foundations of Roman Society: The Status of Persons under the Law

18. Justinian, *Institutes* (Selections)

Law is one of the most fundamental Roman contributions to Western civilization. Its development was the result of a long process. The emperor Justinian I, who reigned at Constantinople from A.D. 527 to 565, ordered the creation in 528 of a legal commission to be headed by the jurist Tribonian, Theophilus, a professor of law at Constantinople, and Dorotheus, a professor of law at Berytus (Beirut). Justinian sought to bring order to the existing law, which was in shambles, with the creation of a definitive collection of legal texts and juridical opinions entitled the *Body of Civil Law*. In 533 the commission revised and published the *Institutes*, as an elementary textbook or short guide to the study of Roman law. The *Institutes* drew on several earlier manuals, including the *Institutes* of Gaius, an excellent second-century jurist. Its subjects include legal definitions of personal status, agency, age of majority, differences in the status of the sexes, classifications of property, and types of Roman law and the manner in which they were created, all essential to any understanding of Roman society and social thought. This text derives from the final period of the formation of Roman law and therefore includes some traces of the Christian influence that modified traditional Roman legal principles.

Titles 1–5, 6 (preface and 6.4–6), 16, 21–23. From *The Institutes of Justinian*, 7th ed., translated by Thomas Corlett Sandars (London: Longmans, Green, 1922), pp. 3–21, 23, 26–29.

Title 1

Justice is the constant and perpetual wish to render every one his due.

1. Jurisprudence is the knowledge of things divine and human; the science of the just and the unjust.

2. Having explained these general terms, we think we shall commence our exposition of the law of the Roman people most advantageously, if our explanation is at first plain and easy, and is then carried on into details with the utmost care and exactness. For, if at the outset we overload the mind of the student, while yet new to the subject and unable to bear much, with a multitude and variety of topics, one of two things will happen—we shall either cause him wholly to abandon his studies, or, after great toil, and often after great distrust of himself (the most frequent stumbling-block in the way of youth), we shall at last conduct him to the point, to which, if he had been led by a smoother road, he might, without great labour, and without any distrust of his own powers, have been sooner conducted.

3. The maxims of law are these: to live honestly, to hurt no one, to give every one his due.

4. The study of law is divided into two branches; that of public and that of private law. Public law is that which regards the government of the Roman Empire: private law, that which concerns the interests of individuals. We are now to treat of the latter, which is composed of three elements, and consists of precepts belonging to natural law, to the law of nations, and to the civil law.

Title 2

The law of nature is that law which nature teaches to all animals. For this law does not belong exclusively to the human race, but belongs to all animals, whether of the air, the earth, or the sea. Hence comes that yoking together of male and female, which we term matrimony; hence the procreation and bringing up of children. We see, indeed, that all the other animals besides man are considered as having knowledge of this law.

1. Civil law is thus distinguished from the law of nations. Every community governed by laws and customs uses partly its own law, partly laws common to all mankind. The law which a people makes for its own government belongs exclusively to that state, and is called the civil law, as being the law of the particular state. But the law which natural reason appoints for all mankind obtains equally among all nations, and is called the law of nations, because all nations make use of it. The people of Rome, then, are governed partly by their own laws, and partly by the laws which are common to all mankind. What is the nature of these two component parts of our law we will set forth in the proper place.

2. Civil law takes its name from the state which it governs, as, for instance, from Athens; for it would be very proper to speak of the laws of Solon or Draco as the civil law of Athens. And thus the law which the Roman people make use of is called the civil law of the Romans, or that of the Quirites; for the Romans are called Quirites from Quirinus. But whenever we speak of civil law, without adding of what state we are speaking, we mean our own law: just as when "the poet" is spoken of without any name being expressed, the Greeks mean the great Homer, and we Romans mean Virgil. The law of nations is common to all mankind, for nations have established certain laws, as occasion and the necessities of human life required. Wars arose, and in their train followed captivity and then slavery, which is contrary to the law of nature; for by that law all men are originally born free. Further, from this law of nations almost all contracts were at first introduced, as, for instance, buying and selling, letting and hiring, partnership, deposits, loans returnable in kind, and very many others.

3. Our law is written and unwritten, just as among the Greeks some of their laws were written and others not written. The written part consists of laws, plebiscites, *senatus-consulta*, enactments of emperors, edicts of magistrates, and answers of jurisprudents.

4. A law is that which was enacted by the Roman people on its being proposed by a senatorian magistrate, as a consul. A plebiscite is that which was enacted by the plebs on its being proposed by a plebeian magistrate, as a tribune. The *plebs* differs from the people as a species from its genus; for all the citizens, including patricians and senators, are comprehended in the people; but the *plebs* only includes citizens, not being patricians or senators. But plebiscites, after the Hortensian law had been passed, began to have the same force as laws.

5. A *senatus-consultum* is that which the senate commands and appoints: for, when the Roman people was so increased that it was difficult to assemble it together to pass laws, it seemed right that the senate should be consulted in the place of the people.

6. That which seems good to the emperor has also the force of law; for the people, by the *lex regia*, which is passed to confer on him his power, make over to him their whole power and authority. Therefore whatever the emperor ordains by rescript, or decides in adjudging a cause, or lays down by edict, is unquestionably law; and it is these enactments of the emperor that are called constitutions. Of these, some are personal, and are not to be drawn into precedent, such not being the intention of the emperor. Supposing the emperor has granted a favour to any man on account of his merits, or inflicted some punishment, or granted some extraordinary relief, the application of these acts does not extend beyond the particular individual. But the other constitutions, being general, are undoubtedly binding on all.

7. The edicts of the praetors are also of great authority. These edicts are

called the *jus honorarium*, because those who bear honours in the state, that is, the magistrates, have given it their sanction. The curule aediles also used to publish an edict relative to certain subjects, which edict also became part of the *jus honorarium*.

8. The answers of the jurisprudents are the decisions and opinions of persons who were authorised to determine the law. For anciently it was provided that there should be persons to interpret publicly the law, who were permitted by the emperor to give answers on questions of law. They were called jurisconsults; and the authority of their decisions and opinions, when they were all unanimous, was such, that the judge could not, according to the constitutions, refuse to be guided by their answers.

9. The unwritten law is that which usage has established; for ancient customs, being sanctioned by the consent of those who adopt them, are like laws.

10. The civil law is not improperly divided into two kinds, for the division seems to have had its origin in the customs of the two states Athens and Lacedaemon. For in these states it used to be the case, that the Lacedaemonians rather committed to memory what they were to observe as law, while the Athenians rather kept safely what they had found written in their laws.

11. The laws of nature, which all nations observe alike, being established by a divine providence, remain ever fixed and immutable. But the laws which every state has enacted, undergo frequent changes, either by the tacit consent of the people, or by a new law being subsequently passed.

12. All our law relates either to persons, or to things, or to actions. Let us first speak of persons; as it is of little purpose to know the law, if we do not know the persons for whom the law was made.

Title 3

The chief division in the rights of persons is this: men are all either free or slaves.

1. Freedom, from which is derived the term free as applied to men, is the natural power of doing each what we please, unless prevented either by force or by law.

2. Slavery is an institution of the law of nations, by which one man is made the property of another, contrary to natural right.

3. Slaves are denominated *servi*, because generals order their captives to be sold, and thus preserve them, and do not put them to death. Slaves are also called *mancipia*, because they are taken from the enemy by the strong hand.

4. Slaves either are born or become so. They are born so when their

mother is a slave; they become so either by the law of nations, that is, by captivity, or by the civil law, as when a free person, above the age of twenty, suffers himself to be sold, that he may share the price given for him.

5. In the condition of slaves there is no distinction; but there are many distinctions among free persons; for they are either born free, or have been set free.

Title 4

A person is *ingenuus* who is free from the moment of his birth, by being born in matrimony, of parents who have been either both born free, or both made free, or one of whom has been born and the other made free; and when the mother is free, and the father a slave, the child nevertheless is born free; just as he is if his mother is free, and it is uncertain who is his father; for he has been conceived promiscuously. And it is sufficient if the mother is free at the time of the birth, although a slave when she conceived; and on the other hand, if she be free when she conceives, and is a slave when she gives birth to her child, yet the child is held to be born free; for the misfortune of the mother ought not to prejudice her unborn infant. The question hence arose, if a female slave with child is made free, but again becomes a slave before the child is born, whether the child is born free or a slave. Marcellus thinks it is born free, for it is sufficient for the unborn child, if the mother has been free, although only in the intermediate time; and this also is true.

1. When a man has been born free, he does not cease to be *ingenuus* because he has been in the position of a slave, and has subsequently been enfranchised; for it has been often settled that enfranchisement does not prejudice the rights of birth.

Title 5

Freedmen are those who have been manumitted from legal servitude. Manumission is the "giving of liberty." For while any one is in slavery, he is under "the hand" and power of another, but by manumission he is freed from this power. This institution took its rise from the law of nations; for by the law of nature all men were born free; and manumission was not heard of, as slavery was unknown. But when slavery came in by the law of nations, the boon of manumission followed. And whereas we all were denominated by the one natural name of "men," the law of nations introduced a division into three kinds of men, namely, freemen, and in opposition to them, slaves; and thirdly, freedmen who had ceased to be slaves.

1. Manumission is effected in various ways; either in the face of the Church, according to the imperial constitutions, or by *vindicta*,[1] or in the presence of friends, or by letter, or by testament, or by any other expression of a man's last will. And a slave may also gain his freedom in many other ways, introduced by the constitutions of former emperors, and by our own.

2. Slaves may be manumitted by their masters at any time; even when the magistrate is only passing along, as when a praetor, or proconsul, or governor, is going to the baths or the theatre.

3. Freedmen were formerly divided into three classes. For those who were manumitted sometimes obtained a complete liberty, and became Roman citizens; sometimes a less complete, and became Latins under the *lex Junia Norbana*; and sometimes a liberty still inferior, and were ranked as *dediticii*, by the *lex Aelia Sentia*. But this lowest class, that of the *dediticii*, has long disappeared, and the title of Latins become rare; and so in our benevolence, which leads us to complete and improve everything, we have introduced a great reform by two constitutions, which re-established the ancient usage; for in the infancy of the state there was but one liberty, the same for the enfranchised slave as for the person who manumitted him; excepting, indeed, that the person manumitted was a freedman, while the manumittor was freeborn. We have abolished the class of *dediticii* by a constitution published among our decisions, by which, at the suggestion of the eminent Tribonian, quaestor, we have put an end to difficulties arising from the ancient law. We have also, at his suggestion, done away with the *Latini Juniani*, and everything relating to them, by another constitution, one of the most remarkable of our imperial ordinances. We have made all freedmen whatsoever Roman citizens, without any distinction as to the age of the slave, or the interest of the manumittor, or the mode of manumission. We have also introduced many new methods, by which liberty may be given to slaves, together with Roman citizenship, the only kind of liberty that now exists.

Title 6

It is not, however, every master who wishes that may manumit, for a manumission in fraud of creditors is void, the *lex Aelia Sentia* restraining the power of enfranchisement.

4. By the same *lex Aelia Sentia*, again, a master, under the age of

1. A *vindicta* was a ceremonial act of claiming as free one who claimed to be wrongly held in slavery.

twenty years, cannot manumit, unless by *vindicta*, and unless this proceeding in regard to the person manumitted has been approved of by the council on some legitimate ground.

5. Legitimate grounds for manumission are such as these: that the person to be manumitted is father or mother to the manumittor, his son or daughter, his brother or sister, his preceptor, his nurse, his foster-father, his foster-child of either sex, or his foster-brother; that the person is a slave whom he wishes to make his procurator, or female slave whom he intends to marry, provided the marriage be performed within six months, unless prevented by some lawful cause; and provided that the slave who is to be made a procurator, be not manumitted under the age of seventeen years.

6. The approval of a ground of manumission once given, whether the reasons on which it is based be true or false, cannot be retracted.

Title 16

Capitis deminutio is a change of *status*, which may happen in three ways: for it may be the greatest *capitis deminutio*, or the less, also called the middle, or the least.

1. The greatest *capitis deminutio* is, when a man loses both his citizenship and his liberty; as they do who by a terrible sentence are made "the slaves of punishment"; or freedmen condemned for ingratitude towards their patrons; or those who suffer themselves to be sold in order to share the price obtained.

2. The less or middle *capitis deminutio* is, when a man loses his citizenship, but retains his liberty; as is the case when any one is forbidden the use of fire and water, or is deported to an island.

3. The least *capitis deminutio* is, when a person's *status* is changed without forfeiture either of citizenship or liberty; as when a person *sui juris* [one's own master] becomes subject to the power of another, or a person *alieni juris* [subject to the power of another] becomes *sui juris*.

4. A slave who is manumitted is not said to be *capite minutus* [deprived of civil rights, freedom], as he has no "*caput*" [head].

5. Those whose dignity rather than their *status* is changed, do not undergo a *capitis deminutio*, and so persons removed from the senatorial dignity undergo none.

6. In saying that the right of cognation remains in spite of a *capitis deminutio*, we were speaking only of the least *deminutio*, after which the cognation subsists. For, by the greater *deminutio*, as, for example, if one of the *cognati* [related by birth] becomes a slave, the right of cognation is wholly destroyed, so as not to be recovered even by manumission. So, too, the right of cognation is put an end to by deportation to an island.

7. The right to be tutor, which belongs to the *agnati* [male blood relations on father's side], does not belong to all at the same time, but to the nearest in degree only; or if there are many in the same degree, then to all in that degree.

Title 21

In some cases it is necessary that the tutor should authorise the acts of the pupil, in others not. When, for instance, the pupil stipulates for something to be given him, the authorisation of the tutor is not requisite; but if the pupil makes the promise, it is requisite; for the rule is, that pupils may make their condition better, even without the authorisation of their tutor, but not worse unless with the tutor's authorisation. And therefore in all cases of reciprocal obligation, as in contracts of buying, selling, letting, hiring, bailment, deposit, if the tutor does not authorise the pupil to enter into the contract, the person who contracts with the pupil is bound, but the pupil is not bound.

1. Pupils, however, cannot, without the authorisation of the tutor, enter on an inheritance, demand the possession of goods, or take an inheritance given by a *fideicommissum*,[2] even though to do so would be to their gain, and could involve them in no risk.

2. A tutor who wishes to authorise any act, which he esteems advantageous to his pupil, should do so at once while the business is going on, and in person, for his authorisation is of no effect if given afterwards or by letter.

3. When a suit is to be commenced between a tutor and his pupil, as the tutor cannot give authority with regard to his own cause, a curator, and not, as formerly, a praetorian tutor, is appointed, with whose intervention the suit is carried on, and who ceases to be curator when the suit is determined.

Title 22

Pupils, both male and female, are freed from tutelage when they attain the age of puberty. The ancients judged of puberty in males, not only by their years, but also by the development of their bodies. But we, from a wish to conform to the purity of the present times, have thought it proper, that what seemed, even to the ancients, to be indecent towards females, namely, the inspection of the body, should be thought no less so towards males; and, therefore, by our sacred constitution we have enacted, that puberty in

2. A *fideicommissum* was a testamentary disposition or bequest in the form of a request.

males should be considered to commence immediately on the completion of their fourteenth year; while, as to females, we have preserved the wise rule adopted by the ancients, by which they are esteemed fit for marriage on the completion of their twelfth year.

1. Tutelage is also determined, if the pupil, before attaining the age of puberty, is either arrogated, or suffers deportation, or is reduced to slavery as guilty of ingratitude on the demand of his patron, or if he becomes a captive.

2. Again, if a person is appointed by testament to be tutor until a condition is accomplished, he ceases to be tutor on the accomplishment of the condition.

3. Tutelage ends also by the death of the tutor, or of the pupil.

4. When, again, a tutor, by a *capitis deminutio*, loses his liberty or his citizenship, his tutelage is wholly at an end. But if he undergoes only the least *capitis deminutio*, as when a tutor gives himself in adoption, then only legal tutelage is ended, and not the other kinds; but any *capitis deminutio* of the pupil, even the least, always puts an end to the tutelage.

5. A tutor, again, who is appointed by testament to hold office during a certain time, lays down his office when the time is expired.

6. They also cease to be tutors who are removed from their office on suspicion, or who excuse themselves on good grounds from the burden of the tutelage, and rid themselves of it according to the rules we shall give hereafter.

Title 23

Males arrived at the age of puberty, and females of a marriageable age, receive curators, until they have completed their twenty-fifth year; for, although they have attained the age of puberty, they are still of an age which makes them unfit to protect their own interests.

1. Curators are appointed by the same magistrates who appoint tutors. A curator cannot be appointed by testament, but if appointed he may be confirmed in his office by a decree of the praetor or the governor.

2. No adolescent is obliged to receive a curator against his will, unless in case of a law-suit, for a curator may be appointed for a particular special purpose.

3. Madmen and prodigals, although past the age of twenty-five, are yet placed under the curatorship of their *agnati* by the law of the Twelve Tables. But, ordinarily, curators are appointed for them at Rome by the praefect of the city or the praetor, in the provinces by the governors, after inquiry into the circumstances has been made.

4. Persons who are of unsound mind, or who are deaf, dumb, or subject to any incurable malady, since they are unable to manage their own affairs, must be placed under curators.

5. Sometimes even pupils receive curators; as, for instance, when the legal tutor is unfit for the office; for a person who already has a tutor cannot have another given him; again, if a tutor appointed by testament, or by the praetor or governor, is unfit to administer the affairs of his pupil, although there is nothing fraudulent in the way he administers them, it is usual to appoint a curator to act conjointly with him. It is also usual to assign curators in the place of tutors excused for a time only, and not permanently.

6. If a tutor is prevented by illness or otherwise from administering the affairs of his pupil, and his pupil is absent, or an infant, then the praetor or governor of the province will, at the tutor's risk, appoint by decree some one to be the agent of the pupil on the nomination of the tutor.

4
Preoccupations of Public and Private Life

19. Cato the Censor, *On Agriculture* (Selections)

Most Romans supported themselves by farming. Land was the most fundamental and the most respectable form of wealth and source of income. Roman political, military, and religious institutions had many ties to agriculture, and a love for agriculture strongly influenced the perspectives of many Roman leaders.

Cato the Censor, or Cato the Elder (234–149 B.C.), was a prominent Roman during the middle period of the Republic. Born about ten miles from Rome in Tusculum, he had a distinguished public career as statesman and orator. He was quaestor in 204 B.C., aedile in 199, praetor in 198, and consul in 195. Yet his greatest fame came during his censorship in 184, when he was in charge of keeping the citizenship rolls and enforcing standards of conduct. Cato strictly enforced taxes and the dress code. He was a strong opponent of the spread of Greek culture and customs. Born into a rural family, he became a shrewd and very successful farmer with a detailed knowledge of farming techniques. About 160 B.C. he wrote his treatise *On Agriculture*, which contains invaluable information about Roman farming practices in Italy, as well as insights into the mentality of the Roman elite. It is the earliest surviving treatise on Roman agriculture. Cato's opinions are also important because of the high esteem in which later generations of prominent Romans held him. His legendary strictness, however, and his views on various subjects, including the economics of agriculture, housing, crops, slaves, and livestock,

De agricultura 1–6, 10–11, 134. From *Cato the Censor: On Farming*, translated by Ernest Brehaut, Records of Civilization, no. 17 (New York: Columbia University Press, 1933), pp. 1–17, 20–27. Reprinted by permission of Columbia University Press.

should not be regarded as necessarily typical of all well-to-do Romans; he was an exceptional man in his own time.

Preface

It is true that it would sometimes be better to seek a fortune in trade if it were not so subject to risk, or again, to lend money at interest, if it were an honorable occupation. But our forefathers held this belief and enacted it into law, that while a thief was compelled to repay double, one who loaned at interest had to repay fourfold. From this one may judge how much worse than a common thief they thought the fellow citizen who lent at interest. (2) And when they were trying to praise a good man they called him a good farmer and a good tiller of the soil, and the one who received this compliment was considered to have received the highest praise.

(3) Now I esteem the merchant as active and keen to make money, but [consider him], as I have said before, exposed to risk and absolute ruin.

(4) Moreover, it is from among the farmers that the sturdiest men and keenest soldiers come, and the gain they make is the most blameless of all, the most secure, and the least provocative of envy, and the men engaged in this pursuit are least given to disaffection.

Now, to come to my subject, this will serve as a preface to the undertaking I have promised.

I. When you think of buying a farm, make up your mind not to be eager to buy, and not to spare any exertion on your own part in going to see farms, and not to think it enough to go over them once. The oftener you visit it the more a good farm will please you.

(2) Notice carefully how prosperous the neighbors are; in a good district they should be quite prosperous. And see that you go on a farm and look around it in such a way that you can find your way off it. See that it has a good exposure to the heavens or it may be subject to disaster. It should have a good soil and be valuable for its own worth. (3) If possible, let it be at the foot of a mountain, looking toward the south, in a healthful situation, and where there is plenty of labor. It should have a good water supply.

It should be near a thriving town or near the sea or a river where ships go up or a good and well-traveled highway. (4) It should be in a region where owners do not often change, and where those who do sell their farms repent of having sold them. See that it has good buildings. Beware of hastily disregarding the experience of others. It will be better to buy from an owner who is a good farmer and a good builder.

When you come to the farmstead, notice whether there is much equipment for pressing and many storage jars. (5) If there are not, be sure the profit is in proportion. . . . Take care that it is not a farm requiring the least possible equipment and expense. (6) Be sure [on the other hand] that a farm is like a man, that however much it brings in, if it pays much out, not a great deal is left.

(7) If you ask me what sort of farm is best, I will say this: One hundred *jugera*[1] of land consisting of every kind of cultivated field, and in the best situation; [of these] the vineyard is of first importance if the wine is good and the yield is great; the irrigated garden is in the second place, the willow plantation in the third, the olive orchard in the fourth, the meadow in the fifth, the grain land in the sixth, forest trees to furnish foliage in the seventh, the vineyard trained on trees in the eighth, the acorn wood in the ninth.

II. When the head of the household comes to the farmhouse, on the same day, if possible, as soon as he has paid respect to the god of the household, he should make the round of the farm; if not on the same day, at least on the next. When he has learned in what way the farm work has been done and what tasks are finished and what not yet finished, he should next day summon the foreman and inquire how much of the work is done, how much remains, whether the different operations have been completed in good season and whether he can complete what remains, and what is the situation as to wine and grain and all other produce.

(2) After he has been informed on these points he should go into an accounting of the day's works and the days. If the work accomplished is not made clear to him, and the foreman says he has pushed the work hard, but the slaves have not been well, the weather has been bad, the slaves have run away, they have done work on the public account—when he has given these and many other excuses, then bring the foreman back to an accounting of the farm tasks and of the day's works spent on them.

(3) When the weather was rainy, [tell him] what work could have been done in spite of the rain: the storage jars could have been washed and tarred, the farm buildings could have been cleaned out, the grain shifted, the manure carried out and a manure pile made, the seed cleaned, the ropes mended and new ones made; the slaves should have mended their patchwork cloaks and hoods.

(4) On festivals they could have cleaned old ditches, repaired the public road, cut briars, dug the garden, weeded the meadow, made bundles of the small wood cut in pruning, dug out thorns, broken up the spelt into grits and made the place neat. When slaves were sick they should not have been given as large an allowance of food.

1. One hundred *jugera* was about 62 acres.

(5) When this has been gone over without irritation, [it is necessary] to consider how the remaining tasks are to be finished; to take account of money, of grain, of what has been stored for fodder, of wine and oil, [reckoning] what has been sold, what paid for, what is still to be collected and what remains to be sold; satisfactory guarantees of payment should be accepted. (6) The balance remaining should be arrived at.

If anything is needed for the year's supply it should be bought; if there is a surplus of anything it should be sold. What needs to be put out under contract should be contracted for. The owner should give directions and leave them in writing as to what work he wishes to be done and what he wishes put out on contract.

(7) He should look over the flock. He should hold an auction and, if he gets his price, sell the oil, the wine and the surplus grain; let him sell the old work oxen, the blemished cattle, the blemished sheep, the wool, the skins, the old wagon, the worn-out iron tools, the aged slave, the slave that is diseased, and everything else that he does not need. An owner should be a man who is a seller rather than a buyer.

III. In his early manhood the head of the household should be eager to plant his land. He should think long before building but he should not think about planting, but plant. When you have approached the age of thirty-six years you should build, if you have your land well planted. Build in such a way that the farm buildings will not find fault with the farm nor the farm with the buildings. (2) It is an advantage to the owner to have a well-built farmstead with storerooms for oil and wine and many storage jars, so that it will be agreeable to wait for high prices. It will prove a source of gain and influence and reputation to him. He should have good press equipment so that the work can be done well. When the olives are gathered the oil should be made at once, to prevent its spoiling. Remember that great storms are wont to come every year and shake the olives down. (3) If you gather them up quickly and the presses are ready, there will be no loss from the storm and the oil will be of a greener color and better. (4) If they remain too long on the ground or on the floor they will begin to decay and the oil will be rank. A fresher and better oil can be made from any kind of olive if it is made in time.

(5) For one hundred and twenty *jugera* of olive orchard there ought to be two presses, if the orchard is a good one and is closely planted and well cared for. There should be good olive-pulping mills, one to each press, of different sizes so that if the millstones are worn you can change them from one to the other; for each press, rawhide press ropes, six levers and twelve crosspieces, press-basket ropes of rawhide and two pulley blocks of the Greek style, worked with fiber ropes, the upper pulleys being eight finger-breadths in diameter and the lower, six. (6) You will draw the press beam up

faster if you wish to make [simple] rollers; [with the blocks] it will be lifted more slowly but with less labor.

IV. The stable for the work oxen should be good and the [summer] pens built in the Faliscan style with lattice work feed racks should also be good. The bars of the lattice work should be a foot apart. If you make them so, the oxen will not toss their fodder out.

Build your farm residence according to your means. In the case of a good farm, if you build well and on a good site, if you dwell comfortably in the country, you will visit it oftener and with greater pleasure; the farm will be the better for it, less mischief will be done and you will get more profit. The face is better than the back of the head. Be a good neighbor. Don't allow your slaves to do mischief. If the neighbors are glad to see you, you will sell your produce more readily, you will put work out on contract more easily, you will hire laborers more easily. If you build, they will help you with day's works, work animals, and building materials. If any need arises—and may it not—they will protect your interests with a good will.

V. The duties of the foreman will be these. Let him keep good order and observe the festivals; let him keep his hands off other people's property and guard his own diligently. Let him hear the slaves' quarrels; if any of them has committed a fault, let him punish him in a good way according to the fault. (2) The slaves should not be badly off and should not be cold or hungry. Let him keep them well employed and he will more easily keep them from wrongdoing and theft. If the foreman refuses to misbehave, they will not misbehave. But if he permits misbehavior the master should not allow it to go unpunished. He should make a return for any favor, so that it will be a pleasure for others to do the right thing. The foreman should not be a stroller, he should never be drunk, and he should not go out anywhere to dinner parties. He should keep the slaves busy and should keep in mind what the master has ordered to be done. He should not believe that he has more sense than his master. (3) He should reckon his master's friends his own.

If he is told to follow anyone's advice he should do so. He should not offer any sacrifice except at the crossroads on the occasion of the *Compitalia*, or at the hearth. He should not give credit to anyone except at his master's direction, and where his master has given credit he should collect the money. He should not lend to anyone seed for sowing, provisions, spelt, wine or oil. He should have two or three households where he can borrow what he needs for current use, or lend, but should lend to no one besides.

(4) He should go over his accounts with his master frequently. As to the laborer working for wages or the share worker, let him not keep the same longer than a day [after finishing?] He should not wish to buy anything

without his master's knowledge or to conceal anything from his master. He should not keep any idle companion nor wish to consult any diviner, augur, inspector of entrails, or astrologer. He should not rob the grain land, for that is unlucky. He should be careful to know how to do every kind of farm work and should work frequently, but not so as to become wearied. (5) If he does this, he will know what is in the minds of the slaves and they will work with better spirit. If he does this, he will be less desirous of strolling and will have better health and will sleep more soundly. Let him first see that the farmstead is locked up and that each one is sleeping in his own place and that the animals have fodder.

(6) Have the work oxen cared for with the greatest diligence and to some degree flatter the ox drivers so that they will more cheerfully care for the oxen. See that you have good plows and plow-shares. Beware of plowing soil that is wet above and dry below, or of driving a wagon or a flock over it. If you do not beware of this you will lose three year's profit where you have driven over the land. (7) The flock and the work oxen should be carefully bedded and their hoofs should be seen to. Be on guard against the scab for your flock and beasts of burden. This usually comes because they are starved or from rainy weather. See that you get all farm work done in time. For farming is of this sort: if you do one thing too late you will do everything too late. If bedding falls short, gather live oak leaves and bed the oxen and sheep with them.

(8) Make it an aim to have a big manure pile. Preserve the manure carefully. When you take it out, remove the unrotted parts and break up the lumps. Carry it out in autumn. Trench around the olive trees in autumn and apply manure. At the right time cut foliage from poplars, elms and oaks and store it away, not too dry, as fodder for the sheep. In the same way store the late crop of grass and the sickle-cuttings from the meadow, these quite dry. After the autumn rains begin, sow turnips and lupins for fodder.

VI. The question of where to plant should be decided thus: where the soil is deep and productive and not occupied by orchards and vineyards should be the grain land. If soil of this kind is often covered with mist, rape, radishes, millet and Italian millet are to be sown above everything else.

On a heavy and warm soil, plant the preserving olive, the larger variety of the *radius* olive, the Sallentine olive, the *orcites* olive, the *posea*, the Sergian olive, the Colminian, the wax-white, planting in greatest numbers the variety which they say does best in the locality. Plant this kind of olive twenty-five or thirty feet apart.

(2) The ground for setting out an olive orchard is that which faces the southwest wind and is exposed to the sun; no other will be good. If the soil is somewhat cold and poor, the Licinian olive should be planted there. If

you plant this on heavy or warm soil the crop will be worthless, the tree will die of bearing, and the red moss will be troublesome.

(3) Along the boundaries and the roads plant elms and some poplars, in order to have foliage for the sheep and work oxen, and timber will be at hand if needed. Wherever in these places there are stream banks or a wet piece of ground, there plant poplar shoots and a reed thicket. Plant it in this way: turn the ground with the spade for deep working; plant there reed buds three feet apart; in the same place set out [the variety of the asparagus plant known as] *corruda* for an asparagus supply. (4) For the reed thicket is suitable for the *corruda* because the ground is dug and burned over, and has shade at the right time. Plant Greek willows around the reed thicket so as to have something with which to tie up the vines.

Decide in this way on what ground the vineyard should be set out. On the ground that is called best for wine and is exposed to the sun plant the small Aminean grape, the twin Eugenean and the little yellowish grape. Where the soil is heavy or the ground somewhat inclined to be covered with mist, plant the large Aminean grape or else the Murgentine, and the Apician and the Lucanian. The remaining grapevines, especially the [variety called] Miscella are suited to any ground.

X. How an olive orchard of two hundred and forty *jugera* should be equipped.

[It should have] a foreman, a foreman's wife, five laborers, three ox drivers, one ass driver, one swineherd, one shepherd, thirteen persons in all; three teams of oxen, three asses equipped with pack saddles to carry out the manure, one ass for mill work, one hundred sheep.

(2) Five oil presses fully equipped including the pulping mills, a bronze cauldron to hold thirty *amphorae* [see n. 3], a cover for the cauldron, three iron hooks, three water pitchers, two funnels, a bronze cauldron to hold five *amphorae*, a cover for it, three hooks, a small vat for water, two *amphorae* for oil, one half-*amphora* measure holding fifty, three skimming ladles, one well bucket, one wash basin, one water pitcher, one slop pail, one small tray, one chamber pot, one watering pot, one ladle, one lamp stand, one *sextarius* measure.

Three wagons of the larger size, six plows with plow-shares, three yokes fitted with rawhide ropes, harness for six oxen; (3) one harrow with iron teeth, four wickerwork baskets for manure, three rush baskets for manure, three pack-saddles, three pads for asses.

Implements of iron: eight heavy spades, eight heavy two-pronged hoes, four spades, five shovels, two four-pronged drags, eight scythes for mowing grass, five sickles for harvesting, five billhooks for trimming trees, three axes, three wedges, one mortar for spelt, two fire tongs, one fire shovel, two portable fire pans.

(4) One hundred storage jars for oil, twelve vats, ten storage jars for the wine-press refuse, ten for oil dregs, ten for wine, twenty for grain, one vat for lupins, ten storage jars of the smaller kind, a vat used for washing, one tub for bathing, two vats for water, separate covers for all storage jars large and small.

One mill to be worked by an ass, one hand mill, one Spanish mill, three harnesses for the mill asses, one kneading table, two round plates of bronze, two tables, three long benches, one stool for the chamber, three low stools, four chairs, two large chairs, (5) one bed in the chamber, four beds with woven thongs and three beds; one wooden mortar, one mortar for fuller's work, one loom for cloaks, two mortars, one pestle for beans and one for spelt, one for [cleaning] spelt for seed, one to separate olive pits, one *modius* measure and one half-*modius* measure.[2]

Eight mattresses, eight spreads, sixteen pillows, ten coverlets, three towels, six cloaks made of patchwork for the slaves.

XI. How a vineyard of a hundred *jugera* should be equipped.

[It should have] a foreman, a foreman's wife, ten laborers, one ox driver, one ass driver, one man in charge of the willow grove, one swineherd, in all sixteen persons; two oxen, two asses for wagon work, one ass for the mill work.

Three presses fully equipped, storage jars in which five vintages amounting to eight hundred *cullei* can be stored,[3] twenty storage jars for wine-press refuse, twenty for grain, (2) separate coverings for the jars, six fiber-covered half-*amphorae*, four fiber-covered *amphorae*, two funnels, three basketwork strainers, three strainers to dip up the flower, ten jars for [handling] the wine juice.

Two wagons, two plows, one wagon yoke, one yoke for the vineyard, one ass yoke, one round plate of bronze, one harness for the mill ass.

One bronze cauldron to hold one *culleus*, one cover for it, three iron hooks, (3) one bronze cauldron for concentrated wine to hold one *culleus*, two water pitchers, one watering pot, one washbasin, one water pitcher, one slop bucket, one well bucket, one small tray, one skimming ladle, one lampstand, one chamber pot, four beds, one bench, two tables, one kneading table, one chest for clothing, one store closet, six long benches.

One well pulley, one *modius* measure, iron bound, one half-*modius* measure, one vat for washing, one bathtub, one vat for lupins, ten storage jars of the smaller size.

(4) Harness for two oxen, three pads for asses and three packsaddles,

2. One *modius* was equal to 9.62 quarts or 1.2 pecks.

3. The *culleus* was the largest measure for liquids and held twenty *amphorae* or 144.5 gallons. Eight hundred *cullei* would be over 115,000 gallons.

three baskets for the wine settlings, three mills worked by asses, one hand mill.

Implements of iron: five sickles for cutting reeds, six billhooks for use in cutting foliage, three for the orchards, five axes, four wedges, two plowshares, ten heavy spades, six spades, four shovels, two four-pronged drags, four wicker-work baskets for manure, one rush basket for manure, forty knives for cutting bunches of grapes, ten for butcher's broom, two portable fire pans, two fire tongs, one fire shovel.

(5) Twenty hampers of the kind used in Ameria, forty baskets of the sort used in planting, or forty wooden picking trays, forty wooden shovels, two dugout carriers, four mattresses, four spreads, six pillows, six coverlets, three towels, six patchwork cloaks for the slaves.

20. Columella, *On Farming* (Selections)

Agriculture did not remain unchanged throughout Roman history. In central Italy there was a trend, in the early first century A.D., to grow less grain and to concentrate instead on the cultivation of grapes and olives. At about the same time, landowners were beginning to rely less on slave labor.

Lucius Junius Moderatus Columella was born in Gades (Cádiz) in southern Spain, early in the first century A.D. He held estates in Spain and in Italy. He wrote a systematic treatise on Roman agriculture entitled *On Farming*, probably between A.D. 60 and 65. Comprising twelve books, it is the most comprehensive extant treatise on Roman agriculture. In it Columella noted and criticized the contemporary trend to enclose landholdings and the growing absenteeism of landlords. He emphasized that landowners must be intelligent, personally interested, and hard working in order to farm efficiently and profitably. His treatise also provides valuable information on the profitability and desirability of slave versus free labor in the first century A.D.

Book 1

VII. After all these arrangements have been acquired or contrived, especial care is demanded of the master not only in other matters, but most of all in

De re rustica 1.7–9. From *Lucius Junius Moderatus Columella: De re rustica*, vol. 1, translated by Harrison Boyd Ash (Cambridge, Mass.: Harvard University Press, 1959), pp. 79–101 (odd-numbered pages). All footnotes deleted. Reprinted by permission of the publisher and the Loeb Classical Library.

the matter of the persons in his service; and these are either tenant-farmers or slaves, whether unfettered or in chains. He should be civil in dealing with his tenants, should show himself affable, and should be more exacting in the matter of work than of payments, as this gives less offence yet is, generally speaking, more profitable. For when land is carefully tilled it usually brings a profit, and never a loss, except when it is assailed by unusually severe weather or by robbers; and for that reason the tenant does not venture to ask for reduction of his rent. But the master should not be insistent on his rights in every particular to which he has bound his tenant, such as the exact day for payment, or the matter of demanding firewood and other trifling services in addition, attention to which causes country-folk more trouble than expense; in fact, we should not lay claim to all that the law allows, for the ancients regarded the extreme of the law as the extreme of oppression. On the other hand, we must not neglect our claims altogether; for, as Alfius the usurer is reported to have said, and with entire truth, "Good debts become bad ones if they are not called". Furthermore, I myself remember having heard Publius Volusius, an old man who had been consul and was very wealthy, declare that estate most fortunate which had as tenants natives of the place, and held them, by reason of long association, even from the cradle, as if born on their own father's property. So I am decidedly of the opinion that repeated letting of a place is a bad thing, but that a worse thing is the farmer who lives in town and prefers to till the land through his slaves rather than by his own hand. Saserna used to say that from a man of this sort the return was usually a lawsuit instead of revenue, and that for this reason we should take pains to keep with us tenants who are country-bred and at the same time diligent farmers, when we are not at liberty to till the land ourselves or when it is not feasible to cultivate it with our own servants; though this does not happen except in districts which are desolated by the severity of the climate and the barrenness of the soil. But when the climate is moderately healthful and the soil moderately good, a man's personal supervision never fails to yield a larger return from his land than does that of a tenant—never than that of even an overseer, unless the greatest carelessness or greed on the part of the slave stands in the way. There is no doubt that both these offences are either committed or fostered through the fault of the master, inasmuch as he has the authority to prevent such a person from being placed in charge of his affairs, or to see to it that he is removed if so placed. On far distant estates, however, which it is not easy for the owner to visit, it is better for every kind of land to be under free farmers than under slave overseers, but this is particularly true of grain land. To such land a tenant farmer can do no great harm, as he can to plantations of vines and trees, while slaves do it tremendous damage: they let out oxen for hire, and keep them and other animals poorly fed; they do not plough the ground carefully, and they charge up the sowing of far more seed than they have actually sown; what they have committed to the earth they do not so foster that it will make the proper growth; and when they have brought it to the threshing-floor, every day during the threshing they lessen the amount either by trickery or by carelessness. For they themselves steal it and do not guard against the thieving of others, and even when it is stored away they do not enter it honestly in their accounts. The result is that both manager and hands are offenders, and that the land pretty often gets a bad name. Therefore my opinion is that an estate of this sort should be leased if, as I have said, it cannot have the presence of the owner.

VIII. The next point is with regard to slaves—over what duty it is proper to place each and to what sort of tasks to assign them. So my advice at the start is not to appoint an overseer from that sort of slaves who are physically attractive, and certainly not from that class which has busied itself with the voluptuous occupations of the city. This lazy and sleepy-headed class of servants, accustomed to idling, to the Campus, the Circus, and the theatres, to gambling, to cookshops, to bawdy-houses, never ceases to dream of these follies; and when they carry them over into their farming, the master suffers not so much loss in the slave himself as in his whole estate. A man should be chosen who has been hardened by farm work from his infancy, one who has been tested by experience. If, however, such a person is not available, let one be put in charge out of the number of those who have slaved patiently at hard labour; and he should already have passed beyond the time of young manhood but not yet have arrived at that of old age, that youth may not lessen his authority to command, seeing that older men think it beneath them to take orders from a mere stripling, and that old age may not break down under the heaviest labour. He should be, then, of middle age and of strong physique, skilled in farm operations or at least very painstaking, so that he may learn the more readily; for it is not in keeping with this business of ours for one man to give orders and another to give instructions, nor can a man properly exact work when he is being tutored by an underling as to what is to be done and in what way. Even an illiterate person, if only he have a retentive mind, can manage affairs well enough. Cornelius Celsus says that an overseer of this sort brings money to his master oftener than he does his book, because, not knowing his letters, he is either less able to falsify accounts or is afraid to do so through a second party because that would make another aware of the deception.

But be the overseer what he may, he should be given a woman companion to keep him within bounds and yet in certain matters to be a help to him; and this same overseer should be warned not to become intimate with a member of the household, and much less with an outsider, yet at times he may consider it fitting, as a mark of distinction, to invite to his table on a holiday one whom he has found to be constantly busy and vigorous in the performance of his tasks. He shall offer no sacrifice except by direction of the master. Soothsayers and witches, two sets of people who incite ignorant minds through false superstition to spending and then to shameful practices, he must not admit to the place. He must have no acquaintance with the city or with the weekly market, except to make purchases and sales in connection with his duties. For, as Cato says, an overseer should not be a gadabout; and he should not go out of bounds except to learn something new about farming, and that only if the place is so near that he can come back. He must allow no foot-paths or new crosscuts to be made in the farm; and he shall entertain no guest except a close friend or kinsman of his master.

As he must be restrained from these practices, so must he be urged to take care of the equipment and the iron tools, and to keep in repair and stored away twice as many as the number of slaves requires, so that there will be no need of borrowing from a neighbour; for the loss in slave labour exceeds the cost of articles of this sort. In the care and clothing of the slave household he should have an eye to usefulness rather than appearance, taking care to keep them fortified against wind, cold, and rain, all of which are warded off with long-sleeved leather tunics, garments of patchwork, or hooded cloaks. If this be done, no weather is so unbearable but that some work may be done in the open. He should be not only skilled in the tasks of husbandry, but should also be endowed, as far as the servile disposition allows, with such qualities of feeling that he may exercise authority without laxness and without cruelty, and always humour some of the better hands, at the same time being forbearing even with those of lesser worth, so that they may rather fear his sternness than detest his cruelty. This he can accomplish if he will choose rather to guard his subordinates from wrongdoing than to bring upon himself, through his own negligence, the necessity of punishing offenders. There is, moreover, no better way of keeping watch over even the most worthless of men than the strict enforcement of labour, the requirement that the proper tasks be performed and that the overseer be present at all times; for in that case the foremen in charge of the several operations are zealous in carrying out their duties, and the others, after their fatiguing toil, will turn their attention to rest and sleep rather than to dissipation.

Would that those well-known precepts, old but excellent in morality, which have now passed out of use, might be held to to-day: That an overseer shall not employ the services of a fellow-slave except on the master's business; that he shall partake of no food except in sight of the household, nor of other food than is provided for the rest; for in so doing he will see to it that the bread is carefully made and that other things are wholesomely prepared. He shall permit no one to pass beyond the boundaries unless sent by himself, and he shall send no one except there is great and pressing need. He shall carry on no business on his own account, nor invest his master's funds in livestock and other goods for purchase and sale; for such trafficking will divert the attention of the overseer and will never allow him to balance his accounts with his master, but, when an accounting is demanded, he has goods to show instead of cash. But, generally speaking, this above all else is to be required of him—that he shall not think that he knows what he does not know, and that he shall always be eager to learn what he is ignorant of; for not only is it very helpful to do a thing skilfully, but even more so is it hurtful to have done it incorrectly. For there is one and only one controlling principle in agriculture, namely, to do once and for all the thing which the method of cultivation requires; since when ignorance or carelessness has to be rectified, the matter at stake has already suffered impairment and never recovers thereafter to such an extent as to regain what it has lost and to restore the profit of time that has passed.

In the case of the other slaves, the following are, in general, the precepts to be observed, and I do not regret having held to them myself: to talk rather familiarly with the country slaves, provided only that they have not conducted themselves unbecomingly, more frequently than I would with the town slaves; and when I perceived that their unending toil was lightened by such friendliness on the part of the master, I would even jest with them at times and allow them also to jest more freely. Nowadays I make it a practice to call them into consultation on any new work, as if they were more experienced, and to discover by this means what sort of ability is possessed by each of them and how intelligent he is. Furthermore, I observe that they are more willing to set about a piece of work on which they think that their opinions have been asked and their advice followed. Again, it is the established custom of all men of caution to inspect the inmates of the workhouse, to find out whether they are carefully chained, whether the places of confinement are quite safe and properly guarded, whether the overseer has put anyone in fetters or removed his shackles without the master's knowledge. For the overseer should be most observant of both points—not to release the shackles from anyone whom the head of the house has subjected to that kind of punishment, except by his leave, and not to free one whom he himself has chained on his own initiative until the master knows the circumstances; and the investigation of the householder should be the more painstaking in the interest of slaves of this sort, that they may not be treated unjustly in the matter of clothing or other allowances, inasmuch as, being liable to a greater number of people, such as overseers, taskmasters, and jailers, they are the more liable to unjust punishment, and again, when smarting under cruelty and greed, they are more to be feared. Accordingly, a careful master inquires not only of them, but also of those who are not in bonds, as being more worthy of belief, whether they are receiving what is due to them under his instructions; he also tests the quality of their food and drink by tasting it himself, and examines their clothing, their mittens, and their foot-covering. In addition he should give them frequent opportunities for making complaint against those persons who treat them cruelly or dishonestly. In fact, I now and then avenge those who have just cause for grievance, as well as punish those who incite the slaves to revolt, or who slander their taskmasters; and, on the other hand, I reward those who conduct themselves with energy and diligence. To women, too, who are unusually prolific, and who ought to be rewarded for the bearing of a certain number of offspring, I have granted exemption from work and sometimes even freedom after they had reared many children. For to a mother of three sons exemption from work was granted; to a mother of more her freedom as well.

Such justice and consideration on the part of the master contributes greatly to the increase of his estate. But he should also bear in mind, first to pay his respects to the household gods as soon as he returns from town; then at once, if time permits, if not, on the next day, to inspect his lands and revisit every part of them and judge whether his absence has resulted in any relaxation of discipline and watchfulness, whether any vine, any tree, or any produce is missing; at the same time, too, he should make a new count of stock, slaves, farm-equipment, and furniture. If he has made it a practice to do all this for many years, he will maintain a well-ordered discipline when old age comes; and whatever his age, he will never be so wasted with years as to be despised by his slaves.

IX. Something should be said, too, as to what tasks we think each kind of body or mind should be assigned. As keepers of the flocks it is proper to place in charge men who are diligent and very thrifty. These two qualities are more important for this task than stature and strength of body, since this is a responsibility requiring unremitting watchfulness and skill. In the case of the ploughman, intelligence, though necessary, is still not sufficient unless bigness of voice and in bearing makes him formidable to the cattle. Yet he should temper his strength with gentleness, since he should be more terrifying than cruel, so that the oxen may obey his commands and at the same time last longer because they are not worn out with the hardship of the work combined with the torment of the lash. But what the duties of shepherds and herdsmen are, I shall treat again in their proper places; for the present it is sufficient to have called to mind that strength and height are of no importance in the one, but of the greatest importance in the other. For, as I have said, we shall make all the taller ones ploughmen, both for the reason I have just given and because in the work of the farm there is no task less tiring to a tall man; for in ploughing he stands almost erect and rests his weight on the plough-handle. The common labourer may be of any height at all, if only he is capable of enduring hard work. Vineyards require not so much tall men as those who are broad-shouldered and brawny, for this type is better suited to digging and pruning and other forms of viticulture. In this department husbandry is less exacting in the matter of thrift than in the others, for the reason that the vine-dresser should do his work in company with others and under supervision, and because the unruly are for the most part possessed of quicker understanding, which is what the nature of this work requires. For it demands of the helper that he be not merely strong but also quick-witted; and on this account vineyards are commonly tended by slaves in fetters. Still there is nothing that an honest man of equal quickness will not do better than a rogue.

I have inserted this that no one may think me obsessed of such a notion as to wish to till my land with criminals rather than with honest men. But this too I believe: that the duties of the slaves should not be confused to the point where all take a hand in every task. For this is by no means to the advantage of the husbandman, either because no one regards any particular task as his own but common to all, and therefore shirks his work to a great extent; and yet the fault cannot be fastened upon any one man because many have a hand in it. For this reason ploughmen must be distinguished from vine-dressers, and vine-dressers from ploughmen, and both of these from men of all work. Furthermore, squads should be formed, not to exceed ten men each, which the ancients called *decuriae* and approved of highly, because that limited number was most conveniently guarded while at work, and the size was not disconcerting to the person in charge as he led the way. Therefore, if the field is of considerable extent, such squads should be distributed over sections of it and the work should be so apportioned that men will not be by ones or twos, because they are not easily watched when scattered; and yet they should number not more than ten, lest, on the other hand, when the band is too large, each individual may think that the work does not concern him. This arrangement not only stimulates rivalry, but also it discloses the slothful; for, when a task is enlivened by competition, punishment inflicted on the laggards appears just and free from censure.

But surely, in pointing out to the farmer-to-be those matters for which especial provision must be made—healthfulness, roads, neighbourhood, water, situation of the homestead, size of the farm, classes of tenants and slaves, and assignment of duties and tasks—we have now come properly, through these steps, to the actual tilling of the soil; of this we shall presently treat at greater length in the book that follows.

21. Cornelius Nepos, *Life of Atticus*

Cornelius Nepos is known to us only as a minor writer from north Italy who made himself a fixture in literary society during the middle of the first century B.C. A friend of Cicero and of the poet Catullus, he dabbled in verse and manufactured historical and biographical compilations in prose. The only part of his work of which anything survives is the biographies, which he wrote to bolster Roman national pride. Nepos grouped the sketches by types (generals, kings, historians, and poets, for example), and organized each group in two parallel sets, parading first the great men of Greece and then those of Rome.

The *Life of Atticus* comes from the series on Roman historians. As Nepos mentions in chapter 18, Atticus wrote a number of specialized works on historical subjects. His most valuable contribution was an aid to historians rather than a history in its own right: he prepared an accurate catalogue of the Roman magistrates, whose terms of office made up the chronological framework by which all events during the Republic were dated. But his truly outstanding accomplishment was to have flourished throughout a half century of strife which carried off many of his more brilliant friends, including Cicero, Brutus, and Mark Antony. To Nepos, writing before the civil wars were ended, the career of Atticus presented a compelling model of behavior.

Nepos does not mention that Atticus was an Epicurean; to more traditionally minded Romans, a philosophy which called on men to maximize pleasure and minimize pain could not help but seem abhorrent. But the biography does reveal how carefully Atticus obeyed Epicurus's admonitions to avoid public life and to seek in friendship the ultimate human pleasures.

---

1. Titus Pomponius Atticus, descended from a most ancient Roman family, held the equestrian rank received in uninterrupted succession from his ancestors. He had a father who was active, indulgent, and, as times then were, wealthy, as well as eminently devoted to literature; and, as he loved learning himself, he instructed his son in all branches of knowledge with which youth ought to be made acquainted. In the boy, too, besides docility of disposition, there was great sweetness of voice, so that he not only imbibed rapidly what was taught him, but repeated it extremely well. He was

From *Justin, Cornelius Nepos, and Eutropius*, translated by John Selby Watson, Bohn's Classical Library (London: George Bell & Sons, 1853), pp. 430–47.

in consequence distinguished among his companions in his boyhood, and shone forth with more lustre than his noble fellow-students could patiently bear; hence he stirred them all to new exertions by his application. In the number of them were Lucius Torquatus, Caius Marius the younger, and Marcus Cicero, whom he so attached to himself by his intercourse with them, that no one was ever more dear to them.

2. His father died at an early age. He himself, in his youth, on account of his connexion with Publius Sulpicius, who was killed when tribune of the people [88 B.C.], was not unapprehensive of sharing in his danger; for Anicia, Pomponius's cousin, was married to Marcus Servius, the brother of Sulpicius. When he saw that the state, therefore, after the death of Sulpicius, was thrown into confusion by the disturbances of Cinna, and that no facility was allowed him of living suitably to his dignity without offending one side or the other (the feelings of the citizens being divided, as some favoured the party of Sulla and others that of Cinna) he thought it a proper time for devoting himself to his studies, and betook himself to Athens. He nevertheless, however, assisted young Marius, when declared an enemy, by such means as he could, and relieved him in his exile with money. And, lest his sojourn in a foreign country should cause any detriment to his estate, he transported thither a great portion of his fortune. Here he lived in such a manner, that he was deservedly much beloved by all the Athenians; for, in addition to his interest, which was great for so young a man, he relieved their public exigencies from his own property; since, when the government was obliged to borrow money, and had no fair offer of it, he always came to their aid, and in such a way, that he never received any interest of them, and never allowed them to be indebted to him longer than had been agreed upon; both which modes of acting were for their advantage, for he neither suffered their debt to grow old upon them, nor to be increased by an accumulation of interest. He enhanced this kindness also by other instances of liberality; for he presented the whole of the people with such a supply of corn, that six bushels of wheat (a kind of measure which is called a *medimnus* at Athens) were allotted to each person.

3. He also conducted himself in such a way, that he appeared familiar with the lowest, though on a level with the highest. Hence it happened that they publicly bestowed upon him all the honours that they could, and offered to make him a citizen of Athens; an offer which he would not accept, because some are of the opinion that the citizenship of Rome is forfeited by taking that of another city. As long as he was among them, he prevented any statue from being erected to him; but when absent, he could not hinder it; and they accordingly raised several statues both to him and Phidias, in the most sacred places, for, in their whole management of the state, they took him for their agent and adviser. It was the gift of fortune, then, in the

first place, that he was born in that city, above all others, in which was the seat of the empire of the world, and had it not only for his native place but for his home; and, in the next, it was a proof of his wisdom, that when he betook himself to a city which excelled all others in antiquity, politeness, and learning, he became individually dear to it beyond other men.

4. When Sulla arrived at Athens in his journey from Asia [84 B.C.], he kept Pomponius in his company as long as he remained there, being charmed with the young man's politeness and knowledge; for he spoke Greek so well that he might have been thought to have been born at Athens; while there was such agreeableness in his Latin style, as to make it evident that the graces of it were natural, not acquired. He also recited verses, both in Greek and Latin, in so pleasing a manner that nothing could have been added to its attractions. It was in consequence of these accomplishments that Sulla would never suffer him to be out of his company, and wanted to take him away with him to Rome. But when he endeavoured to persuade him to go, Pomponius replied, "Do not desire, I entreat you, to lead me with you against those, with whom I quitted Italy in order that I might not bear arms against you." Sulla, commending the good feeling of the young man, directed, at his departure, that all the presents which he had received at Athens should be carried to his house.

Though he resided at Athens many years, paying such attention to his property as a not unthrifty father of a family ought to pay, and devoting all the rest of his time either to literature or to the public affairs of the Athenians, he nevertheless afforded his services to his friends at Rome; for he used to come to their elections, and whatever important business of theirs was brought forward, he was never found wanting on the occasion. Thus he showed a singular fidelity to Cicero in all his perils; and presented him, when he was banished from his country [58 B.C.], with the sum of two hundred fifty thousand sesterces. And when the affairs of the Romans became tranquil, he returned to Rome, in the consulship, as I believe, of Lucius Cotta and Lucius Torquatus [65 B.C.]; and the whole city of Athens observed the day of his departure in such a manner, that they testified by their tears the regret which they would afterwards feel for him.

5. He had an uncle, Quintus Caecilius, a Roman knight, an intimate friend of Lucius Lucullus, a rich man, but of a very morose temper, whose peevishness he bore so meekly, that he retained without interruption, to the extremity of old age, the good will of a person whom no one else could endure. In consequence, he reaped the fruit of his respectful conduct; for Caecilius, at his death, adopted him by his will, and made him heir to three-fourths of his estate, from which bequest he received about ten million sesterces.

A sister of Atticus was married to Quintus Tullius Cicero; and Marcus

Cicero had been the means of forming the connexion, a man with whom Atticus had lived in the closest intimacy from the time that they were fellow-students, in much greater intimacy, indeed, than with Quintus; whence it may be concluded that, in establishing friendship, similarity of manners has more influence than affinity. He was likewise so intimate with Quintus Hortensius, who, in those times, had the highest reputation for eloquence, that it could not be decided which of the two had the greater love for him, Cicero or Hortensius; and he succeeded in effecting what was most difficult, namely, that no enmity should occur between those between whom there was emulation for such eminence, and that he himself should be the bond of union between such great men.

6. He conducted himself in such a manner in political affairs, that he always was, and always was thought to be, on the best side; yet he did not mingle in civil tumults, because he thought that those who had plunged into them were not more under their own control than those who were tossed by the waves of the sea. He aimed at no offices (though they were open to him as well through his influence as through his high standing), since they could neither be sought in the ancient method, nor be gained without violating the laws in the midst of such unrestrained extravagance of bribery, nor be exercised for the good of the country without danger in so corrupt a state of the public morals. He never went to a public auction of confiscated property, nor ever became surety or farmer in any department of the public revenue. He accused no one, either in his own name or as a subscriber to an accusation. He never went to law about property of his own, nor was ever concerned in a trial. Offers of staff positions, under several consuls and praetors, he received in such a way as never to follow any one into his province, being content with the honour, and not solicitous to make any addition to his property; for he would not even go into Asia with Quintus Cicero, when he might have held the office of legate under him; for he did not think it became him, after he had declined to take the praetorship, to become the attendant on a praetor. In such conduct he consulted not only his dignity but his quiet; since he avoided even the suspicion of evil practices. Hence it happened that attentions received from him were more valued by all, as they saw that they were attributable to kindness, not to fear or hope.

7. When he was about sixty years old, the civil war with Caesar broke out [49 B.C.]; but he availed himself of the privilege of his age, and went nowhere out of the city. Whatever was needful for his friends when going to Pompey, he supplied for them out of his own property. To Pompey himself, who was his intimate friend, he gave no offence; for he had accepted no distinction from him like others, who had gained honours or wealth by his means, and of whom some followed his camp most unwillingly, and some

remained at home to his great disgust. But to Caesar the neutrality of Atticus was so pleasing, that when he became conqueror, and desired money from several private persons by letter, he not only forebore to trouble Atticus, but even released, at his request, his sister's son and Quintus Cicero from Pompey's camp. Thus, by adhering to his old course of life, he avoided new dangers.

8. Then followed the time, when, on the assassination of Caesar, the commonwealth seemed to be in the hands of the two Brutuses and Cassius, and the whole state turned towards them. Atticus, at that period, conducted himself towards Brutus in such a way, that that young man was not in more familiar intercourse with any one of his own age, than with him who was so advanced in years, and not only paid him the highest honour at the council, but also at his table. It was projected by some that a private fund should be formed by the Roman knights for the assassins of Caesar; a scheme which they thought might easily be accomplished if even only the leading men of that order would furnish contributions. Atticus was accordingly solicited by Caius Flavius, an intimate friend of Brutus, to consent to become a promoter of the plan. But Atticus, who thought that services were to be done to friends without regard to party, and had always kept himself aloof from such schemes, replied that, "If Brutus wished to make use of any of his property, he might avail himself of it as far as it would allow; but that about that project he would never confer or join with any man." Thus that combination of a party was broken by his dissent alone. Not long after, Antony began to get the advantage; so that Brutus and Cassius, despairing of their fortune, went into exile, into the provinces which had been given them for form's sake by the consuls. Atticus, who had refused to contribute with others to that party when it was prosperous, sent to Brutus, when he was cast down and retiring from Italy, a hundred thousand sesterces as a present; and, when he was parted from him, he ordered three hundred thousand to be sent to him in Epirus. Thus he neither paid greater court to Antony when in power, nor deserted those that were in desperate circumstances.

9. Next followed the war that was carried on at Mutina, in which, if I were only to say that he was wise, I should say less of him than I ought; for he rather proved himself divine, if a constant goodness of nature, which is neither increased nor diminished by the events of fortune, may be called divinity. Antony, being declared an enemy, had quitted Italy, nor was there any hope of bringing him back. Not only his open enemies, who were then very powerful and numerous, but also such as had lent themselves to the party opposed to him, and hoped to gain some share of praise by doing him injury, persecuted his friends, sought to spoil his wife Fulvia of all her property, and endeavoured even to get his children put to death. Atticus, though he lived in intimate friendship with Cicero, and was very warmly

attached to Brutus, yet would not only never give them his consent to act against Antony, but, on the contrary, protected, as much as he could, such of his friends as fled from the city, and supplied them with whatever they wanted. On Publius Volumnius, indeed, he conferred such obligations, that more could not have proceeded from a father. To Fulvia herself, too, when she was distracted with lawsuits, and troubled with great alarms, he gave his services with such constancy, that she never appeared to answer to bail without the attendance of Atticus. He was her surety in all cases, and even when she had bought an estate, in her prosperous circumstances, to be paid for by a certain day, and was unable after her reverse of fortune to borrow money to discharge the debt, he came to her aid, and lent her the money without interest, and without requiring any security for the repayment, thinking it the greatest gain to be found grateful and obliging, and to show, at the same time, that it was his practice to be a friend, not to fortune but to men; and when he acted in such a manner, no one could imagine that he acted for the sake of time serving, for it entered into nobody's thought that Antony could regain his authority. But he gradually incurred blame from some of the nobles, because he did not seem to have sufficient hatred towards bad citizens.

10. Being under the guidance of his own judgment, however, he considered rather what it was right for him to do, than what others would commend. On a sudden fortune was changed. When Antony returned into Italy, every one thought that Atticus would be in great peril, on account of his close intercourse with Cicero and Brutus. He accordingly withdrew from the forum on the approach of the leaders, from dread of the proscription, and lived in retirement at the house of Publius Volumnius, to whom, as we have said, he had not long before given assistance (such were the vicissitudes of fortune in those days, that sometimes one party, and sometimes the other, was in the greatest exaltation or in the greatest peril); and he had with him Quintus Gellius Canus, a man of the same age, and of a character very similar to his own; and this also may be given as an instance of the goodness of Atticus's disposition, that he lived in such close intimacy with him whom he had known when a boy at school, that their friendship increased even to the end of their lives. But Antony, though he was moved with such hatred towards Cicero, that he showed his enmity, not only to him, but to all his friends, and resolved to proscribe them, yet, at the instance of many, was mindful of the obliging conduct of Atticus; and, after ascertaining where he was, wrote to him with his own hand, that he need be under no apprehension, but might come to him immediately; as he had excepted him and Gellius Canus, for his sake, from the number of the proscribed; and that he might not fall into any danger, as the message was sent at night, he appointed him a guard. Thus Atticus, in a time of the greatest

alarm, was able to save, not only himself, but him whom he held most dear; for he did not seek aid from any one for the sake of his own security only, but in conjunction with his friend; so that it might appear that he wished to endure no kind of fortune apart from him. But if a pilot is extolled with the greatest praise, who saves a ship from a tempest in the midst of a rocky sea, why should not his prudence be thought of the highest character, who arrives at safety through so many and so violent civil tumults?

11. When he had delivered himself from these troubles, he had no other care than to assist as many persons as possible, by whatever means he could. When the common people, in consequence of the rewards offered by the triumvirs, were searching for the proscribed, no one went into Epirus without finding a supply of everything; and to every one was given permission to reside there constantly. After the battle of Philippi [42 B.C.], too, and the death of Caius Cassius and Marcus Brutus, he resolved on protecting Lucius Julius Mocilla, a man of praetorian rank, and his son, as well as Aulus Torquatus, and others involved in the same ill fortune, and caused supplies of everything to be sent to them from Epirus to Samothrace.

To enumerate all such acts of his would be difficult; nor are they necessary to be particularized. One point we would wish to be understood, that his generosity was not time-serving or artful, as may be judged from the circumstances and period in which it was shown; for he did not make his court to the prosperous, but was always ready to succour the distressed. Servilia, for instance, the mother of Brutus, he treated with no less consideration after Brutus's death than when she was in the height of good fortune. Indulging his liberality in such a manner, he incurred no enmities, since he neither injured any one, nor was he, if he received any injury, more willing to resent than to forget it. Kindnesses that he received he kept in perpetual remembrance; but such as he himself conferred, he remembered only so long as he who had received them was grateful. He accordingly made it appear to have been truly said, that "Every man's manners make his fortune." Yet he did not study his fortune before he formed himself, taking care that he might not justly suffer for any part of his conduct.

12. By such conduct, therefore, he brought it to pass, that Marcus Vipsanius Agrippa, who was united in the closest intimacy with young Caesar [Octavian], though, through his own interest and Caesar's influence, he had power to choose a wife from any rank whatever, fixed on a connexion with him rather than with any other, and preferred a marriage with the daughter of a Roman knight to an alliance with the most noble of women. The promoter of this match (for it is not to be concealed) was Mark Antony, when triumvir for settling the state; but though Atticus might have increased his property by the interest of Antony, he was so far from coveting money, that he never made use of that interest except to save his friends

from danger or trouble; a fact which was eminently remarkable at the time of the proscription; for when the triumviri, according to the way in which things were then managed, had sold the property of Lucius Saufeius, a Roman knight, who was of the same age as Atticus, and who, induced by a love for the study of philosophy, had lived with him several years at Athens, and had valuable estates in Italy, it was effected by the efforts and perseverance of Atticus, that Saufeius was made acquainted by the same messenger, that "he had lost his property and had recovered it." He also brought off Lucius Julius Calidus, whom I think I may truly assert to have been the most elegant poet that our age has produced since the death of Lucretius and Catullus, as well as a man of high character, and distinguished by the best intellectual accomplishments, who, in his absence, after the proscription of the knights, had been enrolled in the number of the proscribed by Publius Volumnius, the captain of Antony's engineers, on account of his great possessions in Africa; an act on the part of Atticus, of which it was hard to judge at the time, whether it were more onerous or honourable. But it was well known that the friends of Atticus, in times of danger, were not less his care in their absence than when they were present.

13. Nor was he considered less deserving as a master of a family than as a member of the state; for though he was very rich, no man was less addicted to buying or building than he. Yet he lived in very good style, and had everything of the best; for he occupied the house that had belonged to Tamphilus on the Quirinal hill, which was bequeathed to him by his uncle, and the attractions of which consisted, not in the building itself, but in the wood by which it was surrounded; for the edifice, constructed after the ancient fashion, showed more regard to convenience than expense, and Atticus made no alteration in it except such as he was obliged to make by the effects of time. He kept an establishment of slaves of the best kind, if we were to judge of it by its utility, but if by its external show, scarcely coming up to mediocrity; for there were in it well-taught youths, excellent readers, and numerous transcribers of books, insomuch that there was not even a footman that could not act in either of those capacities extremely well. Other kinds of artificers also, such as domestic necessities require, were very good there, yet he had no one among them that was not born and instructed in his house; all which particulars are proofs, not only of his self-restraint, but of his attention to his affairs; for not to desire inordinately what he sees desired by many, gives proof of a man's moderation; and to procure what he requires by labour rather than by purchase, manifests no small exertion. Atticus was elegant, not magnificent; polished, not extravagant; he studied, with all possible care, neatness, and not profusion. His household furniture was moderate, not superabundant, but so that it could not be considered as remarkable in either respect. Nor will I

omit the following particular, though I may suppose that it will be unimportant to some: that though he was a hospitable Roman knight, and invited, with no want of liberality, men of all ranks to his house, we know that he was accustomed to reckon from his day-book, as laid out in current expenses, not more than three thousand sesterces per month, and we relate this, not as hearsay but as what we know, for we were often present, by reason of the intimacy between us, at his domestic arrangements.

14. At his banquets no one ever heard any other entertainment for the ears than a reader; an entertainment which we, for our parts, think in the highest degree pleasing; nor was there ever a supper at his house without reading of some kind, that the guests might find their intellect gratified no less than their appetite, for he used to invite people whose tastes were not at variance with his own. After a large addition, too, was made to his property, he made no change in his daily arrangements, or usual way of life, and exhibited such moderation, that he neither lived unhandsomely, with a fortune of two million sesterces, which he had inherited from his father, nor did he, when he had a fortune of ten million sesterces, adopt a more splendid mode of living than that with which he had commenced, but kept himself at an equal elevation in both states. He had no gardens, no expensive suburban or maritime villa, nor any farm except those at Ardea and Nomentum; and his whole revenue arose from his property in Epirus and at Rome. Hence it may be seen that he was accustomed to estimate the worth of money, not by the quantity of it, but by the mode in which it was used.

15. He would neither utter a falsehood himself, nor could he endure it in others. His courtesies, accordingly, were paid with a strict regard to veracity, just as his gravity was mingled with affability; so that it is hard to determine whether his friends' reverence or love for him were the greater. Whatever he was asked to do, he did not promise without solemnity, for he thought it the part, not of a liberal, but of a light-minded man, to promise what he would be unable to perform. But in striving to effect what he had once engaged to do, he used to take so much pains, that he seemed to be engaged, not in an affair entrusted to him, but in his own. Of a matter which he had once taken in hand, he was never weary; for he thought his reputation, than which he held nothing more dear, concerned in the accomplishment of it. Hence it happened that he managed all the commissions of the Ciceros, Cato, Marius, Quintus Hortensius, Aulus Torquatus, and of many Roman knights besides. It may therefore be thought certain that he declined business of state, not from indolence, but from judgment.

16. Of his kindness of disposition, I can give no greater proof than that, when he was young, he was greatly liked by Sulla, who was then old, and when he was old, he was much beloved by Marcus Brutus, then but young; and that with those friends of the same age as himself, Quintus Hortensius

and Marcus Cicero, he lived in such a manner that it is hard to determine to which age his disposition was best adapted, though Marcus Cicero loved him above all men, so that not even his brother Quintus was dearer or more closely united to him. In testimony of this fact (besides the books in which Cicero mentions him, and which have been published to the world), there are sixteen books of letters, written to Atticus, which extend from his consulship to his latter days, and which he that reads will not much require a regular history of those times; for all particulars concerning the inclinations of leading men, the faults of the generals, and the revolutions in the government, are so fully stated in them that every thing is made clear; and it may be easily concluded that wisdom is in some degree divination, as Cicero not only predicted that those things would happen which took place during his life, but foretold, like a prophet, the things which are coming to pass at present.

17. Of the affectionate disposition of Atticus towards his relatives, why should I say much, since I myself heard him proudly assert, and with truth, at the funeral of his mother, whom he buried at the age of ninety, that "he had never had occasion to be reconciled to his mother," and that "he had never been at all at variance with his sister," who was nearly of the same age with himself; a proof that either no cause of complaint had happened between them, or that he was a person of such kind feelings towards his relatives, as to think it an impiety to be offended with those whom he ought to love. Nor did he act thus from nature alone, though we all obey her, but from knowledge; for he had fixed in his mind the precepts of the greatest philosophers, so as to use them for the direction of his life, and not merely for ostentation.

18. He was also a strict imitator of the customs of our ancestors, and a lover of antiquity, of which he had so exact a knowledge, that he has illustrated it throughout in the book in which he has characterized the Roman magistrates; for there is no law, or peace, or war, or illustrious action of the Roman people, which is not recorded in it at its proper period, and, what was extremely difficult, he has so interwoven in it the origin of families, that we may ascertain from it the pedigrees of eminent men. He has given similar accounts too, separately, in other books; as, at the request of Marcus Brutus, he specified in order the members of the Junian family, from its origin to the present age, stating who each was, from whom sprung, what offices he held, and at what time. In like manner, at the request of Marcellus Claudius, he gave an account of the family of the Marcelli; at the request of Scipio Cornelius and Fabius Maximus, of that of the Fabii and Aemilii; than which books nothing can be more agreeable to those who have any desire for a knowledge of the actions of illustrious men.

He attempted also poetry, in order, we suppose, that he might not be without experience of the pleasure of writing it; for he has characterized in verse such men as excelled the rest of the Roman people in honour and the greatness of their achievements, so that he has narrated, under each of their effigies, their actions and offices, in not more than four or five lines; and it is almost inconceivable that such important matters could have been told in so small a space. There is also a book of his, written in Greek, on the consulship of Cicero.

These particulars, so far, were published by me whilst Atticus was alive.

19. Since fortune has chosen that we should outlive him, we will now proceed with the sequel, and will show our readers by example, as far as we can, that (as we have intimated above) "it is in general a man's manners that bring him his fortune." For Atticus, though content in the equestrian rank in which he was born, became united by marriage with the commander-in-chief, son of the deified [Julius Caesar], whose friendship he had previously obtained by nothing else but his elegant mode of living, by which he had charmed also other eminent men in the state, of equal birth, but of lower fortune; for such prosperity attended Caesar,[1] that fortune gave him everything that she had previously bestowed upon any one, and secured for him what no citizen of Rome had ever been able to attain. Atticus had a granddaughter, the daughter of Agrippa, to whom he had married his daughter in her maidenhood; and Caesar betrothed her, when she was scarcely a year old, to Tiberius Claudius Nero, son of Drusilla, and step-son to himself; an alliance which established their friendship, and rendered their intercourse more frequent.

20. Even before this connexion, however, Caesar not only, when he was absent from the city, never despatched letters to any one of his friends without writing to Atticus what he was doing, what, above all, he was reading, in what place he was, and how long he was going to stay in it, but even when he was in Rome, and through his numberless occupations enjoyed the society of Atticus less frequently than he wished, scarcely any day passed in which he did not write to him, sometimes asking him something relating to antiquity, sometimes proposing to him some poetical question, and sometimes, by a jest drawing from him a longer letter than ordinary. Hence it was, that when the temple of Jupiter Feretrius, built in the Capitol by Romulus, was unroofed and falling down through age and neglect, Caesar, on the suggestion of Atticus, took care that it should be repaired.

Nor was he less frequently, when absent, addressed in letters by Mark Antony; so that, from the remotest parts of the earth, he gave Atticus pre-

1. Here and in the remainder of the life, "Caesar" means not Julius Caesar, but Octavian.

cise information what he was doing, and what cares he had upon him. How strong such attachment is, he will be easily able to judge, who can understand how much prudence is required to preserve the friendship and favour of those between whom there existed not only emulation in the highest matters, but such a mutual struggle to lessen one another as was sure to happen between Caesar and Antony, when each of them desired to be chief, not merely of the city of Rome, but of the whole world.

21. After he had completed, in such a course of life, seventy-seven years, and had advanced, not less in dignity, than in favour and fortune (for he obtained many legacies on no other account than his goodness of disposition), and had also been in the enjoyment of so happy a state of health, that he had wanted no medicine for thirty years, he contracted a disorder of which at first both himself and the physicians thought lightly, for they supposed it to be a bowel disorder, and speedy and easy remedies were proposed for it; but after he had passed three months under it without any pain, except what he suffered from the means adopted for his cure, such force of the disease fell into the one intestine, that at last a putrid ulcer broke out through his loins. Before this took place, and when he found that the pain was daily increasing, and that fever was superadded, he caused his son-in-law Agrippa to be called to him, and with him Lucius Cornelius Balbus and Sextus Peducaeus. When he saw that they were come, he said, as he supported himself on his elbow, "How much care and diligence I have employed to restore my health on this occasion, there is no necessity for me to state at large, since I have yourselves as witness; and since I have, as I hope, satisfied you, that I have left nothing undone that seemed likely to cure me, it remains that I consult for myself. Of this feeling on my part I had no wish that you should be ignorant; for I have determined on ceasing to feed the disease; as, by the food and drink that I have taken during the last few days, I have prolonged life only so as to increase my pains without hope of recovery. I therefore entreat you, in the first place, to give your approbation to my resolution, and in the next, not to labour in vain by endeavouring to dissuade me from executing it."

22. Having delivered this address with so much steadiness of voice and countenance, that he seemed to be removing, not out of life, but out of one house into another,—when Agrippa, weeping over him and kissing him, entreated and conjured him "not to accelerate that which nature herself would bring, and, since he might live some time longer, to preserve his life for himself and his friends,"—he put a stop to his prayers, by an obstinate silence. After he had accordingly abstained from food for two days, the fever suddenly left him, and the disease began to be less oppressive. He persisted, nevertheless, in executing his purpose; and in consequence, on

the fifth day after he had fixed his resolution, and on the last day of February, in the consulship of Cnaeus Domitius and Caius Sosius [32 B.C.], he died. His body was carried out of his house on a small couch, as he himself had directed, without any funeral pomp, all the respectable portion of the people attending, and a vast crowd of the populace. He was buried close by the Appian way, at the fifth milestone from the city, in the sepulchre of his uncle Quintus Caecilius.

22. *The Funeral Eulogy of Turia*

In the last decade of the first century B.C., a well-to-do Roman delivered a eulogy of his deceased wife and then had it inscribed as a memorial to her. The inscription is badly damaged, but close to three-quarters of the speech is tolerably well preserved. The identities of both the husband and the wife are uncertain, since the heading of the inscription is gone, and neither name happens to be mentioned in the sections which remain. Nevertheless, the inscription has become generally known as the "Eulogy of Turia," because the speaker's experiences in some ways parallel the calamities which befell a Roman senator named Quintus Lucretius Vespillo and his wife Turia.

The speech picks up with events that occurred after Julius Caesar led an army from Gaul into Italy in January of 49 B.C. When Pompey and his senatorial partisans were forced to take flight, the speaker and his brother-in-law Cluvius evidently followed them abroad. In the meantime, as public order broke down in Italy, the parents of his wife (or fiancée at that point) were killed, and his house came under attack. After Caesar's victory over the Pompeians, the heroine of the eulogy managed to win a pardon for her husband, who returned home. But worse was in store for him. The assassination of Caesar in 44 B.C. led to a new round of civil war and the takeover of government by the dictatorship of Mark Antony, Lepidus, and Octavian (the later Augustus). Late in 43 B.C., the triumvirs ordered the summary execution of between two and three thousand people and seized their assets, thus settling accounts with enemies and at the same time raising cash to pay their armies. The speaker was among those proscribed, but his wife protected him during the purge and even induced Octavian to reverse the decision.

Women in Rome could not vote or hold office, but they exerted a strong if usually invisible influence on politics. Their influence increased as constitutional processes declined. The "Eulogy of Turia" shows a woman using her power in the years when the Roman Republic was changing to the Principate, and it allows a glimpse of the resources on which her power was based.

You became an orphan suddenly before the day of our wedding, when both your parents were murdered together in the solitude of the countryside. It was mainly due to your efforts that the death of your parents was not left unavenged. For I had left for Macedonia, and your sister's husband Cluvius had gone to the Province of Africa.

So strenuously did you perform your filial duty by your insistent demands and your pursuit of justice that we could not have done more if we had been present. But these merits you have in common with that most virtuous lady your sister.

While you were engaged in these things, having secured the punishment of the guilty, you immediately left your own house in order to guard your modesty and you came to my mother's house, where you awaited my return.

Then pressure was brought to bear on you and your sister to accept the view that your father's will, by which you and I were heirs, had been invalidated by his having contracted a *coemptio* with his wife.[1] If that was the case, then you together with all your father's property would necessarily come under the guardianship of those who pursued the matter; your sister would be left without any share at all of that inheritance, since she had passed under the legal control of Cluvius. How you reacted to this, with what presence of mind you offered resistance, I know full well, although I was absent.

You defended our common cause by asserting the truth, namely, that the will had not in fact been broken, so that we should both keep the property, instead of your getting all of it alone. It was your firm decision that you would defend your father's written word; you would do this anyhow, you declared, by sharing your inheritance with your sister, if you were unable to uphold the validity of the will. And you maintained that you would not come under the state of legal guardianship, since there was no such right

1. *Coemptio* was an old-fashioned form of marriage which brought a wife under the legal control of her husband and, for purposes of inheritance, caused her to be regarded as his child. In the case at issue here, when the father (re)married by *coemptio*, he invalidated his existing will because it took no account of the new wife who had now to be considered a principal heir. At his death, the relatives moved in and insisted that the rules of intestacy applied, under which they would be entitled to be appointed guardians, and to "administer" the estate.

against you in law, for there was no proof that your family belonged to any clan that could by law compel you to do this. For even assuming that your father's will had become void, those who prosecuted had no such right, since they did not belong to the same clan.

They gave way before your firm resolution and did not pursue the matter any further. Thus you on your own brought to a successful conclusion the defence you took up of your duty to your father, your devotion to your sister, and your faithfulness towards me.

Marriages as long as ours are rare, marriages that are ended by death and not broken by divorce. For we were fortunate enough to see our marriage last without disharmony for fully forty years. I wish that our long union had come to its final end through something that had befallen me instead of you; it would have been more just if I as the older partner had had to yield to fate through such an event.

Why should I mention your domestic virtues: your loyalty, obedience, affability, reasonableness, industry in working wool, religion without superstition, sobriety of attire, modesty of appearance? Why dwell on your love for your relatives, your devotion to your family? You have shown the same attention to my mother as you did to your own parents, and have taken care to secure an equally peaceful life for her as you did for your own people, and you have innumerable merits in common with all married women who care for their good name. It is your very own virtues that I am asserting, and very few women have encountered comparable circumstances to make them endure such sufferings and perform such deeds. Providentially Fate has made such hard tests rare for women.

We have preserved all the property you inherited from your parents under common custody, for you were not concerned to make your own what you had given to me without any restriction. We divided our duties in such a way that I had the guardianship of your property and you had the care of mine. Concerning this side of our relationship I pass over much, in case I should take a share myself in what is properly yours. May it be enough for me to have said this much to indicate how you felt and thought.

Your generosity you have manifested to many friends and particularly to your beloved relatives. On this point someone might mention with praise other women, but the only equal you have had has been your sister. For you brought up your female relations who deserved such kindness in your own houses with us. You also prepared marriage-portions for them so that they could obtain marriages worthy of your family. The dowries you had decided upon Cluvius and I by common accord took upon ourselves to pay, and since we approved of your generosity we did not wish that you should let your own patrimony suffer diminution but substituted our own money and gave our own estates as dowries. I have mentioned this not from a wish to commend ourselves but to make clear that it was a point of honour for us to execute with our means what you had conceived in a spirit of generous family affection.

A number of other benefits of yours I have preferred not to mention. [several lines missing]

You provided abundantly for my needs during my flight and gave me the means for a dignified manner of living, when you took all the gold and jewelery from your own body and sent it to me and over and over again enriched me in my absence with servants, money and provisions, showing great ingenuity in deceiving the guards posted by our adversaries.

You resorted to supplications which were the expression of your devotion and because of your entreaties I was shielded by the clemency of those against whom you marshalled your words. But whatever you said was always said with undaunted courage.

Meanwhile when a troop of men collected by Milo,[2] whose house I had acquired through purchase when he was in exile, tried to profit by the opportunities provided by the civil war and break into our house to plunder, you beat them back successfully and were able to defend our home. [about 12 lines missing]

. . . that I was brought back to my country by him, for if you had not, by taking care for my safety, provided what he could save, he would have promised his support in vain. Thus I owe my life no less to your devotion than to Caesar.

Why should I now hold up to view our intimate and secret plans and private conversations: how I was saved by your good advice when I was roused by startling reports to meet sudden and imminent dangers; how you did not allow me imprudently to tempt providence by an overbold step but prepared a safe hiding-place for me, when I had given up my ambitious designs, choosing as partners in your plans to save me your sister and her husband Cluvius, all of you taking the same risk? There would be no end, if I tried to go into all this. It is enough for me and for you that I was hidden and my life was saved.

But I must say that the bitterest thing that happened to me in my life befell me through what happened to you. When thanks to the kindness and judgement of the absent Caesar Augustus I had been restored to my country as a citizen, Marcus Lepidus, his colleague, who was present, was confronted with your request concerning my recall, and you lay prostrate at his feet, and you were not only not raised up but were dragged away and carried off brutally like a slave. But although your body was full of bruises, your spirit was unbroken and you kept reminding him of Caesar's edict with

2. Milo was the political agitator who worked on behalf of senate conservatives in the decade before the civil wars (see document 4). He was exiled after killing Clodius in 52 B.C., but stole back into Italy in 48 B.C.

its expression of pleasure at my reinstatement, and although you had to listen to insulting words and suffer cruel wounds, you pronounced the words of the edict in a loud voice, so that it should be known who was the cause of my deadly perils. This matter was soon to prove harmful for him.

What could have been more effective than the virtue you displayed? You managed to give Caesar an opportunity to display his clemency and not only to preserve my life but also to brand Lepidus' insolent cruelty by your admirable endurance.

But why go on? Let me cut my speech short. My words should and can be brief, lest by dwelling on your great deeds I treat them unworthily. In gratitude for your great services towards me let me display before the eyes of all men my public acknowledgement that you saved my life.

When peace had been restored throughout the world and the lawful political order reestablished, we began to enjoy quiet and happy times. It is true that we did wish to have children, who had for a long time been denied to us by an envious fate. If it had pleased Fortune to continue to be favourable to us as she was wont to be, what would have been lacking for either of us? But Fortune took a different course, and our hopes were sinking. The courses you considered and the steps you attempted to take because of this would perhaps be remarkable and praiseworthy in some other women, but in you they are nothing to wonder at when compared to your other great qualities and I will not go into them.

When you despaired of your ability to bear children and grieved over my childlessness, you became anxious lest by retaining you in marriage I might lose all hope of having children and be distressed for that reason. So you proposed a divorce outright and offered to yield our house free to another woman's fertility. Your intention was in fact that you yourself, relying on our well-known conformity of sentiment, would search out and provide for me a wife who was worthy and suitable for me, and you declared that you would regard future children as joint and as though your own, and that you would not effect a separation of our property which had hitherto been held in common, but that it would still be under my control and, if I wished so, under your administration: nothing would be kept apart by you, nothing separate, and you would thereafter take upon yourself the duties and the loyalty of a sister and a mother-in-law.

I must admit that I flared up so that I almost lost control of myself; so horrified was I by what you tried to do that I found it difficult to retrieve my composure. To think that separation should be considered between us before fate had so ordained, to think that you had been able to conceive in your mind the idea that you might cease to be my wife while I was still alive, although you had been utterly faithful to me when I was exiled and practically dead!

What desire, what need to have children could I have had that was so great that I should have broken faith for that reason and changed certainty for uncertainty? But no more about this! You remained with me as my wife. For I could not have given in to you without disgrace for me and unhappiness for both of us.

But on your part, what could have been more worthy of commemoration and praise than your efforts in devotion to my interests: when I could not have children from yourself, you wanted me to have them through your good offices and, since you despaired of bearing children, to provide me with offspring by my marriage to another woman.

Would that the life-span of each of us had allowed our marriage to continue until I, as the older partner, had been borne to the grave—that would have been juster—and you had performed for me the last rites, and that I had died leaving you still alive and that I had you as a daughter to myself in place of my childlessness.

Fate decreed that you should precede me. You bequeathed me sorrow through my longing for you and left me a miserable man without children to comfort me. I on my part will, however, bend my way of thinking and feeling to your judgements and be guided by your admonitions.

But all your opinions and instructions should give precedence to the praise you have won so that this praise will be a consolation for me and I will not feel too much the loss of what I have consecrated to immortality to be remembered for ever.

What you have achieved in your life will not be lost to me. The thought of your fame gives me strength of mind and from your actions I draw instruction so that I shall be able to resist Fortune. Fortune did not rob me of everything since it permitted your memory to be glorified by praise. But along with you I have lost the tranquillity of my existence. When I recall how you used to foresee and ward off the dangers that threatened me, I break down under my calamity and cannot hold steadfastly by my promise.

Natural sorrow wrests away my power of self-control and I am overwhelmed by sorrow. I am tormented by two emotions: grief and fear—and I do not stand firm against either. When I go back in thought to my previous misfortunes and when I envisage what the future may have in store for me, fixing my eyes on your glory does not give me strength to bear my sorrow with patience. Rather I seem to be destined to longing and mourning.

The conclusion of my speech will be that you deserved everything but that it did not fall to my lot to give you everything as I ought. Your last wishes I have regarded as law; whatever it will be in my power to do in addition, I shall do.

I pray that your spirits will grant you rest and protection.

23. Wills

The revenues of a worldwide empire funneled through Rome, enriching not only the emperor but also the ruling class of senators and knights who assisted him. Rich Romans were extremely rich. Their wealth would have made them powerful figures in any society, but their position in Roman society was strengthened by two factors related to the making of wills. First, wills among the Roman aristocracy typically provided for a much greater number of legacies than modern wills do; etiquette prescribed that a gentleman should remember his friends as well as his kin. This custom naturally encouraged demonstrations of friendship and service toward the rich. Second, increasing numbers of aristocrats were childless. For various reasons (civil war, purges, a declining birth rate), most of the old senatorial families of the Republic had come to an end by the first century A.D. And although they were replaced by a new aristocracy, the newcomers did not establish such long-lived families. Many senators and knights chose not to marry at all, partly because a fortune unencumbered by natural heirs added a powerful hold over the esteem of their associates.

Wills were instruments of social dominance in the testator's lifetime, and they were always newsworthy. In the following letters, Pliny (see the introduction to document 12) moralizes about dispositions made by two members of the senatorial class.

The Will of Ummidia Quadratilla

Gaius Pliny to Geminus: Ummidia Quadratilla has died, just a bit shy of her eightieth year. A sturdy, thick-set figure even for a matron, she was full of pep right up to her last illness. The will she left at the end was exemplary: she made her grandson heir to two-thirds of the estate and her granddaughter heir to one-third. The granddaughter I don't know too well, but I am very close to the grandson. He is an outstanding young man, as dear as flesh and blood could be even to people outside his family. Right from the start he kept clear of spiteful gossip through boyhood and youth, though he was extremely good-looking. He was married by the time he was twenty-four, and would have been a father if god had so willed. Without being undutiful, he led a very upright life under the same roof as his pleasure-loving grandmother. She owned a pantomime troupe, which she promoted rather too exuberantly for a lady of the upper class. Quadratus never

Pliny, *Letters* 7.24. Translated for this volume by Peter White.

watched them, either in the theater or at home, and his grandmother did not insist. Once when she was commending her grandson's education to me, she told me that, being a woman with nothing to occupy her time, she liked to relax with board games or to watch her actors. But whenever she was about to do either, she always told her grandson to go away and study—which I think showed respect as well as love for him. And let me tell you something that will surprise you (it certainly surprised me). At the last priestly games, there was a contest among pantomime artists. Quadratus and I left at the same time, and he said to me, "Do you know, this is the first time I have seen my grandmother's freedman dance?" That shows the grandson's attitude. But meanwhile people who were not even slightly related to Quadratilla paid their "respects" to her (I balk at the word) with obsequious service. They would descend on the theater and clap and jump up and down and ooh and ah; by the end they would be playing back the lady's every gesture with outbursts of song. Well, now they will get tiny legacies in recognition of their theatrical services—from Quadratilla's heir, who never went to the theater.

I tell you all this because you are always glad to hear whatever news there is, and because the pleasure I took in the story comes back to me as I write about it. It makes me feel good to think about the power of family ties seen in the will of the deceased, and about the integrity of the young man. I am also glad that a mansion which once belonged to Gaius Cassius, head and founder of the Cassian school of jurisprudence, will pass into the hands of a new owner just as distinguished. My good friend Quadratus will measure up to the stature of that house, and it will recover its bygone centrality and prestige, once it can boast an orator who is as great as Cassius was a jurist. Goodbye.

The Will of Domitius Tullus

Gaius Pliny to Rufinus: The popular belief that a man's will mirrors his character must be false, since Domitius Tullus has shown himself a far better man in death than in life. Even though he had always encouraged the attentions of fortune hunters, the heir he left was the daughter he shared with his brother (whose daughter he had adopted). He remembered his grandsons in a series of very welcome bequests, and there was also one for his great-granddaughter. All in all, a perfect example of blood being thicker than water, and so quite unexpected. Talk around town varies. Some people go on about his duplicity, ingratitude, or lack of consideration, exposing a most deplorable side of themselves in the course of their attacks

Pliny, *Letters* 8.18. Translated for this volume by Peter White.

on him—as if they were complaining about some old bachelor, and not about a man who had a daughter, grandchildren, and great-grandchildren to provide for. Others applaud him precisely for shattering the impudent hopes of a breed of men whom it is practically a virtue these days to deceive. They also point out that he was not free to draw up his will in any other way: it was not a question of leaving his daughter a fortune, but of returning one which had come to him through her. You see, Curtilius Mancina detested his son-in-law Domitius Lucanus (that was Tullus's brother), and stipulated in *his* will that the granddaughter, Lucanus's daughter, could inherit only if she were legally cut loose from parental control. Well, the father released her, and the uncle adopted her. That was the way they got around the will. Tullus and Lucanus had merged all their affairs in a full and formal partnership, and so through the trick of adoption Tullus brought the emancipated daughter back under his brother's control—and with her, a handsome fortune.

Evidently those brothers were fated to be rich even when the people who made them rich were dead set against them. The same thing happened in the case of Domitius Afer, who adopted and gave them his name. He left a will drafted eighteen years earlier, which was so contrary to his thinking later in life that he was responsible for the confiscation of their father's property. His callousness in stripping away the citizenship of his associate and coparent was as bizarre as the fluke by which the brothers got him in place of the father he had eliminated. But Afer's fortune, like everything else that Lucanus amassed in partnership with his brother, was ultimately supposed to pass to the daughter in her turn: Lucanus had named Tullus sole heir, in preference to the daughter, as a means of promoting harmony between them. So Tullus's will deserves all the more praise as an expression of family feeling, honesty, and plain decency.

In fact, he even rewarded all his in-laws for their various services to him—not least his wife, who inherited attractive country houses and a large sum of money. That excellent and long-suffering woman deserved special consideration because she had taken so much criticism for marrying him. She was a fine person from a distinguished family, already past middle age at the time; her first husband had died some years before, and her childbearing years were long behind her. People thought it unseemly of her to take on a rich old man so desperately sick that he would have been a trial even to a wife who had married him when he was young and healthy. Completely crippled and paralyzed, he could do no more than gaze on his enormous wealth. Even in bed he needed help in order to move, and (this is gross and pathetic) he had to have someone brush and rinse his teeth for him. Over and over as he was railing against the humiliation of his state he was heard to say that every day he licked the fingers of his slaves. But he went on living, and wanted to live, sustained mainly by his wife, who stuck by him and turned to praise the criticism that was heard when she went into the marriage.

That's all the gossip from the city, where the gossip is all about Tullus. Now we're waiting for the estate auction. Tullus had such vast holdings that he could buy up spacious gardens, and on the very same day stock them with dozens of antique sculptures; he had any number of superb pieces buried away in his warehouses.

You must not begrudge me anything out where you are that would justify a letter. Apart from the pleasure we get from hearing news, it furnishes instructive examples for the ordering of our lives. Goodbye.

24. Masters Murdered by Slaves

Slaves were omnipresent in the Roman world—on farms, in commerce, in the state bureaucracy, and in private households; they were one of the most obvious commodities on which the society expended its enormous wealth. But though slavery was a fundamental institution, aspects of it seem paradoxical. Slaves could be and frequently were freed by their masters, and the slave of a Roman, unlike a slave in Athens, automatically became a citizen when freed. In some ways it was easier for a freed slave to become prosperous than for ordinary citizens, and a rich freedman's family needed only a generation or two to achieve respectability. Yet it was in Italy, not in Greece, that slaves revolted by the thousands under such leaders as Spartacus. And it was the Romans who were preoccupied with domestic atrocities like the following.

In the first passage, Tacitus (see the introduction to document 10) reports a senatorial debate of the year A.D. 61, following the murder of the very man who held the highest police authority in the capital. The second text is a letter of Pliny (see the introduction to document 12), describing a similar incident that occurred forty years later.

During the Republic there had been instances when such attacks were punished by putting to death all slaves who were in the house at the time of the crime. During the early years of the Principate, these precedents were invoked as "ancestral practice," and made the basis for laws which became progressively more stern.

Tacitus on the Murder of Pedanius Secundus

Soon afterwards one of his own slaves murdered the city-prefect, Pedanius Secundus, either because he had been refused his freedom, for which he had made a bargain, or in the jealousy of a love in which he could not brook his master's rivalry. Ancient custom required that the whole slave-establishment which had dwelt under the same roof should be dragged to execution, when a sudden gathering of the populace, which was for saving so many innocent lives, brought matters to actual insurrection. Even in the Senate there was a strong feeling on the part of those who shrank from extreme rigour, though the majority were opposed to any innovation. Of these, Caius Cassius, in giving his vote, argued to the following effect:—

"Often have I been present, Senators, in this assembly when new decrees were demanded from us contrary to the customs and laws of our ancestors, and I have refrained from opposition, not because I doubted but that in all matters the arrangements of the past were better and fairer and that all changes were for the worse, but that I might not seem to be exalting my own profession out of an excessive partiality for ancient precedent. At the same time I thought that any influence I possess ought not to be destroyed by incessant protests, wishing that it might remain unimpaired, should the State ever need my counsels. To-day this has come to pass, since an ex-consul has been murdered in his house by the treachery of slaves, which not one hindered or divulged, though the Senate's decree, which threatens the entire slave-establishment with execution, has been till now unshaken. Vote impunity, in heaven's name, and then who will be protected by his rank, when the prefecture of the capital has been of no avail to its holder? Who will be kept safe by the number of his slaves when four hundred have not protected Pedanius Secundus? Which of us will be rescued by his domestics, who, even with the dread of punishment before them, regard not our dangers? Was the murderer, as some do not blush to pretend, avenging his wrongs because he had bargained about money from his father or because a family-slave was taken from him? Let us actually decide that the master was justly slain.

"Is it your pleasure to search for arguments in a matter already weighed in the deliberations of wiser men than ourselves? Even if we had now for the first time to come to a decision, do you believe that a slave took courage to murder his master without letting fall a threatening word or uttering a rash syllable? Granted that he concealed his purpose, that he procured his weapon without his fellows' knowledge. Could he pass the night-guard,

Tacitus, *Annales* 14.42–45. From *The Annals of Tacitus*, translated by Alfred John Church and William Jackson Brodribb (London: Macmillan, 1869), pp. 274–76.

could he open the doors of the chamber, carry in a light, and accomplish the murder, while all were in ignorance? There are many preliminaries to guilt; if these are divulged by slaves, we may live singly amid numbers, safe among a trembling throng; lastly, if we must perish, it will be with vengeance on the guilty. Our ancestors always suspected the temper of their slaves, even when they were born on the same estates, or in the same houses with themselves and thus inherited from their birth an affection for their masters. But now that we have in our households nations with different customs to our own, with a foreign worship or none at all, it is only by terror you can hold in such a motley rabble. But, it will be said, the innocent will perish. Well, even in a beaten army when every tenth man is felled by the club, the lot falls also on the brave. There is some injustice in every great precedent, which, though injurious to individuals, has its compensation in the public advantage."

No one indeed dared singly to oppose the opinion of Cassius, but clamorous voices rose in reply from all who pitied the number, age, or sex, as well as the undoubted innocence of the great majority. Still, the party which voted for their execution prevailed. But the sentence could not be obeyed in the face of a dense and threatening mob, with stones and firebrands. Then the emperor reprimanded the people by edict, and lined with a force of soldiers the entire route by which the condemned had to be dragged to execution. Cingonius Varro had proposed that even all the freedmen under the same roof should be transported from Italy. This the emperor forbade, as he did not wish an ancient custom, which mercy had not relaxed, to be strained with cruel rigour.

Pliny on the Murder of Larcius Macedo

Gaius Pliny to Acilius: Larcius Macedo the ex-praetor has been the victim of an atrocity that calls for more than just a letter. The perpetrators were his own slaves, to whom he had always been a high-handed and brutal master. He let himself forget—or more accurately, he could never manage to forget—that his own father had been a slave. He was having a bath in his country place at Formiae. All of a sudden the slaves surrounded him. One went for his throat while another battered his face and someone else beat him on the chest and stomach and even the genitals, I am embarrassed to say. When they thought he had stopped breathing, they dumped him on the hot flooring to see if he was still alive. Macedo either was past feeling or pretended to be, because he lay there stretched out without moving and so convinced them that the murder was successful. At that point they lugged

Pliny, *Letters* 3.14. Translated for this volume by Peter White.

him outside, as though he had just collapsed from the heat. Some good-hearted slaves took charge of him, and his concubines ran up wailing and shouting. What with the stimulus of the noise and the cool air, he revived. Opening his eyes and moving his limbs, he let it be seen that he was alive, it being now safe to do so. The slaves ran off, but a lot of them have been rounded up and a hunt is on for the rest. Although Macedo died after a few days of touch-and-go recovery, it was some comfort to him that the punishment which usually follows the murder of a master was administered while he was still alive.

You see the perils and injuries and indignities to which we are exposed. And no one has any reason to feel secure because he is gentle and easy-going: viciousness and not reasoning is behind these murders.

But enough on that subject. What else is new? Nothing, otherwise I would include it, since I still have plenty of space, and the holiday today allows time to add more. Actually, I will add one thing about Macedo that I have just remembered. When he was at one of the public bathhouses in Rome, a remarkable thing happened, which was also prophetic, as the aftermath showed. One of Macedo's slaves gently tapped a Roman knight who was standing in their way. The man rounded, not on the slave who had touched him, but on Macedo, and slapped him so hard that he almost fell. Thus the baths went from being the scene of an affront to being the scene of his death.

25. Two Prayers

The Romans considered themselves a god-fearing nation in comparison with the peoples around them. In addition to familiar gods such as Jupiter, Mars, and Apollo, they recognized deities who presided over doorsills, boundary stones, springs, wheat rust, ploughing, grafting, and a host of other sites and functions. Before undertaking any private or public action which might disturb a god's sensibilities, the Romans took precautions to secure divine favor or to avert ill will. The greater part of Roman religion consisted of actions: processions, wordless rituals, sacrifice, and the inspection of heaven-sent signs, all of which it is difficult for us to recapture by the power of imagination. But prayer was also important, and the words of prayers reveal a great deal about the religious mentality of the Romans.

Two religious texts are presented here. The first is a prayer recommended by Cato in his manual of advice to farmers (see document 19); the second comes from the record of a state festival at which Augustus officiated in 17 B.C. The prayers are about a century and a half apart in date, and one is a private utterance on behalf of a single household while the other is a public prayer for the state. Yet despite these differences, the spirit and the language of the two prayers are very much the same.

Cato's Prayer

Father Mars, I beg and entreat thee to be of goodwill and favorable to me and to our house and household, for which purpose I have ordered the swine-sheep-bull procession to be led around my land and fields and farm. And [I beg] that thou wilt check, thrust back and avert diseases seen and unseen, crop failure and crop destruction, sudden losses and storms, and that thou wilt permit the annual crops, the grain crops, the vineyards and tree and vine slips to grow and turn out well. And [that thou] keep safe the shepherds and the flocks and give good health and strength to me and to our house and household; with these purposes in view and in consideration of the purifying procession about my estate, land and fields, and the making of the purifying sacrifice—according to the words as I have spoken them,—receive the honor of this suckling swine-sheep-bull sacrifice. Father Mars, with the same purpose in view, receive the honor of this suckling swine-sheep-bull offering.

Augustus's Prayer

O Fates! As it has been prescribed for you in those books[1]—and by virtue of this may every good fortune come to the Roman people, the Quirites—let sacrifice be made to you with nine ewes and nine female goats. I beseech and pray you, just as you have increased the empire and majesty of the Roman people, the Quirites, in war and in peace, so may the Latins ever be obedient; grant everlasting safety, victory, and health to the Roman people, the Quirites; protect the Roman people, the Quirites, and keep safe and sound the state of the Roman people, the Quirites; be favorable and propitious to the Roman people, the Quirites, to the board of fifteen, to me, to my house and my household; and deign to accept this sacrifice of nine

De agricultura 141. From *Cato the Censor: On Farming*, translated by Ernest Brehaut, Records of Civilization, no. 17 (New York: Columbia University Press, 1933), pp. 120–21. Reprinted by permission of Columbia University Press.

Corpus inscriptionum Latinarum vi.32323, lines 92–99. From *Roman Civilization*, vol. 2, *The Empire*, edited by Naphtali Lewis and Meyer Reinhold (New York: Columbia University Press, 1955; reprint, New York: Harper & Row, 1966), p. 58. Reprinted by permission of Columbia University Press.

1. The books contained the ancient prophecies of the Sibyl, which were kept by a board of fifteen priestly officials and consulted about special rituals.

ewes and nine female goats, perfect for sacrificing. To these ends be you honored by the sacrifice of this ewe, become you favorable and propitious to the Roman people, the Quirites, to the board of fifteen, to me, to my house and my household.

26. Official Reaction to Two Alien Cults

Roman religious practices had the sanction of tradition and of the lawgiver King Numa (ca. 700 B.C.) behind them. But their most powerful sanction derived from their importance in the life of the state. The prosperity of Rome was thought to depend on maintaining correct relations with the gods, and responsibility for these relations rested with persons who served the state, either as regular officeholders or as official priests. Rome's success only complicated the task of safeguarding the state religion; as the empire expanded, the Romans inevitably had to come to terms with alien cults. Although the upper classes typically scorned what they regarded as grotesque superstitions, the policy of the government was usually to tolerate the cults, so long as they did not appear disruptive. The problem is to understand what looked disruptive from a Roman point of view.

The following readings illustrate official attitudes on two occasions when the government acted against foreign cults. On the first occasion, the target was the cult of Dionysus, or Bacchus, which by the early part of the second century B.C. had begun to spread into central Italy from Hellenized areas in the south. The situation is summarized by Livy in book 39 of his *History* (chapters 8–19). The worship of Dionysus, which in Greece was associated with manic rites celebrated by women, in Italy drew together both men and women. A scandal in Rome brought the cult to the attention of the authorities, amid lurid allegations: it was said that the rites took place in secret and at night, progressing from drunkenness through debauchery to murder and offenses against property. After corrective measures were applied in Rome, the consuls took the then unusual step of commanding the "allies" throughout Italy to follow suit. Although their letter of 186 B.C. does not explain why they considered the cult objectionable, it does spell out the kind of activity they were anxious to prevent.

The next two documents concern a nuisance which had to be dealt with three hundred years later. During the first century A.D., the Christians acquired a reputation much like that which clung to the worshippers of Bacchus. They were so unpopular that in A.D. 64 the emperor Nero had them tortured to provide entertainment at public shows, as Tacitus relates in his *Annals* (15.44). By A.D. 110 or 111, when a Roman governor (Pliny, see document 12) inquired how he should treat the Christians in Bithynia (northwest Turkey today), government policy was less extreme but still repressive. The governor was aware of the criminal allegations against the Christians and somewhat perplexed that he could find no basis for them. Yet he had no doubt that harsh proceedings were in order. Some elements in the situation had not existed at the time of the Bacchic scandal: for one thing, the cult of the emperor was now incorporated into the Roman state religion. But official concerns about sectarian gatherings remained much the same.

A Consular Letter concerning Bacchic Associations, 186 B.C.

The consuls Quintus Marcius son of Lucius, and Spurius Postumius son of Lucius, consulted the senate on the seventh day of October in the temple of Bellona. Present as witnesses to the record: Marcus Claudius son of Marcus; Lucius Valerius son of Publius; and Quintus Minucius son of Gaius.

In the matter of the orgies of Bacchus they passed a resolution that the following proclamation should be issued to those who are in league with the Romans by treaties:

"Let none of them be minded to keep a lodge of Bacchus. Should there be some who say that they must needs keep a lodge of Bacchus, they must come to the praetor of the city at Rome, and our Senate, when it has heard what they have to say, shall make decision on those matters, provided that not fewer senators than 100 be present when the matter is deliberated. Let no man, whether Roman citizen or person of the Latin name or one of the allies, be minded to attend a meeting of Bacchant women unless they have first approached the praetor of the city and he have authorised them, by a vote of the Senate, to do so, provided that not fewer Senators than 100 be present when the matter is deliberated." Passed.

"Let no man be a priest. Let not any man or woman be a master or any likewise be minded to institute a common fund; nor let any person be minded to make either man or woman a master or vice-master or mistress, or be minded henceforth to swear, vow, pledge, or make promise with others, or be minded to plight faith with others. Let no one be minded to hold ceremonies in secret; nor let anyone be minded to hold ceremonies in public capacity or in private or outside the city, unless he have first ap-

Corpus inscriptionum Latinarum vi.196. From *Remains of Old Latin*, vol. 4, translated by E. H. Warmington (Cambridge, Mass.: Harvard University Press, 1940). Reprinted by permission of the publisher and the Loeb Classical Library.

proached the praetor of the city and he have authorised them, by a vote of the Senate, to do so, provided that not fewer Senators than 100 be present when that matter is deliberated." Passed.

"Let no single person in a company beyond five in all, men and women, be minded to hold ceremonies, and let men not more than two, and not more than three women be minded to attend there among, unless it be by the advice of the praetor of the city, and a vote of the Senate as recorded above."

You shall proclaim these orders at a public meeting for a period covering not less than three market-days; and that you might be aware of the vote of the Senate, they voted as follows: They resolved that "should there be any persons who act contrary to the purport of the proclamation as recorded above, proceedings for capital offence must be taken against them." And the Senate resolved that it be "right and proper that you engrave this proclamation onto a tablet of bronze and that you order it to be fastened up where it can be most easily read; and that within ten days after the delivery of this State-letter to you, you see to it that those lodges of Bacchus which may exist are dispersed, in the manner recorded above, save if there be concerned anything holy therein." In the domain of the Teurani.

A Consultation Concerning the Christians, A.D. 110 or 111

Pliny to the Emperor Trajan: It is my custom to refer all my difficulties to you, Sir, for no one is better able to resolve my doubts and to inform my ignorance.

I have never been present at an examination of Christians. Consequently, I do not know the nature or the extent of the punishments usually meted out to them, nor the grounds for starting an investigation and how far it should be pressed. Nor am I at all sure whether any distinction should be made between them on the grounds of age, or if young people and adults should be treated alike; whether a pardon ought to be granted to anyone retracting his beliefs, or if he has once professed Christianity, he shall gain nothing by renouncing it; and whether it is the mere name of Christian which is punishable, even if innocent of crime, or rather the crimes associated with the name.

For the moment this is the line I have taken with all persons brought before me on the charge of being Christians. I have asked them in person if they are Christians, and if they admit it, I repeat the question a second and

Pliny, *Letters* 10.96–97. From *Plinius Secundus: Letters and Panegyricus*, vol. 2, translated by Betty Radice (Cambridge, Mass.: Harvard University Press, 1959), pp. 285, 287, 289, 291.

third time, with a warning of the punishment awaiting them. If they persist, I order them to be led away for execution; for, whatever the nature of their admission, I am convinced that their stubbornness and unshakeable obstinacy ought not to go unpunished. There have been others similarly fanatical who are Roman citizens. I have entered them on the list of persons to be sent to Rome for trial.

Now that I have begun to deal with this problem, as so often happens, the charges are becoming more widespread and increasing in variety. An anonymous pamphlet has been circulated which contains the names of a number of accused persons. Among these I considered that I should dismiss any who denied that they were or ever had been Christians when they had repeated after me a formula of invocation to the gods and had made offerings of wine and incense to your statue (which I had ordered to be brought into court for this purpose along with the images of the gods), and furthermore had reviled the name of Christ: none of which things, I understand, any genuine Christian can be induced to do.

Others, whose names were given to me by an informer, first admitted the charge and then denied it; they said that they had ceased to be Christians two or more years previously, and some of them even twenty years ago. They all did reverence to your statue and the images of the gods in the same way as the others, and reviled the name of Christ. They also declared that the sum total of their guilt or error amounted to no more than this: they had met regularly before dawn on a fixed day to chant verses alternately among themselves in honour of Christ as if to a god, and also to bind themselves by oath, not for any criminal purpose, but to abstain from theft, robbery and adultery, to commit no breach of trust and not to deny a deposit when called upon to restore it. After this ceremony it had been their custom to disperse and reassemble later to take food of an ordinary, harmless kind; but they had in fact given up this practice since my edict, issued on your instructions, which banned all political societies. This made me decide it was all the more necessary to extract the truth by torture from two slave-women, whom they call deaconesses. I found nothing but a degenerate sort of cult carried to extravagant lengths.

I have therefore postponed any further examination and hastened to consult you. The question seems to me to be worthy of your consideration, especially in view of the number of persons endangered; for a great many individuals of every age and class, both men and women, are being brought to trial, and this is likely to continue. It is not only the towns, but villages and rural districts too which are infected through contact with this wretched cult. I think though that it is still possible for it to be checked and directed to better ends, for there is no doubt that people have begun to throng the temples which had been almost entirely deserted for a long time; the sacred rites which had been allowed to lapse are being performed again, and flesh of sacrificial victims is on sale everywhere, though up till recently scarcely anyone could be found to buy it. It is easy to infer from this that a great many people could be reformed if they were given an opportunity to repent.

Trajan to Pliny: You have followed the right course of procedure, my dear Pliny, in your examination of the cases of persons charged with being Christians, for it is impossible to lay down a general rule to a fixed formula. These people must not be hunted out; if they are brought before you and the charge against them is proved, they must be punished, but in the case of anyone who denies that he is a Christian, and makes it clear that he is not by offering prayers to our gods, he is to be pardoned as a result of his repentance however suspect his past conduct may be. But pamphlets circulated anonymously must play no part in any accusation. They create the worst sort of precedent and are quite out of keeping with the spirit of our age.

27. Quintilian, *The Training of the Orator*, Book 1 (Selections)

Marcus Fabius Quintilianus was born between A.D. 30 and 40, to a family whose home was in the Ebro valley of northeast Spain. At some point in his youth he moved to Rome, where he studied rhetoric and observed the techniques of practicing orators, but he returned to Spain to pursue his career on home ground. His horizon suddenly expanded in A.D. 68 when Galba, then governor of Spain, set forth with his army to depose the emperor Nero, and took Quintilian back to Rome with him. From then on, under Galba and his successors, Quintilian was one of the most well-connected practitioners in the capital. He argued important cases in the courts, and opened a school of rhetoric which drew the sons of the elite (including Pliny, for one). When the emperor Vespasian established a state-subsidized professorship in Latin rhetoric, Quintilian was appointed to the chair, which he held until his retirement in the late 80s. After that, in the early 90s, the emperor Domitian invited him to the palace, to educate the grandnephews whom he had designated to succeed him.

Institutio oratoria 1 preface to 1.4.5, 1.10.1–2, 1.10.22–27, 1.10.34–38, 1.10.49–1.11.4, 1.11.8–12, 1.11.15–17. From *The Institutio Oratoria of Quintilian*, vol. 1, translated by H. E. Butler (Cambridge, Mass.: Harvard University Press, 1921), pp. 5–65, 159–61, 171–73, 177–79, 183–89 (odd-numbered pages). Reprinted by permission of the publisher and the Loeb Classical Library.

Quintilian evidently died within a couple of years after accepting this assignment.

He wrote the twelve books of *The Training of the Orator* over a three-year period near the end of his life. The friend to whom it is dedicated, Vitorius Marcellus, was a young senator striving to make his reputation in trial oratory; he reached the consulate in the next decade after the book was published. In the preface, Quintilian takes some pains to make it clear that his work is not just another technical manual or treatise. He writes as an experienced teacher offering a very personal summation of his specialty. For the purposes of this volume, what is most important about his approach is the breadth of his perspective on education: he believed that the training of the orator should be a total education, incorporating all branches of knowledge even more perfectly than did the study of philosophy. Yet the limits of Roman schooling perhaps stand more clearly exposed in this account than anywhere else, for the very reason that Quintilian is describing the best that the system could achieve. In book 1, from which these selections are taken, he characterizes the general education a youth should receive by the age of fifteen or sixteen, when professional training with a teacher of rhetoric would begin. But Quintilian's thinking about education even in the early stages is dominated by the criterion of utility to the future orator, and the course of studies he commends differs significantly from a modern school curriculum.

Preface. Having at length, after twenty years devoted to the training of the young, obtained leisure for study, I was asked by certain of my friends to write something on the art of speaking. For a long time I resisted their entreaties, since I was well aware that some of the most distinguished Greek and Roman writers had bequeathed to posterity a number of works dealing with this subject, to the composition of which they had devoted the utmost care. This seemed to me to be an admirable excuse for my refusal, but served merely to increase their enthusiasm. They urged that previous writers on the subject had expressed different and at times contradictory opinions, between which it was very difficult to choose. They thought therefore that they were justified in imposing on me the task, if not of discovering original views, at least of passing definite judgement on those expressed by my predecessors. I was moved to comply not so much because I felt confidence that I was equal to the task, as because I had a certain compunction about refusing. The subject proved more extensive than I had first imagined; but finally I volunteered to shoulder a task which was on a far larger scale than that which I was originally asked to undertake. I wished on the one hand to oblige my very good friends beyond their requests, and on the other to avoid the beaten track and the necessity of treading where others had gone before. For almost all others who have written on the art of oratory have started with the assumption that their readers were perfect in all other branches of education and that their own task was merely to put the finishing touches to their rhetorical training; this is due to the fact that they either despised the preliminary stages of education or thought that they were not their concern, since the duties of the different branches of education are distinct one from another, or else, and this is nearer the truth, because they had no hope of making a remunerative display of their talent in dealing with subjects, which, although necessary, are far from being showy: just as in architecture it is the superstructure and not the foundations which attracts the eye. I on the other hand hold that the art of oratory includes all that is essential for the training of an orator, and that it is impossible to reach the summit in any subject unless we have first passed through all the elementary stages. I shall not therefore refuse to stoop to the consideration of those minor details, neglect of which may result in there being no opportunity for more important things, and propose to mould the studies of my orator from infancy, on the assumption that his whole education has been entrusted to my charge. This work I dedicate to you, Marcellus Vitorius. You have been the truest of friends to me and you have shown a passionate enthusiasm for literature. But good as these reasons are, they are not the only reasons that led me to regard you as especially worthy of such a pledge of our mutual affection. There is also the consideration that this book should prove of service in the education of your son Geta, who, young though he is, already shows clear promise of real talent. It has been my design to lead my reader from the very cradle of speech through all the stages of education which can be of any service to our budding orator till we have reached the very summit of the art. I have been all the more desirous of so doing because two books on the art of rhetoric are at present circulating under my name, although never published by me or composed for such a purpose. One is a two days' lecture which was taken down by the boys who were my audience. The other consists of such notes as my good pupils succeeded in taking down from a course of lectures on a somewhat more extensive scale: I appreciate their kindness, but they showed an excess of enthusiasm and a certain lack of discretion in doing my utterances the honour of publication. Consequently in the present work although some passages remain the same, you will find many alterations and still more additions, while the whole theme will be treated with greater system and with as great perfection as lies within my power.

My aim, then, is the education of the perfect orator. The first essential for such an one is that he should be a good man, and consequently we demand of him not merely the possession of exceptional gifts of speech, but of all the excellences of character as well. For I will not admit that the principles of upright and honourable living should, as some have held, be regarded as the peculiar concern of philosophy. The man who can really play his part as a citizen and is capable of meeting the demands both of public and private business, the man who can guide a state by his counsels, give it a firm basis by his legislation and purge its vices by his decisions as a judge, is assuredly no other than the orator of our quest. Wherefore, although I admit I shall make use of certain of the principles laid down in philosophical textbooks, I would insist that such principles have a just claim to form part of the subject-matter of this work and do actually belong to the art of oratory. I shall frequently be compelled to speak of such virtues as courage, justice, self-control; in fact scarcely a case comes up in which some one of these virtues is not involved; every one of them requires illustration and consequently makes a demand on the imagination and eloquence of the pleader. I ask you then, can there be any doubt that, wherever imaginative power and amplitude of diction are required, the orator has a specially important part to play? These two branches of knowledge were, as Cicero has clearly shown, so closely united, not merely in theory but in practice, that the same men were regarded as uniting the qualifications of orator and philosopher. Subsequently this single branch of study split up into its component parts, and thanks to the indolence of its professors was regarded as consisting of several distinct subjects. As soon as speaking became a means of livelihood and the practice of making an evil use of the blessings of eloquence came into vogue, those who had a reputation for eloquence ceased to study moral philosophy, and ethics, thus abandoned by the orators, became the prey of weaker intellects. As a consequence certain persons, disdaining the toil of learning to speak well, returned to the task of forming character and establishing rules of life and kept to themselves what is, if we *must* make a division, the better part, but presumptuously laid claim to the sole possession of the title of philosopher, a distinction which neither the greatest generals nor the most famous statesmen and administrators have ever dared to claim for themselves. For they preferred the performance to the promise of great deeds. I am ready to admit that many of the old philosophers inculcated the most excellent principles and practised what they preached. But in our own day the name of philosopher has too often been the mask for the worst vices. For their attempt has not been to win the name of philosopher by virtue and the earnest search for wisdom; instead they have sought to disguise the depravity of their characters by the assumption of a stern and austere mien accompanied by the wearing of a garb differing from that of their fellow men. Now as a matter of fact we all of us frequently handle those themes which philosophy claims for its own.

Who, short of being an utter villain, does not speak of justice, equity and virtue? Who (and even common country-folk are no exception) does not make some inquiry into the causes of natural phenomena? As for the special uses and distinctions of words, they should be a subject of study common to all who give any thought to the meaning of language. But it is surely the orator who will have the greatest mastery of all such departments of knowledge and the greatest power to express it in words. And if ever he had reached perfection, there would be no need to go to the schools of philosophy for the precepts of virtue. As things stand, it is occasionally necessary to have recourse to those authors who have, as I said above, usurped the better part of the art of oratory after its desertion by the orators and to demand back what is ours by right, not with a view to appropriating their discoveries, but to show them that they have appropriated what in truth belonged to others. Let our ideal orator then be such as to have a genuine title to the name of philosopher: it is not sufficient that he should be blameless in point of character (for I cannot agree with those who hold this opinion): he must also be a thorough master of the science and the art of speaking, to an extent that perhaps no orator has yet attained. Still we must none the less follow the ideal, as was done by not a few of the ancients, who, though they refused to admit that the perfect sage had yet been found, none the less handed down precepts of wisdom for the use of posterity. Perfect eloquence is assuredly a reality, which is not beyond the reach of human intellect. Even if we fail to reach it, those whose aspirations are highest, will attain to greater heights than those who abandon themselves to premature despair of ever reaching the goal and halt at the very foot of the ascent.

I have therefore all the juster claim to indulgence, if I refuse to pass by those minor details which are none the less essential to my task. My first book will be concerned with the education preliminary to the duties of the teacher of rhetoric. My second will deal with the rudiments of the schools of rhetoric and with problems connected with the essence of rhetoric itself. The next five will be concerned with Invention, in which I include Arrangement. The four following will be assigned to Eloquence, under which head I include Memory and Delivery. Finally there will be one book in which our complete orator will be delineated; as far as my feeble powers permit, I shall discuss his character, the rules which should guide him in undertaking, studying and pleading cases, the style of his eloquence, the time at which he should cease to plead cases and the studies to which he should devote himself after such cessation. In the course of these discussions I shall deal in its proper place with the method of teaching by which students will acquire not merely a knowledge of those things to which the name of art is restricted by certain theorists, and will not only come to understand the laws of rhetoric, but will acquire that which will increase their powers of speech and nourish their eloquence. For as a rule the result of the dry textbooks on the art of rhetoric is that by straining after excessive subtlety they impair and cripple all the nobler elements of style, exhaust the life-blood of the imagination and leave but the bare bones, which, while it is right and necessary that they should exist and be bound each to each by their respective ligaments, require a covering of flesh as well. I shall therefore avoid the precedent set by the majority and shall not restrict myself to this narrow conception of my theme, but shall include in my twelve books a brief demonstration of everything which may seem likely to contribute to the education of an orator. For if I were to attempt to say all that might be said on each subject, the book would never be finished.

There is however one point which I must emphasise before I begin, which is this. Without natural gifts technical rules are useless. Consequently the student who is devoid of talent will derive no more profit from this work than barren soil from a treatise on agriculture. There are, it is true, other natural aids, such as the possession of a good voice and robust lungs, sound health, powers of endurance and grace, and if these are possessed only to a moderate extent, they may be improved by methodical training. In some cases, however, these gifts are lacking to such an extent that their absence is fatal to all such advantages as talent and study can confer, while, similarly, they are of no profit in themselves unless cultivated by skilful teaching, persistent study and continuous and extensive practice in writing, reading and speaking.

1. I would, therefore, have a father conceive the highest hopes of his son from the moment of his birth. If he does so, he will be more careful about the groundwork of his education. For there is absolutely no foundation for the complaint that but few men have the power to take in the knowledge that is imparted to them, and that the majority are so slow of understanding that education is a waste of time and labour. On the contrary you will find that most are quick to reason and ready to learn. Reasoning comes as naturally to man as flying to birds, speed to horses and ferocity to beasts of prey: our minds are endowed by nature with such activity and sagacity that the soul is believed to proceed from heaven. Those who are dull and unteachable are as abnormal as prodigious births and monstrosities, and are but few in number. A proof of what I say is to be found in the fact that boys commonly show promise of many accomplishments, and when such promise dies away as they grow up, this is plainly due not to the failure of natural gifts, but to lack of the requisite care. But, it will be urged, there are degrees of talent. Undoubtedly, I reply, and there will be a corresponding variation in actual accomplishment: but that there are any who gain nothing from education, I absolutely deny. The man who shares this conviction,

must, as soon as he becomes a father, devote the utmost care to fostering the promise shown by the son whom he destines to become an orator.

Above all see that the child's nurse speaks correctly. The ideal, according to Chrysippus,[1] would be that she should be a philosopher: failing that he desired that the best should be chosen, as far as possible. No doubt the most important point is that they should be of good character: but they should speak correctly as well. It is the nurse that the child first hears, and her words that he will first attempt to imitate. And we are by nature most tenacious of childish impressions, just as the flavour first absorbed by vessels when new persists, and the colour imparted by dyes to the primitive whiteness of wool is indelible. Further it is the worst impressions that are most durable. For, while what is good readily deteriorates, you will never turn vice into virtue. Do not therefore allow the boy to become accustomed even in infancy to a style of speech which he will subsequently have to unlearn.

As regards parents, I should like to see them as highly educated as possible, and I do not restrict this remark to fathers alone. We are told that the eloquence of the Gracchi owed much to their mother Cornelia, whose letters even to-day testify to the cultivation of her style. Laelia, the daughter of Gaius Laelius, is said to have reproduced the elegance of her father's language in her own speech, while the oration delivered before the triumvirs by Hortensia, the daughter of Quintus Hortensius, is still read and not merely as a compliment to her sex. And even those who have not had the fortune to receive a good education should not for that reason devote less care to their son's education; but should on the contrary show all the greater diligence in other matters where they can be of service to their children.

As regards the boys in whose company our budding orator is to be brought up, I would repeat what I have said about nurses. As regards his *paedagogi*,[2] I would urge that they should have had a thorough education, or if they have not, that they should be aware of the fact. There are none worse than those, who as soon as they have progressed beyond a knowledge of the alphabet delude themselves into the belief that they are the possessors of real knowledge. For they disdain to stoop to the drudgery of teaching, and conceiving that they have acquired a certain title to authority—a frequent source of vanity in such persons—become imperious or even brutal in instilling a thorough dose of their own folly. Their misconduct is no less prejudicial to morals. We are, for instance, told by Diogenes of Babylon, that Leonides, Alexander's *paedagogus*, infected his pupil

1. Chrysippus was a philosopher of the third century B.C. who elaborated much of the Stoic doctrine embraced by the Romans.

2. A *paedagogus* was not an educator but a slave attendant who accompanied a child to school and on his walks through town.

with certain faults, which as a result of his education as a boy clung to him even in his maturer years when he had become the greatest of kings.

If any of my readers regards me as somewhat exacting in my demands, I would ask him to reflect that it is no easy task to create an orator, even though his education be carried out under the most favourable circumstances, and that further and greater difficulties are still before us. For continuous application, the very best of teachers and a variety of exercises are necessary. Therefore the rules which we lay down for the education of our pupil must be of the best. If anyone refuses to be guided by them, the fault will lie not with the method, but with the individual. Still if it should prove impossible to secure the ideal nurse, the ideal companions, or the ideal *paedagogus*, I would insist that there should be one person at any rate attached to the boy who has some knowledge of speaking and who will, if any incorrect expression should be used by nurse or *paedagogus* in the presence of the child under their charge, at once correct the error and prevent its becoming a habit. But it must be clearly understood that this is only a remedy, and that the ideal course is that indicated above.

I prefer that a boy should begin with Greek, because Latin, being in general use, will be picked up by him whether we will or no; while the fact that Latin learning is derived from Greek is a further reason for his being first instructed in the latter. I do not however desire that this principle should be so superstitiously observed that he should for long speak and learn only Greek, as is done in the majority of cases. Such a course gives rise to many faults of language and accent; the latter tends to acquire a foreign intonation, while the former through force of habit becomes impregnated with Greek idioms, which persist with extreme obstinacy even when we are speaking another tongue. The study of Latin ought therefore to follow at no great distance and in a short time proceed side by side with Greek. The result will be that, as soon as we begin to give equal attention to both languages, neither will prove a hindrance to the other.

Some hold that boys should not be taught to read till they are seven years old, that being the earliest age at which they can derive profit from instruction and endure the strain of learning. Most of them attribute this view to Hesiod, at least such as lived before the time of Aristophanes the grammarian, who was the first to deny that the *Hypothecae*, in which this opinion is expressed, was the work of that poet. But other authorities, among them Eratosthenes, give the same advice. Those however who hold that a child's mind should not be allowed to lie fallow for a moment are wiser. Chrysippus, for instance, though he gives the nurses a three years' reign, still holds the formation of the child's mind on the best principles to be a part of their duties. Why, again, since children are capable of moral training, should they not be capable of literary education? I am well aware that during the whole period of which I am speaking we can expect scarcely the same amount of progress that one year will effect afterwards. Still those who disagree with me seem in taking this line to spare the teacher rather than the pupil. What better occupation can a child have so soon as he is able to speak? And he must be kept occupied somehow or other. Or why should we despise the profit to be derived before the age of seven, small though it be? For though the knowledge absorbed in the previous years may be but little, yet the boy will be learning something more advanced during that year, in which he would otherwise have been occupied with something more elementary. Such progress each successive year increases the total, and the time gained during childhood is clear profit to the period of youth. Further as regards the years which follow I must emphasize the importance of learning what has to be learnt in good time. Let us not therefore waste the earliest years: there is all the less excuse for this, since the elements of literary training are solely a question of memory, which not only exists even in small children, but is specially retentive at that age.

I am not however so blind to differences of age as to think that the very young should be forced on prematurely or given real work to do. Above all things we must take care that the child, who is not yet old enough to love his studies, does not come to hate them and dread the bitterness which he has once tasted, even when the years of infancy are left behind. His studies must be made an amusement: he must be questioned and praised and taught to rejoice when he has done well; sometimes too, when he refuses instruction, it should be given to some other to excite his envy, at times also he must be engaged in competition and should be allowed to believe himself successful more often than not, while he should be encouraged to do his best by such rewards as may appeal to his tender years.

These instructions may seem but trivialities in view of the fact that I am professing to describe the education of an orator. But studies, like men, have their infancy, and as the training of the body which is destined to grow to the fulness of strength begins while the child is in his cradle and at his mother's breast, so even the man who is destined to rise to the heights of eloquence was once a squalling babe, tried to speak in stammering accents and was puzzled by the shapes of letters. Nor does the fact that capacity for learning is inadequate, prove that it is not necessary to learn anything. No one blames a father because he thinks that such details should on no account be neglected in the case of his own son. Why then should he be criticised who sets down for the benefit of the public what he would be right to put into practice in his own house? There is this further reason why he should not be blamed. Small children are better adapted for taking in small things, and just as the body can only be trained to certain flexions of the limbs while it is young and supple, so the acquisition of strength makes the mind offer greater resistance to the acquisition of most subjects of knowledge. Would Philip of Macedon have wished that his son Alexander should be taught the rudiments of letters by Aristotle, the greatest philosopher of that age, or would the latter have undertaken the task, if he had not thought that even the earliest instruction is best given by the most perfect teacher and has real reference to the whole of education? Let us assume therefore that Alexander has been confided to our charge and that the infant placed in our lap deserves no less attention than he—though for that matter every man's child deserves equal attention. Would you be ashamed even in teaching him the alphabet to point out some brief rules for his education?

At any rate I am not satisfied with the course (which I note is usually adopted) of teaching small children the names and order of the letters before their shapes. Such a practice makes them slow to recognise the letters, since they do not pay attention to their actual shape, preferring to be guided by what they have already learned by rote. It is for this reason that teachers, when they think they have sufficiently familiarised their young pupils with the letters written in their usual order, reverse that order or rearrange it in every kind of combination, until they learn to know the letters from their appearance and not from the order in which they occur. It will be best therefore for children to begin by learning their appearance and names just as they do with men. The method, however, to which we have objected in teaching the alphabet, is unobjectionable when applied to syllables. I quite approve on the other hand of a practice which has been devised to stimulate children to learn by giving them ivory letters to play with, as I do of anything else that may be discovered to delight the very young, the sight, handling and naming of which is a pleasure.

As soon as the child has begun to know the shapes of the various letters, it will be no bad thing to have them cut as accurately as possible upon a board, so that the pen may be guided along the grooves. Thus mistakes such as occur with wax tablets will be rendered impossible; for the pen will be confined between the edges of the letters and will be prevented from going astray. Further by increasing the frequency and speed with which they follow these fixed outlines we shall give steadiness to the fingers, and there will be no need to guide the child's hand with our own. The art of writing well and quickly is not unimportant for our purpose, though it is generally disregarded by persons of quality. Writing is of the utmost importance in the study which we have under consideration and by its means alone can true and deeply rooted proficiency be obtained. But a sluggish pen delays our thoughts, while an unformed and illiterate hand cannot be deciphered, a circumstance which necessitates another wearisome task, namely the dictation of what we have written to a copyist. We shall therefore at all times and in all places, and above all when we are writing private letters to our friends, find a gratification in the thought that we have not neglected even this accomplishment.

As regards syllables, no short cut is possible: they must all be learnt, and there is no good in putting off learning the most difficult; this is the general practice, but the sole result is bad spelling. Further we must beware of placing a blind confidence in a child's memory. It is better to repeat syllables and impress them on the memory and, when he is reading, not to press him to read continuously or with greater speed, unless indeed the clear and obvious sequence of letters can suggest itself without its being necessary for the child to stop to think. The syllables once learnt, let him begin to construct words with them and sentences with the words. You will hardly believe how much reading is delayed by undue haste. If the child attempts more than his powers allow, the inevitable result is hesitation, interruption and repetition, and the mistakes which he makes merely lead him to lose confidence in what he already knows. Reading must therefore first be sure, then connected, while it must be kept slow for a considerable time, until practice brings speed unaccompanied by error. For to look to the right, which is regularly taught, and to look ahead depends not so much on precept as on practice; since it is necessary to keep the eyes on what follows while reading out what precedes, with the resulting difficulty that the attention of the mind must be divided, the eyes and voice being differently engaged. It will be found worth while, when the boy begins to write out words in accordance with the usual practice, to see that he does not waste his labour in writing out common words of everyday occurrence. He can readily learn the explanations or *glosses*, as the Greeks call them, of the more obscure words by the way and, while he is still engaged on the first rudiments, acquire what would otherwise demand special time to be devoted to it. And as we are still discussing minor details, I would urge that the lines, which he is set to copy, should not express thoughts of no significance, but convey some sound moral lesson. He will remember such aphorisms even when he is an old man, and the impression made upon his unformed mind will contribute to the formation of his character. He may also be entertained by learning the sayings of famous men and above all selections from the poets, poetry being more attractive to children. For memory is most necessary to an orator, as I shall point out in its proper place, and there is nothing like practice for strengthening and developing it. And at the tender age of which we are now speaking, when originality is impossible, memory is almost the only faculty which can be developed by the teacher. It will be worth while, by way of improving the child's pronunciation and distinctness of utterance, to make him rattle off a selection of names and lines of studied difficulty: they should be formed of a number of syllables which go ill together and should be harsh and rugged in sound: the Greeks call them "gags." This sounds a trifling matter, but its omission will result in numerous faults of pronunciation, which, unless removed in early years, will become a perverse and incurable habit and persist through life.

2. But the time has come for the boy to grow up little by little, to leave the nursery and tackle his studies in good earnest. This therefore is the place to discuss the question as to whether it is better to have him educated privately at home or hand him over to some large school and those whom I may call public instructors. The latter course has, I know, won the approval of most eminent authorities and of those who have formed the national character of the most famous states. It would, however, be folly to shut our eyes to the fact that there are some who disagree with this preference for public education owing to a certain prejudice in favour of private tuition. These persons seem to be guided in the main by two principles. In the interests of morality they would avoid the society of a number of human beings at an age that is specially liable to acquire serious faults. I only wish I could deny the truth of the view that such education has often been the cause of the most discreditable actions. Secondly they hold that whoever is to be the boy's teacher, he will devote his time more generously to one pupil than if he has to divide it among several. The first reason certainly deserves serious consideration. If it were proved that schools, while advantageous to study, are prejudicial to morality, I should give my vote for virtuous living in preference to even supreme excellence of speaking. But in my opinion the two are inseparable. I hold that no one can be a true orator unless he is also a good man and, even if he could be, I would not have it so. I will therefore deal with this point first.

It is held that schools corrupt the morals. It is true that this is sometimes the case. But morals may be corrupted at home as well. There are numerous instances of both, as there are also of the preservation of a good reputation under either circumstance. The nature of the individual boy and the care devoted to his education make all the difference. Given a natural bent toward evil or negligence in developing and watching over modest behaviour in early years, privacy will provide equal opportunity for sin. The teacher employed at home may be of bad character, and there is just as much danger in associating with bad slaves as there is with immodest companions of good birth. On the other hand if the natural bent be towards virtue, and parents are not afflicted with a blind and torpid indifference, it is possible to choose a teacher of the highest character (and those who are wise will make this their first object), to adopt a method of education of the strictest kind and at the same time to attach some respectable man or faithful freedman to their son as his friend and guardian, that his unfailing companionship may improve the character even of those who gave rise to apprehension.

Yet how easy were the remedy for such fears. Would that we did not too often ruin our children's character ourselves! We spoil them from the cradle. That soft upbringing, which we call kindness, saps all the sinews both of mind and body. If the child crawls on purple, what will he not desire when he comes to manhood? Before he can talk he can distinguish scarlet and cries for the very best brand of purple. We train their palates before we teach their lips to speak. They grow up in litters: if they set foot to earth, they are supported by the hands of attendants on either side. We rejoice if they say something over-free, and words which we should not tolerate from the lips even of an Alexandrian page are greeted with laughter and a kiss. We have no right to be surprised. It was we that taught them: they hear us use such words, they see our mistresses and minions; every dinner party is loud with foul songs, and things are presented to their eyes of which we should blush to speak. Hence springs habit, and habit in time becomes second nature. The poor children learn these things before they know them to be wrong. They become luxurious and effeminate, and far from acquiring such vices at schools, introduce them themselves.

I now turn to the objection that one master can give more attention to one pupil. In the first place there is nothing to prevent the principle of "one teacher, one boy" being combined with school education. And even if such a combination should prove impossible, I should still prefer the broad daylight of a respectable school to the solitude and obscurity of a private education. For all the best teachers pride themselves on having a large number of pupils and think themselves worthy of a bigger audience. On the other hand in the case of inferior teachers a consciousness of their own defects not seldom reconciles them to being attached to a single pupil and playing the part—for it amounts to little more—of a mere *paedagogus*.

But let us assume that influence, money or friendship succeed in securing a paragon of learning to teach the boy at home. Will he be able to devote the whole day to one pupil? Or can we demand such continuous attention on the part of the learner? The mind is as easily tired as the eye, if given no relaxation. Moreover by far the larger proportion of the learner's time ought to be devoted to private study. The teacher does not stand over him while he is writing or thinking or learning by heart. While he is so occupied the intervention of anyone, be he who he may, is a hindrance. Further, not all reading requires to be first read aloud or interpreted by a master. If it did, how would the boy ever become acquainted with all the authors required of him? A small time only is required to give purpose and direction to the day's work, and consequently individual instruction can be given to more than one pupil. There are moreover a large number of subjects in which it is desirable that instruction should be given to all the pupils simultaneously. I say nothing of the analyses and declamations of the professors of rhetoric: in such cases there is no limit to the number of the audience, as each individual pupil will in any case receive full value. The voice of a lecturer is not like a dinner which will only suffice for a limited number; it is like the sun which distributes the same quantity of light and heat to all of us. So too with the teacher of literature. Whether he speak of style or expound disputed passages, explain stories or paraphrase poems, everyone who hears him will profit by his teaching. But, it will be urged, a large class is unsuitable for the correction of faults or for explanation. It may be inconvenient: one cannot hope for absolute perfection; but I shall shortly contrast the inconvenience with the obvious advantages.

Still I do not wish a boy to be sent where he will be neglected. But a good teacher will not burden himself with a larger number of pupils than he can manage, and it is further of the very first importance that he should be on friendly and intimate terms with us and make his teaching not a duty but a labour of love. Then there will never be any question of being swamped by the number of our fellow-learners. Moreover any teacher who has the least tincture of literary culture will devote special attention to any boy who shows signs of industry and talent; for such a pupil will redound to his own credit. But even if large schools are to be avoided, a proposition from which I must dissent if the size be due to the excellence of the teacher, it does not follow that all schools are to be avoided. It is one thing to avoid them, another to select the best.

Having refuted these objections, let me now explain my own views. It is above all things necessary that our future orator, who will have to live in the utmost publicity and in the broad daylight of public life, should become accustomed from his childhood to move in society without fear and habituated to a life far removed from that of the pale student, the solitary and recluse. His mind requires constant stimulus and excitement, whereas retirement such as has just been mentioned induces languor and the mind becomes mildewed like things that are left in the dark, or else flies to the opposite extreme and becomes puffed up with empty conceit; for he who has no standard of comparison by which to judge his own powers will necessarily rate them too high. Again when the fruits of his study have to be displayed to the public gaze, our recluse is blinded by the sun's glare, and finds everything new and unfamiliar, for though he has learnt what is required to be done in public, his learning is but the theory of a hermit. I say nothing of friendships which endure unbroken to old age having acquired the binding force of a sacred duty: for initiation in the same studies has all the sanctity of initiation in the same mysteries of religion. And where shall he acquire that instinct which we call common feeling, if he secludes himself from that intercourse which is natural not merely to mankind but even to dumb animals? Further, at home he can only learn what is taught to himself, while at school he will learn what is taught others as well. He will hear many merits praised and many faults corrected every day: he will derive equal profit from hearing the indolence of a comrade rebuked or his industry commended. Such praise will incite him to emulation, he will think it a disgrace to be outdone by his contemporaries and a distinction to surpass his seniors. All such incentives provide a valuable stimulus, and though ambition may be a fault in itself, it is often the mother of virtues. I remember that my own masters had a practice which was not without advantages. Having distributed the boys in classes, they made the order in which they were to speak depend on their ability, so that the boy who had made most progress in his studies had the privilege of declaiming first. The performances on these occasions were criticised. To win commendation was a tremendous honour, but the prize most eagerly coveted was to be the leader of the class. Such a position was not permanent. Once a month the defeated competitors were given a fresh opportunity of competing for the prize. Consequently success did not lead the victor to relax his efforts, while the vexation caused by defeat served as an incentive to wipe out the disgrace. I will venture to assert that to the best of my memory this practice did more to kindle our oratorical ambitions than all the exhortations of our instructors, the watchfulness of our *paedagogi* and the prayers of our parents. Further while emulation promotes progress in the more advanced pupils, beginners who are still of tender years derive greater pleasure from imitating their comrades than their masters, just because it is easier. For children still in the elementary stages of education can scarce dare hope to reach that complete eloquence which they understand to be their goal: their ambition will not soar so high, but they will imitate the vine which has to grasp the lower branches of the tree on which it is trained before it can reach the topmost boughs. So true is this that it is the master's duty as well, if he is engaged on the task of training unformed minds and prefers practical utility to a more ambitious programme, not to burden his pupils at once with tasks to which their strength is unequal, but to curb his energies and refrain from talking over the heads of his audience. Vessels with narrow mouths will not receive liquids if too much be poured into them at a time, but are easily filled if the liquid is admitted in a gentle stream or, it may be, drop by drop; similarly you must consider how much a child's mind is capable of receiving: the things which are beyond their grasp will not enter their minds, which have not opened out sufficiently to take them in. It is a good thing therefore that a boy should have companions whom he will desire first to imitate and then to surpass: thus he will be led to aspire to higher achievement. I would add that the instructors themselves cannot develop the same intelligence and energy before a single listener as they can when inspired by the presence of a numerous audience.

For eloquence depends in the main on the state of the mind, which must be moved, conceive images and adapt itself to suit the nature of the subject which is the theme of speech. Further the loftier and the more elevated the mind, the more powerful will be the forces which move it: consequently praise gives it growth and effort increase, and the thought that it is doing something great fills it with joy. The duty of stooping to expend that power of speaking which has been acquired at the cost of such effort upon an audience of one gives rise to a silent feeling of disdain, and the teacher is ashamed to raise his voice above the ordinary conversational level. Imagine the air of a declaimer, or the voice of an orator, his gait, his delivery, the movements of his body, the emotions of his mind, and, to go no further, the fatigue of his exertions, all for the sake of one listener! Would he not seem little less than a lunatic? No, there would be no such thing as eloquence, if we spoke only with one person at a time.

3. The skilful teacher will make it his first care, as soon as a boy is entrusted to him, to ascertain his ability and character. The surest indication in a child is his power of memory. The characteristics of a good memory are twofold: it must be quick to take in and faithful to retain impressions of what it receives. The indication of next importance is the power of imitation: for this is a sign that the child is teachable: but he must imitate merely what he is taught, and must not, for example, mimic someone's gait or bearing or defects. For I have no hope that a child will turn out well who loves imitation merely for the purpose of raising a laugh. He who is really gifted will also above all else be good. For the rest, I regard slowness of intellect as preferable to actual badness. But a good boy will be quite unlike the dullard and the sloth. My ideal pupil will absorb instruction with ease and will even ask some questions; but he will follow rather than anticipate his teacher. Precocious intellects rarely produce sound fruit. By the precocious I mean those who perform small tasks with ease and, thus emboldened, proceed to display all their little accomplishments without being asked: but their accomplishments are only of the most obvious kind: they string words together and trot them out boldly and undeterred by the slightest sense of modesty. Their actual achievement is small, but what they can do they perform with ease. They have no real power and what they have is but of shallow growth: it is as when we cast seed on the surface of the soil: it springs up too rapidly, the blade apes the loaded ear, and yellows ere harvest time, but bears no grain. Such tricks please us when we contrast them with the performer's age, but progress soon stops and our admiration withers away.

Such indications once noted, the teacher must next consider what treatment is to be applied to the mind of his pupil. There are some boys who are slack, unless pressed on; others again are impatient of control: some are amenable to fear, while others are paralysed by it: in some cases the mind requires continued application to form it, in others this result is best obtained by rapid concentration. Give me the boy who is spurred on by praise, delighted by success and ready to weep over failure. Such an one must be encouraged by appeals to his ambition; rebuke will bite him to the quick; honour will be a spur, and there is no fear of his proving indolent.

Still, all our pupils will require some relaxation, not merely because there is nothing in this world that can stand continued strain and even unthinking and inanimate objects are unable to maintain their strength, unless given intervals of rest, but because study depends on the good will of the student, a quality that cannot be secured by compulsion. Consequently if restored and refreshed by a holiday they will bring greater energy to their learning and approach their work with greater spirit of a kind that will not submit to be driven. I approve of play in the young; it is a sign of a lively disposition; nor will you ever lead me to believe that a boy who is gloomy and in a continual state of depression is ever likely to show alertness of mind in his work, lacking as he does the impulse most natural to boys of his age. Such relaxation must not however be unlimited: otherwise the refusal to give a holiday will make boys hate their work, while excessive indulgence will accustom them to idleness. There are moreover certain games which have an educational value for boys, as for instance when they compete in posing each other with all kinds of questions which they ask turn and turn about. Games too reveal character in the most natural way, at least that is so if the teacher will bear in mind that there is no child so young as to be unable to learn to distinguish between right and wrong, and that the character is best moulded, when it is still guiltless of deceit and most susceptible to instruction: for once a bad habit has become engrained, it is easier to break than bend. There must be no delay, then, in warning a boy that his actions must be unselfish, honest, self-controlled, and we must never forget the words of Virgil, "So strong is custom formed in early years." [*Georgics*, 2.272]

I disapprove of flogging, although it is the regular custom and meets with the acquiescence of Chrysippus, because in the first place it is a disgraceful form of punishment and fit only for slaves, and is in any case an insult, as you will realise if you imagine its infliction at a later age. Secondly if a boy is so insensible to instruction that reproof is useless, he will, like the worst type of slave, merely become hardened to blows. Finally there will be absolutely no need of such punishment if the master is a thorough disciplinarian. As it is, we try to make amends for the negligence of the boy's *paedagogus*, not by forcing him to do what is right, but by punishing him for not doing what is right. And though you may compel a child with blows, what are you to do with him when he is a young man no longer amenable to such threats and confronted with tasks of far greater difficulty? Moreover when children are beaten, pain or fear frequently have results of which it is not pleasant to speak and which are likely subsequently to be a source of shame, a shame which unnerves and depresses the mind and leads the child to shun and loathe the light. Further if inadequate care is taken in the choices of respectable governors and instructors, I blush to mention the shameful abuse which scoundrels sometimes make of their right to administer corporal punishment or the opportunity not infrequently offered to others by the fear thus caused in the victims. I will not linger on this subject; it is more than enough if I have made my meaning clear. I will content myself with saying that children are helpless and easily victimised, and that therefore no one should be given unlimited power over them. I will now proceed to describe the subjects in which the boy must be trained, if he is to become an orator, and to indicate the age at which each should be commenced.

4. As soon as the boy has learned to read and write without difficulty, it is the turn for the teacher of literature. My words apply equally to Greek and Latin masters, though I prefer that a start should be made with a Greek: in either case the method is the same. This profession may be most briefly considered under two heads, the art of speaking correctly and the interpretation of the poets; but there is more beneath the surface than meets the eye. For the art of writing is combined with that of speaking, and correct reading precedes interpretation, while in each of these cases criticism has its work to perform. The old school of teachers indeed carried their criticism so far that they were not content with obelising lines or rejecting books whose titles they regarded as spurious, as though they were expelling a supposititious child from the family circle, but also drew up a canon of authors, from which some were omitted altogether. Nor is it sufficient to have read the poets only; every kind of writer must be carefully studied, not merely for the subject matter, but for the vocabulary; for words often acquire authority from their use by a particular author. Nor can such training be regarded as complete if it stop short of music, for the teacher of literature has to speak of metre and rhythm: nor again if he be ignorant of astronomy, can he understand the poets; for they, to mention no further points, frequently give their indications of time by reference to the rising and setting of the stars. Ignorance of philosophy is an equal drawback, since there are numerous passages in almost every poem based on the most intricate questions of natural philosophy, while among the Greeks we have Empedocles and among our own poets Varro and Lucretius, all of whom

have expounded their philosophies in verse. No small powers of eloquence also are required to enable the teacher to speak appropriately and fluently on the various points which have just been mentioned. For this reason those who criticise the art of teaching literature as trivial and lacking in substance put themselves out of court. Unless the foundations of oratory are well and truly laid by the teaching of literature, the superstructure will collapse. The study of literature is a necessity for boys and the delight of old age, the sweet companion of our privacy and the sole branch of study which has more solid substance than display. . . .

10. I have made my remarks on this stage of education as brief as possible, making no attempt to say everything, (for the theme is infinite), but confining myself to the most necessary points. I will now proceed briefly to discuss the remaining arts in which I think boys ought to be instructed before being handed over to the teacher of rhetoric: for it is by such studies that the course of education described by the Greeks as *enkyklios paideia* or general education will be brought to its full completion. . . .

10.22. But let us discuss the advantages which our future orator may reasonably expect to derive from the study of Music. Music has two modes of expression in the voice and in the body; for both voice and body require to be controlled by appropriate rules. Aristoxenus divides music, in so far as it concerns the voice, into *rhythm* and *melody*, the one consisting in measure, the latter in sound and song. Now I ask you whether it is not absolutely necessary for the orator to be acquainted with all these methods of expression which are concerned firstly with gesture, secondly with the arrangement of words and thirdly with the inflexions of the voice, of which a great variety are required in pleading. Otherwise we must assume that structure and the euphonious combination of sounds are necessary only for poetry, lyric and otherwise, but superfluous in pleading, or that unlike music, oratory has no interest in the variation of arrangement and sound to suit the demands of the case. But eloquence does vary both tone and rhythm, expressing sublime thoughts with elevation, pleasing thoughts with sweetness, and ordinary with gentle utterance, and in every expression of its art is in sympathy with the emotions of which it is the mouthpiece. It is by the raising, lowering, or inflexion of the voice that the orator stirs the emotions of his hearers, and the measure, if I may repeat the term, of voice or phrase differs according as we wish to rouse the indignation or the pity of the judge. For, as we know, different emotions are roused even by the various musical instruments, which are incapable of reproducing speech. Further the motion of the body must be suitable and becoming, or as the Greeks call it *eurythmic*, and this can only be secured by the study of music. This is a most important department of eloquence, and will receive separate treatment in this work. To proceed, an orator will assuredly pay special attention to his voice, and what is so specially the concern of music as this? Here too I must not anticipate a later section of this work, and will content myself by citing the example of Gaius Gracchus, the leading orator of his age, who during his speeches had a musician standing behind him with a pitchpipe, or *tonarion* as the Greeks call it, whose duty it was to give him the tones in which his voice was to be pitched. . . .

10.34. As regards geometry, it is granted that portions of this science are of value for the instruction of children: for admittedly it exercises their minds, sharpens their wits and generates quickness of perception. But it is considered that the value of geometry resides in the process of learning, and not as with other sciences in the knowledge thus acquired. Such is the general opinion. But it is not without good reason that some of the greatest men have devoted special attention to this science. Geometry has two divisions; one is concerned with numbers, the other with figures. Now knowledge of the former is a necessity not merely to the orator, but to any one who has had even an elementary education. Such knowledge is frequently required in actual cases, in which a speaker is regarded as deficient in education, I will not say if he hesitates in making a calculation, but even if he contradicts the calculation which he states in words by making an uncertain or inappropriate gesture with his fingers. Again linear geometry is frequently required in cases, as in lawsuits about boundaries and measurements. But geometry and oratory are related in a yet more important way than this. In the first place logical development is one of the necessities of geometry. And is it not equally a necessity for oratory? Geometry arrives at its conclusions from definite premises, and by arguing from what is certain proves what was previously uncertain. Again are not the problems of geometry almost entirely solved by the syllogistic method, a fact which makes the majority assert that geometry bears a closer resemblance to logic than to rhetoric? But even the orator will sometimes, though rarely, prove his point by formal logic. For, if necessary, he will use the syllogism, and he will certainly make use of the enthymeme which is a rhetorical form of syllogism. Further the most absolute form of proof is that which is generally known as linear demonstration. And what is the aim of oratory if not proof? . . . . It will suffice for our purpose that there are a number of problems which it is difficult to solve in any other way, which are as a rule solved by these linear demonstrations, such as the method of division, section to infinity, and the ratio of increase in velocity. From this we may conclude that, if as we shall show in the next book an orator has to speak on every kind of subject, he can under no circumstances dispense with a knowledge of geometry.

11. The comic actor will also claim a certain amount of our attention, but only in so far as our future orator must be a master of the art of deliv-

ery. For I do not of course wish the boy, whom we are training to this end, to talk with the shrillness of a woman or in the tremulous accents of old age. Nor for that matter must he ape the vices of the drunkard, or copy the cringing manners of a slave; or learn to express the emotions of love, avarice or fear. Such accomplishments are not necessary to an orator and corrupt the mind, especially while it is still pliable and unformed. For repeated imitation passes into habit. Nor yet again must we adopt all the gestures and movements of the actor. Within certain limits the orator must be a master of both, but he must rigorously avoid staginess and all extravagance of facial expression, gesture and gait. For if an orator does command a certain art in such matters, its highest expression will be in the concealment of its existence.

What then is the duty of the teacher whom we have borrowed from the stage? In the first place he must correct all faults of pronunciation, and see that the utterance is distinct, and that each letter has its proper sound. There is an unfortunate tendency in the case of some letters to pronounce them either too thinly or too fully, while some we find too harsh and fail to pronounce sufficiently, substituting others whose sound is similar but somewhat duller. . . . He will also see that final syllables are not clipped, that the quality of speech is continuously maintained, that when the voice is raised, the strain falls upon the lungs and not the mouth, and that gesture and voice are mutually appropriate. He will also insist that the speaker faces his audience, that the lips are not distorted nor the jaws parted to a grin, that the face is not thrown back, nor the eyes fixed on the ground, nor the neck slanted to left or right. For there are a variety of faults of facial expression. I have seen many, who raised their brows whenever the voice was called upon for an effort, others who wore a perpetual frown, and yet others who could not keep their eyebrows level, but raised one towards the top of the head and depressed the other till it almost closed the eye. These are details, but as I shall shortly show, they are of enormous importance, for nothing that is unbecoming can have a pleasing effect.

Our actor will also be required to show how a narrative should be delivered, and to indicate the authoritative tone that should be given to advice, the excitement which should mark the rise of anger, and the change of tone that is characteristic of pathos. . . .

11.15. I will not blame even those who give a certain amount of time to the teacher of gymnastics. I am not speaking of those, who spend part of their life in rubbing themselves with oil and part in wine-bibbing, and kill the mind by over-attention to the body: indeed, I would have such as these kept as far as possible from the boy whom we are training. But we give the same name to those who form gesture and motion so that the arms may be extended in the proper manner, the management of the hands free from all trace of rusticity and inelegance, the attitude becoming, the movements of the feet appropriate and the motions of the head and eyes in keeping with the poise of the body. No one will deny that such details form a part of the art of delivery, nor divorce delivery from oratory; and there can be no justification for disdaining to learn what has got to be done, especially as *chironomy*, which, as the name shows, is *the law of gesture*, originated in heroic times and met with the approval of the greatest Greeks, not excepting Socrates himself, while it was placed by Plato among the virtues of a citizen and included by Chrysippus in his instructions relative to the education of children.

5 Problems of the Later Roman Empire

28. Diocletian, *Price Edict* (Selections)

The Roman Empire experienced drastic inflation in the third century A.D., from causes that included civil strife, external wars, and imprudent fiscal and monetary policies. Emperor Diocletian, who reigned from A.D. 284 to 305, contributed to a substantial reorganization of Roman political and military institutions. Inflation, already endemic earlier in the century, had rapidly accelerated in the 260s and 270s. The situation was further worsened by the expansion of the army, which probably reached its maximum size under Diocletian, and construction of new elaborate border fortifications. Diocletian's introduction of a new coinage in 296 failed to halt the price spiral, and in 301 he decreed the fixing of the prices of goods and services throughout his empire. Fragmentary inscriptions in Greek and Latin from various parts of the empire, and especially from the eastern provinces, have enabled the text of his edict to be reconstructed. This legislation provides an extremely valuable record of this unique effort to impose price controls and also provides information about the specific kinds of desirable goods and services available in the empire.

The hatred of Christians for Diocletian, who harshly persecuted them, contributed to the refusal of the public to accept this program. Diocletian's price controls failed, as the Christian apologist Lactantius narrated in his treatise *On the Deaths of the Persecutors*. Diocletian retired in 305 and died in 313 or 316 at Salona (near the Dalmatian port of Split, in

From "Edict on Maximum Prices," in *Roman Civilization*, vol. 2, *The Empire*, edited by Naphtali Lewis and Meyer Reinhold (New York: Columbia University Press, 1955; reprint, New York: Harper & Row, 1966), pp. 463–73. Reprinted by permission of Columbia University Press. Adapted for this volume with additional passages translated by Walter Emil Kaegi, Jr.

Yugoslavia). The introduction of a new gold coinage, by Constantine I in the fourth century, eventually helped check the inflation, about which much remains poorly understood. Because the history of prices in antiquity is badly documented, this text, although written during a period of exceptional price rises, is extremely valuable to the historian.

The Emperor Caesar Gaius Aurelius Valerius DIOCLETIAN Pius Felix Invictus Augustus, *pontifex maximus*, Germanicus Maximus for the sixth time, Sarmaticus Maximus for the fourth time, Persicus Maximus for the second time, Brittannicus Maximus, Carpicus Maximus, Armenicus Maximus, Medicus Maximus, Adiabenicus Maximus, holding the tribunician power for the eighteenth year, seven times consul, acclaimed *imperator* for the eighteenth time, father of his country, proconsul; and the Emperor Caesar Marcus Aurelius Valerius MAXIMIAN [corresponding titles]; and Flavius Valerius CONSTANTIUS [corresponding titles], most noble Caesar; and GALERIUS Valerius Maximian [corresponding titles], most noble Caesar, declare:

As we recall the wars which we have successfully fought, we must be grateful to the fortune of our state, second only to the immortal gods, for a tranquil world that reclines in the embrace of the most profound calm, and for the blessings of a peace that was won with great effort. That this fortune of our state be stabilized and suitably adorned is demanded by the law-abiding public and by the dignity and majesty of Rome. Therefore we, who by the gracious favor of the gods previously stemmed the tide of the ravages of barbarian nations by destroying them, must surround the peace which we established for eternity with the necessary defenses of justice.

If the excesses perpetrated by persons of unlimited and frenzied avarice could be checked by some self-restraint—this avarice which rushes for gain and profit with no thought for mankind, not annually or monthly, but even from hour to hour and from minute to minute; or if the general welfare could endure without harm this riotous license by which, in its unfortunate state, it is being very seriously injured every day, the situation could perhaps be faced with dissembling and silence, with the hope that human forbearance might alleviate the cruel and pitiable situation. But the only desire of these uncontrolled madmen is to have no thought for the common need. Among the unscrupulous, the immoderate, and the avaricious it is considered almost a creed, swelling and consuming with fluctuating desires, to desist from plundering the wealth of all only when necessity compels them. Through their extreme need, moreover, some persons have become acutely aware of their most unfortunate situation, and can no longer close their eyes to it. Therefore we, who are the protectors of the human race, are agreed, as we view the situation, that decisive legislation is necessary, so that the long-hoped-for solutions which mankind itself could not provide may, by the remedies provided by our foresight, be vouchsafed for the general betterment of all.

Common knowledge recognizes and the credibility of the facts themselves announces that our consideration for this situation is almost too late, insofar as we have developed plans and kept our considered remedies to ourselves, in the hope that, as was to be expected through the laws of nature, men, caught red-handed in the most serious crimes, could correct themselves. Indeed, we believe that it is far more desirable that the marks of infamy from this intolerable depredation be removed by the collective judgment of opinion and by the will of those same men who, as they inclined to more and more serious acts and turned with a certain blindness of mind to crimes against the state, by their serious offenses had made enemies of individuals and the general public, being guilty of the most atrocious inhumanity.

We hasten, therefore, to apply the remedies long demanded by the situation, satisfied that no one can complain that our intervention with regulations is untimely or unnecessary, trivial or unimportant. These measures are directed against the unscrupulous, who have perceived in our silence of so many years a lesson in restraint but have been unwilling to imitate it. For who is so insensitive and so devoid of human feeling that he can be unaware or has not perceived that uncontrolled prices are widespread in the sales taking place in the markets and in the daily life of the cities? Nor is the uncurbed passion for profiteering lessened either by abundant supplies or by fruitful years, so that, without a doubt, the men who engage in such businesses are intent on controlling the very winds and weather, even by the movements of the stars. Because of their iniquity, they cannot tolerate, in their hope for future harvests, that the fertile fields may be flooded by waters from heaven. Thus they regard the clemency of the sky, which is the source of the abundance of produce, as a personal loss.

And the men who plan incessantly to draw gain from divine generosity and to diminish the occurrence of general prosperity, by means of famine which causes the reduction of harvests and by means of their agents' trading, are men who, already personally abounding in immense riches which could generously satisfy entire nations, try to capture small profits and pursue oppressive and ruinous rates of interest. Respect for the common interests of humanity persuades us to impose, O our subjects, a limit to the avarice of these men.

But now we must set forth in detail the causes which have pressed and driven us to cease our long-enduring forbearance and to take steps. So that, although it is difficult to reveal, by resort to a specific argument or fact, the avarice that rages in the entire world, nevertheless the adoption of a remedy may be considered more just when men who are completely deprived of limits are forced by some sign and proof to recognize the unchecked desires of their own minds. Who does not know that wherever the common safety requires our armies to be sent, the profiteers insolently and covertly attack the public welfare, not only in villages and towns, but on every road? They charge extortionate prices for merchandise, not just fourfold or eightfold, but on such a scale that human speech cannot find words to characterize their profit and their practices. Indeed, sometimes in a single retail sale a soldier is stripped of his donative and pay. Moreover, the contributions of the whole world for the support of the armies fall as profits into the hands of these plunderers, and our soldiers appear to bestow with their own hands the rewards of their military service and their veterans' bonuses upon the profiteers. The result is that the pillagers of the state itself seize day by day more than they know how to hold.

Aroused justly and rightfully by all the facts set forth above, and in response to the needs of mankind itself, which appears to be praying for release, we have decided that maximum prices of articles for sale must be established. We have not set down fixed prices, for we do not deem it just to do this, since many provinces occasionally enjoy the good fortune of welcome low prices and the privilege, as it were, of prosperity. Thus, when the pressure of high prices appears anywhere—may the gods avert such a calamity!—avarice, which, as though diffused in some vast expanse cannot be restrained, will be checked by the limits fixed in our statute and by the restraining curbs of the law.

It is our pleasure, therefore, that the prices listed in the subjoined schedule be held in observance in the whole of our Empire. And every person shall take note that the liberty to exceed them at will has been ended, but that the blessing of low prices has in no way been impaired in those places where supplies actually abound because there is special provision when avarice is calmed. Moreover, this universal edict will serve as a necessary check upon buyers and sellers whose practice it is to visit ports and other provinces. For when they too know that in the pinch of scarcity there is no possibility of exceeding the prices fixed for commodities, they will take into account in their calculations at the time of sale the localities, the transportation costs, and all other factors. In this way they will make apparent the justice of our decision that those who transport merchandise may not sell at higher prices anywhere.

It is agreed that even in the time of our ancestors it was the practice in passing laws to restrain offenses by prescribing a penalty. For rarely is a situation beneficial to humanity accepted spontaneously; experience teaches that fear is the most effective regulator and guide for the performance of duty. Therefore it is our pleasure that anyone who resists the measures of this statute shall be subject to a capital penalty for daring to do so. And let no one consider the statute harsh, since there is at hand a ready protection from danger in the observance of moderation. To the same sanction will also be subject the person who by immoderate acquisitive desire will have engaged in collusion, in contravention of the laws, with the avidity of the seller. Nor will he be exempt from the same penalty who, possessing the necessary products for eating and for daily use, after this moderate legislation will have decided to withdraw them from commerce, because there should be an even more severe penalty for the person who causes poverty than for the one who disturbs it, contrary to the law. We therefore exhort the loyalty of all, so that a regulation instituted for the public good may be observed with willing obedience and due scruple, especially as it is seen that by a statute of this kind provision has been made, not for single municipalities and peoples and provinces but for the whole world to whose ruin a few men have raged, whose avarice neither propitious time nor riches, accumulated by every effort, have succeeded in moderating or satiating.

The prices for the sale of individual items which no one may exceed are listed below.

1. Wheat	1 army *modius*[1]	100 *denarii*[2]
Barley	1 army *modius*	60 *denarii*
Rye	1 army *modius*	60 *denarii*
	. . . .	
2. Likewise, for wines:		
Picene	1 Italian *sextarius*	30 *denarii*
Tiburtine	1 Italian *sextarius*	30 *denarii*
Sabine	1 Italian *sextarius*	30 *denarii*
	. . . .	
Ordinary	1 Italian *sextarius*	8 *denarii*
	. . . .	
3. Likewise, for oil:		
From unripe olives	1 Italian *sextarius*	40 *denarii*
Second quality	1 Italian *sextarius*	24 *denarii*
	. . . .	
Salt	1 army *modius*	100 *denarii*
	. . . .	

1. A normal *modius* was equal to 16 *sextarii*, with 1 *sextarius* being equal to 0.546 liter. An army *modius* is variously estimated to have been 1.5 or 1.3 times larger than a normal *modius*.

2. By this time the *denarius* had greatly depreciated. It had become a small copper coin with a nominal value of seven hundred fifty-six to one gold *aureus*. At that time, 60 *aurei* equalled 1 pound. These rates could not be sustained, and the *denarius* continued to depreciate rapidly relative to precious metals.

4. Likewise, for meat:		
Pork	1 Italian pound	12 *denarii*
Beef	1 Italian pound	8 *denarii*
	. . . .	
7. For wages:		
Farm laborer, with maintenance	daily	25 *denarii*
Carpenter, as above	daily	50 *denarii*
	. . . .	
Baker, as above	daily	50 *denarii*
Shipwright working on a seagoing ship, as above	daily	60 *denarii*
	. . . .	
Shepherd, with maintenance	daily	20 *denarii*
	. . . .	
Scribe, for the best writing	100 lines	25 *denarii*
	. . . .	
Elementary teacher, per boy	monthly	50 *denarii*
Teacher of arithmetic, per boy	monthly	75 *denarii*
	. . . .	
Teacher of rhetoric or public speaking, per pupil	monthly	250 *denarii*
Advocate or jurist, fee for a complaint	monthly	250 *denarii*
Advocate or jurist, fee for pleading	monthly	1,000 *denarii*
	. . . .	
25. Wool from Asturia, washed	1 pound	100 *denarii*
Wool, best medium quality, washed	1 pound	50 *denarii*

29. *On Military Matters* (Selections)

The author of *On Military Matters* is unknown, but he probably wrote his Latin treatise in about A.D. 368 or 369 for Emperor Valens and his brother, Emperor Valentinian I. This relatively short treatise is a unique attempt to analyze and propose solutions for the principal internal problems of the empire. There is no evidence whether any emperor or his counsellors ever read or discussed it or attempted to implement any of its recommendations. It was, however, extensively recopied and illustrated in the Middle Ages and the Renaissance. The author examines the material causes of the present crisis without considering supernatural causes, such as divine wrath. He even offers technological solutions, however fanciful, to the empire's problems with manpower. The existence of this treatise raises the question of why other technological solutions were not proposed or tested. The author is conscious of contemporary bureaucratic and military weaknesses and external perils that confronted the imperial leadership. His discussion of the problems of the coinage reflects the difficult period of adjustment to the new coin introduced by Constantine I, the *solidus* (a gold piece of approximately 22.5 karats and weighing about 4.5 grams), which became the key to the new monetary policy after the failure of Diocletian's Price Edict. The illustrations are omitted here.

Preface

1. Most Sacred Emperors: In order to ensure the successful realization of your divine policies, proposals should be put forward on suitable occasions for the profit of your Commonwealth, ever flourishing under Heaven's inspiration. 2. Hence, in so far as my ability allows, I have composed a chapter in this tract on the subject of the Public Grants—not that this is an adequate treatment of that vast institution, but I hope by placing first this specimen of my modest talents to win your confidence in the utility of what follows. Accordingly, to ensure that the confidence you repose in my promise may not become a burden on my conscience for the future, I claim no reward if my promise should not be fulfilled but rather a penalty instead, so certain am I that I speak truth. Let no praise or [reward] be bestowed upon me, for in this part of my work it is more than enough to escape your indig-

De rebus bellicus, preface, i–vi, xx–xxi. From *A Roman Reformer and Inventor*, translated by E. A. Thompson (Oxford: Oxford University Press, 1952), pp. 106–14, 122–23.

nation at my presumption. 3. However, it will be fitting for the Head of the State to learn of desirable reforms from a private person, as useful measures sometimes escape his inquiries. 4. That is why persons who have been proved to have correct ideas on any subject should occasionally be called upon, for, to quote an excellent orator, "It is to the man of natural gifts that the majority of men turn for counsel." In this connexion one has always to examine what a man means rather than what he says; for it is universally agreed that in the technical arts (among which we include the invention of weapons) progress is due not to those of the highest birth or immense wealth or public office or eloquence derived from literary studies but solely to men of intellectual power (which is the mother of every excellence), depending as it does on a happy accident of nature. And in fact this is a quality which we see granted without respect of persons; for although the barbarian peoples derive no power from eloquence and no illustrious rank from office, yet they are by no means considered strangers to mechanical inventiveness, where nature comes to their assistance.

5. Wherefore, Most Merciful Emperors, who in your everlasting felicity esteem the glory of good repute, and transmit to your sons the affection due to the Roman name, deign to regard the useful projects with which Divine Providence has inspired my mind.

6. While, therefore, all men, whether they are members of the Imperial services, or persons content with the leisure of a private station, or tillers of the soil, or engaged as businessmen in the pursuit of commerce, alike rejoice in the felicity of your age, you will learn from this work of mine the interests of each, the details of which interests you will find set out at the appropriate places under various headings in the subjoined discourse.

I shall in fact describe how the taxes can be reduced by a half, thus [restoring] the provincial farmer to the strength that was his; 7. how, too, by [bringing down] the imposts and halting the outrage offered to our frontiers the settler may be enabled, once fortifications have been erected, to develop uninhabited lands without anxiety; how, further, the amount of your gold and silver may be doubled without hardship to the taxpayer, and the soldier gratified by the heaping on him of rewards beyond your customary lavishness. To these suggestions I have felt it necessary to add the prerequisites for victory on land and sea amid the exigencies of war. From these I shall select for description a few mechanical inventions so as to sustain your interest.

I shall, in fact, demonstrate how a particularly fast type of warship is able through a brilliant invention to outmatch ten other ships, sending them to the bottom without the aid of a large crew. 8. Again, an ingenious contrivance has been worked out for use in engagements by land: a horse, when charging the line in order to break it or pressing upon fleeing troops, is equipped with a device by which he lashes himself on independently of any human control, thus wreaking great havoc among the foe. 9. Further, to counter the difficulties caused by rivers, a new type of bridge has been invented which is not at all burdensome to transport, for, essential as it is for negotiating rivers and swamps, it can be carried by a very small number of men and about fifty pack-horses.

10. The foregoing account having now given, I think, some indication of what is to follow, I beg leave to say that I am bringing you by divine permission a great boon, and I declare that through the foresight of Your Pious Majesties the vigour of your arms together with the entire State will be sustained by the above-mentioned remedies. True, these are not unknown to those closest to Your Clemencies, men harassed by many other cares to which I am a stranger. But preoccupied as they are, many points escape them; whereas I, prompted by my leisure and not being entirely unversed in the subject, have been anxious to collect and assemble from all sources what can be of use to your felicity.

But where the exigencies of the case have forced me to speak somewhat freely on any point, I think I should be protected by your indulgence, for if I am to carry out my promise I must be assisted for the sake of the freedom of science.

The Reduction of Public Grants

I. 1. The Treasury always imitates martial praise and the pomp of triumphs [gap in original text] lest extravagant grants should rather arouse the seeds of war. If the foresight of the Imperial Majesty restrain these grants, the evil of war will flourish no longer, and the enfeebled resources of the taxpayers will be restored. If, however, unrestrained grants dissipate what ought to be conserved, the ever welcome aid of riches will no longer be able to relieve our needs as it did in ancient times.

2. We must therefore recall for a moment the prudence exercised by our forefathers in their needy circumstances—or what seems prudence nowadays amid our unbridled resources. During our early history our rulers rejoiced not in riches left to lie idle but in the construction of buildings, to adorn which they contributed their entire supply of gold and silver. Their stock of bronze, too, they fashioned into their own likenesses to testify to their worth. But in order that the convenience of trade and the means of royal largesse might be supplied, in place of bronze they made use of clay skilfully refined and hardened by fire and stamped with recognized types: their gold and silver they laid aside. Later generations, however, disdained the inexpensive measures of olden times, and fashioned disks of leather which they stamped with a thin coating of gold. These disks served the

bounty of kings and the needs of commerce without detriment to the taxpayers. 3. But in the following age the stock of bronze became abundant and was now rejected as a decoration for public buildings. The men of this period, like their predecessors, had durable specimens in mind, and consequently at greater expense they coined bronze, whose very weight lent it strength. As we have remarked, coins of this sort were more durable because of their weight; but mighty kings, in their prodigal way, stamped their own portrait only upon the gold and silver, which portrait, inspiring awe for the figure it represented, served no useful purpose, but remained a perpetual tribute to the royal glory. 4. The stock of bronze, however, which was now cheaper owing to its abundance, was stamped for use in donatives to the troops and in the various commercial transactions of the peoples. In order that the truth which I have told may be more readily believed I have caused the appropriate types and denominations of the various periods together with the different devices of the ancients to be depicted in a variety of colours.

The Date of the Origin of Extravagance and Greed

II. 1. It was in the age of Constantine that extravagant grants assigned gold instead of bronze (which earlier was considered of great value) to petty commercial transactions; but the greed I speak of is thought to have arisen from the following causes. When the gold and silver and the huge quantity of precious stones which had been stored away in the temples long ago reached the public, they enkindled all men's possessive and spendthrift instincts. And while the expenditure of bronze itself—which, as I have said, had been stamped with the heads of kings—had seemed already vast and burdensome enough, yet from some kind of blind folly there ensued an even more extravagant passion for spending gold, which is considered more precious. 2. This store of gold meant that the houses of the powerful were crammed full and their splendour enhanced to the destruction of the poor, the poorer classes of course being held down by force. 3. But the poor were driven by their afflictions into various criminal enterprises, and losing sight of all respect for law, all feelings of loyalty, they entrusted their revenge to crime. For they often inflicted the most severe injuries on the Empire, laying waste the fields, breaking the peace with outbursts of brigandage, stirring up animosities; and passing from one crime to another supported usurpers, whom they brought forth for the glorification of Your Virtuous Majesty: it was not bravado that inspired them. 4. Therefore, Most Excellent Emperor, you will take care in your prudence to limit public grants and thereby look to the taxpayers' interests and transmit to posterity the glory of your name.

5. Wherefore, do you reflect for a little on the story of those happy times, and ponder upon those famous kingdoms of antique poverty, which had learned to till the fields and abstain from riches: remember how their uncorrupted frugality commends them to all history with honour and praise. Assuredly we term "golden" those realms which had no gold at all.

The Fraudulent Practices of the Mint and Their Correction

III. 1. Among the intolerable mischiefs from which the State suffers is the debasement of the solidus arising from the fraudulent practices of certain persons. This inflicts hardship in various ways on the peoples of the Empire, and diminishes the prestige of the Sovereign's likeness in that coins are repudiated through the fault of the Mint. For the unscrupulous cunning of the purchaser of the solidus and the pernicious dilemma of the seller have combined to introduce considerable difficulty into the actual contracts, so as to preclude the possibility of straight dealing in business transactions. 2. Therefore Your Majesties' correction must be applied in this matter, too, as in all others: I mean, the workers of the Mint must be assembled from every quarter and concentrated in a single island so as to improve the utility of the coinage and the circulation of the solidi. Let them, in fact, be cut off for all time from association with the neighbouring land, so that freedom of intercourse, which lends itself to fraudulent practices, may not mar the integrity of a public service. 3. Confidence in the Mint will there be maintained unimpaired thanks to its isolation; there will be no room for fraud where there is no opportunity for trade. 4. But so that the character of a future issue may be made clear, I have subjoined an illustration showing the types and sizes of the bronze as well as of the gold coinage.

The Corruption of the Provincial Governors

IV. 1. Now in addition to these injuries, wherewith the arts of avarice afflict the provinces, comes the appalling greed of the provincial Governors, which is ruinous to the taxpayers' interests. For these men, despising the respectable character of their office, think that they have been sent into the provinces as merchants, and are all the more burdensome in that injustice proceeds from the very person from whom a remedy should have been expected. And as if their own iniquity were not enough, every one of them directs in the work of ruin Exactors of such character that they completely exhaust the resources of the taxpayers by various methods of extortion—evidently the Governors assume that they would be insufficiently distinguished were they alone to transgress. For what opportunity afforded by the collection of the taxes remains unexploited by the Exactors? When do they enforce payment of arrears without filling their own pockets? As for the Governors, the buying of recruits, the purchase of horses and grain, the monies intended for city walls—all these are regular sources of profit for them and are the pillage for which they long. But were the provinces to be governed by spotless men, jealous of their integrity—then there will be no room left anywhere for fraud, and the State will be strengthened by new reserves of morality.

Methods of Economy in Military Expenditure

V. 1. I have now described, as I intended, the distresses of the State, which should rightly be removed by Imperial measures. Let us turn now to the vast expenditure on the army which must be checked similarly, for this is what has thrown the entire system of tax payment into difficulties. 2. But in case one as busy as Your Majesty should be wearied by such a mass of confusion, I shall explain the solution of this chronic problem briefly. A member of the forces, after completing some years' service and attaining to a rate of five annonae [grain ration] or more, should be granted an honourable discharge and go into retirement to enjoy his leisure, so that he may not burden the State by receiving the annonae any longer. The next in rank will take his place, and at fixed intervals will save the whole company very heavy expenses. 3. But if the troops of the following drafts, who are summoned to take the place of those retiring, prove too numerous, let them also go into retirement with an equally liberal [gratuity] or be attached to some other company where troops are lacking, so as to bring it up to strength. This procedure will not only relieve the State, oppressed as it is by its expenditure, but will also diminish the worries of the Imperial Foresight. Further, it will encourage more men to enter the service, men who were formerly deterred by the slowness of promotion. 4. A provision of this kind will increase the population of the provinces by supplying veterans enriched with Imperial gifts who will still be strong enough to cultivate the land. They will live upon the frontiers, they will plough the areas which they recently defended, and having won what they longed to obtain from their toil they will be taxpayers instead of soldiers. 5. But since the total strength is sometimes reduced by military disaster or by desertions from the service arising from boredom with camp duties, such losses must be made up with some such remedy as the following: groups of 100 or 50 younger men, over and above those listed in the registers, should be held in readiness with some training, and maintained on a lower rate of pay (seeing that they are new recruits), to make up losses if circumstances should so require. When these provisions have been put into effect, the army will be maintained at full strength without difficulty and at the same time losses will be replaced in good time by trained reserves.

Military Machines

VI. 1. Above all it must be recognized that wild nations are pressing upon the Roman Empire and howling round about it everywhere, and treacherous barbarians, covered by natural positions, are assailing every frontier. 2. For usually the aforesaid nations are either covered by forests or occupy commanding mountain positions or are defended by snow and ice, while some are nomadic and are protected by deserts and the burning sun. Others are defended by marshes and rivers and cannot easily be tracked down; yet they mutilate our peace and quiet by unexpected forays. 3. Nations of this kind, then, which are protected by such defences or by city- and fortress-walls, must be attacked by means of a variety of new military machines. 4. But in case any difficulty should arise in constructing these types of weapon I have attached to my discourse a very accurate coloured picture of the hurling engines, so that the task of imitating them may be easy.

The Defence of the Frontiers

XX. 1. Among the measures taken by the State for its own advantage there is also the effective care of the frontier-works which surround all the borders of the Empire. Their safety will be better provided for by a continuous line of forts constructed at intervals of one mile with firm walls and very powerful towers. These fortifications should be constructed without public expenditure on the individual responsibility of the local landowners, with watches and pickets kept in them so that the peaceful provinces may be surrounded by a belt of defences, and so remain unimpaired and at peace.

On Removing the Confusion of the Laws and Justice

XXI. 1. Most Sacred Emperor, when the defences of the State have been properly provided both at home and abroad through the operation of Divine Providence, one remedy designed to cure our civilian woes awaits Your Serene Majesty: throw light upon the confused and contradictory rulings of the laws by a pronouncement of Your August Dignity and put a stop to dishonest litigation. For what is so alien to decent conduct as to give vent to one's passion for strife in the very place where the decisions of Justice distinguish the merits of individuals?

30. *The Theodosian Code* (Selections)

The emperor Theodosius II, who reigned at Constantinople from A.D. 408 to 450, was the grandson of Theodosius I, or Theodosius the Great. Many forms of intellectual activity flourished at the court of Theodosius II, including the creation of ecclesiastical and secular literature and the study of history, but he particularly encouraged the study of law. He ordered the collection, categorization, and publication in A.D. 438 of a definitive code of Roman legislation, selecting laws that had been enacted since the empire had become Christian under Emperor Constantine I in the early fourth century. This Latin compilation, which is usually called *The Theodosian Code*, included legislation from both eastern and western parts of the empire. It is a fundamental source for the understanding not only of law, but also of late Roman bureaucratic, fiscal, agricultural, religious, commercial, and military policies and conditions. The following selection sheds light on the development of the dependent sharecropping farmer, or *colonus*, whose freedom to move became restricted by law partly because the government needed dependable tax revenues; it also describes the perennial problem of inefficiency and dishonesty in government.

Title 5.17: Fugitive Coloni, *Inquilini*,[1] and Slaves

1. Emperor Constantine Augustus to the Provincials

Any person in whose possession a colonus that belongs to another is found not only shall restore the aforesaid colonus to his birth status but also shall assume the capitation tax for this man for the time that he was with him.

1. Coloni also who meditate flight must be bound with chains and reduced to a servile condition, so that by virtue of their condemnation to slavery, they shall be compelled to fulfill the duties that befit freemen.

Given on the third day before the kalends of November in the year of the consulship of Pacatianus and Hilarianus.—October 30, 332.

From *The Theodosian Code and Novels and the Sirmondian Constitutions*, translated by Clyde Pharr (Princeton, N.J.: Princeton University Press, 1952), pp. 23, 28, 115–17, 315.

1. *Inquilini* were probably cottagers who worked as laborers or craftsmen, living on estates but not leasing land.

Title 11.22: Transfer of Tax Payments Shall Not Be Requested

4. Emperors Honorius and Theodosius Augustuses to Anthemius, Praetorian Prefect

We have learned that some landholders have disregarded the custom of the ordinary tax collections and have progressed so far in lawlessness that some of them by the authority of impetrated rescripts elude the insistence of tax collectors, under the pretext that of their own free will they would more readily deliver the payments sought. Since this usurpation has been detected, We promulgate the regulation that this new method of impetration shall be annulled, which is commonly called automatic tax collection, and the entire custom of demanding payment, as it formerly existed, shall be revived. The desired objectives of this compulsory public service shall be managed by the decurions and the provincial apparitors [a magistrate's attendants or clerks], with the exception of those persons whom the consideration of your most eminent office has registered.

Given on the fourteenth day before the kalends of June in the year of the eighth consulship of Honorius Augustus and the third consulship of Theodosius Augustus.—May 19, 409.

Title 5.18: Inquilini and Coloni

1. Emperors Honorius and Theodosius Augustuses to Palladius, Praetorian Prefect

If a person who is a colonus or inquilinus by birth status has departed from a landholding thirty years before and if, through a continuous period of silence, he has not been brought back to his native soil, every unfounded action against him or the person who perchance now possesses him shall be completely excluded. It is Our will that this same number of years shall be observed likewise for future times.

1. But if within this period of thirty years any colonus by birth status has departed from a landholding, whether he escaped through flight or was abducted by his own wish or through solicitation, and if there should be no doubt concerning his status, We order that all controversy shall be removed and that he, together with his family, shall be restored without delay to the status to which he was born. . . .

Given on the sixth day before the kalends of July at Ravenna in the year of the consulship of Monaxius and Plinta.—June 26, 419.

Title 1.12: The Office of Proconsul and Legate

2. The Same Augustus [Constantine] to Proculus

It is to the interest of the public discipline, and it likewise befits the proconsular dignity, that you should bring under your power the administration and cognizance of the collection of the public revenues, and likewise the administration and cognizance of all other matters, in such a way that you shall not be content with the prepared reports and fraudulent statements of the apparitors. But you shall acquaint yourself with the administration of the judges themselves and the depositions of the prefect of the annona [grain supply and allotment] and those of the fiscal representatives, as to whether the aforesaid prepared reports are trustworthy. For thus it will be possible to give relief to the provincials against unjust exactions.

Given on the seventh day before the kalends of January in the year of the fifth consulship of Constantine Augustus and the consulship of Licinius Caesar.—December 26, 319.

Title 1.16: The Office of Governor of a Province

7. The Same Augustus to the Provincials

The rapacious hands of the apparitors shall immediately cease, they shall cease, I say; for if after due warning they do not cease, they shall be cut off by the sword. The chamber curtain of the judge shall not be venal; entrance shall not be gained by purchase, the private council chamber shall not be infamous on account of the bids. The appearance of the governor shall not be at a price; the ears of the judge shall be open equally to the poorest as well as to the rich. There shall be no despoiling on the occasion of escorting persons inside by the one who is called chief of the office staff. The assistants of the aforesaid chiefs of office staff shall employ no extortion on litigants; the intolerable onslaught of the centurions and other apparitors who demand small and great sums shall be crushed; and the unsated greed of those who deliver the records of a case to litigants shall be restrained. 1. Always shall the diligence of the governor guard lest anything be taken from a litigant by the aforesaid classes of men. If they should suppose that anything ought to be demanded by them from those involved in civil cases, armed punishment will be at hand, which will cut off the heads and necks of the scoundrels. Opportunity shall be granted to all persons who have suffered extortion to provide for an investigation by the governors. If they should dissemble, We hereby open to all persons the right to express complaints about such conduct before the counts of the provinces or before the praetorian prefects, if they are closer at hand, so that We may be informed by their references to Us and may provide punishment for such brigandage.

Given on the kalends of November at Constantinople in the year of the consulship of Bassus and Ablavius.—November 1, 331.

31. Priscus, *History* (Selection)

Priscus of Panium, who probably was a rhetorician, was born in Thrace. He wrote a work in Greek comprising seven books and entitled *Byzantine History and Attila*, which probably included events up to A.D. 472; only fragments of it survive. Inspired by earlier Greek historical models, it is both a reminder of the persistent strength of Greek historical writing to the end of the Roman Empire in western Europe and a unique record of the obscure but critical years of the middle of the fifth century. Particularly important is Priscus's eyewitness account of his participation in an embassy sent in 449 by Emperor Theodosius II to the court of the powerful and dreaded Attila, king of the Huns (reigned A.D. 434–53), who was then at the zenith of his power, in what now is Hungary. Maximin, who was a socially prominent diplomat and military officer, led the embassy. The conversation of Priscus with a Roman exile at the court of Attila provides some insights into contemporary relations between Romans and barbarians. It includes explanations why some Romans disliked their own government and were ready to consider the possibility of an alternative life among even the most notorious of barbarians. Earlier internal problems continued to plague the Roman government until its disappearance in parts of western Europe. For stylistic reasons, Priscus deliberately uses the anachronistic and inexact term "Scythians" when referring to the Huns.

When Attila entered the village he was met by girls advancing in rows, under thin white canopies of linen, which were held up by the outside women who stood under them, and were so large that seven or more girls walked beneath each. There were many lines of damsels thus canopied, and they sang Scythian songs. When he came near the house of Onegesius, which lay on his way, the wife of Onegesius issued from the door, with a number of servants, bearing meat and wine, and saluted him and begged him to partake of her hospitality. This is the highest honour that can be

From John B. Bury, *History of the Later Roman Empire: From the Death of Theodosius to the Death of Justinian*, 2d ed., vol. 1, translated by John B. Bury (London: Macmillan, 1923), pp. 283–85.

shown among the Scythians. To gratify the wife of his friend, he ate, just as he sat on his horse, his attendants raising the tray to his saddlebow; and having tasted the wine, he went on to the palace, which was higher than the other houses and built on an elevated site. But we remained in the house of Onegesius, at his invitation, for he had returned from his expedition with Attila's son. His wife and kinsfolk entertained us to dinner, for he had no leisure himself, as he had to relate to Attila the result of his expedition, and explain the accident which had happened to the young prince, who had slipped and broken his right arm. After dinner we left the house of Onegesius, and took up our quarters nearer the palace, so that Maximin might be at a convenient distance for visiting Attila or holding intercourse with his court. The next morning, at dawn of day, Maximin sent me to Onegesius, with presents offered by himself as well as those which the Emperor had sent, and I was to find out whether he would have an interview with Maximin and at what time. When I arrived at the house, along with the attendants who carried the gifts, I found the doors closed, and had to wait until some one should come out and announce our arrival. As I waited and walked up and down in front of the enclosure which surrounded the house, a man, whom from his Scythian dress I took for a barbarian, came up and addressed me in Greek, with the word *Chairē*, "Hail!" I was surprised at a Scythian speaking Greek. For the subjects of the Huns, swept together from various lands, speak, besides their own barbarous tongues, either Hunnic or Gothic, or—as many as have commercial dealings with the western Romans—Latin; but none of them easily speak Greek, except captives from the Thracian or Illyrian sea-coast; and these last are easily known to any stranger by their torn garments and the squalor of their heads, as men who have met with a reverse. This man, on the contrary, resembled a well-to-do Scythian, being well dressed, and having his hair cut in a circle after Scythian fashion. Having returned his salutation, I asked him who he was and whence he had come into a foreign land and adopted Scythian life. When he asked me why I wanted to know, I told him that his Hellenic speech had prompted my curiosity. Then he smiled and said that he was born a Greek and had gone as a merchant to Viminacium, on the Danube, where he had stayed a long time, and married a very rich wife. But the city fell a prey to the barbarians, and he was stript of his prosperity, and on account of his riches was allotted to Onegesius in the division of the spoil, as it was the custom among the Scythians for the chiefs to reserve for themselves the rich prisoners. Having fought bravely against the Romans and the Acatiri, he had paid the spoils he won to his master, and so obtained freedom. He then married a barbarian wife and had children, and had the privilege of eating at the table of Onegesius.

He considered his new life among the Scythians better than his old life among the Romans, and the reasons he gave were as follows: "After war the Scythians live in inactivity, enjoying what they have got, and not at all, or very little, harassed. The Romans, on the other hand, are in the first place very liable to perish in war, as they have to rest their hopes of safety on others, and are not allowed, on account of their *tyrants*, to use arms. And those who use them are injured by the cowardice of their generals, who cannot support the conduct of war. But the condition of the subjects in time of peace is far more grievous than the evils of war, for the exaction of taxes is very severe, and unprincipled men inflict injuries on others, because the laws are practically not valid against all classes. A transgressor who belongs to the wealthy classes is not punished for his injustice, while a poor man, who does not understand business, undergoes the legal penalty, that is if he does not depart this life before the trial, so long is the course of lawsuits protracted, and so much money is expended on them. The climax of the misery is to have to pay in order to obtain justice. For no one will give a court to the injured man unless he pay a sum of money to the judge and the judge's clerks."

In reply to this attack on the Empire, I asked him to be good enough to listen with patience to the other side of the question. "The creators of the Roman republic," I said, "who were wise and good men, in order to prevent things from being done at haphazard, made one class of men guardians of the laws, and appointed another class to the profession of arms, who were to have no other object than to be always ready for battle, and to go forth to war without dread, as though to their ordinary exercise, having by practice exhausted all their fear beforehand. Others again were assigned to attend to the cultivation of the ground, to support both themselves and those who fight in their defence, by contributing the military corn-supply. . . . To those who protect the interests of the litigants a sum of money is paid by the latter, just as a payment is made by the farmers to the soldiers. Is it not fair to support him who assists and requite him for his kindness? The support of the horse benefits the horseman. . . . Those who spend money on a suit and lose it in the end cannot fairly put it down to anything but the injustice of their case. And as to the long time spent on lawsuits, that is due to concern for justice, that judges may not fail in passing correct judgments, by having to give sentence offhand; it is better that they should reflect, and conclude the case more tardily, than that by judging in a hurry they should both injure man and transgress against the Deity, the institutor of justice. . . . The Romans treat their servants better than the king of the Scythians treats his subjects. They deal with them as fathers or teachers, admonishing them to abstain from evil and follow the lines of conduct which they have esteemed honourable; they reprove them for their errors like their own children. They are not allowed, like the Scythians, to inflict death on them. They have numerous ways of conferring freedom; they can manumit not only during life, but also by their wills, and the testamentary wishes of a Roman in regard to his property are law."

My interlocutor shed tears, and confessed that the laws and constitution of the Romans were fair, but deplored that the governors, not possessing the spirit of former generations, were ruining the State.

Index